BOOKS BY JUDITH MARTIN

Miss Manners' Guide to

Rearing Perfect Children

Miss Manners'® Guide to Rearing Perfect Children

Judith Martin

Illustrated by Gloria Kamen

ATHENEUM *New York* *1984*

Miss Manners *is a registered trademark
of United Feature Syndicate, Inc.*

Library of Congress Cataloging in Publication Data
Martin, Judith, ———
    Miss Manners' guide to rearing perfect children.
    Includes index.
    1. Etiquette for children and youth. I. Title.
BJ1857.C5M32 1984   395   84–45041
ISBN 0–689–11489–3

For my parents

Contents

1. Theory and Skills

For the Enrolled (Parents, Including Stepparents,
Adoptive Parents, Foster Parents, and
Guardians)   7

6. *Collegiate*

7. *Postgraduate*

8. *Extra Credit*

9. *Conclusions*

Illustrations

Introduction

On the subject of manners for children, many adults believe that the opposite of "polite" is "creative." Poor little mannerly children, they think—how suppressed and inhibited they must be. Actually, the opposite of "polite" is "rude." If you think that rude children are better off emotionally than well-behaved ones, you are in luck, because there are so many of them around. What an increasingly joyful world it is getting to be as they all grow up and take charge.

Miss Manners, as you may guess, believes in manners for children. As a small lady in her jurisdiction replied, when asked in pitying tones if she was expected to be polite all the time, "You bet your Aunt Fanny I am." Miss Manners has also observed that when children are truly allowed to express their preferences, uninfluenced by the dreary adult expectation that they must all be artistic and original little noble savages, they come out resoundingly in favor of rigid traditionalism. The devotion to ritual exhibited by the average toddler in regard to his bedtime routine would make a nineteenth-century English butler look like a free spirit.

Children instinctively accept the idea of right behavior and wrong behavior, even if they cannot, or do not care to, sort the human possibilities into the proper categories. There is hardly anyone more forlorn than a child who, on being thrust into a new social situation, is instructed to do "whatever makes you feel comfortable." The fright of a basically decent child on finding himself on a solo visit to a friend's house, without having been warned what the common standards are in the way of pleasantries to adult hosts and table manners, is exceeded only by the terror of a pubescent child anxious to appear as if he knows what he is doing, or should be doing, at his first boy-girl party.

By the time a child who has been subjected to manners instruction since birth gets to this point, polite behavior has become second nature, and he is free to enjoy himself without fear of inadvertently doing wrong. A good parent owes it to a child to teach manners as an interesting and useful skill, and not as a subject that is invoked to condemn whatever the child happens to be doing when the adult is feeling irritable.

This means that during the training period (birth to marriage), the entire household will have to conform to the practice of exchanging greetings and simple conversation; a pattern of consuming food in ways that are aesthetically and socially presentable; civilized restraints upon anger that allow it to be expressed without throwing out all respect; a pretense that one is interested in the comforts and adventures of others; and the principle that guests, regardless of age or personal charms, deserve to be treated hospitably.

Once a parent learns to live this way, he will find it not unpleasant. For the child, such standards are much less strict, rigid, cruel, inhibiting, and pitiless than peer pressure standards, which are always quick to fill any vacancy left by lackadaisical adults.

What follows is Miss Manners' curriculum for child-rearing, beginning with a discussion of theory and skills and proceeding through postgraduate work. Miss Manners warns you to pay attention: This course has a final examination, and you-know-who will grade it.

Mrs Geoffrey Perfect and the late Mr. Perfect

Jonathan Rhinehart Awful, father of....

daughter, Daffodil Louise Perfect wed....

and divorced Jonathan Awful, junior

Daffodil Louise Right + Theodore B. Right

Kimberly, (the second Mrs. Awful)

Jonathan Rhino, Jr. (Rhino revised)

Heidi Right (first Mrs. Right) (and the three Right children)

Heather

Lauren

Orville

Adam

Lisa

Jason (The four Awful children)

Kristen

THE FAMILY TREE OF CHARACTERS IN THIS BOOK:
The Awfuls Get More Awful, and the Perfects Turn Right

Preface

The Perfect Saga, continued

Well-wishers of Daffodil Louise Awful, née Perfect, formerly residing in *Miss Manners' Guide to Excruciatingly Correct Behavior*, may recall that she was perfectly brought up by her parents, Clara and Geoffrey Perfect, with the sidelines assistance of Mr. Perfect's late brother's wife, Mrs. Plue Perfect.

What went wrong? Why cannot the Perfect tradition simply be handed down through the generations until everyone is perfect?

One thing that went wrong was Mr. Awful, whom Daffodil insisted on marrying, even after her father pointed out how thoroughly unattractive he found that young gentleman. But we'll let that pass, as, indeed, he eventually did out of the family.

Another was that the tradition did not pass on as smoothly as previous generations had managed, a few secret scandals and black sheep notwithstanding. It was interrupted, for the best of motives, at about the time that the Awful children were coming into the world. Daffodil and Rhino were seduced by the charming idea of allowing their children to be free, creative, and honest, qualities that less doting people called, when they saw the results, unmannerly, ignorant, and rude. Even the fond parents had to admit that the results, while not disastrous, were less than Perfect.

But Daffodil got a fresh start in mid-life. When we left her, so had her husband....

As a middle-aged divorcée, Daffodil found that she could manage everything except the etiquette problems. It hardly seemed fair to her that she should end up with all of those, and all the Awful children as well.

When Jonathan Rhinehart Awful, junior,* left his dutiful wife of many years for someone named Kimberly whom he had met on a nudist beach, Mrs. Awful's friends were quick to assure her that they were not surprised, as they had always figured he was a rotter. Daffodil Awful never knew how to respond to these kind remarks; a simple ''Thank you'' did not seem right. She was left with the dreadful feeling that during the years they had been a popular couple, everyone had actually been snickering and awaiting disaster.

Dealing with her old friends was not a major problem of Daffodil Awful's post-marital life, however, as many dropped her for the social crime of making their dinner tables uneven. If they hadn't, she might have dropped them for the worse crime of addressing their ''We must have lunch sometime'' notes to ''Mrs. Daffodil Awful.'' She would not have minded ''Ms. Daffodil Awful,'' although she preferred to use the old-fashioned form of combining maiden and married surnames and be ''Mrs. Perfect Awful.'' But, true to her upbringing (her mother was the former Clara Grace Proper), she reacted to ''Mrs.'' with a lady's given name as to watching a fish stabbed with a meat knife.

Once Daffodil and her lawyer had pointed out to Rhino that she had entirely fulfilled her part of a contract that was understood to provide job security, and that she was therefore entitled to ample compensation, she behaved perfectly. She never spoke ill of the current Mr. and Mrs. Jonathan Rhinehart Awful† but said, instead, ''Rhino was always a wonderful husband to me, and while I don't really know his wife, she is quite striking-looking, and seems to be an extremely agreeable girl.'' Thus Daffodil made everyone understand that Rhino really loved her but had been victimized by mid-life insanity, and that Kimberly was flashy-looking, absurdly immature, and pathetically overanxious to please.

With great dignity and willpower, Daffodil did not behave in the manner common to women in her situation: She did not call acquaintances at three in the morning to confide that she was depressed, she did not allow her gray hairs to go blond, and she did not tell everyone within hearing distance that she was interested in meeting men.

She did, however, enroll in law school. This was not so much from financial necessity (her father had prudently tied up all the Perfect money the first time he saw Rhino) as from etiquette necessity. Her hope was to solve the ''Mrs. Daffodil'' problem by joining the Supreme Court of the United States, whereupon she would be addressed as Justice Daffodil Awful, or even Mrs. Justice Awful.

In school, and in the community, Daffodil made an advantage of her age by cultivating a kindly, maternal interest in people of all ages and sexes. At a time when other people were all busy asserting themselves, being their own best friends,

---

*(He was 3d when Daffodil's choice, but was promoted when his grandfather expired— and probably died, as well, but the club servants were reluctant to move him because nobody was sure—upon being told that Joe Kennedy's son represented the hope of idealism in America.)

†(The "junior" was dropped because Rhino's father dropped, when Kimberly broke into his welcome-to-the-family speech to ask under what sign of the zodiac he had been born.)

and being good to themselves, she was an instant social hit. Because she never seemed to notice that she was unpaired, but cheerfully filled her house with young law students, elderly neighbors, children, and other single women, they all decided she needed help, and brought her their widowed fathers, bachelor nephews, and divorced brothers. Daffodil could never quite stifle her indignation at the vulgarity of her older friends' asking whether she "had a man," her mother's term for finding a satisfactory butler, but, indeed, she soon had her choice of them.

Then, at the age of fifty, she met Mr. Right. Theodore Bishop Right's sterling inner qualities, and the sterling way his hair was just graying at the temples, persuaded her to marry again, as much as the prospect of finally, once again, being properly addressed.

Mr. Right had also been wronged. The first Mrs. Right, Heidi, had unceremoniously departed some time ago in order to find herself, and had gotten lost. Daffodil thus acquired, upon her marriage, resident stepchildren.

It had been Heidi Right's belief that child-rearing interfered with the freedom of the parent as an individual, and therefore she had done none. Teddy Right was so softhearted that he had indulged the children in whatever they wanted, a policy Daffodil, while appreciating the intention, considered softheadedness and, ultimately, very unkind indeed to the children.

When she got them, Heather, Lauren, and Orville Right were almost as innocent of manners as the children of Daffodil's first husband by his second marriage: Lisa, Adam, Jason, and Kristen Awful. (Kimberly Awful believed that child-rearing interfered with the freedom of the child and its growth as a creative individual. As for Rhino, the only service he could ever perform, as his first father-in-law used to say, was to serve as a bad example.)

Daffodil, who is now practicing domestic law with a vengeance, did not solve her personal etiquette problem. Although she should be called Ms. Daffodil Louise Right professionally and Mrs. Theodore Bishop Right socially, people keep addressing her in both spheres as Mrs. Daffodil Awful Right, which is worse than before. She is determined to solve the etiquette problems of her stepchildren and, knowing that the world is full of Awful children, at least restore to these their Rightful heritage.

It is for her and for them that this book is written.

Theory and Skills

There is no quick and easy way to rear a child. It takes eighteen years of constant work to get one into presentable enough shape so that a college will take him or her off your hands for the winter season, and it can easily take another ten years of coaching and reviewing before someone will consent to take the child on permanently. Then, if you are lucky, you may get a few years' break—itself broken by the occasional necessity of dealing with children who are not your direct descendants, but those of friends, neighbors, lovers, or strangers who may have shirked the task entirely—before beginning again as a grandparent.

Miss Manners can, however, offer you some tools that will make the job possible. Be grateful that she does not suggest that you seek professional help. This is professional help: Manners are the basis of civilized society, and passing on the civilization to the young, so that they do not run around in a natural and savage stage but can live easily and comfortably within the accumulated traditions and standards of their society, is what child-rearing is all about.

Miss Manners abhors the idea, fashionable for the last two decades (and in the years immediately preceding the French Revolution), that the child is born good, creative, and wise, and that education should therefore consist of drawing out what is there—feelings and even opinions—rather than putting things in, such as the accumulated experience and wisdom of society. We are all born ignorant and oafish. What infant ever considers, when it can't sleep, that someone else might want to?

The chief tools of child-rearing are example and nagging. You cannot teach a child honesty if he hears you talking about cheating on your income tax or watches you outfit your home with supplies from your office and the public accommodations you frequent. If you are rude to your spouse, or to the child (within the standards of parent-child etiquette, which are different from child-parent etiquette), you will never be able to teach politeness. Shouting at someone to shut up may work in that short period between oblivious infancy and the development of a cunning thinking process, but it is doomed when the child is able to recognize paradox. Neither can you train a child by telling him something once. Exasperating as it is to have to keep repeating things—and Miss Manners has the feeling she has told you this a hundred times before, so please pay attention so she doesn't have to go through it all again—the reward is that after six thousand four hundred and twelve times of prompting a child to say "Thank you," he or she will shock you, and probably himself, too, by saying it before he has had a chance to think what he is doing.

An essential tool, for use in public, is the parental signal to the child that he is getting into trouble. One tries to avoid humiliating a child in front of others, although there is a stage in life when most children consider the mere fact of having parents to be humiliating, and not much can be done about that. Every parent should have a particular facial expression that looks pleasant to observers—it is usually some peculiar type of smile—but clearly conveys to the child that if he

"Just wait 'till the company leaves....."

"We're thrilled and proud but we won't embarrass you by kissing you....."

"Please tell your friends we don't do things like that"

"Don't forget to say thank you..."

ESSENTIAL PARENTAL FACIAL EXPRESSIONS

doesn't stop what he is doing this instant, the minute he is left alone with his parent, he is going to be sorry.

All adults need a similar technique for curbing the destructive behavior of children over whom they have no actual authority. The method Miss Manners recommends is to feign interest in the child's safety, and say, while grabbing the child's wrist, "I wouldn't do that, dear, because you might get hurt." It is the invisible pressure on the wrist that suggests to the child the source of that hurt. Those who are temporarily put in charge of ill-mannered children, such as grand-parents, may invoke the rules-of-the-house decree, by which the children are told that whatever standard prevails in their own home (which one must bite one's tongue to avoid condemning), they must nevertheless yield to the different policies of a different authority. Should a temporary authority become a permanent one, as for instance when a dear friend of the family becomes a stepparent, the desire to ingratiate oneself should never be viewed as a conflict to asserting full authority. Contrary to all logic, children actually prefer adults who set standards and limits to those whose easier ways they interpret to be indifference.

An invaluable skill, without which sensible parenting is not possible, is the ability to say no. The fun of being a parent consists partly of the fact that you get a fresh start with each baby, and may have a go at imposing the standards in which you believe, before you have to take on any conflicts with those of the society. Extreme youth is the time to introduce the manners and customs with which you would like to live, rather than ones you find to be common in both senses of the word. At that stage, the poor defenseless child is not aware that he is supposed to prefer junk food to good, that most of his peers are not required to address adults respectfully, that television is considered to be a cultural necessity by most of the population, or that it is possible to get through life without learning to put your toys away. He will find out soon enough, but by then he will be saddled with the knowledge that it is possible to improve on the lowest common standards.

Oddly, it is only after the child has learned that his parents' "No" prevails that he can be trusted to perform this exercise himself. Saying "No" probably is a human instinct, judging from the ease with which toddlers catch on to the practice, but the civilized use of it (to refuse to do what one thinks wrong), as opposed to the more natural use of it (to get out of doing what one knows is right), has to be learned. This is accomplished by allowing the school-age child to argue the merits of a decision with his parents and even, if he makes the better argument, to win. The pretense of infallibility is a dangerous one, and not necessary to assert-ing authority. This is known as "I do things the way I believe is right, not just what everybody else does; I may, occasionally, make a mistake, but I'm doing the best I can." Later, the child must be gradually permitted to make his own nonfatal mistakes.

Nevertheless, if the child wins too often—that is, if he is admittedly superior to his parents at making judgments—something is terribly wrong. Grown-up au-thority is based not so much on the idea of because-I'm-bigger-than-you-are as on the assumption that grown-ups have spent more years acquiring experience, knowledge, and judgment. Adults who take their general standards from children, copying, for example, dietary or drug-taking habits of the young, their romantic practices, and even their clothing, should not be rearing children, and possibly not even running around loose. If they are parents, they deprive their children not only of guidance, but of the valuable opportunity of growth that comes from shocking one's parents. If you can't tell the adults from the children, if everybody in the society yearns to live the childish life, none of the incentive for development that comes from youthful yearning for the privileges of the mature will take place. Thus for personal as well as cosmic reasons, nobody, young or old, will be looking forward to the future.

For her part, Miss Manners looks forward to a future in which the world will be populated with civilized people. If every parent will do the job of child-rearing, that should happen any generation now.

They Need a Parent

DEAR MISS MANNERS:

I want my kids to feel that I am their friend, but I can't make them understand why I can't stand it when they and their friends call me ''Pops'' and tell me to get snacks for them and come in and turn on the television when I'm trying to read the paper. I wasn't brought up that way myself, and I can't get used to it.

GENTLE READER:

If you took the role of the father, you wouldn't have to, because you could set the rules. Why don't you, as your children seem to have other friends, anyway?

For the Enrolled

(Parents, Including Stepparents, Adoptive Parents, Foster Parents, and Guardians)

Real Selves at Home

DEAR MISS MANNERS:

Lately, I have discovered that my husband's family believes that "manners are for company," and now that I am, alas, no longer an outsider, everyone feels comfortable to be his or her real self. My husband complains that in private he should be able to eat as he wishes, while my belief is that one owes oneself the same courtesy one would extend to strangers. He is angry at my refusal to eat meals with him at home, but when I walk into the dining room and am faced by him hunched over his plate, gobbling, smacking, and belching to himself, I cannot really feel privileged that he is so "relaxed" in my presence.

Do you see a resolution here? I do not like being in the position of teaching table manners to a grown-up man or of making ultimatums; neither do I like the idea of eating alone or of feeling repulsed by unappetizing habits.

GENTLE READER:

What a peculiar idea it is that one's "real self" is one's worst behavior. There is nothing false about being good, in Miss Manners' opinion, and the effort to live up to one's better self is the noblest career on which one can embark. Her view is entirely the opposite of your husband's and even different from yours that "one owes oneself the same courtesy one would extend to strangers." One owes one's family much more. Manners toward strangers are a fine thing, but in family life, they are essential. If you offend strangers, you can move on, but if you disgust members of your family—well, you can still move on, and many people do, but it is emotionally and otherwise rather expensive. Thus, while Miss Manners admires your belief (which is one of her rules, too) that one should not attempt to teach manners to grown-ups, she feels that something has to be done here. You will never find happiness, or even ordinary peace, with a man who repulses you three times a day.

The arguments for your husband's improving his table manners are:

1. You both want to share meals, but you want them to be agreeable.

2. Good manners always take precedence over bad, so there is no use arguing that it is a question simply of his comfort against yours.

3. Good manners do not preclude stylistic differences between informal, family eating and company behavior. Picking up chicken bones and going after the last slurp of sauce are permissible in the informal family environment, but not in formal situations.

4. The habit of eating pleasantly is quickly acquired, and one is less apprehensive about being on display in business or social situations when the correct thing has become second nature.

5. Your children will need a single standard of household behavior. It will be greatly to their advantage, for reason 4, to have this be a high standard.

6. Any activity likely to lead to your having children is apt to be adversely affected by the daily practice of your being repulsed by your husband's physical behavior.

(For specific rules of table manners and methods of teaching them, please see *Review*, in Chapter 9, and *Mealtime*, in Chapter 8.)

❧ FAMILY PRIDE AND TRADITIONS

Stocking Up on Childhood Memories

"Be kind to your biographer," Miss Manners' dear father used to say when carefully dating his letters, diaries, and memorabilia. It is an idea that takes on a whole new meaning when you consider that your most likely biographer is your own child.

That few parents will end up as the leading characters in films or books written by their children is probably just as well. But there is a natural and not unreasonable human hope that one will be remembered as a supporting character when that child comes to bore his descendants with his reminiscences. What the overall judgment will be on the parent's performance is a gamble. The easygoing parent may well be remembered as uncaring, and the demonstrative one as suffocating. There is hardly a parental instinct that cannot be perverted into a grievance by the efforts of a thoughtful child, especially if aided by an enthusiastic therapist.

It is a mistake, therefore, to guide one's parental behavior with the risky business of reputation in mind. The rule is to do the best you can, in what you believe to be the child's ultimate interests, and be prepared to suffer through the child's later explanation of how he (by that time a childless young adult who knows everything) would have done it better. Nature has its own revenge, in that these people usually eventually have children of their own.

There are, however, certain factors that can enhance childhood in a memorable way. The most effective of all, according to Miss Manners' dear mother, is the simplest. A teacher, she often heard the parental lamentation of "But we give him everything" from those whose children confided to their teacher, separately, how much they cheerfully hated their parents. The parental complaint was followed by a list itemizing valuable goods given.

"I could never find a correlation between the parents' generosity and the child's feeling about them," noted Miss Manners' mother. "Then I began to notice a connection between the child's feelings and the parents' facial expressions when they came to pick him up at school, or even when they just talked about him. The parent who beamed at the child had a loving child, and the one who didn't, didn't. After that, it didn't seem to matter what else the parents did or didn't do."

Miss Manners is happy to present such unmaterialistic news, although she does not deny that many people's fondest childhood memories have to do with toys or other presents. Yet the parent who gives whatever is asked, when it is asked, seems to get no return except increased expectation. The generally sensible parent, who restricts giving to fixed occasions and the choice of presents to items that are educational, useful, or apt to be of lasting, rather than fleeting, enjoyment, will give enormous pleasure by a rare wild deviation from this policy.

A gentleman of Miss Manners' acquaintance once, while out to lunch with his teenaged daughter, impulsively stopped in a jewelry store and bought her diamond stud earrings. Miss Manners' own father achieved the same effect, at somewhat less cost, when she was eleven and on an educational sightseeing trip—by suddenly, without apparent cause or warning, buying flowers and pinning them on her coat. It is of such that memories are made, and incidentally, standards for future entrance into the family. A young lady who has experienced spontaneous romanticism is unlikely to fall in love with someone of grudging manners.

That, too, is what creating memories is all about. A whiff of immortality may be unlikely ("If your memoirs start out, 'My life really began at twenty-five,' " said the parents of a young gentleman given his dream trip at sixteen, "we'll come back and kill you"), but one can at least hope that the memory of a happy childhood will be reflected in a perpetuation of the parents' attitudes and standards. (For more on proper present-giving, please see pp. 32–39.)

Parental Passion

DEAR MISS MANNERS:
Would you discuss the etiquette of kissing—parents doing so upon the foreheads, cheeks, etc.?

GENTLE READER:

Children must be kissed regularly by their parents, and the cheeks and fore-heads are excellent target areas. Tops of heads are good, provided the parent is able to identify a plastic ponytail holder before receiving it in the eye, and the tips of noses are especially tasty. Toes are not recommended beyond infancy.

Why, you may ask, should respectable people have to put up with all this sloppy passion on the part of their elders? Why was the human child's ambulatory ability purposely made so that it requires months to master sufficiently well to be able to escape from this unseemly attention? The answer is that Nature devised parental passion as a protection for the species. No sensible person would voluntarily nur-ture a creature of yelps, messes, and no conversation unless rendered foolish by extreme fondness. This is no less true as the child grows older and acquires dread-ful traits of a more complicated nature. It is therefore in the child's self-interest to cooperate in maintaining a proper state of affection between the generations. It is a wise child who submits gracefully to a kiss on the forehead, and who also understands the value of a childish kiss on a withered cheek or clenched jaw.

Pride and Embarrassment

There was a time when the greatness of America was presumed to require em-barrassment about one's family. The idea was that poor foreigners arrived, and produced children who didn't care for either attribute, and set about turning themselves into well-to-do Americans.

That was all very well, but Miss Manners, who is basically in the business of preserving and refining folk custom under its grander name of etiquette, never cared for the aspect of it that contained shame of origins. She is very pleased that that is now passed, and it is more chic to brag about differences than to attempt to conceal them. Nevertheless, pride in distinguishing characteristics is a feeling that must be cultivated in small children, who are born conformists and spend the first parts of their lives striving to be inconspicuous and vainly attempting to persuade their relatives to do the same.

Stylistically, one permits them to adopt the more or less reasonable standards of their peers in appearance, language, and social habits—the disclaimer about reason is there because anything that violates the health, moral, or financial stan-dards of the family is definitely not permitted—outside of the house, if they con-form to the rules within. This is also useful for teaching the concept of multiple styles (as in ''I'm sorry, jeans may be all right on the playground, but we do not wear them to church''), which is in danger of being lost in these simplistic times.

Many things in a child's life, however, cannot be changed to suit his fancies of what would be acceptable. Race, religion, ethnic origin, and economic class are among these, but so are the composition of the family (number of parents, chil-dren, and odd residents in the home) and the stylistic preferences of those people. The family could consist of Papa, his lady friend, and her children; or Aunt Annabelle, who tipples and tends to shout at the postman; or an elder brother who has dyed his hair pink and an elder sister who has just been made a partner in her law firm and has gone ultrarespectable.

Humiliated by the fact that his own particular family does not conform to his idea of family as developed by pictures on greeting cards and other sources of cultural information, the child attempts to renovate it. As no family ever does conform completely—many a nonsmoking parent has been puzzled by the present of a kindergarten-made ashtray, not realizing that the idea that Papa is supposed to smoke a pipe has made a stronger impression on the child than living half a dozen years with this individual—every child goes through these exercises.

This is a natural but unpalatable form of shyness. For the family's own protection against harassment from within, it must be replaced with proper pride. This is done with lectures in two categories.

First is the one on family pride. The history of the people from whom the child is descended is told, with an emphasis on achievements and ideals, and stories about Great-Grandpa the Horse Thief thrown in for comic relief, believability, and examples of things going wrong. One starts with the historical part and proceeds to the particular family, finally arriving at the personal history of the parents and other living relatives. Extolling one's own virtues is not an easy thing to do gracefully, but, mixed in with funny anecdotes of one's mistakes, it should be done in such a way as to let the child know that his family has redeeming qualities that make up for its oddity.

Next comes the lecture—lecturing, in Miss Manners' opinion, is one of the rewards of child-rearing—on the child's own worth. The idea is to build up the child's confidence to the point where he takes a fond view of his own distinguishing characteristics—his looks, his interests, his talents—rather than one of shame at not conforming to the crowd or duplicating those of the most admired member of his class.

This includes an attack on shyness. "You are as good as anyone else" is the theme of this part, and never mind the contrast with such other staples of child-rearing as "Why can't you find out what the homework is when everybody else manages to?"

Miss Manners' dear mother used to put it, "As long as you are honest and kind, you don't have to be timid about doing what you want to do." How she managed to engrave this principle without her children's applying it to defying her standards, Miss Manners does not remember. It was, however, very useful for going out into the intimidating world.

The Right to Reminisce

DEAR MISS MANNERS:

My husband is fond of reminiscing, and often tells the children stories of when he was a little boy, the pranks he pulled in college, and so on. There isn't one left that the children haven't heard a hundred times, or that I haven't heard a thousand times. Isn't it rude to bore people who can't get away? Can we stop him?

Gentle Reader:

Probably not. However, the etiquette aspect of this problem is different in the family circle than it is on the outside; repetition, of stories, jokes, and ways of doing things, is one of the distinguishing characteristics of family life. In other words, boring your relatives is known as family tradition.

Creating Traditions

Ritual, or at least a common share of peculiar habits, is what gives a family identity. Miss Manners figures that that must be why, when so many persist in regarding the sacred subject of etiquette as one of life's frills, the highest emotions, on such basic occasions as weddings and funerals, are spent on quarreling about details of behavior. Who wore what, who sat where, what was said in the receiving line, and what was served to eat and drink—these are the issues of which lifetime feuds are made. That is why Miss Manners is always after you to follow the conventions on such matters. You become free from being criticized for individual choices, and can even blame Miss Manners, should anyone try. She is big enough to take it.

Even she acknowledges, however, that there are social patterns in which there is no right or wrong, but only family custom. Does Father serve the family meal, or does Mother? Is Sunday dinner eaten at midday or in the evening? Is breakfast a time for conversation or newspaper reading? Miss Manners advises all co-heads of families to make decisions on such questions, so as not to let them be taken over by secret judgments that one's spouse, coming from a different tradition, simply doesn't know how to behave. Couples need the strength of unity here, in order to weather such charges from the side of the family whose custom was not adopted.

Beyond that, those starting families need to develop some customs and rituals of their own. Such routines, not only pleasant in themselves, soon become so emotionally laden as to bind together the members of the family and serve as a standard for those of flimsier backgrounds wishing to enter the family. A married couple should develop rituals from their respective heritages and prejudices, but it is in the nature of the job that once developed, the routine must be repeated religiously. It is advisable to claim the privilege of being hosts early, even if only at the least popular holidays when there are senior claims.

Religious and national holidays are obvious occasions for these, as are birthdays. Miss Manners believes in stating the nature of the occasion, in as sentimental a fashion as possible (discussing democracy on the Fourth of July, telling baby stories about the family member whose birthday it is), although she knows she is supposed to be letting you decide these things for yourself. She also recommends family dinner and children's bedtime as occasions for which patterns are needed. Even the small child's last stalling tactic of a request for a drink of water is amusing if set into a ritual, so that the parent understands it cannot be skipped, and the child understands it cannot be executed twice.

Other possibilities include:

- Sunday-afternoon teatime, at which one child prepares tea or hot chocolate, another makes the bread-and-butter or other snack, and the family members take turns providing entertainment. Perhaps everyone has to have memorized a poem and must recite it (the parents will keep trying to appear with excuses, but the children must not let them get away with that), or a book is read aloud.
- Lunch downtown in a grown-up restaurant, between one child and one parent on a school holiday, possibly in combination with a shopping trip.
- A family sport, including assigned tasks for the preparation of equipment.
- Sickbed luxuries, including special trays and privileges. These should also be available to parents, who are not allowed to be sick but could declare temporary emotional illness on school holidays.
- Opening of the season—the first picnic, nature walk, snowman-building, planting.

In each of these, it must be decided what foods are appropriate, what reminiscences, and what each person's task is. When you vary one of these ever so slightly, and a child screams, ''No, that's not right!'' you will know that you have succeeded. You will have established a tradition. (For more on these questions, please see *Family Gatherings*, next section, and *Mealtime*, Chapter 8.)

An Example: Christmas

There are no etiquette problems at family Christmas celebrations, because among people who love one another, everything is done easily and informally, in a spirit of love and tolerance. If you believe that, you are probably looking in the Yellow Pages right now for a chimney sweep, so that Santa Claus will not get his fur trim dirty when he visits.

Important occasions are just the time when relatives squabble most fiercely, and etiquette is generally the weapon, although it is not identified as such. It is dressed up as the question of whether one part of the family ''does the right thing'' as defined by another part, or whether one branch is either not up to another's standard or thinks itself above it. The fact is, as many a parent of a bride or bridegroom has ruefully noticed, that it is impossible to sustain a family for any length of time without bringing in some new blood. And with new blood come new customs. Right behind that comes trouble.

Let us take a fictitious young couple who have somehow managed to get themselves married without encountering clashes of etiquette between their two families. (Miss Manners told you this was fictitious.) They approach their first Christmas together, in their own cozy home, which has been such a bower of happiness.

His family has always hung colored electric lights on everything they own, including the cat, the day after Thanksgiving; her family thinks three dull-green satin balls on a living potted tree on the coffee table is as much as one can do to make the house festive without its being garish.

Her family opens presents on Christmas Eve; his opens them on Christmas morning.

His family always goes to late services on Christmas Eve; hers goes caroling.

Her family sends cards only to faraway friends and checks off those received in a red notebook before sending them to a children's hospital; his sends cards to everyone, including next-door neighbors and live-in siblings, and sticks those received in the slats of the Venetian blinds.

His family eats Christmas dinner at three in the afternoon; hers eats it at eight in the evening.

Her family serves roast goose and plum pudding; his serves glazed turkey and fruitcake.

His family gathers in New Hampshire for Christmas and expects them to be there; hers gathers in Chicago and expects them to be there.

Do you begin to see what chance this couple has of making it to the New Year?

What can Miss Manners do to save this marriage, let alone the extended family, should they all gather with their individually inherited beliefs? First, like all good busybodies, she must get them to admit that their problem falls within her particular field. When presents are opened is a question of custom, not of who knows how to behave and who belongs in a tree. Having established this, she will then step neatly aside by proclaiming that unlike everything else in etiquette, where the sense of right and wrong so lacking in our other moral spheres usually prevails, any of these Christmas customs is as valid as any other.

What? You say you feel cheated? Did you suppose that Miss Manners was mad enough to impose her own frail body between those of two near relations with blood in their eyes? Besides, she always takes Christmas off.

Unemployed Parent

DEAR MISS MANNERS:

My husband has lost his job. He worked sixteen years for the same company, bad shifts and all, and now they just throw him out like he was a dog. He's not old, either. His union wants to fight, but he hasn't got the heart. I'm working, but I don't make much. I'm not sure how we are going to get by.

This sounds like I'm asking for a handout, but I'm not. My question is, what do we tell the children? We always said work hard, and you'll be okay. My daughter, who's sixteen and talks about leaving school, says what's the use. What do you tell young people when something like that happens?

GENTLE READER:

Not to put their trust in businesses; but that is not the same as telling them not to put their trust in people, including themselves. The contribution their father has made through his work is still to be admired by those who know him, beginning with the family, even if others chose not to reward it. It is the family's job to remind him of his worth when he is discouraged, and not to conclude that some company had the ability to cancel that with his job. Tell your daughter to stay in school. The more education and skills a person has, the more easily he is able to transfer his working ability from one company to another.

🌹 FAMILY GATHERINGS

Giving Thanks

DEAR MISS MANNERS:

Every year, I spend three days preparing a magnificent Thanksgiving feast for the whole family—between thirteen and seventeen people—from the small children (who yell that it isn't fair if they each don't get a drumstick) to Dad (who tells us all the details about what any food is going to do to his comfort a few hours later). This year, my sister has even warned us that she is going to be miserable (because her boyfriend is spending Thanksgiving with his ex-wife and children). I'm not asking for any thanks, but I can't stand all that carping one more year. What can I do, besides hide in the kitchen to avoid giving one of them a fast yam to the mouth?

GENTLE READER:

Ask for thanks. Hasn't anybody noticed what the purpose of the holiday is? Thanksgiving is God's day off from receiving complaints, and Miss Manners urges you to direct the conversation to appropriate expressions of gratitude for what is right in their lives. With a little luck, you will even hear them thank you for your efforts.

Avoiding Family Dinners

DEAR MISS MANNERS:

Due to illness in my husband's family, it has become the custom for the daughters and daughters-in-law to hold the traditional holiday dinners. The menu and guest list are always in accordance with the mother-in-law's wishes. However, I prefer to have an intimate family dinner (myself, my husband, and our children) with possibly an invitation to one or both sets of the children's grandparents.

With this arrangement, my children are allowed to celebrate at the dining table with the adults, not banished to the kitchen with cousins. It does hamper adult conversation, but my husband and I prefer the childish chatter to the banality of so-called adult conversation. Also, by being seated at the dining table, they improve their table manners and conversational skills.

Upon occasion, I have tried to use this arrangement, only to have my mother-in-law pleading with a daughter to hold "the family dinner," leaving me looking like the terrible person who wants no family ties. How does one tactfully inform one's in-laws that she does not care to entertain brothers, sisters, and their children for holiday dinners? We see the other families occasionally, and we all live reasonably close. No such problem exists on my side of the family, since we all are considerate of one another's wishes. One idea would be to have the families over for just dessert and coffee or gift-exchanging, but I feel certain my mother-in-law would arrange some means of having a formal dinner through one of her other children, thereby pointing the finger at me for not taking my turn. How does one stop this vicious circle without offending the parties involved?

GENTLE READER:

Is it possible that Miss Manners has understood you correctly? Do you wish not only to withdraw your husband and children from this traditional family dinner, but to find a way to prevent an ill old lady from having her usual holiday dinner with her other children? Do you really think you can convince Miss Manners that you are only doing this to teach the children manners, and that your family, in contrast to your husband's, understands what it is to be considerate of another's wishes?

Truly, the holiday spirit is upon us. You must do a better job of hoodwinking Miss Manners if you expect her to produce the zeal with which to assist you in hoodwinking others. The business about the children won't do at all. Miss Manners heartily endorses the civilizing ritual of the family dinner table that you describe, but, as she naturally assumes you practice this 363 nights a year, having special dinners with others on Thanksgiving and Christmas will not ruin the children.

It would seem, then, that the choice is declining to participate in the holiday dinner—and letting the others celebrate and gossip about you as they wish—or participating. In claiming the right to do as you wish, you surely cannot fail to understand that you must grant that to others. No, wait, there is another way. You can claim to be absenting yourself to celebrate in your family tradition, such as it is. See if you can get away with that one. Merry Christmas.

Gender and Tradition

DEAR MISS MANNERS:

Who cleans up at a family meal? I have two brothers and their wives and children coming for Thanksgiving dinner, as well as an aunt and some stray friends. If I were having that big a crowd for a regular dinner party I would get someone in to help, but obviously I'm not going to do that for family, both because of the expense and because I couldn't get anyone to work the holiday, anyway. I could just pile the dishes and leave them, of course, but some will insist on helping me do them right away, and I don't really relish the idea of millions of gummy plates at night, when everyone's gone home.

But I resent the idea that the women have to do the cleaning up while the men go in the family room, and I have one sister-in-law who always goes with the men when this happens, and the rest of us resent this, too.

What's the answer? In order to have a traditional Thanksgiving, do we have to have the traditional division of labor by sex? Bear in mind that if you say yes, my husband, Butterfingers, will have to carve the turkey.

GENTLE READER:

You misread tradition. People often used the terms "men" and "women" when they really meant to describe tastes, habits, and talents that, we have learned, do not properly belong to one gender or another. For example, Miss Manners still believes in the tradition of separating smokers from nonsmokers after dinner, but that would be defeated by separating the ladies from the gentlemen.

The head of the family traditionally carves the turkey. Miss Manners assumes that you each occupy this position at times and suggests that the person least likely to carve a thumb into the stuffing assume it for the day. You might also have recourse to the tradition of honoring a guest by asking him or her to perform such a ceremonial task.

The people least likely to disrupt interesting conversation by being absent from the table should clear the table between courses. If this suggests to you the entire collection of children—well, Miss Manners, who just said she doesn't believe in assigning people tasks by sweeping categories, didn't actually say it was they.

After dinner, those who have a weakness for televised football or for dozing off while digesting unusual quantities of food should retire to a room that has well-upholstered chairs. Those who wish to criticize their behavior or otherwise indulge in conviviality of a quasi-confidential nature should assemble in the kitchen.

Extended Family Conversation

By today's standards of conversation, anyone can talk easily with a new acquaintance. You need only exchange first names before entering into a recital based on one of the standard polite topics, such as what went wrong with your marriage or how much you paid for your house.

These conventions make it dangerous to agree to listen to polite conversation, but that is another problem. The one on which Miss Manners wishes to dwell now is how the habit of self-gossip has extinguished the ability of its practitioners to hold conversation with their own relatives. It is the most socially glib people, she has noticed, who tend to find themselves tongue-tied when faced with holiday tables populated by people of their own blood or choosing.

The reason, of course, is that your family circle knows perfectly well what went wrong with your marriage and how much you paid for your house. What is worse, they have developed their own opinions on these subjects, and are prepared to dispute your premises and conclusions by bringing in irrelevant material, such as how you treated your spouse or what investment opportunities you missed.

Naturally, this kills that form of table talk; or, if it doesn't, it soon brings on the desire to kill the talkers. How, then, are you supposed to talk your way through an entire meal with a bunch of people who sit on the other side of the turkey, looking like you?

There are special rules applying to extended families for each of the usual levels of conversation, which are, going from bottom to top, exchanging information, exchanging opinions, recounting stories, and playing with ideas.

1. You cannot exchange the sort of information that one does socially, such as where you went to school and which old movies you regard fondly. But the satisfaction of discovering common ground is nothing compared to the license one has only among family, for blatantly reeling off triumphs ("I got an A-minus in Man and His Environment"; "We had the whole house recarpeted") and trials ("My liver is acting up again"; "They're beginning to lay people off in my office") and for feeling entitled to warm expressions of congratulations or sympathy.

2. The unsolicited exchange of opinions ("Why do you always fall in love with the same type?"; "That haircut makes your face look even wider") is disastrous under all circumstances, but it is more freely practiced, and with even worse results, among family members. However, with relatives, unlike friends, you can request professional advice ("Come look at my sink"; ". . . at Anastasia's rash"; ". . . at our tax returns"), on the presumption that all good family members put their expertise at the disposal of all others.

3. Long narrations are awful socially, as they generally hold the attention only of those whom they are about, who also happen to be the narrators. But in families, you can reminisce more freely, on the grounds that the characters are all part of the heritage of the listeners.

4. Playing with general ideas, amusingly or philosophically, has always been Miss Manners' concept of real conversation. In family circles, you are likely to have to pick a topic to meet a wider range of ages and interests than at parties ("Are the schools any good?" will rivet any generation), but you need not be shy about ones involving great sentiment ("What do you think the real spirit of Christmas is?"). And you should know only too well which topics are safe and which had better be avoided.

Remarking on the Unremarkable

Life is full of situations that cry out not to be commented upon. It should, for example, be obvious that everyone eats, that some people eat more than others, that individuals nearly all have food preferences, and that many never eat certain foods, for one reason or another. Yet nearly all the talk at mealtimes, and a great deal of that in between, forms a running commentary on the eating that is or is not taking place.

For family gatherings, this is often the only form of conversation:

"You didn't touch your dessert. . . . I thought you were on a diet. . . . Are you going to have seconds? . . . You have to finish this because I don't want any left over. . . . Didn't you like the soup? . . . I'm not supposed to eat salty things. . . . Where do you buy your meat? . . . Oh, come on, I made this specially for you. . . ."

It's enough to make Miss Manners queasy. Some time ago, she told you to cut out all that talk about wine, as it was getting to be vulgar, and now she must tell you the same thing about food. Gather around the table, and enjoy yourselves, by all means, or don't enjoy yourselves if that is what you prefer, but please stop talking about what you or anybody else is eating.

Miss Manners hopes she need not remind you that certain unscheduled events at the dinner table, or anywhere else, should pass unremarked. The answer to "Excuse me" is not "Where are you going?"

There is also altogether too much comment these days about how people look. The only way you are supposed to notice that someone looks is "nice," as in "My, don't you look nice!" or some equally innocuous variation. In fact, if your proposed comment would not sound right after an opening of "My," whether or not you use this colloquialism, it should not be said. One can imagine, for example, "My, what a pretty dress," "My, how rested you look after your vacation," and "My, how grown-up you look," but not "My, how stout you're getting," "My, what a terrible haircut," or "My, you're going to be a squirt like your father, aren't you?"

Miss Manners does not believe in commenting at all upon emotional appearance, unless it is being displayed with obvious provocative theatricality. "Why do you look so depressed?" is a rude question unless the person has been clamoring for your attention in order to show you ravages for which you are responsible.

Even "Why are you crying?" is a question that should be put only by parents, those temporarily in charge of weepers under the age of six, and people who recognize that the chief effort of the crier is to project the sobs rather than to conceal them. The therapeutic effect of unburdening one's sorrows is often exaggerated in comparison with the comfort of believing that one's lapse has gone unnoticed.

It is, in fact, a basic human dignity, all too often ignored these days, to be allowed to exercise one's taste and get through the vicissitudes of ordinary life, without having to subject it all to the critical scrutiny of those whose taste and judgment we do not remember requesting.

Dietary Differences

DEAR MISS MANNERS:

This will be the first holiday season following my sister's recent marital separation. My panic concerns her current boyfriend, who has impressed me as a know-it-all. In addition, this man is a devout vegetarian. The normal fare at our family Christmas dinner is ham, turkey, dressing, gravy, and vegetables seasoned with fatback.

Our potential brother-in-law will probably eat cranberry sauce or nothing at all. On overnight visits, he has said things like "I hope you aren't having pork, beef, or chicken." I personally try not to fix anything offensive when they visit—I do not think I should have to make special things, but I do. What is the proper behavior of a vegetarian when visiting and dining at nonvegetarian houses? This is especially a problem for my parents, as they are probably not going to understand, much less fix the traditional dinner differently.

GENTLE READER:

For both vegetarians and know-it-alls, the rule is different for guests than for brothers-in-law. It sounds to Miss Manners as if this person is more likely to remain the former than become the latter, especially if family approval is a factor, but that you will have to decide.

Guests are allowed to get away with being know-it-alls, but are not invited to meals at which foods they don't eat are being featured—set-menu holiday meals, barbecues, chicken-frying contests, or whatever. They are not supposed to dictate what everyone else will eat, but to fortify themselves before arriving, and spend the meal idly pushing the food around the plate while enjoying the opportunity to hog the conversation. If their diets are known, they should be invited only when they can enjoy most, if not all, of the food.

Brothers-in-law, or other regular fixtures of the family, are teased, good-naturedly but unmercifully, about being know-it-alls, but they are provided with food they can eat, even if the rest of the family is having something else. Efforts are made by those others, however, to refrain from saying, "Boy, you don't know what you're missing."

Private Media Events

DEAR MISS MANNERS:

My problem is with the use of videocassette recorders and cameras at family gatherings. There is no problem for the children (who love to perform for the camera) or, in my experience, for the men (who seem to be able to ignore the camera), but all of the women present objected strenuously to being on camera and even to having conversations picked up on the audio. This made last Christmas a very tense affair, with some women leaving the gathering for other parts of the house, or not talking when the camera operator was in the room.

What is to be done? The offending parties just cannot understand the negative reaction to their own understandable desire to preserve some tangible reminder of the gathering, and they and the children take great pleasure in playing back their recording later in the day. They are the proud grandparents who are hosting the family, or the proud young father, and it is not easy or politic to try to modify their behavior. Strong protests by most of the women at both gatherings had no effect.

GENTLE READER:

Miss Manners is trying to make allowances for the desire of photographers to immortalize their relatives, and for the madness of photographers in general who are unable to understand that it's difficult to produce a remembrance of an event if you prevent it from taking place by recruiting the participants to do modeling instead. Still, it distresses her to hear that strong protests by their own relatives have no effect on these people.

Very well, then. Let us set some rules. Miss Manners suggests that you set out photo opportunities, much the way the White House does, and ban other camera-roaming. A certain room could be set aside for the activity, in which those who enjoy it could spend as much time as they like. Others could agree to make limited appearances there, with the understanding that candid photography elsewhere is prohibited. The resulting photographs will all be of children horsing around, saying things like ''Take me!'' But so be it.

UNPAIRED PARENTS

Divorce for the Children's Sake

That people will do anything to please their children is evident from the number of people who explain that they are getting divorced for their sake. ''We felt it was better for the children than living in a house with tension,'' they will confide.

Miss Manners does not consider it her business whether or not people get divorced, or claim the ability to judge whether they will be better off doing so or not. She only hopes that the fashionable cliché, replacing the earlier one of ''staying together for the sake of the children,'' is not obliging perfectly happy couples to sacrifice their unions.

Admittedly, the children of divorced parents are better off in many ways. It is easier to play one parent off against the other if they are rivals, and nicer to have two houses to play in than only one. It is up to divorcing parents to ensure that the children are not too much better off for their own good.

To begin with, Miss Manners suggests that divorcing couples stop making that excuse. The habit of invoking children as excuses for adult behavior is all too easy to fall into, and children understandably resent it. Household tensions, however casual or profound, should be decently clothed in politeness, and if parents are polite to each other, their children are not apt to speculate on whether they are deeply in love or fulfilled in their very souls.

Divorcing is an adult decision, for which adults must take full responsibility. No child should ever be asked his opinion on the advisability, or allowed to think that he has any influence in the matter. The selfish declaration ''We're doing this because we think we would both be better off living apart'' is, in this case, much kinder than any suggestion of doing it for the benefit of the child.

It is announced as a *fait accompli*, preferably before the child hears it from the neighbors. Once the principle of doing it for the sake of the adult, rather than the child, is established, the usual bad effect it produces will not seem so illogical. No one expects anyone else to be delighted to hear that the former's convenience is prevailing over the latter's wishes. ''I'm sorry, but this suits us, and you're going to have to live with it'' is easier to take than attempts to persuade the child that he really should be glad.

Announcements of impending marriages or other household arrangements should be made at the same time in the same spirit. There's no use asking, ''How would you feel about having Roderick for a stepfather?'' unless you want an honest answer.

If that is enough brutality for one day, Miss Manners will now help the parent back into the natural parental state of reassurance and optimism. The arms open,

DRS

Dear Polly,

Theodore Bishop
Right and I were
married very quietly
on July seventh.
Teddy has three children,
Heather, Lauren and
Orville, and I very
much look forward
to introducing my new
family to you.

Affectionately yours,

Daffodil

A LETTER ANNOUNCING A SECOND MARRIAGE. *It is always correct to announce a marriage by letter, rather than with the more formal, third-person, engraved announcement. For second (or fifth) marriages, it is actually preferable, as well as cheaper, and less likely to inspire mean people to exclaim: "What does she expect us to do? What happened to the teaspoon we sent her the first time—Rhino probably hocked it. Anyway, how many times is she going to pull this on us?"*

the beaming look returns, and the firm tone used for the announcement turns to one of warmth at the cozy place of honor one has reserved, smack in the middle of the new plans, for the children.

You will see that none of this allows for that currently popular family sport, the unburdening of the soul. Miss Manners is not of the stiff-upper-lip school so much as to fail to recognize that need, but she heartily disapproves of dumping such burdens on children. If at all possible, the divorcing parents should use this occasion to learn to present a united front. Eventually, they will need it. A few years of competition, along the child-induced lines of "But Mommy always lets me do that" and "But Daddy bought me this," can deplete anyone's stock of principles and cash very quickly.

Instead, the divorce may be viewed as an opportunity for demonstrating to the children the beauty and virtue of good manners under stress.

Here are some useful phrases for the well-mannered divorcing parent:

"No, darling, I think Mommy is a wonderful woman, and just because we're not going to be living together, that doesn't mean that I don't appreciate her."

"Well, now, I'm sure Daddy had his reasons for saying that."

"He can't be that bad. It's not easy being a stepfather. Why don't you try to give him a chance?"

"No, when you're in their house, it's only fair that you obey her, as well as Daddy."

"All right, but try to understand that it's not easy for Mommy, managing alone, and she needs all the help you can give her."

"Of course, Daddy loves you. We don't count love by how many presents or phone calls we get, do we?"

What's that? You say it sticks in the throat? All right, if virtue itself isn't enough to convince you of the wisdom of being polite throughout divorce, Miss Manners will propose another motivation. Part of the development of the childish brain consists of disbelieving everything that is said, and cherishing the notion that the opposite is true. The parent who attempts to enlist the child in a dislike of an absent parent will eventually be disbelieved, with the diagnosis that the misstatements are delivered out of meanness. The parent who says only polite things about the other will also be disbelieved, but the assumption will be that the motivation is kindness. Which would you prefer?

The Child Exchange

New social forms require new rules of etiquette, and the current rage for divorce as a source of human drama has inspired Miss Manners to set laws for the exchanging of children.

The child exchange is not a system whereby parents can trade in children who do not suit them, but a social routine that has grown around weekends, holidays, and other occasions when a child is transferred from the residence of one parent to the other's care. It has been used to act out many interesting emotions, many of which should probably not be expressed at all, certainly not in front of minors.

La Ronde

The Divorced Family Weekend

Friday Afternoon

Friday Night

Saturday

Sunday Morning

The Divorced Family's Favorite Meeting Place

Sunday Evening

Miss Manners does not want to hear tales of mistreatment or other motivations for uncontrollable behavior. She is well aware that such exchanges are often the only occasions on which formerly married people see each other, and that they therefore naturally want to pack into them all their accumulated conflicts.

Her position is that anyone who is mature enough to get divorced ought to be able to behave; and that anyone regularly possessed by uncontrollable feelings ought not to have the custody of small children.

The proper exchange begins with simple courtesy. We do not accept the standards that commercial delivery services have tried to impose: that the only convenience counted is the one of the person coming to the house, making it reasonable to require the one who lives there to stay put, on call, all day if necessary. Appointments to pick up or deliver children must be set exactly, and exactly kept. The obligation of the parent turning the child over is to see to it that the child is ready, and the necessary equipment—appropriate clothing, toys, needed school books—is also handed over.

Failure to observe all these rules by either parent is not a proper way of demonstrating contempt for the other parent. It merely demonstrates what a rude person one is, which, while not legally a cause for divorce, is certainly a cause for the other's looking back upon the fact of the divorce with satisfaction.

One does not bring or (in the case of the person who is at home) display guests at such an occasion, if the presence of such people is known to be provocative. If the replacements for the respective spouses have any sense at all, they will remain in the car, upstairs, or in another state during exchanges of children between currently unfriendly people. This does not mean that failure to observe such a nicety is an excuse for bad behavior in the person so provoked. One can hardly imagine a better occasion for demonstrating to children the necessity of restraining oneself to a semblance of civilized behavior under all circumstances.

The other great principle to be demonstrated is that one does not take over the ordinary lives of other people, especially one's children, with an insistence on returning to one's own problems. To dominate an event important to a child—whether it is the arrival of the weekend in the life of a schoolchild, or a grown-up child's wedding—with a reenactment of the parents' own nasty drama is unforgivable. This is the manners reason—there are also moral reasons—why one does not use up custody time with the apparently popular pastime of collecting information or delivering insults about the other parent with the child.

Besides, as Miss Manners keeps telling the maritally disgruntled, rude behavior to an ex-spouse or that person's subsequent spouse is counterproductive if the motive is to make someone feel terrible. It is the cheerful, happy, cooperative parent who both wins the heart of the child and rubs it in to the former spouse just how happy living without that person can be.

The Divorced Weekend

Why lions and tigers should have the full task of amusing the children of divorced parents on weekends Miss Manners does not know. She does know that the combined efforts of every creature in the zoo are not enough to cement a relationship between small children and a nonresident parent.

Weekend custody is often the occasion for a rivalry between parents that does nothing for their offspring except ruin their appetites for dinner. The parent who wishes to make his or her time seem like a holiday, in contrast to the everyday child-rearing of the chief custodial parent, is making a mistake. People with whom we only make whoopee never turn out to mean as much to us as those with whom we share our everyday lives.

Miss Manners will not concede that this means that the weekend parent hasn't a chance to weave himself into the fabric of the child's life. The advantage of not having to do the daily nagging about getting ready to go to school, getting to bed early, and so on remains with the weekend guardian. There are greater blocks of time with which to work, uninterrupted, and fewer tasks for the child.

Filling that time with an occasional excursion is all very well, but only as a part of sharing the parent's life and interests, and his sharing the child's. First, the child must learn that he has a permanent place in that parent's life, and a realistic one, as opposed to that of the pal one goes partying with, so to speak.

This means that the parent reveals his household routine, whatever it is, and asks the child to share it. The chores of running a household, as well as the rules concerning meals, bedtime, and manners standards, are made explicit. It is one of the great ironies of child-rearing that children who are allowed to do anything they feel like end up feeling resentful, as they all harbor, against what one would think to be their own interests, the strict and conservative notion that a parent who truly loved them would take the trouble to bring them up.

If there are other people in Papa's or Mamma's life and household, that fact should not be hidden, only because it cannot be done successfully. That does not mean that a parent brings a date to all the time spent with his children, even such a respectable date as a new spouse. The concept that one can love several people and yet want time alone with each, as well as the pleasure of having them all together, is a difficult one—no child really understands why, having him, his parents still felt they needed another child—but essential for an understanding of the logistics of any family, no matter what its composition.

So much for the theory. What happens when the children arrive on Friday night, spoiling for the opportunity to be spoiled? What on earth does one do with them?

The first thing is the briefing. No, no, not their briefing the parent on the other parent's social life or character faults. That should really be discouraged, for the psychological toll it exacts, not to mention the dearth of amusement to children. The briefing comes from the parent on what has happened in his life, since they were last there, and what to expect for the weekend; and from the child, on his activities since last seen and his hopes for the weekend.

Here is a sample dialogue:

Parent: "I'm a little edgy, because I've been working on a tough case this week." (Story follows, geared to understanding of the child, but sharing in some way what the parent's thoughts and concerns have been.) "I've got about two hours' work left, and we need to plan a study period, when I can do that and you can do your homework. Henrietta and her children will be here Saturday night, and I'd appreciate it if you would help me amuse those kids. Otherwise, here are some things I thought we might do.'' (There follows a list of real interests the parent wants to share, whether it is painting the garage or going out with some definite mission and preparation, such as heading for the local museum after a discussion of a particular topic to be studied there, reading aloud something from which they can all find amusement and instruction, or practicing a sport together. The zoo is fine if they go there because everybody wants to see something, not because nobody can think of anything else to do.)

Child: "Why can't we go to the movies? Why do you have to have those stinky kids here? Can we have a pizza for dinner? I can't do my homework, because I forgot my history book. Why do we have to paint the garage? I'd rather watch television while you do it.''

At this point, it is useful to the parent to imagine himself in full custody. Would he treat the children then as somewhat unpleasant houseguests, who have to be indulged because they are only around temporarily, or would he assert himself as a parent and reply that he expects his children to eat sensibly, perform their duties, be pleasant to his guests, participate in the household responsibilities, and make an effort to exert themselves intellectually, rather than allowing their minds to lie around doing the easiest thing?

It is that that makes the real difference between a parent and a host. It is possible to be a parent on a part-time basis, and worth it, if for no other reason, because children have amazingly little emotional attachment to those who only want to entertain them.

Joint Custody

DEAR MISS MANNERS:

Does joint custody mean I always have to be polite to someone I can't stand?

GENTLE READER:

Yes. But think of the benefits. You will set an unparalleled example of civilized behavior to your children and impress your admirers as one to be trusted even under adversity.

New Parent

The ancient Greek code of hospitality is the one to which Miss Manners still subscribes. You may never murder a guest while he is in your house. It is so much more polite to get him off the premises first, by sending him on an impossible mission from which you are quite certain he cannot return alive.

In the crude modern translation, this means that everybody in the household has to be nice to all the guests, even if he personally didn't want them there, and even to the extent of letting them get away with the murder of etiquette rules. Guests can leave their beds unmade, start eating before their hostess, leave

CHILDREN PERFORM THE DUTY OF BEING SHOWN OFF TO ADULT GUESTS. *At great personal sacrifice these children have dressed in parent-pleasing clothes, and are cheerfully allowing themselves to be patronized senseless by visitors. The gentleman at left is explaining at length what things were like when he was a boy, while the lady at right has just expressed her amazement at how nicely the hors d'oeuvres are being passed.*

dirty dishes around the house, and mess up the paper in the morning so that nobody can find anything.

They can also stay home next time. Nothing unites a family so strongly as the presence of someone who is an annoyance to all. The difficulty is with one whose faults are invisible to the individual who invited him and a constant trial to everyone else. Nothing divides a family so strongly as that. Miss Manners seems to recall that there are some ugly examples in ancient Greek literature of what can happen then.

For short-term visiting, the only defense is endurance, with some temporal and geographical protection. Children can arrange to be excused after saying hello and submitting with grace to the routine nonsensical inquiries about their growth by particularly disliked adults, for example. Siblings may be told to keep their own friends out of other people's rooms. Sometimes conditions may be set for future invitations: Aurora is not allowed to come here again unless it is understood that there is to be no crank telephoning from this house. You can ask Brian over to play, but not to dinner.

That is harder to do if the guest is a relative. Unpleasant relatives are one of the burdens of life, and the only comfort is the virtue of being meek to them and the relief when they leave. (For examples, please see *Houseguests*, Chapter 7.)

What, however, if the guest never leaves? Suppose it's Mamma or Papa's adored friend, who has been installed as something less than a stepparent but more than a temporary nuisance?

Well, any guest is, in some way, a family project, but there's no use pretending that the family can rule as a committee on who comes and what limits must be set. The parent, who is presumed to act with some maturity in everybody's greater interests, decides those things alone, and it is just as well, or no parent would ever be allowed to have a guest who stayed more than an hour and didn't bring candy. It is therefore up to the parent to do these things responsibly.

A live-in adult will, by necessity, have some authority over the children. What this is ought to be understood by all, and the person who is abused by someone in either position ought to be able to take this case directly to the parent for a fair decision. Miss Manners is a great believer in investing stepparents with full parental authority, and none of that I-don't-have-to-unless-my-mother-says stuff, but not in giving it to temporaries. Melding two theories of child-rearing into a consistent system that satisfies both and can be more or less understood by the children is hard enough with presumably permanent parents, even the original ones living together, and should not, if possible, be attempted more than—oh, say, twice— to a childhood.

It is unfortunate when a parent's own social insecurities interfere with presiding fairly in such a household. The adult who is anxious to make a good impression on someone and perhaps to encourage permanent residence can plead with the inmates to be polite and kind to him or her. That, in fact, should be done routinely; please see obligations to guests (above). Siding with that person, regardless of the merits of the case, and allowing that person to be rude to the children is unconscionable. So is allowing the children to be rude, on the grounds that their offended sensibilities excuse them from normal social duties.

In the end, no one will benefit from the existence of a household in which the legitimate interests of some of the members have been suppressed in the interest of making up to any of the others. Propagandist that she is, Miss Manners nevertheless truly believes that no one will ever live happily for more than three days, and never mind ever after, in a home where manners have been cast aside on any excuse whatsoever. (For servants' authority, please see pp. 328–331. For the parent's friend's side, please see pp. 73–74.)

The Stepmother Myth

DEAR MISS MANNERS:

Ten years ago, my mother passed away. Two years later, my dad remarried. I call her by her first name. My children call her Grandma.

When introducing her to my friends, what do I say? "This is my dad's wife"? "My stepmother"? No way will I say "This is my mother" or call her Mother.

Yet I am very fond of her, and respect her as well. She and my dad feel it is very disrespectful to say she is my stepmother. Please answer as soon as possible as this is causing some friction in the family.

GENTLE READER:

My, my, my. Will you all please stop putting your own emotional connotations onto perfectly good words? What is the good of devising conventional terms for everyday use if people insist on rejecting them for idiosyncratic reasons?

It is nonsense to say that "stepmother" is a disrespectful term. It describes a perfectly respectable relationship, and Miss Manners refuses to concede to it that fairy-tale association with wickedness. It seems to her that assuming the task of motherhood to someone with whom one has not been associated through birth is an honorable undertaking. Neither does she think that using the shorter term "mother" to describe a stepmother or a mother-in-law takes anything away from one's original mother.

Among these prejudices, Miss Manners advises deferring to the preferences of one's elders. You are a grown-up woman, and it seems to Miss Manners that you can manage to choke out describing her as your mother, if you are unable to convince her that the affection and respect in which you hold her has made the term "stepmother" very dear to you.

Reserving Titles

DEAR MISS MANNERS:

I am a mother of two, and have been married to my second husband for eight years. I had been a widow since my first husband died in Vietnam. My problem is that my second husband objects to the way I introduce my first husband's father at social gatherings.

My present husband's father has been dead for nearly seven years, and he never got a chance to meet his grandchildren. I loved him very much, and always refer to him as Grandfather Ben to our children. They call my first father-in-law Uncle, as we have a very close relationship and I never wanted to sever our ties. My husband feels that our children should call him Mr. Smith, and that I should introduce him as either my ex-father-in-law, Mr. Smith, or simply as Bill Smith; I feel that to use the first would indicate that I was divorced, not widowed, and the second seems very cold. All I want is to continue to introduce this fine man to our friends and acquaintances, as he is a stranger to this area and knows no one. My husband's family, including his mom, have no objections to including Bill in our family circle, and I don't feel it's disrespectful of his father's memory to do so.

GENTLE READER:

Tricky as this little etiquette problem is, you have no idea how grateful Miss Manners is to work on it. The reason is that it is only an etiquette problem; everybody in the situation is full of goodwill. Most of what Miss Manners gets along this line turns out to be only nominally about etiquette, with the problem really being only an excuse for acrimonious people who want the sanction of etiquette as an excuse to make each other feel terrible.

All your husband is asking is that you reserve family titles for your current family. He is not asking you to sever your ties, and, indeed, his family is apparently generous about taking in this man to whom you feel a tie. Accept that, and do not annoy them with the detail. It is not cold to address the man by his name, and you can still find opportunities privately to tell him that you will always cherish him as having a unique place in your life.

Sequential Mothers

DEAR MISS MANNERS:

Recently, I attended a bar mitzvah of a boy whose parents are divorced. The father, who has remarried, gave a corsage to both his former and his current wife on this occasion. The boy's mother politely declined to wear her corsage on account of allergies. Later, she expressed to me her resentment that her ex-husband had also given the identical corsage to his current wife, saying that it made her feel like part of a harem. She pointed out (correctly) that she had been solely responsible for her son's religious education and the planning of the bar mitzvah, and that the stepmother had taken no role in this. My question is, did the boy's father behave correctly? Is there any way he could have made this apparently well-meaning gesture without wounding everyone's feelings?

GENTLE READER:

Probably not. People adore taking umbrage at well-meaning gestures these days. Why, Miss Manners cannot fathom. It is not as though the world were so crowded with people in a kinetic state of making well-meaning gestures that we had better discourage some of them and restore the balance of rudeness in the world.

Corsages seem to be particular harbingers of insult, but who is to say that we would not be troublemakers also if we were tied together at the ankles and hung upside down? If they don't clash with ladies' dresses, they spoil the neckline, and if four grandmothers and three mothers are given them for a ceremonial occasion, not only do the recipients complain about the aesthetics, but a great-aunt sulks at having been omitted. This poor man, in a futile attempt to avoid conflict, figured (correctly) that if he gave different corsages, each lady would consider that the other's was "better" than hers. Developing allergies begins to seem like the only peaceful solution. (For more on stepparents at family ceremonies, please see pp. 277–282.)

Dramatic Reunion

DEAR MISS MANNERS:

I was divorced from my first husband more than ten years ago, moved to a new city, remarried, and now have three children. My husband travels for business and suggested that I may join him (with our kids) in the very town, 1,500 miles away, where my ex and his new wife and child live.

Would it be appropriate to write in advance and suggest coming for dinner or a drink, if my husband agrees? We separated fairly amicably, all things considered.

Gentle Reader:

One can hardly ask for a more interesting social event than the reunion of formerly married people, especially when the current families are present, observing their spouse/parent carefully for signs of renewed interest, demonstrations of current loyalties, and so on. The exes must satisfy them, with whom, after all, they have to live, and at the same time evaluate and show off to the former spouse— all the while maintaining faultless politeness because any tiny slip will be overinterpreted by everyone present as deeply symbolic.

At least, that is Miss Manners' idea of good drama. It is not everyone's, especially when he or she is emotionally connected to the situation. It is certainly, therefore, a good idea to obtain your husband's consent, and to obtain from him a little advance goodwill by explaining that your curiosity has to do with your present happiness and the desire to indulge in your relief that things turned out as they did.

For the same reason, do not be disappointed if your former husband does not accept the invitation because he and his wife do not feel up to this frolic. By all means, issue the invitation. Just remember, if the event does take place, that generous charm is your best proof that you are not being eaten up by regrets.

PRESENTS

Blessedly Receiving

"Here."

"I've already got one."

This seems to be the natural way of giving and accepting a present, according to Miss Manners' careful observation of the ritual among people in their most nearly natural state. It is not only children, who, in their uncharming guilelessness, manage to take the satisfaction out of generosity and acquisition alike. You would think, from the ungraciousness with which present-giving is usually accompanied, that it takes place between people who wish no credit for their kindness, and those who want to discourage the practice of which they are the beneficiaries.

The correct way to give a present is to accompany it by a shy smile. The correct way to receive one is with a look of astonished delight. The appropriate words are "Thank you, I love it, how kind of you, this is marvelous" and "I'm so glad, I hoped you might like it." Instead of this pleasant ritual, present-givers tend to shove their offerings with such statements as "You probably won't like this, but I couldn't think of anything else" or "You're so hard to get presents for because you have everything" or "I was going to get you [naming something more expensive than the actual present], but I was afraid you'd never use it." There are also an amazing number of present-receivers who think it appropriate to say, "I'm never really going to use this, so there's no use in my taking it," or "It's really too expensive—you don't mind if I trade it in for something more practical, do you?"

All of this comes from the natural inclination to assess an object for its intrinsic, rather than its symbolic, value. The latter is the civilized, rather than the natural thing to do. Do not mistake Miss Manners' preference for the common naiveté of "it's the thought that counts," which would have it that all presents are equal. They are not. It takes some sophistication to assess an object in terms of the trouble the donor has taken with it, first in observation, and then in either effort or money.

What makes any present valuable is that it confirms that the giver was interested enough in the receiver to take careful note of his or her needs or preferences. Deprecating statements on the part of the giver demonstrate that he has not cared to take that trouble; grudging statements on the part of the receiver indicate that any such attempt has been a failure.

The other value that needs assessing by one who receives a present is what sacrifice, however small, it represents on the part of the giver. Homemade presents are universally deemed to be charming, chiefly because hardly anyone has time and effort to spare. Few people have extra money, either, which is one reason that diamonds and automobiles, for example, make successful presents—unless given by a husband whose regular jewelry bill the bracelet will be a small part of, or by a wife who was planning to trade in the old car anyway.

Now—once you have accurately assessed a present, how does this alter your behavior at the time of its exchange? Only by the degree of enthusiasm you supply when engaging in the ritual Miss Manners described. The difference, whether you have worked on a present for months or merely grabbed the nearest thing, or whether you recognize that the giver has done the former or the latter, is in the glow that accompanies the shy smile or the astonished delight.

Greed

Small and innocent children make marvelously skilled extortionists, Miss Manners has observed. There seems to be a completely natural feeling that leads them, in a wonderfully open way with no prompting necessary, to say such things as "Buy me that!" and "What did you bring me?"

Adults, operating under the disadvantage of having been more or less civilized, rarely have a comparable ability to reply with equally charming candor, "Don't be silly, dear." This state of affairs is an example of why Miss Manners is always so puzzled to hear well-meaning people rattling on about not wanting to inhibit the naturalness of their children. Why not, pray? Repressing the dear things, an activity of bygone days that was known as child-rearing, can only improve the state of the world.

Certainly Miss Manners cannot be alone in being uncharmed by unbridled greed. The child who is allowed to express this universal but nevertheless unattractive urge will end up the poorer. A parent therefore has an obligation to the child, as well as to the household budget, to refuse all such demands. Even for occasions on which presents can reasonably be anticipated—birthdays, Christmas—a child should be encouraged to engage in hinting, rather than ordering. (''What a beautiful doll!'' and ''I wish I had a bicycle'' are not much more subtle than ''Gimme,'' but they are more charming.)

Miss Manners recommends a strict policy of demonstrating that attempts to establish other present-giving occasions backfire. The childish imagination, not to mention the childish legalistic inclination, is deft at proposing such events. Many parents have found themselves unwittingly accepting rules that they must bring presents from trips, that a sick child is entitled to material compensation, or that any excursion, whether it is ostensibly for the purpose of sightseeing, going to the circus, or visiting the doctor, is fundamentally a shopping expedition. The clever parent counters this by showing that, left alone, he or she is subject to generous whims, but that petitioning drives all such impulses away. ''Actually, I was thinking of getting you that to surprise you, but you've taken all the fun out of it, so never mind.'' Or ''You're making me sorry I brought you—I thought the show would be a treat, but I wouldn't have bothered to take you out just to buy souvenirs.''

The resourceful child will then turn to blackmailing grandparents or other likely suckers. Some of these can be enlisted to cooperate in the parental policy, but the only legitimate object of training is the child. All suspect loot should be rigidly analyzed (''How did Grandpa happen to get you that gun you've been talking about?'') and treated like either diamond earrings offered to a respectable young lady by a gentleman of evil intentions (given back) or, if that would cause etiquette problems among the adults, like the door prize won by the chairman of the ball committee (given to the needy).

In sum, the child must learn that his own apparent surprise is a major ingredient of the pleasure and gratitude that encourage others to give you what you want. It is an appeal to base emotions, but isn't that just what children have abundantly available?

Reciprocity

DEAR MISS MANNERS:

Most of our large family is moderately to very well-off, and they can afford to give us fine gifts. We are very grateful, but we feel guilty about not being able to reciprocate appropriately. We barely pay our bills for an average month with my husband's salary and my home sewing for the public.

Every year, I spend many hours making handmade gifts for our relatives. Since I do not spend this time making money, we are left very short and are forced to borrow and spend the rest of the year repaying it. We have suggested to our families that we draw names or give gifts only to the children, but these were turned down because our families really enjoy the gift-giving ceremony. Since there are twenty of them and three of us, we are clearly the minority. Please tell us what we can properly, graciously, and self-respectingly do.

GENTLE READER:

You certainly managed to knock off the standard solutions to the problem of burdensome present-giving, didn't you? Making things by hand, or limiting the exchanges to one each, or giving presents only to children are all fine, time-honored techniques to avoid the problem in large families of spending half the year buying presents and the other half paying for them. Yet a present-opening ceremony is one of the few occasions on which you cannot show up empty-handed. The rule is that if the presents are part of the entertainment, as they are at children's birthday parties and at showers, you must bring one, however small. Note that last adjective, which is your last hope. The present may be very inexpensive indeed, provided it seems well chosen, genuinely amusing, or best-of-its-class in an object, such as a hanger or toothpicks, on which one ordinarily spends almost nothing. Miss Manners trusts that among decent, loving families, no one ever notices or thinks about the cost of a present.

Equality Among Steps

DEAR MISS MANNERS:

I'm married fifteen years to my second husband. My first marriage ended after nine years and two children. I have another child from my second marriage. For the past fifteen years, my two children from number one have received nothing from my mother-in-law and her daughter (their aunt). My daughter from marriage number two always receives many expensive gifts. They are all given something at Christmas. Am I wrong to feel deeply hurt, as I feel it's so unfair for one child to receive birthday presents year after year and my other two nothing?

My mother-in-law says our daughter is her natural grandchild, and a present for her is expected, and gives her pleasure to buy. I say they are all my children and they should be treated equally. I haven't spoken to my mother-in-law and sister-in-law for more than a month, as I finally expressed my feelings and I feel I'm justified. Please give me your opinion. My husband takes their side and says I'm making a big deal over nothing. Am I?

GENTLE READER:

Yes, and not only that, but you are making a worse deal for yourself for the future in attempting to establish among your children the idea that everyone must treat them all alike. It cannot be done, even by you. You may think you are carrying out a policy of equality now, but one day, perhaps when your children are an advanced age themselves and you are hoping for a little peace in which to end your days, one of them will suddenly snap out a memory of the day you gave her sister one more chocolate-chip cookie than you gave her, and another will snap back about not having been allowed to stay up as late as she distinctly remembers her sister was allowed to do when she reached the same age.

That, Miss Manners assures you, is what can happen to a mother who really does love all of her children equally, and who is trying very hard to pursue a policy of treating them all the same. What of people who do not actually have the same feelings about each? You are expecting your present mother-in-law to think of all your children as having equal claims to being her grandchildren. It would be nice if she did, but she obviously does not, so you are claiming that it is her duty to do so.

Let Miss Manners ask you this: The children of your first marriage have relatives that your third child does not. Must they also treat all your children alike? Must your former mother-in-law and your ex-husband, for that matter, match whatever attention they pay to the children related to them by an equal tribute to your next child? Of course not. You don't really believe, deep in your heart, that people do not distinguish their blood relatives from connections acquired through re-marriage. Your true motive is to protect your older children, who are perhaps neglected by their paternal relatives, from the consequences of your divorce, by demanding that others act as substitute relations. You cannot do this. It is the responsibility of a parent to help children deal with any difficulties caused by divorce—not to force others to pretend that there are no consequences. Miss Manners heartily recommends that you abandon all futile desires to prove to your children that they may expect to be treated identically by anyone. If you can succeed in convincing them that you have unbounded love for each of them, you will have done something far more important.

Curbing Present-Giving

Dear Miss Manners:

My husband and I would like to discontinue our long-standing practice of giving gifts to our nieces and nephews at Christmas and on their birthdays. All are still under eighteen. We have no children to receive gifts in return. Can you suggest the least awkward way out?

Gentle Reader:

Although Miss Manners can imagine many good reasons for discontinuing the giving of presents—that the expense is too great, that the recipients have not performed the courtesy of expressing any thanks—she doesn't much care for yours of dwelling on the fact that you will not get your investment back in kind. In any case, the way to do it is to send letters or cards with personal notes on them, congratulating the children on their birthdays or wishing them a merry Christmas. That way, they will know that you have not forgotten them, but have changed the practice.

The Purpose of Thank-you Letters

Dear Miss Manners:

At Christmas, I had occasion to talk by phone to my niece and I made the remark that she probably didn't remember me or my husband very well. I hadn't seen her since her marriage about nine years ago, and prior to that, I rarely saw her. I later learned through her grandmother that my remark had hurt her, because she well remembered us and the unusual gifts we used to send her.

I, too, had an aunt who did lovely things for me when I was a child: gave me my first roller skates, a lovely small cedar chest, etc. I have never forgotten her or ceased to love her, although we rarely see each other. I think the secret of joyful gift-giving lies in the lack of thought about how much we intend to spend or how practical the gift should be. Anybody can stick a check in an envelope along with a card and consider his "duty" done, but the person who goes out looking for something a little different will sometimes end up with an ideal gift for very little. He'll have all the fun of selecting it, and anticipating the surprise at the receiving end of the line.

And perhaps we make too much over failure to receive thank-you notes, particularly from children. It's the parents' responsibility to teach children that it's nice to say thank you, but shouldn't our gifts be given with no thought for thanks? "The Lord loveth a cheerful giver" applies to nieces, nephews, and grandchildren, every bit as much as it does to a contribution placed in the collection plate.

GENTLE READER:

As you have so charmingly mastered the art of present-giving, why do you expect so little on the receiving end? The Lord probably also loveth a graceful receiver, but in any case, the givers certainly do. You mention the pleasure one anticipates in the surprise one's present produces. What about the pleasure of knowing for sure? The purpose of a thank-you letter is not only, as some people seem to believe, to force a payment in labor in exchange for a present, but to allow the giver to know that his generosity has been appreciated.

This, unfortunately, does not come naturally. Left to their own meager devices, children or anyone else will accept all kinds of offerings as no more than their due, without the least thought of expressing genuine pleasure in them, much less of simulating pleasure when there is none, as a way of showing appreciation for the spirit of the giver, if not for the item chosen. It is not selfishness to want to know that your kind intentions have had the desired effect—you expect the dog to wag its tail when you pet it, don't you? Would you be just as satisfied if it growled and walked away, knowing that you had performed your side well? Yes, it is the job of parents to teach this, but other relatives can sometimes encourage it, too, with gentle inquiries about whether the present was received and if it suited.

Speaking of which, why don't you write your aunt a thank-you letter right now, and tell her how much you remember, after all these years, those lovely things she did for you? Do you suppose that her interest ended with her own behavior and that such a reaction would mean nothing to her? Wouldn't you have liked that niece to have let you know, now and again, that she remembers you warmly?

The Proper Results

DEAR MISS MANNERS:

Between the first part of April and the middle of June, we sent out nine presents for graduations, weddings, new babies, a housewarming, and one bouquet of flowers to a sick friend.

In return, we got eight thoughtfully worded thank-you notes and one thank-you call, from our friend with M.S. who can no longer write. Perhaps this news will make your day more pleasant. It certainly made many of ours bright beyond measure.

GENTLE READER:

Make that ten wonderful presents you sent out, and here is the tenth expression of gratitude from someone whom you have made happy.

Heirlooms

DEAR MISS MANNERS:

I am very lucky to have a loving mother who has been giving me some of her family heirlooms through the years.

My husband's two adolescent daughters have been living with us for the last year and "eye" each item as it enters our home or is used, often expressing their choice for their (future) ownership. We are planning to have our own children in the near future. The girls still have close relationships with their mother and both sets of grandparents. They are not close to my family, although they do live nearby. Is it correct to believe that the girls should expect their "heirlooms" to come from their mother or grandparents? And that it is my right to save or give these gifts to my children without hurting anyone's feelings?

GENTLE READER:

First things first. If you teach your stepdaughters some manners, you will be leaving them a more valuable heritage than your mother's jewels.

The key point here is not what will happen after you are dead, but the fact that you are alive. No matter how valuable the property, no matter how clear the lines of inheritance, it is incredibly rude to speculate on one's spoils in the event of the death of the person with whom you are discussing the matter. Even a crown prince does not (if properly reared) try on his father's crown before the father is certain not to sit up in bed and object. Only the person with the property can bring up the subject, and then the proper response from the heir is "I can't bear to think about it."

Your response to your stepdaughters should be a pleasant "Well, I'm not planning to die for a while yet, so if you don't mind, I would rather not hear this discussed." You may then do what you wish and leave them to find out your decision when your will is read.

Miss Manners' Christmas List

It is considered extremely charming to make one's wish list of presents entirely of intangibles. If a spouse asks what you want for Christmas, the proper reply is "You." If children ask their parents, the reply is "That you be happy." If a less intimately connected person is so queried, the reply is "Peace in the world."

This is no help whatsoever to the person begging assistance before going out to purchase something—anything—that he suspects the recipient will find useless, the wrong size, and in poor taste. But it is not considered fair to express exasperation at these smugly unhelpful answers—you must reflect upon what a lovely person that is, not to say "A new car," "A trip to Europe," or "A decent salary."

To circumvent this unsatisfactory exchange, Miss Manners recommends the family tradition of a gentleman of her acquaintance, which is the privilege of speaking to others without their official knowledge. Middle names are used instead of first names. If Sean Melvin's wife wants to know what he wants, she announces that she wants to have a private conversation with Melvin, who must first promise not to tell Sean. A mite on the cute side, Miss Manners admits, but a useful device.

In the meantime, Miss Manners, who is not without pretenses to charm herself, would like to give her Christmas list of intangibles that she would prefer to receiving diamond necklaces (although she would certainly make an effort to be gracious if one of those should, by the decree of fate, come her way instead).

Here, then, are the presents Miss Manners would like for Christmas. They are smaller than peace in the world, but also for everybody, and easier to wrap.

1. Last names. Weary of the cheekiness of being addressed by her first name by those who have not waited to have this privilege granted to them—sometimes because she has never met them before in her life—and even wearier of the patently false friendship of being instructed to do this to those she hardly knows, Miss Manners would like to see the return of the use of last names in what used to be adult society. What is more, she wants them with titles, rather than the prep-school style of calling people "Longworth" and "Byers."

2. A ban on computer talk at the dinner table.

3. The handshake as a standard form of greeting. The grasping of another person's hand was once thought to be an honorable, and even warm, gesture of goodwill. It has been devalued by the social kiss, which no two people perform alike, and which leaves a lot of lipstick and other confusion in its wake.

4. The conventional, routine, and not-to-be-taken-literally compliment, such as "My, you're looking well," in place of the well-thought-out, individual, sincere critique, such as "You look awful; are you depressed?"

5. A ban on reading material on clothes and, in fact, on clothes making personal statements of any kind. Miss Manners is for freedom of speech for all people, but believes that it is time that clothes shut up.

Well, that's enough. Miss Manners doesn't want to appear greedy. Incidentally, she wears a size 6.

(For more on presents and thanks, please see *Birthday Parties*, Chapter 3.)

DISCIPLINE

Maintaining Inequality

One of the most reasonable of childish protests is "If you can do it, why can't I?" No sensible parent will admit that as a basis of argument. The best answer is

''Because,'' and the next best is ''Because I'm grown up and you're not,'' or ''Because I'm the parent and you're the child,'' or ''Because I'm bringing you up, you're not bringing me up.''

A belief in the arguability of every premise is, Miss Manners assures you, a tremendous handicap in dealing with children. A belief that children and adults must be subject to identical rules is plain silly. If children are entitled to all the privileges of adulthood, why don't they take some of the responsibilities? Does your child ever think of paying the electric bill or reminding you that it's time for your annual checkup?

Do not suppose that you have trapped Miss Manners on that one, and that you can now pad the expense account, sass your sister-in-law, and chew with your mouth open while forbidding your children to do anything of the sort. Indeed, fundamental morality and manners are not negotiable. They will do as you do, not as you say.

Nevertheless, anyone who has gotten to the stage of parenthood has of necessity been navigating the murky waters of life for some time, and acquired some sense of its shoals and currents. (Would someone please bail Miss Manners out of nautical metaphors that are closing over her head? Thank you.) The two basic excuses for doing something that you have forbidden your child ever to do are:

1. The situation is more complicated than you can understand, or than I am in a position to explain to you. You'll have to believe that I'm using the best judgment I have to do the right thing, however it looks. (I know you're supposed to respect your parents, but I finally had to stop Grandpa from calling Mommy That-Woman-You-Call-Your-Wife.)

2. My function here is to serve as a bad example to you. (I do believe smoking is bad, but I'm unfortunately addicted to it and I will not allow you to develop the same problem.)

Excuses are not needed, once one has comfortably accepted the principle of the double standard for different generations. Adults can do things that children can't, such as staying out late when one has to get up early the next day and not even saying what time one expects to get home, or even the great privilege of getting up and going to work the day after a fever, instead of giving it a day's rest.

The most delicate area is that of child-rearing itself. Controlling someone else's life, bossing that person around, creating expectations and goals for him to achieve, serving, in other words, as both playwright and critic, is lots of fun. That's why people have children at all. You get into trouble trying to practice this sort of thing on a spouse, acquaintance, or stranger. (Miss Manners saw an interesting example of the last only recently. A frail old lady got onto the bus with some difficulty, only to be stopped by a hefty matron, obviously a total stranger, who said, ''Now, you're too weak to be out like this. Don't you have a brother? You tell him he has to drive you in his car.'')

Children understand the joy of being the boss, and are only too ready to issue instructions to one another. While not disputing the parent's right to correct them, they fail to see why they can't play, too. Why is setting a child straight a dutiful thing to do, while reciprocating brings on a snippy ''Don't talk back to me''? Because.

Actually, Miss Manners is not all that authoritarian about it. She believes in an occasional "Yes, you're right; you caught me. Parents aren't always perfect, either, and I shouldn't have done it." This is not out of fairness, but because it is such a thrill to the child, because not claiming to be perfect is itself a disarmingly ingenuous protection for the parent, and because it actually reinforces the standard. Everybody understands that what is left unsaid is ". . . but I am perfect most of the time, a demonstration of which is my graciousness in admitting fault." It even stores up a bit of sympathy against the inevitable day when the grown child has a true moral difference with the parent, and overruling is no longer possible.

Until then, Miss Manners will concede only one etiquette advantage to the child that the parent must not employ. It is never proper for a parent to use an innocent child as an excuse, as in "No, I'm sorry, I can't help you fund-raise because Daniela gets upset when I leave her with a baby-sitter." A child, however, has blanket permission to refuse to do anything (except his duty) "because my parents won't let me."

Enlightened Punishment

Whamming someone smaller than oneself in order to teach that person civilized behavior is not within Miss Manners' concept of propriety, much less logic.

She is not saying that she doesn't understand the parent who is driven beyond endurance and administers a good smack to someone who, however small, has patently been asking for it, but only that she considers it unwise. The parent who understands how to rule will not normally need crude weapons, and will also find that it is the indignity of the occasional last-resort smack that is effective, not the actual physical tap. (Let it be understood that we are still talking only about symbolic taps. A person who even risks injuring a child no matter what the provocation needs to be restrained by something a lot stronger than the gentle bonds of etiquette.)

It would be nice to say that the proper parent need not be concerned with proper forms of punishment, because if he or she has properly practiced proper child-rearing, there will be no crimes to punish. Even Miss Manners doesn't dream she could get away with that. Besides, her respect for civilization itself, which it is the goal of child-rearing to instill, is so great that she does not believe it can be absorbed without a struggle. Show her a child who has never rebelled against becoming civilized, and she will show you a child who isn't smart enough to realize what those people are trying to do to him.

One surprising but useful by-product of being a doting parent is that the child doted upon gets upset when that parent is unhappy with him. The more cheerful and satisfied the normal state of the parent, the easier it is to register displeasure. Thus, a surly parent may have to resort to terrible measures to convince the child that there has been any loss of satisfaction, since none was apparent anyway; but a happy parent may be able to instill awe and remorse with only a severe look. This is an incentive, if any were needed, for maintaining an affectionate and pleasant household. Truly devoted parents have incredible power. Miss Manners has known them to wither children into fearful obedience with only the quiet statement "I am disappointed in you."

Along with physical violence, emotional violence is outlawed by Miss Manners as a means of punishment. It is not necessary to assassinate a person's entire character in order to clear it of undesirable practices. "Clean up that mess this minute" is a permissible parental remark; "You're a slob" is not. Keeping the complaint within boundaries is, she admits, difficult. Family life is conducive to the development of amateur lawyers, and there is always a temptation to make a more significant case. But "Why do you always get everything wrong?" is not a question that leads to self-improvement, whereas "Why are you leaving that dish in the sink instead of washing it?" may be, even though in fact it is no more sensible.

Public humiliation is another illegitimate weapon. It is one of the least attractive features of childhood that any toddler can reason, even before he has the words to do it in, along the lines of "She's not going to make a scene here in the grocery store, in front of all these people who are bound to side with a chubby little angel over a harassed-looking woman. I can therefore do what I like, and she will be powerless to protest." Miss Manners has already mentioned the necessity of the parent's teaching the child a signal that, unnoticable to others, is understood by him to mean "Stop that or I'll get you later." In the case of a very small child whose concern for his image is not fully developed and, more to the point, who would be incapable of associating a delayed punishment with a crime committed more than five minutes before, she will allow such warnings as "Do you want to get down now, or do you want me to grab you and pull you down in front of all these people?" If necessary, that must be done. Tantrums must be demonstrated to be ineffectual, no matter how many onlookers are cheering on the child.

After parental disapproval itself—in which it is carefully demonstrated that, contrary to what children believe, parents are capable of loving and disapproving at the same time—the best punishments classically fit the crimes. Not coming home when told results in not being allowed to go out. Destroying property results in having to replace it, through one's allowance or work. Lying takes away the privilege of trust and subjects one to being checked up on instead of believed.

In this society, we believe in telling people what the limits of their punishments will be, presuming that the infractions are not repeated, and in rehabilitation. Yes, motivations are considered. Few children swipe things in order to feed the poor, but we believe in this country that everyone is entitled to a hearing, and at least the opportunity to convince those in charge that it really wasn't so bad after all, that it sprang from a misunderstanding or common human failing, and so on.

The Orphan Act

DEAR MISS MANNERS:

We have a foster child, whom we hope to adopt, but who is becoming a discipline problem. Just when we had her cured of swearing at us, or kicking, or breaking things, she started in with something new. She cries when she is asked to do something perfectly ordinary (take out the trash, do her homework, go mail the letters) and says, ''I guess that's the only reason you want me here,'' or ''What else do I have to do to stay here?''

We love this child, and have shown her so as best we know how. It hurts us very much that she doesn't seem to understand, after all this time. And the worst thing is that the other children are picking it up, too.

GENTLE READER:

With any luck, you'll soon have a home that sounds like the orphanage scene in *Annie.* If it is any comfort, Miss Manners will tell you that the orphan routine is by no means confined to foster or adopted children or their new siblings. Pampered heirs do it to their original parents all the time. Complaints along the lines of ''You wouldn't do that if you were my real mother'' are ubiquitous, too—children who are not adopted have only to say, ''I bet you're not really my real mother, or you wouldn't do that.''

Just because all this seems to be natural, Miss Manners does not believe it should be tolerated. The first rule is not to be hurt by it; and the second is to learn to laugh it out of use by means of teasing that is built on the fact that the child does know that you love her. For example, when she cries, you make a teary face, too, stretch out your arms and, once she is securely held in your embrace, say, ''Oh, the poor little outcast. If Mommy really loved her, what would she do? Would she never make her do anything? Oh, what a terrible mommy!''

No child can keep up that line when it has been preempted, and the echoed wailing should finally get a giggle from among the sobs. A few such sessions, and you should be able to reduce your response to ''Come on, Cinderella, help clean up and we'll all go to the ball.''

Insults

DEAR MISS MANNERS:

My children are always saying dreadful things to each other—derogatory personal remarks that I consider downright rude. They, and sometimes my wife, call them ''just teasing.'' What would you consider the polite side of teasing, and where, even in a family, is it just nastiness?

GENTLE READER:

Insulting is such a favorite human pastime that it is always creeping up again under one supposedly virtuous name or another—teasing, honesty, helpfulness.

The rule about proper teasing is: If it has to do with something the person can't help, such as physical appearance, it is only allowable if the characteristic is obviously much admired. If it has to do with behavior, it must be behavior of which the doer is, however bashfully, proud. You tease someone for being popular, not for biting his nails. In other words, family teasing is designed to take note of the successes and idiosyncrasies that make one beloved, not the traits that have been driving everyone crazy.

Secrets

DEAR MISS MANNERS:

Everybody in my family is mad at me. We have a new neighbor, and I told my new friend about my family. He wanted to know how much money my father makes and if it was more than his father, and also I told him about my sister having her ears fixed so they don't stick out. I got a big lecture on family secrets. Why is something that is true such a big family secret, and what's so wrong about telling it except that they get mad?

GENTLE READER:

A family secret is something a member of your family doesn't want known outside the family. The reason to keep family secrets, besides the fact that you don't want your family to be unhappy or mad, is that they know so much about you that you don't want blabbed around.

🌹 TRAVEL

Modified Togetherness

DEAR MISS MANNERS:

Why are our family vacations always a torture instead of a treat? My husband and I figure that we will finally get to spend undivided time with the children, that we only have so many years in which they will want to go with us, instead of with their own friends or families, and that we will have our well-earned rest and fun together. But every year we end up bickering and going off for the day to do separate things, or I with one child and he with the other, because everyone has different ideas and no one is willing to cooperate.

GENTLE READER:

Family holidays often sound better than they are. What you are really trying to do is to put together the recreational wishes of people of different generations and tastes, satisfying them all. It's marvelous if it can be done, but as in family life itself, love alone, without tolerance and planning, is not enough.

The family that has a common sport has it comparatively easy. Occasionally one dissenting member can be accommodated—if, for example, everybody skis except one person, but that person's sport happens to be drinking hot toddies at ski lodges —but it is not fair to stick a nonparticipant with the chores. Different levels of skills must be taken into account with the sport, and intrafamilial competition kept within pleasant bounds. But some general vacation spots lend themselves to diversified activity—one person on the beach, one in the water, one on the boardwalk shopping, and one in playing the video games; or one group sightseeing while the other goes to a matinee. Trade-offs may also be arranged—''We'll sit through the game if you'll sit through *Sound and Light.*''

Supervisory requirements aside, mealtime reunions are quite enough in the way of togetherness for related people with unrelated ideas. Would you feel better if Miss Manners described this as an opportunity for each person to scout out something different to report back to the family for its amusement?

Packing Fights

DEAR MISS MANNERS:

My mother and I always fight before vacations, because she wants me to take along dresses and boots and other things I hate and won't have a good time if I have to wear. How can I make her understand that I need to feel right to have fun?

GENTLE READER:

''Never fight about packing,'' a much-too-clever child of Miss Manners' acquaintance advises. ''Your mother has too much energy then. Let her put in whatever she wants, as long as you can also put in what you want. Then wear her down during the vacation, when she will not be in the mood for arguments each day over what you will wear.''

Children of Unbroken Homes

DEAR MISS MANNERS:

All my friends are going away for the holidays. I won't have anyone to play with or invite over. This happens every time we have a vacation, and lots of times on weekends. Everybody goes to visit his father in nice places, and I have to stay home because my parents aren't divorced. Also, they get more presents.

GENTLE READER:

That is hard, and Miss Manners sympathizes with you, but you must learn that life is difficult and we can't always get what we want. Your parents have their own lives to live, and if they insist on finding happiness with each other, you have to accept and respect that, no matter how deeply you feel that it interferes with your having a normal life like your friends. One day you may be a parent yourself and come to understand that a good marriage is so important that it should not be sacrificed, even to the children's understandable desire to get more presents and trips.

Traveling Abroad

DEAR MISS MANNERS:

We are planning to take our children abroad for the summer, and would like some suggestions on keeping them amused. We want this to be a happy experience, but we hope it will be an educational one as well.

GENTLE READER:

Miss Manners makes it a rule to avoid traveling in foreign countries with anything under the age of eight. Even then, she makes them wait until they beg to go, plead that they are being slighted when others go off without them, and promise to do whatever she says in return.

She then drives a hard bargain. The child must demonstrate that he actually enjoys trying unfamiliar foods, and is willing to take afternoon naps if these are presented as foreign customs rather than childhood ones. He must learn a few words and phrases of the language: "Excuse me," "Please," "Do you speak English?" and "Could you please tell me where I might find a public restroom?" He must explain what he is taking along to amuse himself with during travel time and other enforced idle periods, and undertake to carry a reasonable share of the luggage. He must learn a rudimentary history of the country, as well as its most glaring differences with his own in matters of etiquette, so that he doesn't make some awful mistake. He must agree to a schedule that includes such adult pastimes as café sitting, as well as sightseeing, resting, eating, and partaking of whatever the country has to offer that is most different from his own, rather than trying to duplicate what he is used to.

Then, if he still wants to go, she gives him a delighted smile, a small budget in foreign currency to be spent as he wishes, a foreign phrase book, and her dressing case to carry.

At Home Abroad

DEAR MISS MANNERS:

After many years of living in the same city, we are moving abroad. My husband's company has made it clear that that is where the career development opportunities are, and even considering the adverse effects the jolt of moving to a foreign country has on children (I have been reading up expert opinion on the subject, and most of it is discouraging), we must do it. Anyway, we're going.

I have also been reading up on what to expect in a foreign land, and how to handle the customs and the different style of living and entertaining we are bound to encounter, even though we are being provided with American-style housing. My question is about the children's aspect of this, which isn't covered. One woman sent by the company to advise me on what to expect finally confided (I think she had been told to paint a rosy picture for me, but she broke down) that there has been a terrible effect on her own children. She says they are arrogant, that they and their friends go around acting superior because they're Americans, and that they constantly complain about the hardship of living away from home, even though they have servants and all sorts of things they would never dream of here.

I would be heartbroken if my children got that way, although I realize that the fact of being uprooted explains why that happens. How can I prepare them to at least act polite so that my husband will not be embarrassed in front of foreign businessmen, and, I hope, to develop an attitude that will keep them from feeling the bad effects of this situation?

GENTLE READER:

Dear, dear. What a terrible thing you are doing to your children in showing them the world. If only you would leave them where they are; American children at home are never arrogant or dissatisfied.

Miss Manners is sorry to resort to sarcasm in explaining to you the first thing you must do, which is to change your attitude before the children catch that negative one from you, and look forward to an endless source of blackmail and blame in the mere fact of their living abroad. Perhaps some families react as you described; others, fired with a sense of adventure, not only learn and grow, but find themselves drawn more closely together from sharing an experience new to all.

To accomplish all this, you must require that they join you in preparing for your new life. Few study conditions are as satisfying to children as taking language classes with their parents, because if you all start together from the beginning, the children will soon have the pleasure of correcting your grammar and giggling at your accent. This is your chance, also, to learn comparative etiquette, or the different set of customs that will reveal how many of the behavior patterns you believe instinctive and take for granted are merely a set of social customs.

Once you are there, you will have an endless source of family amusement in sharing your observations and cultural confusions. There is, however, one rule that Miss Manners insists upon. You must never allow your children to be rude or condescending to the people of your host country. You would not, she trusts, allow them to get away with this at home. If standards were relaxed abroad, either because of the poor behavior of their peers or out of a false guilt you have at transplanting them, the children would have a legitimate cause to complain.

EQUIPMENT AND FACILITIES

The Perfectly Appointed House

To keep a house in which every object, down to the smallest bibelot, is in perfect taste is in shocking taste. No house can be truly elegant unless it contains at least half a dozen atrocities of varying sizes and uses. This must not include the residents, though.

Such an apparent attack of madness on the part of Miss Manners is not to be confused with the unfortunate notion that a house should have the look of being "lived in," or, as Miss Manners terms it, "slovenly." If disorder were indeed sweet, we could solve the teenage summer unemployment problem by leasing adolescents out as decorating consultants.

It is, rather, in the selection of furnishings that care must be exercised to include enough dreadful items to avoid the appearance of being mercenary, heartless, and socially aggressive. The discriminating person always has on hand a few things that could not possibly have been chosen for their aesthetic value, thus emerging as a person of tradition and sentiment. For those who find it difficult to commit errors of taste, here is a small list of horrible things from which to choose. If one does not come by them naturally, it may be possible to purchase them at yard sales.

Child-Made Objects

No household, even one which is blessed with no children, should fail to have at least one item whose provenance is clearly Arts and Crafts Hour at school or camp. Ceramic ashtrays, a favorite present from children to parents they never have noticed don't smoke, are good, as are yarn potholders, because they are relatively permanent. Things made out of cardboard, straws, and pipe cleaners tend to disintegrate, although not as quickly as one would like. Art work must be rotated on the standard exhibit space (the refrigerator door), because it is produced in such prodigious quantities.

Hideous Presents Donated by Adults

These should be displayed and cherished in proportion to the sacredness of the bond between giver and receiver, divided by the number of miles they live apart. Thus, wedding presents from friends may be quietly returned, but a spouse's poor choice should be tolerated unless you are willing to exchange the giver at the same time. Inviolate are presents from one's servants. We are not all as fortunate as the lady whose faithful butler returned from a trip to his ancestral land of Egypt with an electrically lighted sphinx for his employer's living room, but we should all be as wise as that lady, who considered what her friends would think if she kept it, considered what the butler would think if she expelled it, and gave it a place of honor. One can always make new friends, but a good butler is not easy to find.

Souvenirs

This category includes sports trophies, wedding albums, framed awards, family photographs (as long as they do not include famous people), and items pertaining to happy vacations (as long as they are not of the sort that could only have been stolen from public accommodations). No member of the family should be allowed to contribute items from more than one of these categories to the general decor, and they must all be kept in places that indicate the owner's embarrassment for having them at all. The powder-room walls are an excellent place for awards, the photographs go in the master bedroom, and the trophies are used as doorstops in the guest rooms.

What Miss Manners does not want to see are awards hung in the library, children's artwork professionally framed and put in the drawing room, wedding albums on coffee tables, photographs of any member of the family shaking hands with the president hung anywhere at all, or any restaurant or hotel property, including matchbooks. The ostentatious display of bad taste is in extremely poor taste.

You Call That Living?

Congratulations on the new sofa. Try not to think about what it cost, and remember that it is supposed to last forever and is just what you always wanted. Miss Manners knows what you are really thinking. You are plotting to keep it looking new, and to protect it from those filthy savages your relations and friends. First you fit on the extra pieces of material that come with it, to protect its arms from their arms. You need another piece for over the back, to protect it from their greasy heads, but you can also use a doily for that. Of course, you warn everyone to keep feet off it, and it's too bad you can't make them keep their bottoms off it as well. But perhaps you can. You can slipcover the whole thing (remembering to get extra protective pieces to save wear on the slipcover), or you can just bar everyone from the living room and let the sofa have it for itself, to preside over in grandeur and safety.

Just one question, please. Why did you buy a sofa?

The concept of ''best'' as it applies to household equipment is usually not as in ''Why not the best?'' so much as in ''The best is yet to be.'' Only it never says when. Miss Manners rather likes the old-fashioned distinction between ''everyday'' and ''special'' provided that specials are held with some frequency. The fine china, the real silver, the good linens—those who can afford them enjoy the luxury of festivity. They can, that is, if they consider their guests and even sometimes their own families good enough to use the best. Surprisingly few people do.

Assigning best status to a piece of furniture stretches the idea toward the ridiculous. You might shoo dogs and other creatures on all fours, such as small children, off the good furniture, but the general household idea is supposed to be that the furniture is there to serve the people, not the other way around.

If the sofa is that good, put a velvet rope over it so that nobody ever makes the mistake of sitting on it. Or donate it to a museum. You could also put a velvet rope across the doorway to that room that is too good for anyone you ever associate with to use. It's amazing to Miss Manners how many people have preserved the tradition of the unused front parlor in these days of small houses, tight real estate, and parsons who don't make house calls.

It is true that the living room will get dirty if it is lived in. The sofa in which people sit occasionally needs cleaning or recovering, which is expensive, but hardly more so than all those slipcovers and doilies. Nice things deserve to be treated nicely, of course, but some of those nice things are people. Looking pretty no longer excuses anyone from performing a useful function in life.

A reasonable rule, Miss Manners suggests, would be: Never buy anything for ''best'' that is too good for your best friend. And if your family can't be trusted to be livable enough for the living room, something needs doing over immediately.

The "Formal" Living Room

Dear Miss Manners:

In this day and age, you hear so many people talking about their "formal" dining room or living room. I would like to know when a dining or living room becomes formal.

Gentle Reader:

When it's kept clean all the time, and family members who so much as enter it are accused by the person who does that cleaning of "tracking through" there.

We had the same arrangement in another day and age, except that the living room was called the front (or best) parlor, and the real living room, now called the recreation or family room, was called simply the parlor. The first-ranking dining room was then called the dining room, and the runner-up the breakfast room, or in really grand houses the family dining room.

Sharing

Most parents make some stab at teaching their children to share their toys—a gesture that goes directly against human nature and is therefore an important step in the opposite direction, toward civilization. When it comes to sharing their own toys, however, many of the same parents simply give up, let the children take them over, and then sulk about it. Miss Manners knows many households in which the telephones, television sets, phonographic equipment, and hair dryers have simply been duplicated to avoid the problem of sharing between parent and child. Sometimes each child is issued all this equipment.

This strikes Miss Manners as being rather an expensive way of dealing with the situation. As computers increasingly become a part of household equipment, it is also ceasing to strike parents as the solution to go out and purchase several. So the parents will have to learn to share and even to teach sharing. This time around, it is harder because the concept of strict equality does not—should not—exist between parent and child. Is it fair, after all, that one of them should have to do all the child-rearing?

Let's see if we can do this without resorting to the ugliness of "Well, it belongs to me. If you want one, go out and buy your own."

The first question is whether the person who wants to use the equipment knows how to operate it properly and take care of it. Miss Manners has always thought it a shame that manufacturers of television sets do not make them impossible to use by anyone who cannot read and understand complicated instructions.

The next question is whether the use of the appliance will annoy others. That is usually in the nature of the item. Phonographs annoy everyone who did not select the record; dishwashers never do.

So far, the standards apply to everyone. Enough of that. The question of whether the activity interferes with something else that the user ought to be doing applies only to children. Children with homework to do cannot be on the telephone (although they all claim they are only inquiring around to find out the homework assignment, which no one in the class seems to have heard). Parents with tax forms to fill out may chatter all they wish. Children who have to be up early to go to school may not watch television until all hours of the night. Parents who have to be up early to go to work may, because what they are actually doing is "unwinding."

Even less fair are restrictions on items that might logically be shared, but that the use of by others drives the owners crazy. Only grown-ups are allowed to have such quirks, and even then they are only allowed a few that they do not have to explain, with however twisted logic. Children are allowed to apply this privilege only to appliances they have bought with their own money. A child who has bought a phonograph with summer-job money is allowed to stipulate that no one else use it without his permission—a stance that would look dreadful in a parent. Miss Manners does not pretend that this evens things out. But time will.

Non-Sharing

Just about everyone seems to have at least one oddity that is completely indefensible by any standards of reason, logic, or importance. That is no reason not to take such things seriously in the people with whom one tries to live in harmony. They are, in fact, items of faith to their owners, however reluctant they may be to declare this. One violates them at one's peril.

"So what if I changed the margins on your typewriter—change them back, if you like." "It's just us—who cares if the cereal bowl has a plate under it or not?" "What's the point of hanging that up when I'm going to wear it again tomorrow?" "Only a crazy person would even notice whether the window shades are all at the same level." "I guess I used the hammer last—it must be around somewhere." "It tastes better from the carton." "I straightened up your desk for you."

These are the matters of which broken families are made. Do not be fooled by the fact that the aggrieved parties cite differences of sex or money. They just think that sounds more respectable. You will notice that many of these have to do with neatness, table manners, noise, or property rights. Indeed, it is the ability to adjust in these areas that is the most crucial factor in determining the success of a marriage in a country where the ballot is secret.

Miss Manners will now set forth some principles for adjudicating these conflicts.

The higher value takes precedence over the lower; the less intrusive condition takes precedence over the disruptive one. Does this mean that Miss Manners always sides with the quiet, neat, generous person with the beautiful table manners? Naturally. Does she expect the messy, the noisy, the sloppy, the cranky always to be the one to change? No, not quite.

This uncharacteristic tolerance comes of the realization that orderly people would then be expected to share—to let their less fortunate relatives make off with their scissors, get into their tool and sewing boxes, and use up their stamp supplies. That would never do. The modified law, then, is that in household places that are shared, the higher standard is maintained, but that there will be recognized private areas in which people may induge as they see fit, without interference or criticism. Respect, or, better, blindness, should be accorded to whatever takes place within these boundaries. The chief point is that no one has to justify his taste or conduct there. The closet, the desk, the unshared meal, and the individual's hobby, sports, or occupational equipment obviously are such areas. Separate bathrooms are nice; separate cars and separate bedrooms should not be snickered at. One need be limited only by one's financial resources and the extent of one's inability to tolerate the other person's habits. It is, in Miss Manners' view, this sort of apartness that keeps families together.

The Bathroom

There are a few areas that Miss Manners would like to declare out of her jurisdiction. This is her year for rereading dear Charles Dickens, and if she has to look after everyone's behavior every minute, she will never get through. Surely you would not be so unfeeling as to wish her a lifetime of Barnaby Rudging and Tiny Timming. But each time Miss Manners piously intones that she does not interfere in God's province, someone reports an epidemic of giggling in church; and every time she sighs with relief at having everyone bedded down for the night, the murmur of complaints begins about nocturnal noises and stolen covers.

So it is with the jurisdiction of the bathroom. In vain does Miss Manners cry that she doesn't care what people do in the bathroom—she doesn't want to think about it—if only they will shut the door first. To deaf ears does she moan that her dear mother did not rear her to be the instructress of people who have not mastered the proper use of the water closet. Still she is besieged by complaints about the proper use of the water closet. Still she is besieged by complaints about the proper placement of the toilet-seat cover, and the correct direction of unravelment of the tissue roll.

All right. Here are the basic rules of bathroom etiquette, and then Miss Manners wishes the subject and the door closed.

The only proper announcement of departure for a bathroom is ''Excuse me.'' The question ''Where are you going?'' is so rude that it should never be asked, but it unfortunately often is, the human mind being unaccountably subject to lapses of imagination.

A lady may answer, ''To powder my nose''; a gentleman of Miss Manners' acquaintance replies, ''Where even the emperor must go on foot.'' The remarks ''To comb my hair'' and ''To make a telephone call'' are suitable for both genders.

''How long are you going to be in there?'' is not a nice question. ''Would it be possible for me to get in there soon?'' is not a nice question, either, but it is an improvement.

Not every item in every bathroom is for the use of all who use the bathroom, even if those who share the room are related by marriage or blood. (The luxury of separate bathrooms is, in Miss Manners' opinion, a help in preventing marriages from splitting and blood from spilling.)

Shared territory must be scrupulously maintained, and agreements should be firmly made about the distribution of such possibly limited properties as hot water or space for hanging laundry. Individual matters, such as towels and shed hair, are the responsibilities of their owners.

Miss Manners has previously pointed out that guests who endeavor to save their hosts toil by refraining from using the guest towels only laden these people with worries about what on earth they did use. Guests must also realize that any private items in a host's bathroom, such as pills or cosmetic devices, are invisible, which means not only that the guest doesn't see them, but that he doesn't mention them afterward, either to their owners or to third parties.

There is a prohibition on attempts to conduct general conversation through a shut bathroom door. Miss Manners cannot think of a sociable remark that cannot wait until the door is opened voluntarily—with the one exception of ''I noticed that something's dripping through the ceiling downstairs.''

What No Gentleman Hears

DEAR MISS MANNERS:

It has long been my practice as a young gentleman to open a water faucet upon entering the bathroom of a private residence. This, as I have believed, tends to drown out, as it were, the possibly distasteful sounds associated with a man going about his business there.

After having heard what it sounds like without this practice, I wonder why this is not a crucial part of male behavior in our society. I have never seen or heard of any endorsement concerning appropriate bathroom behavior to guard the eating and drinking sanctity of guests nearby.

GENTLE READER:

Your argument, which seems to be sparkling with exquisite refinement, has one flaw. No gentleman or gentlewoman would ever listen to what is going on inside a bathroom with a closed door. Therefore, the problem does not exist officially. Therefore, the solution to it, however charming, is superfluous.

Do not let this discourage you from your practice. Miss Manners appreciates the thought, even though she will not be able to hear the difference.

What Really Occurs in the Bathroom

DEAR MISS MANNERS:

How can a host or hostess indicate to their guests—adults and children alike—the necessity of washing their hands after using the bathroom? Among the couples we know no one observes the essential hygienic function. Our powder room is stocked with soaps and towels. We certainly don't want to post a sign in there. What can we say to our guests?

GENTLE READER:

Nothing whatsoever. Unless your bathroom is also equipped with a peephole, you do not know what they are or are not doing, and it would be rather disquieting to them to pretend that you do.

However, Miss Manners, who is omniscient, will tell you what they are doing. They are washing their hands by just barely touching the edge of the soap, and drying them on toilet paper or their own handkerchiefs. This is because the misbegotten rule their parents taught them, of not using the guest towels or guest soap in their own houses, seems to be the only rule to last everyone a lifetime.

Bathroom Sins

DEAR MISS MANNERS:

I grew up one of three daughters in a largely feminine household. Though not a born gentleman, my father was well trained by my mother in the aspect of civility. In my home, I was never faced with the appalling sight of a raised toilet seat.

My mother, who is quite the lady, considers negligence in this matter on the part of males the cardinal sin. A recent gentleman caller failed in this regard, and my mother, with dignity, tact, and some indignation, tried to remind this man that the facilities should be left in readiness for ladies, because the ladies live here. He was very dense about it, and she had to spell out the situation using the ugly word "toilet." How can we make ourselves clear in a ladylike way in this repugnant matter?

GENTLE READER:

What you report is a sin, but it is not the cardinal sin. The cardinal sin is correcting the manners of one's guests. A true lady does not acknowledge that there is such a thing as a toilet. When someone leaves the room, she does not think about where that person is going, and when she leaves the room herself, she is confident that everyone assumes she is retiring to powder her nose.

This makes it difficult to devise a ladylike way to say, "Hey, put down the toilet seat after you relieve yourself, will you? I don't want to fall in." In fact, it makes it impossible. And that, in turn, saves you and your mother and all your sisters from committing the cardinal sin. Whatever happened to your father, by the way? Being a lady, Miss Manners cannot tell you what manner of egress your story has suggested to her.

Role Models and Television

No, Miss Manners will not critique manners on television. She can hardly think of any occupation sillier than that of waggling her finger at shadows. So please stop telling her about this series in which family members say rude things to one another, or that commercial in which those who are acquainted with a certain product insult to their faces those who are not.

Let them.

It is not only that Miss Manners has enough trouble, as she keeps murmuring, in getting human beings to behave themselves, but that she understands the difference between them and dramatic characters. Television programs may be about all sorts, and the requirements of their behavior is not that it be mannerly, but that it be appropriate to the characters being represented. Commercials are intended to sell dry goods, not to teach deportment.

As a drama critic in another life (did you think she had no other pleasure but the hope of catching you in social error?), Miss Manners is upset by the behavior of dramatic characters only when it is plainly out of character. She does not expect television to provide role models; neither does she think that expectation should be held by those, such as parents, who ought to be doing that job themselves.

Indeed, it is when television programs do attempt to emulate refined manners that they go furthest wrong. Aristocrats are invariably represented as being snobbish to their dependents and scornful of any life but their own lavish one—as if boredom, *noblesse oblige* (not to mention fear of offending the help), and parsimony were unheard of among the upper classes. The very programs that are the most meticulous about historical research in representing period costumes and settings are utterly ignorant of historical manners. You always find the Victorians eating with their gloves on, and chummily addressing one another by their first names. Dreadful.

You must understand that these pettish complaints are made in the name of dramatic veracity, not the general intolerance Miss Manners exhibits when she encounters unseemly behavior in real life. She will direct that, instead, to the people who complain about television, as if they had no neighbors or relatives to turn in when the reckoning on manners is done.

Role models for children must be parents, grandparents, teachers, and other exemplary adults. (Using other children as examples is a poor idea. If there is one thing that a self-respecting child cannot endure, it is a perfect child, and rightly so. Nature did not intend children to behave perfectly until they have been thoroughly reared.) It is part of this job to interpret the world, and if the child's world includes watching people behave badly on television, why, that must be interpreted, too. Unless, of course, the television is turned off, a simple mechanical process whose lack of popularity among parents Miss Manners cannot understand.

The traditional conversation begins when the child has gleefully discovered an example of someone doing something he or she has been enjoined from doing, and says, "If he can do it, why can't I?"

The answer is, "Because you see how dreadful it is. We would never behave that way, would we?"

The question is not intended to be thought over; it is supposed to suggest its own answer and will, if repeated often enough, eventually succeed. For this exchange, poor examples are necessary and helpful, and Miss Manners, for one, thinks it generous of television to provide them for those who can't find any errors worth reporting in real life.

Television and Guests

DEAR MISS MANNERS:

Is there such a thing as television etiquette?

My specific questions relate to TV watching and guests, visiting relatives and the role of the host. When is it proper for a host to ask for quiet from the visitors when watching TV? Does this depend on whether the visitors are relatives or other guests? Does it matter if the situation involves dinner, a casual visit, or a transactional situation?

Is it proper for a guest to request a specific show or none at all? When is it right for TV to be the focus of a social situation? May the television be on during dinner? What about the place of the remote control? What about the volume?

If someone has made an advance call and received permission to visit, and upon arrival is offered a refreshment, is the visitor required to accommodate him/herself to the TV show in progress? Is the regular TV watcher ever expected to alter his/her habits? Or should those socializing with the TV addict take into consideration this affliction?

What about reading and telephone addicts? Is there hope for socializing among people of different TV traditions?

GENTLE READER:

Not while that thing is on. Please turn it off so that we can converse.

Conversation is, in fact, the chief feature (nicely supplemented by food and drink) of all social engagements unless another activity has been announced in advance. You can invite people to watch television—or roller skate, play whist, paint the house, spin the bottle, stuff envelopes, or move the piano—but only if you specify the activity, so that the guest can plead a previous engagement to attend a funeral that day.

The host should be alert to setting the volume at an agreeable level and, unless the invitation specified the program to be watched, consider suggestions on what to watch.

Communal television watching has no point if it does not include the exchange of smart remarks. You can thus only shush people to the extent of saying something like "Hey, wait a minute, I think they're about to announce the results."

Television watching should not be even an incidental part of any other visiting, unless during a visit that is either long—a weekend or more—or of such a frequent nature—someone who drops by often—that the actual socializing is intermittent. The same goes for reading or telephoning. You need not suspend your normal activities for someone who is always there, although Miss Manners assumes here the normal household politeness of checking to see that one is not interfering with the comforts of another.

Mind you, Miss Manners is not condemning the television addicts. All they need do to watch their program uninterrupted is to refrain from inviting people or from agreeing to visits that are proposed to them. She will even forgive them for saying, "Oh I'm so sorry, eight tonight is a bad time for me—I have a firm commit-

ment then, and won't be free until quite late,'' instead of explaining why they always seem to be tied up during prime time. (For more on children and television, please see pp. 131–132 and 360.)

The Car

DEAR MISS MANNERS:

When they lock me up, tell everyone it was the driving that drove me crazy. I have three children, widely spaced, and each one has a schedule that involves either keeping me on the road all day or leaving me stranded without a car when I need one.

The seven-year-old goes to private school, and not only needs to get there, but has made friends with classmates from way over on the other side of the city, and needs to be driven back and forth just to have an afternoon of play. The twelve-year-old is starting to go to dances and other evening events, from which I don't want him coming home alone. He also complains about taking the bus during the day, since his sister gets door-to-door service everywhere.

Then there is my sixteen-year-old. He doesn't want to be driven—he just wants to take over my car. I thought it would be easier on me when I had someone to help with the driving, but he doesn't see it that way. All it means is that I often don't have the car when I need it, and can't sleep at night until I hear him come in. Help!

GENTLE READER:

How did you manage to bring up children of such different ages without establishing the principle of Higher the Age, More the Privileges, and Bigger the Responsibilities? Did you put them all to bed at the same time, and do all the chores yourself?

Here are basic locomotion rules for different ages:

Children who are too young to use public transportation must register their requests (above the basic trips to school, lessons, and medical appointments) in advance, with the understanding that minimizing the driving is something to keep always in mind. It is simply a fact of life that a child who wants to be driven somewhere must fit in with the schedule of the driver, and your seven-year-old could get quite clever about visiting the friend who lives near the shopping center while the driver is doing the shopping, timing other visits for parents' trips home from work or an older child's nearby appointment, and, when all else fails, being the hostess, who doesn't have to stir out of her house.

The middle child should be taught that getting around by oneself is a privilege and an adventure. (Miss Manners dearly hopes you have also taught him the basics of public transportation: giving precedence to adults in boarding and seating, and refraining from shoving and other rowdiness.) To deserve this glorious freedom, he should register at home where he is going to use it, and when return from it. In return for getting picked up when he needs to be, he occasionally extends his services in fetching the younger child by bus, with all the accompanying privileges of lording it over his sister that he is in charge.

With the privilege of using the family car goes the even greater responsibility of sharing the driving. With the privilege of having children who can share the driving comes the responsibility of worrying until they get home. (For car pools, please see pp. 158–159.)

Well-Mannered Safety

Dear Miss Manners:

My daughter was saved from extensive injury and maybe death because she was wearing a seat belt. About the same time, the daughter of a friend of mine was not wearing a seat belt and was involved in an accident not far from her home, in good weather, in the afternoon. Her face hit the instrument panel. She had to have a knee fused, and a great deal of plastic surgery, which did not restore her former beauty.

I insist that my passengers use seat belts in my car, and have them set up so they are easy to fasten. I try to do this in a tactful way, saying that I can be a better driver knowing that I am taking every precaution for the safety of my friends. Some tell me about people being trapped in a car and burned. More often, they protest at the bother, with an air of amusement and condescension at my foolishness.

I try to use a seat belt when I am riding in another's car, but they are stuck down inside the seat, or they won't pull out, or I feel I am putting the driver to a lot of bother and implying he or she is not a good driver. What are the rules in these cases?

Gentle Reader:

Miss Manners makes rules of etiquette, not safety rules, although she must admit that matters of safety do take precedence. (In the choice between the impoliteness of criticizing a friend unasked or allowing him to drive you while drunk, for example, politeness loses.)

But etiquette will help you here, because the driver of a car is entitled to the prerogative of the captain of a ship, in setting the rules that passengers must obey. You may soften your commands by assuming an air of lovable fastidiousness ("Well, I know, but it just makes me feel better") but you need not—you should not—abdicate your power.

Similarly, in another's car, you merely murmur, "I feel happier with the seat belt on," while digging it up. Grisly stories with sobering morals are not necessary.

If a Child Calls ...

Dear Miss Manners:

Our eleven-year-old has been taught to say who he is when making a telephone call, and to ask politely to speak to whomever he is calling. His school friends are apt to hit me with "Is Chris there?" or "C'n I talk to Chris?" with no preamble, and I find it offensive, especially since I've usually had to drop what I'm working on and change my position to answer the phone.

Also, there is the problem of children tying up the phone and how to get them off without offense, and the problem of coming on the line or extension after another person is already talking on the telephone.

GENTLE READER:

Miss Manners is not above jumping at any opportunity to interrupt her work, either, but doesn't feel it quite fair to do so by involving other people's callers in chitchat. Unless Chris is in a business requiring his calls to be screened—in which case, why doesn't he hire a secretary?—politeness does not require that his callers identify themselves and deliver preambles to whomever answers the telephone.

Miss Manners believes that family members are entitled to receive calls, as they should letters, without having them scrutinized by other members of the family. While there is nothing wrong with volunteering one's identity and guessing that one is talking to Chris's father and asking him how he is, all that is strictly necessary is, "May I please speak to Chris?" The answer (unless it is "This is he") is "Just a moment, please" (not "Who is this?" or "Is this Nicole again?") or "I'm sorry, but he's not here right now. May I take a message?" (In this context, "here" only means "available"; one does not say "Chris is in the bathroom now" or "He can't talk to you until he finishes his homework" or "He says he won't talk to you.")

General rules about the use of the telephone by children must be made clear to them, and one is that a silent signal from the parent means, "Wind that up immediately." It will have to be explained that the child is better off saying, "I'm sorry I have to go now" than bringing on a spoken parental protest that could be heard on the other end of the line. When someone picks up a telephone line that is in use, the polite statement is, "I'm on this line," to which the polite reply is "Oh, sorry," followed by CLICK! Failure to produce the click also has its consequences—an immediate "So please hang up," followed, after the telephone call, with high parental sarcasm such as, "How would you like it if I listened in when you were on the phone?"

If a Child Answers . . .

DEAR MISS MANNERS:

Please say something about children answering the telephone. Experiences with children on the phone are often frustrating.

Of course, the first responsibility lies with the caller. The first question should not be "Is your mother home?" This is likely to get a plain "Yes" or "No" or perhaps "She's in the bathroom." Also, a "No" answer may give dangerous information to the wrong person. When a child answers the phone, why not say, "May I speak with your mother?" The child's reply should be, "Yes, I'll call her." What she shouldn't do, but sometimes does, is shout, "Mom, some woman wants to talk to you.'' This starts the conversation off on three wrong feet.

Can't we teach the kids to use simple cordiality in tone, as well as words? A little family role-playing could help. How would you feel if John called and I was rude to him? I'm also a believer in not letting the children answer the phone at all until they are old enough to write a very simple message, preferably name and number, which should be repeated carefully after being written down. The small child can babble sixteen dollars worth of long distance without benefit to anyone but the telephone company.

GENTLE READER:

Miss Manners quite agrees with you that children should not be answering telephones until they have acquired the ability to do so politely. She would only like to make two small adjustments in your suggestions for the adults involved.

The first has to do with teaching techniques. In Miss Manners' experience, the statement "How would you feel if . . ." should be used with caution. Perhaps the child would secretly think it hilarious if you were rude to his friend John. A small child can learn by rote to say "Just a minute, please" much more easily than he can deal with the psychological underpinnings.

The second is that the question "May I speak with your mother?" presumes that the childish voice belongs to an immediate descendant of the person you are calling, when, in fact, it could be a visitor or a high-pitched adult. A child who is old enough to answer the telephone is old enough to learn that his mother has a name other than Mommy.

Surliness on the Telephone

DEAR MISS MANNERS:

When I call my friend Mrs. Goodtaste, and inquire if she is at home, it would be pleasing if daughter Nola or son Midas would utter something in addition to a curt "No," followed by complete silence.

Some alternatives might include (1) "Mumsy is out just now, but she will be home around five—would you care to call her then?"; (2) "Mother is unable to come to the phone just now—may she return your call?" (3) "Dear Ma-Ma will be so dreadfully sorry to have missed your call—may I take a message?"

Having known these children since infancy, driven them to Scout meetings, entertained them, and remembered all their special days, perhaps they might add something like: (1) "I do hope that you and Mr. Friendly have been well"; (2) "It is nice to hear from you"; (3) "We all hope you'll come by and see us when you can."

Of course, we have to face the fact that many of their parents aren't much better.

GENTLE READER:

Do we have to? You are quite right, both in the problem you identify and the desirability of the sample dialogue you propose, but Miss Manners is not ready to concede that the ability to be courteous has been bred out of the human race, or perhaps has died out for lack of use.

This is another instance of the need to teach children hypocrisy. You and their parents know that they don't care whether you are well or visible because they took all your kindnesses as no more than their due. If they were forced to repeat these pleasantries by rote, however, one day they might listen to the words and wonder whether you and Mr. Friendly are not as human as themselves and as in need of kindness.

For Auditors

(Grandparents and Other Relations;

Friends of the Family, Intimate to Casual;

Families Dealing with the Rudeness of Others,

and Vice Versa)

If people feel they absolutely must criticize and correct others, Miss Manners recommends having children. All those wonderful teaching instincts that spoil marriages and send friends fleeing have their natural outlet in pushing children around. (No, no, Miss Manners meant to say guiding them, for their own good.)

Still, there are limits. Here, for the benefit of both parent and child, are the rules about giving and receiving criticism—the parent giving and the child receiving, of course. The child who, having been brought up in one of those strange households that gives lip service to fairness regardless of age, endeavors to offer helpful and instructive criticism to a parent is just asking for trouble. Strictly speaking, one may criticize only one's own children and stepchildren. They are fair game, the term for such criticism being ''bringing them up to be civilized human beings.'' Any attempt to dispute this jurisdiction, such as a plea ''You're not my real mother,'' must be immediately overruled.

Grandparents, temporary resident friends of parents, hosts who are related to the children, and housekeepers should be invested with full authority by the parent if they are left in charge, but this must be exercised with subtlety. If one cannot honestly say ''I know your father expects you to do this, even if he's not here,'' then one says something like ''Well, this is the way I prefer to do things; at your house, you may do differently.'' This is, incidentally, an excellent way to

62

For Auditors
63

offer an alternative to the laxness of the parents. Friends' children and your children's friends may not be criticized at all. But you can say to them, "I'm afraid you'll have to get down—that table isn't strong enough to hold you," and "You're going to get hurt if you keep that up." (The earlier-described unpleasant leer, disguised as a smile, indicates that this may be a real possibility.)

There are also rules about what types of criticism may be offered, and how. No critiques of congenital defects, including inherited stupidity, may be offered, even by the child's immediate ancestors. If humanly possible, it is advisable to address one fault at a time, rather than attempting to condemn a lifelong pattern. Neither is it allowable to criticize children for not being perfect, as so few of us are. Miss Manners' dear mother, a teacher, reported sadly that it was the rule when a child had a report card of four A's and a B or a test score of 96 for the parents' reaction to be "Why'd you get a B?" or "What were the four points you missed?" rather than "How wonderful."

Unfortunately, children must always accept criticism, whether it is properly offered or not. They cannot answer even the worst offenders, who offer free-lance critiques of looks, clothes, behavior, and speech to all children within hearing distance, by pointing out what they don't like about the adult's looks, clothes, behavior, or speech, especially the most recent speech. That would only prove that they are, indeed, rude children. The answer to unwarranted criticism is "Thank you for setting me straight." As humble as this may sound, Miss Manners promises all children who use it that they will make the adults very, very nervous. If they can manage to add "sir" or "ma'am" to the statement, the adult will reply with an apology.

To the criticism of authorized people, the response is never to offer an excuse, unless it is an inviolable one, because it only gives the adult more material for his anger and criticism. The most unscrupulous child Miss Manners knows always looks very contrite, and answers, "I know. It was awful. I feel terrible." This is unfair, because it leaves the adult nothing more to say, and, after repeating his original complaint three times and receiving the same answer, the adult can only mutter, "Oh, all right. Let's forget it."

Improver, Heal Thyself

If you wish to improve yourself for the New Year, Miss Manners will register no objections. Not a few of you, she has noticed, could—how can she put this delicately?—stand it. She would just appreciate it if you would get to work from the outside in, improving those sloppy manners before you begin on the mess in the soul.

Please do not resolve to improve others. It would be far better to resolve to accept others cheerfully as you find them.

Let us not descend to the personal here, and notice the fact that Miss Manners spends her life in the quixotic task of improving others. She only does so when asked. No such restraint is generally practiced in the society. On the contrary, there seems to be a notion about that we are all presenting ourselves, in every aspect of our persons and our lives, to be criticized by relatives, friends, acquaintances, and utter strangers.

"You ought to get out more."

"You'd look younger with your hair shorter—let me give you the name of my hairdresser."

"That baby is going to catch cold if you don't put something on his head."

"She's not right for you."

"Stop worrying about calories and enjoy yourself."

"Do you know what that's doing to your health?"

"Stop holding everything in—you'd feel better if you got it all off your chest."

"That color makes you look fat."

"If you got some real exercise, you wouldn't feel so tired."

"Let me tell you why you seem to have trouble getting along with people."

"You shouldn't just let your money sit around like that doing nothing."

"You look terribly overworked."

"You two should get away from each other once in a while."

"Are you sure you're all right?"

None of these is the opening of a declaration of deep concern from one intimate friend throwing out a lifeline to another—it is what passes, these days, for the pleasantries of ordinary conversation. The idea that one is not constantly submitting one's looks, habits, and philosophy for critical scrutiny occurs only to those to whom these remarks are addressed. Even they merely complain to Miss Manners of the tactlessless of the phrasing, without questioning the premise of whether we all really do want to live up to our best potential, or at least whether we want to be helped to do so. The only fair game for social missionaries are their own minor children, certain victims of the social professions (pupils, patients, apprentices), and one's very own self.

Whatever happened to "Oh, really? I never noticed it. Well, don't improve yourself too much. I like you just the way you are."

Glaring

Glaring is one of the few social skills—one cannot exactly call it a grace—that has not disappeared in these troubled times. One sees it best at concert halls and other public arenas. In a darkened hall, one person looks back over his or her shoulder and gives the Glare Direct to a person who has made noise. The eyes widen, a beam of shocked fury goes forth, and without the lips or the eyebrows of the glarer moving, a zap is sent out that freezes the offender with humiliation. This is an effective weapon, much preferable, under the circumstances, to the "Shhh" that adds to the noise it purports to stop, or the withering remark that so often leads to symphonic brawls.

Do not think for a minute that Miss Manners wishes to disarm the glarers, confiscating their flashing eyeballs for the sake of saving the feelings of noisemakers.

She only wants to limit its use. (Isn't that what all weapons-control people claim?) In this case, the abuses have to do with innocent children. The second most popular use of the glare is to direct it at parents whose children are making noise or indulging in other childhood activities in public places. Notice that Miss Manners is defending only innocent children. There are plenty of guilty children behaving intolerably in public, and whatever eye signals strangers can transmit to inform their parents that they have not properly performed their child-rearing tasks, are fine with Miss Manners. The proper duty of a parent is to bring children to optional public events only if they are capable of following the etiquette of the event, and to assume reasonable control over children unable to grasp the protocol at mandatory public appearances.

Let us define some of these terms. A visit to a grocery store is not an optional excursion; other people's weddings are. Teaching a child the rules means allowing him to attend nonobligatory events only if he will not disturb other members of the public; assuming control of a child whom you must have with you means telling him to stop annoying others and tending to his physical needs in such a way as to put a quick end to the child's source of complaint.

To get back to glaring: With this in mind, one can see that glaring is permissible only when the parent-child team is in flagrant disregard of the proper formula. Thus, you may glare at a parent whose child is kicking the back of your airplane seat, unchecked; you may not glare at a parent whose child is being airsick. You may not glare at a quiet child at the opera, on the assumption that the child plans to make trouble; you may glare at one there who has been given crackly candy to keep it quiet. You may glare at a child who is running about under the tables of an otherwise subdued restaurant; you may not glare at a fretful baby whose parents are attempting to quiet it down at a travelers' restaurant. In other words, you may glare at a child for being improperly brought up or controlled, but you may not glare at a child for existing or for parents at failing to keep their children locked in a closet until they reach the age of discretion.

Unsolicited Comments

DEAR MISS MANNERS:

I'm a sixteen-year-old male who enjoys going out to dinner as often as I can, but what I don't enjoy is those nosy old women who mumble to each other about how terrible someone else's manners are. Why can't they keep their comments to themselves?

I mean, I could understand if someone was bobbing his face in his plate, but not little things like clicking his fork or smacking his lips. I think if someone pays hard-earned money for a nice dinner, he shouldn't have to listen to rude comments while he dines. I have something to say to all those elderly folks—"The bad manners are in the bad comments."

GENTLE READER:

You are correct, of course, much as Miss Manners hates to side with you because of the uncharitable tone of your letter. The breach of manners by those who make audible comments about others is, indeed, worse than the manners that excited their comments.

On the other hand, you mention that these ladies are mumbling. Is it possible that you were straining to eavesdrop on others, an instance of bad manners that would be worse than whatever it is you heard? Let's call this one a draw, shall we?

RELATIONS

Civilizing Others

DEAR MISS MANNERS:

I recently acquired a son-in-law who came complete with a fifteen-year-old son from his first marriage. While my relationship with the son-in-law is just about cordial, I do have excellent rapport with said "grandson," whom I enjoy—that is, except for two areas.

First, his table manners are barbaric! It is as though he is not accustomed to using a fork (his roots are upper-middle-class). His father makes no effort to correct this situation, and the only time he eats in an acceptable manner, according to my daughter, is when I am at the table, having previously read him the riot act as to what I expect from him. The same is true of his appearance—he lives in torn jeans, T-shirt, and dirty sneakers. His father brought him over to my home for holiday dinner in that garb. I explained the cliché "When in Rome," he went home and changed—no scene, no problem.

Now—do I "take over" in the role as Keeper of the Manners, which only covers the infrequent visits, or do I read out my son-in-law and let the chips fall where they may? I should add, my daughter is not concerned where the chips fall.

GENTLE READER:

You are wildly succeeding as a grandmother, against great odds, in exactly the manner Miss Manners prescribes for combining pleasure and duty in civilizing the young. Why would you then consider turning into an unpleasant and impolite mother-in-law?

We all have a great obligation toward the children who come under our sphere of influence, which few people seem to understand; and we have an equal obligation to refrain from messing with the adults in our spheres, which even fewer people seem to understand. The world is full of children whose parents have not bothered to teach them any manners, which you may perhaps have noticed. Occasionally, one of them will get lucky, and find a stepparent, adult friend, grandparent, or other relative or teacher who will take over that task. It is a more difficult task for such people than it is for the original parents, who get a fresh start and a presumption of authority.

Anyone stepping in later, with less clear authority, must first obtain the child's desire to please him or her. Affection, tact, and a myriad of qualities that the child will admire and want to imitate are needed for this, in tremendous quantities. But if a child observes a pleasantly ordered way of life different from that to which he has become accustomed, and if he is led into this by someone of whose love he is convinced, he will respond. Your grandson has already done this.

There is no way that you can be expected to perform the same feat with your son-in-law, or, for that matter, with your grown-up daughter. Your chance with her is past, and whether she decides to enforce manners in her household is now out of your control. Perhaps she will see, from your relationship to her stepson, that manners do combine extremely well with love; perhaps not.

In any case, the boy is learning proper behavior from you, and will have it at his command in the future, whether or not he practices it now at home. It is Miss Manners' firm belief that children of bilingual behavior, so to speak, will choose the better when they are independent.

Training a Step-Grandmamma

DEAR MISS MANNERS:

I have been dating a man for four years, and I have a six-year-old son. When "Mother" (his) comes for a visit (every two years or so) we go out to dinner quite often.

Here's the problem: My child is well behaved in public, but as soon as the meal is served, "Mother" starts picking at my son to "hold your napkin like this—use a knife and fork to cut the drumstick"—he just learned to master a fork—"leave your milk on this side—your spoon stays on your plate," etc. Needless to say, dinner is quite unpleasant, and my son is so frustrated that he often refuses to eat, hangs his head, and pouts.

I have told "Mother" that I will take charge of my son when on outings, but she will not let go. He has manners and is not a slob. I plan to marry her son, so I want to stop this now.

GENTLE READER:

Once you marry her son, will you have dinner with Mother more often? If not, Miss Manners is not going to take the time to prepare you for an event that will not occur until your child is of an age to eat properly. What you heavily suggest, however, is that no one will ever eat properly enough for this lady, who does not seem willing to allow you the task of bringing up your child.

Why, since she will be the child's grandmother, don't you let her try? Leave the child with her, sometime when you and your husband need a holiday, and suggest that they forge a relationship. This is not so cruel to the child as it sounds, as no person in her right mind would spend all her time carping at a child who is old enough to show resentment and to tell tales. With temporary total responsibility, she is likely to soften her criticism with reason and perhaps affection, and it may turn out well for both of them.

Vulgar Connections

DEAR MISS MANNERS:

I have a nephew who is delightful and has charming manners. However, he has regrettably become enamored of a young woman beneath his station. The young woman (I cannot call her "lady") delights in recording offensive but humorous (in her mind) messages on my dear nephew's telephone answering device. How can I convey to my nephew the shock I feel upon hearing these vulgarisms without sending him straight to the woman's defense—and her arms?

GENTLE READER:

You are indeed correct that any attempt to drive your nephew away from his friend would have the opposite effect. Why do you not, therefore, reverse directions? Naturally, if you criticized her, he would defend her. What you must do is to say what a lovely person she is, and suggest that he offer to help her with her unfortunate taste lapses. If that doesn't do it, nothing will.

The Small Rude Guest

DEAR MISS MANNERS:

My husband has out-of-town relatives who visit once or twice a year. My problem is how to handle what I consider the transgressions of a seven-year-old child.

This child invariably gets into things, such as desk drawers, cupboards, etc. I don't feel I can hover around the child to see that she is never unsupervised; besides, it seems to me that a child of this age, who is quite bright, should know better than to go through drawers in other people's houses, even that of a relative. The parents' response to this is "When Susie wants something, she usually finds it." I might add that the parents believe in using psychology to discipline this child. Should I take the mother aside and ask her to please keep an eye on her daughter —that I do not appreciate this sort of behavior? Or should I request that the family bring along toys to entertain the child and keep her out of mischief? Or am I overreacting?

GENTLE READER:

Overreacting? Miss Manners hardly thinks it possible to overreact to the heinous crime of going through another person's drawers, no matter what the age or relationship. She once had great difficulty understanding the situation of a lady of her acquaintance whose husband had discovered her infidelity through a search of her bureau drawer. Miss Manners thought it was a question of whether the lady ought ever to forgive such a breach of marital trust. She also has trouble understanding what you or Susie's parents can possibly mean by "psychology" or "discipline" if saying "When Susie wants something, she usually finds it" is an example of their behavior. Perhaps you mean that they believe in using philosophy to explain their failure to discipline this child.

"Oh, dear," you are probably saying by this time, "now Miss Manners is off on a tirade and I shall never get my question answered."

Let's see. What was it? It wasn't how to bring up this child, who isn't yours (let us be thankful for that), or how to insult your husband's relatives by pointing out their failures. It was simply how to keep that child out of mischief. A hostess can only properly be concerned about the immediate safety and happiness of her guests; she is not allowed to involve herself in the long-range planning. Say to the parents, "I'm so afraid that Susie is bored when she comes here, and I'm terrified when she tries to amuse herself, poor thing, by getting into all sorts of dangerous places. Can you suggest how we can keep her busy where you can keep an eye on her? This house is simply not childproof, and I would never forgive myself if she hurt herself because I can't always watch her for you."

Horrid Houseguests

DEAR MISS MANNERS:

My favorite cousin's daughter and her best friend's visit to me last week is the cause of my present unhappiness. Mary and Jill arrived from a tiny country town on the bus, and my husband and I planned a wonderful week for the two girls. It soon became apparent that these two shy girls from the country were here to kick up their heels and have a ball, with no thought of our plans of the zoo and many other things our city has for fifteen-year-olds.

After four days, in which I learned that these two were capable of anything just short of delinquency, I called my cousin and asked if they could return home—not giving any of the real reasons we had for wanting them to go. But here are a few: When I asked for a napkin at a local restaurant, Jill said—loud enough for everyone to hear—"I didn't come down here to be her maid," and "These two oldies are weird." They ransacked the refrigerator as we slept, and left half-filled Cokes under the bed, dripping all over the new wall-to-wall carpeting. They left the guest bathroom in worse shape than did Elvis Presley and his entourage at a Holiday Inn.

Yesterday, my cousin sent a cold letter (she is fifty-five and I am fifty-seven—my children are married and out of town) in which she rebukes us for not enjoying the "zest for living" teenagers have today. And how "sorry" she is that we were unfair in implying malicious intent to natural, youthful fun. I must have known this would be the end of our friendship. I have learned that in some households, teenagers are permitted any kind of what I call rude behavior.

GENTLE READER:

Miss Manners must warn you that she is probably not going to salvage your relationship with your formerly favorite cousin. The only way to do that would be for you to say that, yes, you probably are unused to the ways of today's teenagers, and should have realized that you were not up to enjoying their youthful zest before you invited them.

That would stick in your throat, wouldn't it? Miss Manners hardly blames you, and must quickly point out that she offers it merely as a face-saving device for your cousin, not in any way as an assessment of the situation. Of course those horrible girls behaved abominably, and you were quite right to cut the visit short and commendably tactful for not specifying why. Please understand that Miss Manners is in complete sympathy with you on that.

Perhaps you would have been mollified if your cousin had called you up in tears, endorsed your repulsion, and admitted that she had been utterly incapable of teaching her daughter how to behave or encouraging her to associate with those who knew.

But as that would have stuck in her throat—and the lump would have been all the greater for its truth—she chose, instead, to save face by attacking you. That was not a particularly nice thing to do, but neither would vilifying her own daughter have been. The correct thing for her to have done would have been to bring up her child to behave decently.

The choice is now yours. Drop the closeness or accept the false demurrals. Miss Manners admits she would be hard put to make a decision between two such equally galling moves.

Relative Titles

DEAR MISS MANNERS:

Our large and loving family consists of three generations, some in their sixth and seventh decades, some in their third and fourth decades, and some ranging in age from a few months to five years. The first generation and most of the second generation object to little ones' addressing their elders on a first-name basis. Some second-generation family members do not object.

How does one solve this minor dilemma without causing resentment among the elders and total confusion among the tykes? What title is appropriate for a toddler to use in addressing a first cousin once removed who is an aunt or uncle to another toddler of the same age?

"Cousin Mary" and "Cousin John" are too archaic for any of us; "Miss Mary" and "Mr. John," widely used in the South, are not for relatives. Couldn't "Aunt Mary" and "Uncle John" be used by all the children until the age of reason?

GENTLE READER:

Gather round, kiddies, and we will explain this system to you.

"Aunt Mary" isn't really your Aunt Mary, dear; she's your cousin, but we didn't like the sound of that. Josie here is your cousin, you see, but you don't have to call her Cousin because she's the same age you are and doesn't mind just being called Josie. Okay, she's not exactly the same age, but to us grown-ups, all of you are more or less the same age, even if she's eighteen and you are ten.

Okay? Now, Uncle John is your grandmother's husband and Josie's father is your uncle, but he thinks "Uncle" sounds too old—no, for him, not for Grandpa . . .

And so on. At this rate, these children are never going to reach the age of reason. Miss Manners maintains that each child is capable of learning the relationship to himself or herself of each of the others and using the correct title or the first name alone, as that individual prefers.

Relations Great and Grand

DEAR MISS MANNERS:

This question may not be in your category, but I hope you can answer it.

When there is a niece or nephew to a person, what are their children and grand-children to the person? I believe they are great-nieces and great-great-nieces. Some friends disagree. They say grand-nieces and grand-grand-nieces.

GENTLE READER:

You would be surprised what creeps into Miss Manners' category these days. She certainly is.

It is always a pleasure to her to mediate an argument when she can say that everybody is wrong. (It is less of one if readers then write in to say that she was wrong, too.) In this case, Miss Manners' understanding is that "grand" is the adjective, and "great" the adverb. No, no, wait a minute. Your grandmother is your parent's mother. From then on up, you add "greats" for each generation: great-grandmother, great-great-grandmother, and so on. Going down, you get your niece, your grandniece, and then your great-grandniece.

Nonmarital Families

DEAR MISS MANNERS:

The situation is this: There is a marital family and a nonmarital family. The man involved has tried to keep secret his involvement with the nonmarital family. The nonmarital wife all along has tried not to keep things secret. The nonmarital child knows what the dynamics are. The marital children sense something amiss, but are met with denial from their father. The marital wife knows, but tries to ignore everyone connected with the nonmarital family. There are legal and financial ties between the father and his nonmarital child, plus sexual and emotional ties between the father and the nonmarital wife.

What, in your view, would be the ideal social relationship between the half-siblings? Between the marital wife and the nonmarital wife? Between the father and the nonmarital child? Between the maternal grandparents and the nonmarital family? Nonmarital children have equal legal rights to inheritance, child support, etc., in most states now. But social recognition and cordiality between the families, the clans, involved is not clearly defined.

Please help. In this case, the fears and denials of the father are so great as to be contributing to mental-emotional problems. The nonmarital child is nine; the others are in their late teens.

GENTLE READER:

The ideal social relationship, since you ask, would be one big happy family, all gathered together at Thanksgiving to enjoy this interesting and varied network of relationships. Do you want to know the chances of that's happening?

We have precedent for two opposite social attitudes toward second families, as they were called before legal second families through sequential marriage became so fashionable.

One is the royal approach, which is to establish the nonmarital (Miss Manners admires your term) wife and children in recognized positions which are nevertheless subservient in rank to those of the legal family. Making one's mistress a duchess was considered a gracious way of handling a difficult situation, and an effective one in mitigating any shadow that may otherwise lie on the relationship. The Princess of Wales is proud to be able to claim some of the same ancestors as the Prince, for example, and never mind that her branch of that tree grew, shall we say, in the shade.

An example of the other system is that described by a nonmarital child named Eva Duarte, later Peron, who cited lack of the recognized right to attend her father's funeral as a crucial factor in determining her feelings toward the landowning class to which he belonged. Her feelings were not at all nice, and Miss Manners considers a historical and social lesson to be apparent in the outcome.

Insofar as it is emotionally possible, she believes that tolerance and kindness should be summoned, at least to those who are nonvoluntary participants in the relationship, the legal wife and all the children. That is, one does not expect her to recognize the claim socially (as a divorced wife should that of a second wife), but the children of the marriage and grandparents should make what concessions they can to the blood relationship with the other children, if they are able to do so without forgetting their responsibilities to the legal relatives.

Although Miss Manners is willing to concede extenuating circumstances in the nonmarital wife's having assumed that position, she believes that recognition of the legal wife's superior social claim is part of the deal. Miss Manners is also trying to work up some sympathy for the father, but is finding it difficult, because you present him as such a weasel. It is, after all, his establishment of the second family on a nonlegal basis that created the problem, and his social cowardice now that is exacerbating the situation.

As you asked about an ideal solution, Miss Manners confesses that she would be pleased if the two families got together and eliminated their common problem, namely him.

Whew. Would someone please ask Miss Manners a nice, quiet question about which fork to use?

Choosing Relatives

DEAR MISS MANNERS:

I am a divorced woman who has no nieces or nephews on my side of the family. There are nieces and nephews on my ex-husband's side. Am I still considered an aunt?

GENTLE READER:

It is said that one cannot choose one's relatives, but the fact is that you can. You are an aunt if you want to be one.

🌹 INTIMATE FRIENDS

The Parent's Friend

One of the most thankless positions one can fill in family life is that of the good friend of the parent who does not have custody of the children. However much the parent may love you on his own time, he will hardly be able to help, during the children's visits, slipping into the otherwise universal desire to cast you as villain.

Are you determined to go on with the life you and the parent normally lead, rather than casting it all aside to allow the children to dictate everything? How selfish, and how callous you are to the tender feelings of both children and anxious parent. Do you put aside all your own wishes and devote yourself entirely to their happiness? How selfish you are, using small children to promote your own romantic interests.

Do you set some rules, according to your best ideas of what is in the long-term interests of the children? How mean you are, to expect discipline during the few free hours the children share with the parent. Do you indulge them? How mean you are to subvert the child-rearing of the custodial parent.

Do you insist on being a part of the group? How egotistical you are to insert yourself into that fragment of family. Do you absent yourself when the children arrive? How egotistical of you to avoid a difficult but important time in the life of someone you claim to love.

Miss Manners is reluctant to acknowledge that any etiquette situation is hopeless, but this one is close. Assistance is really needed from the children's parent, to defend this person's right to exist at all, and to insist upon interpreting kindly-meant behavior when all others jump to condemn it.

The parent, however, is generally emotionally overwrought during filial visits. Being a nonresident parent isn't easy, either, and the natural instinct of children is to understand this and attempt to make it even more difficult. If everyone would take to heart Miss Manners' advice about making such periods into periods of family life, with all its duties and pleasures, rather than into holiday-ish visits when constant treating is apt to begin to cloy, it would be better for all. The first step in playing this thankless part therefore consists of making the parent face what his hopes in regard to the children really are—whether they are of establishing himself firmly as parent, or of outbribing and outshining the custodial parent—and forming a plan to achieve them. (For more on weekend custody, please see pp. 25–29.)

Concealing altogether a person who is an important part of the parent's life is, in Miss Manners' opinion, a mistake. Life after divorce is compartmentalized enough without that, and anyway, one doesn't want to run the risk of that person's being represented to the children entirely in the words of the former spouse. Nor should an unrelated adult interfere with a child's right to have private time with a parent. Even original parents, as well as stepparents, ought to know enough to allow individual children undisturbed time with each parent.

Especially when the time the children are there is limited, it is necessary to plan periods that are private between each child and the parent, as well as times, such as meals and some excursions or other activities, that bring the whole circle together. The adults' interests should be considered, too, but, without being unnecessarily explicit, Miss Manners suggests that the time for adults to be together in private is after the children's bedtime.

Dignity must be allotted to everyone, at all times. Insisting that the child treat the friend of the family (or at least one member of the family) with respect is of highest importance. Under no circumstances does Miss Manners accept emotional distaste, however understandable, as an excuse for rudeness. She would not think it necessary to add that the friend must also be respectful of the children, assuming that no adult worth tolerating would be otherwise, but this may involve some explanation of what politeness to children is. Condescension can be rudeness, and so can the exercise of authority in those not used to combining this with tact.

What would family life be without the right to register complaints about one another? Nevertheless, Miss Manners is aware that this, too, is a no-win situation for the friend. If the children's behavior is criticized, the critic is told one has to make allowances for them and is made to feel callous toward the victims of a broken home. Let us assume, instead, that no one not genuinely interested in the welfare of children would consider it worthwhile to associate with them at all, under these trying circumstances.

Too Good Friends

DEAR MISS MANNERS:

I am thirty-six, divorced and going with a man, forty-two, who is also divorced. I love him very much. He has two boys, two and five, by a previous marriage; the ex-wife has custody. I have been with them only a few times, and the last time was the first night we all stayed over at Gene's house (I have my own house and Gene stays here most of the time).

I have no children of my own and don't know any, so I'm not used to small children and am just slowly figuring out how they think and what to expect from them, and I'm just slowly getting to like them (they aren't bad or mean—they are just undisciplined, loud, and neurotic).

Gene's house is out in the woods. The house has no lock on the front door, no lock on the bathroom door, and you can't lock the bedroom door because there is no door. You go up some stairs, and you're in the bedroom.

Last night, the five-year-old was following me around (we get along pretty well and he seems to like me) and I said excuse me, I was going to the bathroom, and went in, closed the door, and sat down. I was just getting started and in he comes! I was so startled I started yelling "Out! Out! Out!" and when he didn't make a move, I physically propelled him out the door and slammed it as hard as I could. He cried, and Gene acted like I was overreacting. I said I thought a five-year-old boy should know better than to barge in on some lady when she was sitting on the throne.

This morning at six, the boys got up and were running through the downstairs screaming bloody murder and having a howling good time. Pretty soon I heard little feet on the stairs; they were heading for the bedroom. I panicked and woke up Gene and said the babies were coming in! He said, "So what?" I put the covers over my head and felt totally helpless and invaded. I'm really proud that I didn't start screaming. I finally said, "I am freaking out! I can't handle it! I cannot deal with this!" and Gene made the boys leave.

I was so shook I was fighting tears (and won) and I got dressed (need I mention I skipped my shower this morning—no shower curtain, either). Gene acted like I was nuts. No one ever apologized to me for the five-year-old's barging in on me in the bathroom or pulling on my covers this morning. Gene asked me what was going on with me, and I said, "Oh, nothing, I was just in bed—with you—stark naked—and two little boys I don't even know well start pulling at my bedclothes!"

Is this normal behavior for little boys? Am I supposed to run around naked in front of them and defecate in front of them? Am I uptight and old-fashioned? I was so shook up I couldn't talk for about an hour. By the way, I had rape dreams all night long—someone peeking in the unlocked windows and rattling the door, and I felt real sick. I say they are uncivilized.

Do I expect too much from them? I know the five-year-old won't go barging in on someone on the toilet again—it was a rude way for him to learn that. As for their assaulting us in bed—that won't happen again because I am never again going to spend the night in the same house with them. That did me in.

GENTLE READER:

You may not have doors in this household, but you certainly have labels. Miss Manners started listing them: undisciplined, loud, neurotic, overreacting, uptight, old-fashioned—but then she got bored. It seems such a tiresome way of stating the obvious, which is that some people like to run around naked at home and others don't.

You are something more than a houseguest in this house, and something less than a stepparent, but in either case, your wishes should be consulted without prejudice while you are in residence, unless they prefer their habits to your presence. Otherwise, the preferences of the modesty people take precedence over those of the nakedness advocates, simply because naked people are presumed to have thicker hides.

Gentlemen Callers

DEAR MISS MANNERS:

Please address yourself to the etiquette of how divorced or widowed women inflict their children on gentlemen callers. As it happens, I like children all right in small doses and with the understanding that children are to the human race as tadpoles are to frogs—they will, God willing, one day get there, but they are not there yet.

But you might be surprised at the number of perfectly well-brought-up women who think they are doing a man the most wonderful favor by inviting, or allowing, the children to participate in conversations, to play under the man's feet during dinner, to have him read a favorite bedtime story, or otherwise compete with the family dog during the time the gentleman is trying to pay court to Mamma. "The children just love you!" she will say. Which is all right, but not while the gentleman caller is trying to figure out a way to love Mamma.

Of course, many men no doubt deserve this treatment, and on occasion this can be a ploy to discourage unwanted affection, but not always. I speak now of the not always. It is a puzzle that an intelligent woman, basking in this display of the fruit of her womb, should think a man pleased to see the evidence that another man was there first. Discussion please.

GENTLE READER:

Miss Manners can well imagine that the affections of a man who regards the children of someone he admires in the light of "evidence that another man was there first," and wishes such evidence suppressed, could well be unwanted by their mother. Nevertheless, Miss Manners can understand that even a kindhearted gentleman who loves children as much as frogs, or even frogs' legs, might wish to distinguish between courtship and family life, experiencing one before he has decided whether he wishes to consider the other.

In the early stages of courtship, children are in more or less the same position to the lady's suitor that her parents would be if she should live with them. In neither case should she associate with someone who finds her family unacceptable. She should expect any visitor to the house to meet them on friendly terms during his visit. Such an exchange is brief when the gentleman is taking her out, but if intimacy increases, she will probably grant him the privilege of being a guest at dinner and other family occasions, when they will be present.

The analogy ends when the courtship becomes serious, because a gentleman should expect to live with the children of a lady he marries, but not necessarily with the parents. Such intimacies as playing footsie under the table with the children or participating in their bedtime rites should by no means be granted to a gentleman until he has expressed a strong desire to be auditioned for the role of stepfather.

Mother's Overnight Guests

DEAR MISS MANNERS:

I am a divorcée with three children, ranging from four to twelve, and I don't want to bring them up to think that love is something fleeting, and indiscriminate sex is perfectly okay. In spite of my unhappy marriage, and another relationship that didn't work out, I believe in monogamy, and I pray that they will all make good marriages someday. I am trying to bring them up to avoid some of the mistakes I suffered from.

But, listen, I'm only human. I get lonely, and it's not realistic to think that I'm going to date the way I did before I was married. There are not that many guys around for someone like me, and they're not going to be the ones who want to sit and hold hands in the movies forever. And it's not just them; it's me, too.

So what do I do without setting a bad example? I've tried spending the night out, but I don't have a baby-sitter I trust, and the few times I did it I was so nervous about the kids that I didn't enjoy myself. Finally, I had a guy stay over at my place, and had him sneak out before the kids were up. But he made a racket, and my eldest gave me a funny look when I said it was the man come to read the meter.

Frankly, I want to have him stay over again, even though it will probably never be anything serious. What is the proper behavior for a mother who wants to teach her kids the right thing, but can't live like a nun? The kids are no dopes.

GENTLE READER:

No children are, to the extent that they do not eventually figure out that their parents have experienced sex, at least the number of times as there are children in the family. It is, however, in the nature of even bright children to assume that this was accomplished as fastidiously as possible, and with no untoward enjoyment. These assumptions would eventually be doubted even if you were still married to their father. The occasional novelty of a houseguest—that is the way you should describe him—will probably prompt speculation sooner. Do not join in this speculation, or abet it in any way, such as flirting in front of the children. Neither should you keep things interesting by surprising them as to who will come to breakfast.

Invite your friend to arrive before the children go to bed, and treat him, in front of them, as you would any nonromantic friend. What you do after you put the children to bed, Miss Manners will not ask. If the children ask, the response is "We were visiting. It got late, and he stayed over." You are not allowed to smile or be otherwise coy when you say this. It is a great mistake to open a parent's life for the inspection of the children—would you, if you were married?—and a worse one to deprive them of the comfort of believing that no matter what Mother does, it couldn't possibly, because of her dignified age and position, be exciting.

STRANGERS AND ACQUAINTANCES

Compliments

How ingenious it was of Nature to design small children to be adorable. As they cause a great deal of trouble, and have no other redeeming qualities, their existence and continued survival ultimately depend on the tremendous appeal they have for most otherwise sensible and discriminating people.

That is how it should be. Children, in a sense, belong to all of humanity, and all of humanity should be looking out for their best interests. This makes it rather a chummy relationship, and therefore adults are allowed more leeway in expressing their interest and admiration of children than they are with other adults. Exclaiming ''What a darling baby!'' to a stranger on a bus is not the same thing as calling out ''You've got terrific legs'' to a stranger on the street. Asking a toddler her age is not the equivalent of asking your hostess hers. Winking at a baby to whom one is being introduced is quite different from winking at a gentleman to whom one is being introduced.

Nevertheless, some well-intentioned grown-ups go too far. Even enthusiasm must be controlled if it is apt to damage the fledgling feelings of the little one, and perhaps the more strongly developed ones of the big ones in whose custody they are.

You do not, for example, compliment one child at the expense of another: ''What lovely curls—too bad his sister doesn't have them.''

You do not try to pass off as compliments remarks that are likely to be interpreted as criticisms: ''You're so much finer-looking than those big rough boys in your class.''

You do not give speculative compliments that may be based on mistaken assumptions: ''I'll bet you're a straight-A student, aren't you?''

You do not compliment children on their mistakes: ''Look, isn't this cute? Look at the way she spelled 'friend.' ''

And you do not extol what you perceive as a desirable oddity as if it were an accomplishment, or the children's predominant characteristic.

Miss Manners has particularly noticed violations of this last rule in regard to twins and redheads. She would not have thought that the statistics justified the unhinged amazement displayed by adults when they come across two or more siblings of the same age or even one bright-haired child, but she has observed that it is practically universal.

No adult seems capable of greeting a red-haired child correctly (''Hello''), much less a pair of twins (''Hello . . . Hello''). Miss Manners doesn't mind routine compliments in these cases, but the adult should bear in mind that the children, having been born to these conditions, sometimes wish that others would contain their excitement, stop pointing out their observations (the children, no matter how young, already know all about it), and treat them with ordinary courtesy.

Ordinary courtesy toward children may still consist of tiresome questions (''Now, who do you look like?'') or unanswerable remarks (''My, how you've grown''), but there is at least in them no assumption that the child is a freak of nature. Incidentally, the parents of these children, themselves accustomed to dealing with questions that range from the exasperating (''Can you tell them apart?'') to the offensive (''Were you on fertility drugs?''), should teach them to answer the standard one (''Where did you get that red hair?'') with patient good humor. There is no use setting a bad example for adults by being snippy in return. But Miss Manners will offer a prize to any adult capable of meeting identical redheads and remarking to one, ''Where do you go to school?'' and to the other, ''How do you like this weather we've been having?''

Conversation

DEAR MISS MANNERS:

How do you talk to a child? Don't tell me it's just like talking to a grown-up—I can always ask a grown-up what he does or what he thinks of the economy, but "What grade are you in?" and "How do you like school?" definitely do not produce interesting conversation.

My friends are into bringing their children around to parties with them. I feel sorry for the children left standing there, but don't really know what to do, other than suggest that they go watch television. But I could never succeed in getting a conversation going. Some of them just won't talk.

GENTLE READER:

Almost any child will talk. All you have to do is to ask him to tell you the plot of the last movie he saw. But you are right; that is not conversation, and debatably preferable to silence. The idea is to get him going on an interest, and that is rarely schoolwork. The child's equivalent of "What do you do?" is to fish for what hobbies, sports, or entertainment he likes, and then let him tell you something about it, making sure that there is some room for you to slip in questions and observations, too, so that it seems like a two-way conversation. You could ask computer questions, or where a good place would be to entertain houseguests of about his age (if you had them), or what the difference seems to be between his school and its rival. None of these is riveting, Miss Manners admits, but, then, neither is asking an adult's occupation or opinion of the economy. The point, with a child, is to talk to him on a more or less equal level, assuming that you both have access to some knowledge. The adult who tries to get the child to talk to his own previous childlike self—"I hated math when I was your age"—or the child's future self—"When you're older, you'll see what I mean"—is bound for failure.

One last warning. Someday you will ask an interesting child whether he wouldn't rather watch television while the adults are talking, or whether he wouldn't like you to fry him up a hamburger when the adults are having filet mignon, and you will insult him for life.

Rude Strangers

DEAR MISS MANNERS:

I'm not at all sure there is a kind and witty answer for my question, but I'd like you to try to come up with one. My daughter is almost five, and is a bit small for her age. She is multiply handicapped with Down's syndrome (no speech—only sounds) and she must crawl, as she has loose knee ligaments. Luckily, her handicaps are not easily visible.

My question is, what do I say when people ask her age? They are being kind and interested, and if I said she was a large two-year-old (very large), that might not be believable. If I say four and soon five they might ask questions which I'd just as soon not get into in a very casual meeting in a grocery store. What is the answer for the parent of a retarded child? I don't feel witty as I ask this question, but I do hope you'll be able to put this in a form suitable for your column. It is a question a number of people do have to face.

GENTLE READER:

It is true that Miss Manners will do nearly anything for a laugh, but the "nearly" is there for a reason. In this case, she is less interested in your putting rude strangers in their place than she is in your teaching your daughter the skill she will need of refusing to feel on the defensive just because others do not know how to behave. Give her age accurately. How humiliating it would be for her to have you lie. When they ask, as you anticipate, "What's wrong with her?" simply reply, "Why, she feels fine. We both feel fine today. How are you?"

Responding to Rude Questions

DEAR MISS MANNERS:

What is the proper response to the people whose curiosity outweighs their intelligence? Specifically, when my youngster's leg braces are noticed, it seems to become the Event of the Day for strangers on buses, clerks in grocery stores, kids in parks—mostly people I feel should know better. But no, it's "What's wrong with his legs?" "Is he crippled?" "Can't he walk?" "Is he paralyzed?" "What's the matter with him?"

Now, I realize that we have to accommodate reality, too: The boy does wear braces. But just how much medical history do we owe these inconsiderate people without stooping to rudeness or shaming them? My very first consideration is that my response be the most healthy one for my child to hear me say.

GENTLE READER:

Miss Manners is gratified that you are willing to deal with the reality of the situation, which is that people always will be asking those rude questions, and that there is no percentage in your son's learning to return the rudeness. You do not even mention the rudeness of being asked questions about your son in front of him, as if he were an object, which Miss Manners finds appalling, too.

Only when the temporarily able-bodied come to accept disabilities as a common human condition will we have a truly civilized society. In the meantime, you must continue, politely and firmly, to refuse to satisfy unseemly curiosity about his person. Miss Manners suggests you meet all questions with the cheerful statement "Oh, the braces are utilitarian. I assure you, he doesn't just wear them for decorative purposes."

Siblings and Sympathy

DEAR MISS MANNERS:

I have two children, one a dear little boy with multiple sclerosis, and his sister, who is, thank God, healthy, but hard to get along with. Our family life is not easy, but we try to make life as pleasant for little Peter as we can. It is very discouraging when Debby yells at him for something he can't help, or otherwise shows a complete lack of sympathy. She is older, and capable of helping out with him if she tried. Is there anything we can do to develop a true brother-sister relationship between them?

GENTLE READER:

True sibling relationships have a varied lot of ingredients, but sympathy is rarely one of them. It should be demanded in emergencies, but a permanent state of affairs, no matter how difficult, cannot be defined as an emergency. In Miss Manners' opinion, the receiver of such sympathy would be even worse off than a child unnaturally asked to put aside her own demands for attention and consideration. Brother and sister must be required to treat each other civilly, but to favor the needs of one over the other, for whatever reason, is to destroy any possibility of affection between them.

Non-obvious Disability

DEAR MISS MANNERS:

I have a beautiful eight-year-old daughter who has mild paralysis in her right arm. This means that she is unable to shake hands or use utensils "properly" and has difficulty in some social situations. Because she wears no brace, people often are unaware of her limitations and criticize her for poor manners when she tries her best. She really wants to be a lady, and it really hurts when other people comment. Can you help us with polite responses? Our problem is complicated by the fact that some of these people are being deliberately cruel. They simply do not recognize her limitations, and she feels too self-conscious to engage in a lengthy explanation of her arm.

GENTLE READER:

By all the evidence you provide, your daughter is a little lady; it is those who comment on her behavior who need the etiquette lessons.

Nevertheless, Miss Manners believes that their rudeness is not deliberate cruelty —just plain old busybody, unthinking rudeness. It is natural to expect everyone to perform such a commonplace gesture of society as a handshake—although the reasons not to range from arthritis to a religious injunction against touching a member of the opposite sex—and it is a convention of this society that a refusal to do so is a deliberate insult.

The person who cannot shake hands must therefore offer some brief explanation. Your daughter could either say "I have trouble with my arm" without elaborating (the reply to further inquiries is "It's not important, don't worry about it") or she could offer her left hand.

On the whole, Miss Manners does not believe that one needs to recite one's medical history socially, in order to satisfy the rudeness or curiosity of others, but when she once instructed a mother who asked how to teach her child to avoid this, she was soundly berated by those who interpreted it as "being ashamed" of the disability. Although Miss Manners is far from associating privacy with shamefulness, she feels that the decision to reply to those who want to know what is "wrong" is strictly voluntary. In any case, tell your daughter that the reply to those who criticize one's manners, for whatever reason, is a cold stare that clearly shows, plainer than words, what one thinks of *their* manners.

The Ultimate Rudeness

Dear Miss Manners:

In 1971, I had a mastectomy due to cancer. Now, I'm doing great. No recurrence. I am now sixty-two years old.

My only problem is a fifteen-year-old grandson of a friend, who walks into the room when I visit my friend and greets me with "Hi, disease," or "Hi, cancer." I told the grandmother I object to this, and she tries to pass it off as "teenager talk." She even smiles about it. Our friendship has really been on the rocks. Today, I received a letter which says, "Just about everything that befalls mankind is called a disease. It is not a dirty word. It is a medical term." I agree with that, but feel it surely is not a way to greet a person, especially someone who had to battle for life.

The grandmother thinks I'm objecting to make her angry. She went to several of the boy's teachers to ask if he is rude, but she failed to say what the real issue is. I believe she feels this is a reflection on her, as she has raised him. Rather than correct him, she calls it "teenagers' ways."

Gentle Reader:

Your friend, if you wish to continue calling her that, is correct in one thing: The child's manners are, indeed, a reflection on her as the person who brought him up. To permit rudeness on the grounds that it is the way of teenagers is the last pitiful defense of someone who has failed at child-rearing. And to adopt the childish reasoning that "medical terms" (which would, of course, include all bodily parts and functions) are permissible in polite society because they are not by definition obscene is even worse. By this reasoning, you and the child could properly have a rousing discussion speculating on when the grandmother might be expected to die, an eventual medical surety.

The issue here is that this woman has elected to defend her grandchild's rudeness, rather than attempt to coerce him into refraining from one of the most tasteless and blatant insults it has ever been Miss Manners' privilege to hear about. Her weakness is at least as unfortunate for the child as for you, but you, at least, have the opportunity to remove yourself from it.

A Tall Tale

Dear Miss Manners:

I am seven feet tall. This is the source of some difficulty, as everywhere I go I am accosted by imbeciles demanding to know how tall I am. Perfect strangers then name every near or distant relative or acquaintance whom they consider tall: "I've

got an uncle who is six-foot-two, and I thought *he* was tall! But you're really tall."
Please comment on their behavior and advise me of a proper response to this
imposition.

GENTLE READER:

The behavior of people who feel compelled to comment on obvious physical characteristics is, as you say, imbecilic, and Miss Manners trusts that you scrupulously
refrain from making such observations when you meet twins, redheads, very short
people—and, indeed, anyone at all.

You may not be rude in response, but Miss Manners will allow you to say, "I
really don't know—I haven't measured myself for some months," if you do so
pleasantly.

Inviting Children to Stay Home

DEAR MISS MANNERS:

Is it proper to ask, and is there a tactful way of asking, friends not to bring
their children along when they are invited to your house?

It's not that we hate children. It's just that (1) We don't have children ourselves
and there isn't anything for them to do at our house to keep them entertained; and
(2) if children are present, they seem to end up at the center of conversation when
we are interested in more adult conversation. In the event we all go on a picnic
or to the beach, of course the children are welcome. I just know, and have seen,
so many parents who feel their children are an unquestioned permanent appendage
to their own bodies, like their arms and legs.

GENTLE READER:

There is something wrong with your simile. Nobody ever tried and failed to
get a baby-sitter to sit with his arms or legs so that he could go out dancing without
them.

Parents should not, of course, include their uninvited children automatically.
Miss Manners would go so far as to say that it is only for daytime, weekend, or
vacation parties that they should inquire, "Does this include children?"—to
which a perfectly proper answer may be "No, I'm afraid this is an adult party."

If you confine your invitations to evening parties, and the parents still are
likely to bring their children, you may be forgiven for specifying when you invite
them that yours is a "grown-up" party. Miss Manners only asks that you not
attribute refusals you may get entirely to an excess of parental devotion.

What Do You Say to a Frozen Cat?

DEAR MISS MANNERS:

Several times recently, a similar situation has caused me discomfort enough to
generate an intense self-examination not only of my feelings about graciousness
and courtesy toward guests in my home, but also of my basic feelings about children and parenting. Let me say that I am childless and have told myself that perhaps I am also too intolerant.

What is the correct position of the hostess with regard to destructively mis-behaving children?

I realize that the most appropriate action would be to take my cues from the accompanying parent, but when that parent is chatting amicably about whatever in the midst of a whirlwind, oblivious to the fact that her child is attempting to shot-put my sofa cushions into the fireplace where there is a—you guessed it—fire blazing away, am I permitted to speak? Whom do I address? Is it more gracious (if possible, civil if not) to keep silent, wring my hands, and hope their visit is blessedly brief? I have spoken, wishing later to bite off my tongue; and I have bitten my tongue, wishing later I had spoken. Neither affords me noticeable comfort.

May the hostess speak before a small guest puts her cat in the freezer? May she speak afterward? Should she rather keep still, emulating the blind parent, and try to resuscitate the cat at a later date?

Please help. The knowledge that I have acted correctly may be my only consolation.

GENTLE READER:

Miss Manners has been trying to think of an appropriate thing for a hostess to say after she has allowed her cat to remain in the freezer for a polite interval, but none of them seems quite right.

"Oh, my, what have we here?"

"I'm sure you were just playing, but Kitty doesn't like that."

"Would you like some ice cream, dear, or would you prefer some of *this*?"

Let us therefore find you some other consolation, or rather, let us allow you to head off the need for consolation. It is the firm belief of all parents who abdicate the responsibility of child-rearing that (1) it is kinder, healthier and wiser to allow children to do whatever they wish than it is to bring them up and pass along to them the benefits of civilization; and that (2) childless people who do not understand this are heartless. Do not allow them to persuade you of either of these premises. A parent who does not civilize his child leaves civilization the task of defending itself, and you had better save your premises from such children.

It would be rude, not to mention futile, to enter into a discussion or contest on the subject of child-rearing. It also seems selfish to value your possessions above a human being, even a nasty little one. The only grounds on which you can enter into the fray, then, is as protector of a child's and a guest's health. "I'm afraid that Tinkerbell is vicious—you'd better discourage Natasha from teasing her, because we wouldn't want that pretty face to get all torn up." "Oh, dear, I know the sweetest child who got terribly burned playing near the fire like that. Please make her stay a safe distance."

You will get a pitying look for being so timid about danger, but never mind. It will work; or, if it doesn't, you can appeal to the child directly, using Miss Manners' time-honored "you-might-get-hurt" method of persuading other people's children to behave.

The time for tolerance is when the parent actually is attempting to discipline the child, but having a bit of trouble. A parent who is bravely doing his duty by saying, through a clenched-teeth smile, "Come on, now, Jonathan, cut that out," should be encouraged by murmurings of "Oh, he's really such a dear child—maybe I can find something to amuse him besides Tinkerbell, who's not used to children."

Furry Children

DEAR MISS MANNERS:

My husband and I have three small children. We always hire a baby-sitter when we are invited to spend an evening with friends. But today, many of our friends have decided to remain "childless by choice" and raise dogs instead. These canine children are always more rowdy and rambunctious than my own small human children. Their "parents" either smile indulgently when the dog sniffs the canapés or keep interrupting the conversation to yell at the little furry darlings—but never are the four-legged creatures banished from the room. If I go to the expense and trouble of leaving my children with a sitter during an adult party, shouldn't my host return the courtesy and not inflict animal children on me?

GENTLE READER:

There is a great advantage in one's friends' having animal, rather than human, children in that it is permissible to confess to a mild dislike for them. The most one can say to complain about the presence of children is "I'm sorry, but I'm not very good with children." For animals, however, it is possible to declare an allergy or, if that is not strictly true, to imply it with "I'm afraid I have problems with animals; I hate to ask this, but could you keep him away from me?" Once the dog is safely shut away, you can be gracious and say what an adorable dog it is, and what a shame that you can't enjoy it.

Hypocritical Compliments

DEAR MISS MANNERS:

I recently viewed a friend's granddaughter performing on TV, and the friend asked me how I liked it. I told her that I enjoyed it very much, which pleased her. Actually, I hated it. Was I a hypocrite? How does one cope with such a situation?

GENTLE READER:

Miss Manners tries very hard to understand the concept of emotional human duty in a society whose members are bothered by their consciences for the deed of having pleased a grandmother by complimenting her granddaughter. Presumably, had you admitted that you hated the performance, you would not be suffused with self-satisfaction at your own honesty, and never mind the fact that you had wiped out your dear friend Grandmamma. Hypocrisy is not generally a social sin, but a virtue.

The Nursery

Pregnancy and Birth

It worries Miss Manners to hear new parents speak of the birth itself as the most rewarding moment in their lives. Like brides who say something similar about the wedding day, they seem to be suggesting that they expect it to be all downhill from then on.

The enormous amount of preparation some couples put into the birth is, in her opinion, rather sweet. In case it doesn't go quite as planned, however, or for parents whose attitude, with which Miss Manners also sympathizes, is "Wake me up when you've got something to tell me," or to protect participatory parents from finding the end product—the child—an anticlimax to the drama, she has other forms of preparation to suggest. There is enough etiquette to fill the nine months and then some. If nothing else, the time of pregnancy is, for both parents, a continuous course in how to weather personal remarks, unsolicited advice, and poor jokes.

As distraction from that, the new parents ought to make some agreements about their separate and joint contributions to child-rearing. Miss Manners tries hard not to dictate private matters between married couples, but is unequivocally in favor of the sharing of parental duties. In any case, a discussion of such matters as who gets up how often, dispelling any lingering prejudice about a soiled baby's always needing its mother and a cranky baby's always needing its father, is useful.

89

If this is not the first child, certain courtesies are owed to existing children. One of them is not the senseless but ubiquitous inquiry "How would you like a little brother or sister?" to which an honest answer would be "Like a hole in the head." Propaganda is what is required here, not the examination of unacceptable feelings. Only in a weak moment does an only and therefore inexperienced child have the delusion that he needs a rival, but any fleeting and mistaken positive feelings may be enlarged upon until the child is actually half convinced that the project is partly his idea, and will be to his advantage. After the birth, this is sustained by giving the older child as many ceremonial duties and honors as possible. The baby, being too young to understand his own dignity, will not object if the role of the elder brother or sister is aggrandized at his expense.

Pregnancy is the usual time of the baby shower, in which the mother, and now sometimes both parents, is cornered for a full party of the kind of kidding they have been taking since they first announced the event. Showers are not supposed to be given by relatives, but by friends, and the presents given at them should be of the token variety, as close friends will pay ceremonial calls when the baby is born, at which point they will present the handsmocked dresses and fuzzy animals that will be their major contributions to the new person's worldly goods. Prospective parents should discourage multiple showers, or those held early in the pregnancy, as these will wear out the patience of their friends, who cannot understand why they seem to be taking so long for production.

Considering how long a period that is, Miss Manners is always amazed to hear of parental discussions in the maternity ward of what the baby is to be called. Aside from the rudeness of having such a close association with the fetus without knowing its name, she would think that the fact that there must be a name, and that it should apply to one of only two sexes, would suggest that the parents should apply themselves to the task. It is not necessary, however, to announce what it is. Public debates about the desirability of certain names, or who needs to be honored with a namesake, may be skipped if the parents claim a touchingly superstitious reluctance to divulge their decision, and reveal it only after it has been put on the birth certificate.

This is also the time to decide on the form of the announcement. The father gets a list of close relatives and friends who should be notified by telephone immediately (with some judgment exercised about who really would welcome being awakened at the popular birth hour of three in the morning); the mother gets the address book and a box of writing paper, because she's the one lying in bed in need of a nontaxing task. Miss Manners loathes cute little fill-in announcements with pictures of storks and superfluous expressions of printed joy. The dignified way to announce a birth, which doesn't take any longer, is to write a note on one's card or usual paper, saying, "Gregory and I are delighted to tell you of the birth of our daughter, Romola Jean ..." with the date and, if you must, the birth weight. (Miss Manners has always disliked including information that can only seem to be of a competitive nature, inviting unkind comments about the significance of one's production or how much excess weight the mother must have left, but acknowledges that it is customary.)

Hospital stays tend to be short, so there is less need than formerly for feathered bedjackets and lists of who is to be allowed and who told by the hospital officials that no visitors are permitted. Except for being expected to endure funny faces from their fathers and grandparents, from which hospitals generally try to protect the newborn by placing them behind glass, the newborn does not take up true social duties until going home, at which point he is expected to receive well-wishers graciously. A baby is allowed to sleep through such visits, but the polite baby will sleep so that his face may be at least partially seen.

This is also the time to choose godparents, if there are to be any. The request to serve as such, although a great honor, may be declined without offense by those who claim they will not have the time—because, for instance, they have twelve other godchildren—to do the office justice. A godparent is expected, in addition to the traditional service of taking an interest in the child's religious training, to present the baby with something silver and relatively useless, to remember its future birthdays, graduations, and weddings, and to be available for parental functions when the child is seeking a refuge from his parents. Therefore, one accepts only when one's feeling about the parents is warm enough to make one feel that one would enjoy knowing someone like them.

Miss Manners trusts that all this, and fixing up the nursery, will be sufficient to consume all excess leisure time of any couple finding themselves impatient at enforced waiting. It is a problem they will not have again for many years.

A Lady's Birth

DEAR MISS MANNERS:

After the birth of my child several months ago, I called the newspaper and had her birth announcement printed. My mother was appalled. She said that birth announcements in the paper were considered tasteless and low-class. Does this still apply in modern times?

GENTLE READER:

It is one of Miss Manners' deepest beliefs, which you will appreciate now that you have a child, that mothers are never wrong. However, yours is, Miss Manners regrets to say. The old-fashioned social rule was "A lady has her name in the paper only three times: when she is born, when she marries, and when she dies." Notice of a person's birth has never been considered to tarnish her reputation. This has been adapted to fit times when a lady can find herself being married three times. After that, she should stop making public announcements about it—saying on successive occasions that one is marrying "positively for the last time" is only courting disaster for a lady who is probably busy already. This rule applies, of course, to a lady's personal rather than her professional life. Making a profession out of one's personal life is as vulgar as ever.

My, we did stray from your mother and daughter, didn't we? Please forgive Miss Manners, who has an unfortunate tendency to ramble at hyacinth time.

The First Announcement

DEAR MISS MANNERS:

I have learned recently that I am expecting a child, and my husband and I are delighted. Is there a "proper" time to announce to relatives, close friends, and office colleagues our happy news? Unlike some acquaintances of mine who, in recent years, have announced their condition to all and sundry barely a day after the results have come back from the laboratory, I am determined to wait a decent interval for such a pronouncement, if only to delay as long as possible my colleagues' expectant stares at my waist as they await the day I begin "showing."

But, oh, Miss Manners, there is something I dread even more, and that is the most horrible of impertinences, the question "Was it a surprise?" I have heard this question asked several times in the past, by people who are only the most casual of acquaintances of the expectant mother. Frankly, is it really anyone's business? Is there a proper response to this that will convey the message without offending too greatly the unthinking—although well-meaning—questioner? I have considered simply answering the question with "We are so thrilled" and quickly changing the subject. Will this be sufficient to let the questioner know that I am not prepared to give out this information?

GENTLE READER:

Miss Manners welcomes your question. The concept of the respectable secret has all but disappeared from this society, leaving it a duller place. At your stage, most people would already have discussed with anyone who would listen the fact that they had been "trying to" conceive, such an unfortunately vivid term, and all the reasons leading up to that decision. This is not only vulgar, but dangerous. If you admit to having had any doubts about having a child, let alone to the pregnancy's having been a surprise, people will remember this every time they see your child, who will go through life bearing the reputation of someone whose parents didn't want him, however fleeting their doubts may have been.

The time to announce a pregnancy is just before everyone else announces it to you. The only method Miss Manners permits for letting people know they have asked a rude question is to pretend not to understand the question. A few replies of "Why, what do you mean? We are so happy to have received this great blessing," suggesting that you are not clear about what made the pregnancy occur but are delighted that it did, should eventually embarrass the most hardened snoop. Your "We are so thrilled" is more polite; say it firmly in answer to each improper question until they stop.

Congratulations to you. Miss Manners trusts that she can count on you to teach the child that, contrary to current popular belief, the great moral quality of honesty does not require blurting out everything you know all the time.

Public Pregnancy

DEAR MISS MANNERS:

I am a professional woman, six months pregnant. At work, I am confronted daily with what I consider highly personal questions from mere acquaintances (or even strangers) regarding my condition. People I barely know will approach me and ask, "When are you due?" or "Do you want a boy or a girl?" or, worst of all, "How much weight have you gained?"

I attempt to keep my personal life as separate from my business life as I can, but this one happy aspect of my personal life is quite obvious, and people seem compelled to comment upon it. How can I convey to these nosy, if well-intentioned, people that I consider these matters none of their business? I don't want to offend —although they have offended me—because I value peaceful business relationships. Yesterday, a man shouted at me from the end of the hall, "Hey, when's the happy day?" I was speechless.

Am I being too sensitive? I don't mind these kinds of questions from friends, or even close business acquaintances, but should I really be expected to discuss intimate details with the elevator operator?

GENTLE READER:

Actually these people are performing a service for you. They are trying to teach you how to be patient when you are endlessly asked the same silly question —one of the essential skills of parenthood. As nosy questions go, these are not the worst. If they had previously asked you, for example, whether you were planning to have children, or whether you were pregnant, Miss Manners would have been the first to encourage you to stare them down with a frozen smile and silence.

Being obviously pregnant is tantamount to a public announcement, and when an event is announced, it is not untoward to inquire when it is going to happen. Answer the question about when the birth is expected—not with an exact date, which can easily be wrong, but by saying "around the end of the summer" or whatever—and Miss Manners will help you avoid the others.

"Do you want a boy or a girl?" is surely one of the most stupid questions imaginable. What is more, if you guess wrong and say, "Well, we have five girls so we thought it would be nice to have a boy now," and you have a girl, people will remember for the rest of her life that she was "unwanted" and blame whatever trouble she gets herself into as an adult on this blighted start. The correct answer is always "We really don't care, as long as it's healthy"—or simply "Yes." However, if you do, in fact, know the sex of the unborn child, Miss Manners will reluctantly allow you to startle these people and perhaps cure them of asking the question. Say that you want whatever you know it to be, and you may add, "and what's more, we only want a girl. We won't take a boy. I told the doctor that. If it's a boy, we're going to leave him out on the hillside to starve."

The answer to how much weight you gained, and to any similar questions, such as what you're eating or whether you are drinking, is a firm "My doctor says everything is going normally.'' You may repeat this as many times as you are asked any such questions. And just in case you can't learn to treat silly questions cheerfully by the time your child learns to ask them, these people will help by asking you, after the birth, whether you are breast-feeding, whether you think that baby isn't overheated in those clothes, where he got hair that color, and whether you don't think it would be less dangerous for him to be sleeping facing the other way.

Nature's Helpers

DEAR MISS MANNERS:

During the last year, I have had two miscarriages. I am now just beginning the fifth month of my third pregnancy, and it looks as if I'll carry this one to term. My co-workers and friends, who know about the past, are constantly hounding me with the following comments: ''Are you sure you're pregnant?'' ''When are you going to gain weight?'' (I'm very petite, and am just starting to show.) I have tried such comments as ''Everything's fine, don't worry,'' but they still have to ''say their piece.'' Because of the miscarriages, I am sensitive and find it hard not to be defensive. How can I respond tactfully, yet bluntly enough so they'll stop questioning me?

GENTLE READER:

Ah, yes, the helpful people, who believe that wombs need lots of friendly advice and encouragement to function. Your sample comment is really very good, and Miss Manners is sorry to have to tell you that the reason it doesn't work is that nothing will stop some people. A tearful look and a blurted ''I'm not supposed to get upset'' would, but Miss Manners will understand if you do not want to resort to that.

Truly Unpleasant Comments

DEAR MISS MANNERS:

One of our co-workers is apparently carrying on a liaison with another co-worker (of the opposite sex). At least, they are seen together frequently enough that even people who don't know them have begun to comment. Ordinarily, this would be the kind of thing that makes life in the office interesting. In this case, however, the situation is complicated by the fact that the male co-worker is married to a close friend of ours and is about to become a father. Should we say anything, and if so, to whom?

GENTLE READER:

Undoubtedly, you are saying a great deal, to one another. ''Did you see the way they exchanged glances in the boardroom?'' ''Poor Annie, she probably doesn't suspect a thing.'' ''This is the third time this week that neither of them came back from lunch until four-thirty.'' And so on. That is about as much office fun to which you co-workers are entitled. To extend it by making a pregnant woman miserable is not nice.

Besides, you don't really know what is going on. They may be plotting a corporate takeover for the purpose of establishing a trust fund for the unborn baby, and the gentleman's wife may be directing it all from the sidelines. The days when you could safely assume that romance was the only possible motivation for a lady and a gentleman to seek each other's society are over.

Miss Manners noticed that you asked her only to whom something might be said —not what should be said. She is unpleasantly curious about what you had in mind. Perhaps "My, you must be about due. How do you feel? And by the way, do you know that your husband has been running around with someone from the office?" Or "Do you really think you ought to be carrying on like this?" Observations and questions, indeed, that so many people have thought must add to the general happiness of the world.

Shower Signatories

DEAR MISS MANNERS:

Many of my thirty-plus-year-old women friends are now expecting their first babies. I have been invited to a number of showers recently to celebrate this happiness, but I am puzzled as to how to sign the note card I've enclosed with the gift. I'm a working woman who pools my salary with my husband's, so do I sign the card "Gloria and Michael"? Or do I sign only my name, because I was the one who was invited to the shower—and admittedly shopped for and selected the gift? Also, should I include the name of my child who's a prospective friend of the new baby?

GENTLE READER:

The following facts are irrelevant: that you work, that your friends are over thirty, that your money is pooled with your husband's, that you did the shopping and selected the present, and that you are promoting a friendship with the next generation, sight unseen. What remains, for your guidance, is the fact that the party was not for couples or families, but for individuals. Just sign your own name.

Sharing Pregnancy

DEAR MISS MANNERS:

An acquaintance is five months further along in her pregnancy than I am in mine. She is continually offering and loaning me maternity clothes, books, advice, etc. Thus far, I have accepted her generosity with appreciation. We are not, however, such close friends that I feel entirely comfortable in her continuing this practice. The baby clothes and gadgets are probably coming next. How can I turn down her offers without hurting her feelings or jeopardizing her acquaintance?

GENTLE READER:

Have a child of the opposite sex, and insist on dressing it exclusively in old-fashioned, gender-specific clothes. Or just say, "Thank you, I'm pretty well supplied, but I'm glad to think I can draw on your generosity if I need to later."

You will soon find, however, that there are few things you can do with outgrown baby things except to have another baby, and when you find yourself looking for someone to pass them on to, you will realize that this service, while a kindness, need not be a sign of intimate friendship.

Office Labor

DEAR MISS MANNERS:

I am in my ninth month of pregnancy. I have been fortunate, in that I have been able to maintain a state of excellent health, and intend, therefore, to continue my professional activities as long as I am able. This brings up the distinct possibility that I might go into labor at my office. While I have no intention of making a fuss, out of consideration for my co-workers (some of whom appear to be highly emotional with respect to my condition), should this situation arise, I would like to handle it with as much discretion as possible. Are there rules of etiquette for going into labor while pursuing one's professional activities? If there are none, could you please suggest some appropriate guidelines.

GENTLE READER:

There are rules of etiquette for everything.

Offices are sometimes the scenes of unanticipated medical emergencies, such as heart attacks, and the rule for the patient is first to alert someone who can take charge of the situation, then to cooperate with legitimate assistance that is offered, and third, if it is possible, to minimize the fuss, in order to avoid involving others who will only clutter up the scene. As you can anticipate your need for help, you can arrange for it now. Enlist a trusted colleague to be on the alert to remove you from the office to the hospital quickly and discreetly when you announce that it is time. The general rule to remember is that births are properly announced at the conclusion, not the onset, of the event.

Prenatal Wisdom

DEAR MISS MANNERS:

We belong to a childbirth class, and have gotten to know several couples who are expecting babies at the same time that my wife and I are. Obviously that's why we're all in the class. We have begun to visit one another, and of course the subject of discussion at many of these social events is how to bring up children. I have thought a great deal about this, and do not say what I say lightly. I believe you must mean what you say to children, so that they know where they stand, and not make idle threats, but carry things through. Once a child knows you might weaken, he doesn't respect you. This is not what I am asking you about. My wife and I agree perfectly—at least in private. What happened was that a heated argument occurred at a party, and a friend of my wife's called me a fascist, and my wife did not support me but hedged, leaving people the impression that she might think differently. I found this disloyal. What do you think?

GENTLE READER:

Miss Manners thinks:

- That this is your first child.
- That you will revise your policy when you say, "You do that one more time, and I'll kill you," and the child does it one more time.
- That God gives each child two parents in order to get a second opinion.

Sharing Magical Moments

DEAR MISS MANNERS:

As my wife and I prepare for the birth of our first child, we are learning that the social conventions surrounding these blessed events are fertile ground for miscommunication and hurt feelings.

First, there is the longstanding subtle, but firm, pressure to invite (or allow) one or the other of our mothers to "come help out" when the baby is born. My wife and I do see merit in having three generations under our roof at such a magical time, and neither of us objects to giving Grandma a bathtub to scrub if it will make her feel better—but family politics being what they are, inviting one will exclude the other, and we have nearly decided to opt for neither.

We also find ourselves under pressure to attend a baby shower which a dear, well-meaning friend is organizing. I have expressed polite reservations about our embarrassment, because it seems the ticket of admission is a gift. We cringe at the vision of driving home with our car full of expensive plastic baby entertainment centers. It is more our style to forearm ourselves with a working minimum of yard-sale odds and ends and family hand-me-downs and a few boxes of new diapers, all to be deployed when we get back from the hospital, and to be augmented as the need arises.

GENTLE READER:

Miss Manners hopes you will not think her patronizing if she assures you that you have a lifetime of magical moments ahead of you, and that the understandable reluctance of new parents to share any of them will pass.

In a sense, babies belong to everyone, and lucky for them that they do. The attentions of grandparents, the showering of presents that may not be in your taste but may turn out to be in your child's, and, indeed, the general obligations of the society, including paying taxes for schooling, will all be of inestimable benefit to your baby. Nevertheless, this will undoubtedly be your baby, as you will discover when the first flurry of attention is past and you are sharing very private magical moments with the baby at two in the morning.

Accept the shower presents graciously (you can always give them to other babies later).

"Helping out" is a tradition impossible to avoid. The only effective solution is to hire a baby nurse, so that all grandparents and the parents can join in mutual resentment of her monopolizing the baby, but that is expensive. If there is not an open feud between your mothers, Miss Manners suggests your inviting them together. Their strained attempts to be civil to each other will then free you to play with your baby. Otherwise, invite your mother to stay with you while your wife is in the hospital, the tradition of the husband's helplessness at such a time persisting even when he is famous for his cookery. Hospital stays tend to be short now, and her tour of duty will be over after the gala day of homecoming.

It is considered the prerogative of the wife's mother to interfere in the household from the day the baby is home until the wife is truly up and around. There is sometimes a cause-and-effect relationship there that also makes that period short. Remember that the grandmothers will be back regularly from then on. Also remember that there will be plenty of magical moments to go around.

Cradle Courtesy

What Child Is This . . . ?

DEAR MISS MANNERS:

I am expecting a baby at about the time I usually send out Christmas cards. I don't like the idea of sending out birth announcements because it sounds like a plea for a gift, but I would like the people on my mailing list to know about the event, especially because they live in various other parts of the country, and I don't see them often. I was wondering if it would be proper for us to enclose a little note with each card telling them of the event. Could I also enclose a picture and the baby's vital statistics?

GENTLE READER:

Miss Manners admits that she has, in the past, railed against using Christmas as an excuse for bragging of the year's trivial triumphs to people with whom one is not close enough to correspond regularly. However, she believes that anyone who would not rejoice at Christmastime over a new baby must be an old poop.

The Unwed Mother's Mother

DEAR MISS MANNERS:

I am a thirty-year-old single woman who is expecting her first child. This child was planned, and I feel very celebratory about my pregnancy. My parents have a very different value system from my own, and while they are not going to disown me, they would not have agreed with my decision to have a child sans matrimony, had they been consulted.

My mother is wondering what and/or how to tell their friends and neighbors, as well as people like my aunts, uncles, and cousins. I haven't seen these people in more than ten years and don't plan to, so this does not affect me socially, but I think it might make my parents act guilty or apologetic when they need not do so. What could they say to announce or explain the birth/existence of their eighth grandchild that is tactful and nonjudgmental? (I had not planned to send these people birth announcements.)

GENTLE READER:

What you call a different value system, your parents' circle may call something less attractive. The idea, therefore, is to announce the joyous event without debating the preliminaries. The times are with you, not only bcause others have chosen as you have, but because the idea of marriage as an irrevocable condition has been shattered among your parents' generation, as well as those younger. Even the most conventional of their friends will have learned by now that marriages are made and unmade with a speed that does not allow onlookers the luxury of analyzing them for the fun of placing blame.

Your parents should say or write, "Hester has a beautiful baby ..." with the name, the birth date, and an expression of their pleasure. Miss Manners doubts that many people will reply, "When did she get married?" or "Who's the father?" Those who do should be told firmly, "He and Hester are no longer together." (It is not, Miss Manners hopes, against your principles to acknowledge that you were once together.)

Adoption

The new mother proudly introduced her recently adopted daughter.

"Do you have any real children?" was the reply.

"What did she think this one was?" asked the mother in recounting the incident. "Polyester?"

There are perfectly good conventional statements to make on all of life's major occasions, and the appropriate one for this was "Congratulations," with perhaps some babbling on about the charm of the child and the good fortune of the parents. It is when people start making up their own comments, reflecting their thoughts, sentiments, and philosophy, that Miss Manners begins to worry. Nearly all of these are ill-thought-out and, if subject to the slightest scrutiny, crude and rude. So much for the natural impulses. Anyone who has ever been subjected, when bereaved, to the improvised consolation of people who refuse to let it go at "I'm so terribly sorry" will know what Miss Manners means.

Now, adoption is a happy occasion. But you would never know it from the usual comments it elicits. Most people seem to assume that it is a last-resort move to settle for an arrangement that was far from what was actually wanted; further, they assume that they should feel free to indicate this when talking to the parents and to or in front of the child.

Typical remarks, adoptive parents report, are:

"Couldn't you have any of your own?"

"Didn't his family want him?"

"Why didn't his family want him?"

"How can you be sure that there's nothing wrong with her?"

If there are children in the family who were not adopted, the question is "Which ones are real?"

If the adoptive mother becomes pregnant, she is subjected to the popular belief that tenseness from wanting children had prevented her pregnancy until adoption got her mind off it. "See, it worked—you got pregnant," and "Well, you didn't have to adopt, after all—you're going to have your own" are the standard remarks in this instance.

If the child is adopted at an age old enough to have insults delivered to him directly, he is generally asked, "Why didn't your parents want you?" or "How come you had to be adopted?" or "Why weren't you adopted when you were little?" But subtle people prefer to address these questions to the parents while the child is standing there.

Miss Manners is running through all this nastiness that poses as social conversation among friends not only for the purpose of telling those who indulge in it to cut it out this minute, but to remind adoptive parents of the importance of teaching their children not to answer rude questions simply because they were asked. Actually, this is a social skill that all of us badly need in these nosy days, when "Can you tell us how you felt when you saw your family being killed?" is considered to produce a commodity oddly labeled "news."

Although Miss Manners is not ordinarily partial to the snappy comeback, she will not try to discourage those who teach their children to look the questioners straight in the eye and reply, "Why do you ask?" For parents, however, she prefers something more sophisticated. How about a small laugh and the observation "My, we had no idea how curious people are about where babies come from."

Mildly Misleading Announcements

DEAR MISS MANNERS:

My husband and I are adopting an infant between the ages of one to six weeks, early this spring. We would very much like to have announcements printed to send to our friends and relatives. We are opposed to using the word "adoption" on the announcement. Is there an appropriate way of having such an announcement printed without implying that we have given birth, just avoiding the use of the word "adoption"?

GENTLE READER:

Miss Manners is tempted to stray into the question of why you are avoiding the word "adoption," but will control herself. Perhaps she can make enough trouble

Gunpoint Haven

First Manassas, Virginia

General Trevor Nuisance and Mrs. Awful-Nuisance

We are delighted to announce the arrival of our new son, Duong Tran, who is eleven.

ADOPTIONS AND BIRTHS *are best announced in one or more full sentences, written on the parents' informal card or plain or marked adult paper (as opposed to fill-in cards with lewd storks on them). The proud parents have restrained themselves from mentioning their son's weight, which is ninety-five pounds. General Nuisance uses his military title socially, but his wife does not use hers except on duty; if the reverse were true, the correct wording would be Admiral Stacey Awful-Nuisance and Mr. Trevor Nuisance.*

by stating her opposition to printed (or engraved) birth announcements in general. She prefers letters. In your case, you need only describe the event as an arrival, rather than a birth: "Sylvester and I are delighted to tell you of the arrival of our daughter, Tatiana, who was born on . . ." for example. (The birth date is not necessary, but some people may jot it down and remember your child's birthday in future.)

If you must involve a stationer, have one of those cards made with your and your husband's names, to which a tiny card with the baby's name is attached by a wee bow. Miss Manners considers the idea of an infant visiting card, which is what this is designed to represent, plain silly. But many people mistakenly think of it as the formal way to announce a baby. She only suggests it here as a way to send an announcement with no verbs.

Stop Being Such a Baby

DEAR MISS MANNERS:

My dearest friend from college, for whom I was maid of honor, and with whom I have kept in close touch since, surprised me with a formal birth announcement (the baby was three weeks early) with a handwritten note. She does live out of state, and I realize they have new costs to consider, but I had thought she would give me a short call to let me know.

During the week prior to and for several weeks after the baby's birth, I was occupied with unexpected surgery in the family; thus I did not call or write my friend, though I admit I was still a bit tardy even then with replying. When I called to congratulate her, she explained that those friends who had kept contact were informed by phone, and those who had not were informed by letter. Since I had not expected the baby to arrive ahead of schedule, I had planned to contact her later, a few weeks before the due date, to see how she was coming along.

I feel, though maybe without cause, that I have been slighted. I realize that since I don't correspond on the most regular of schedules, some may feel this treatment was correct. Am I being childish? How do I respond to this friend? I think that the friendship may be ending, but do want to keep her as a friend. I do not want to offend her, but I'd like to let her know how I feel, and have her stand in my shoes, so to speak.

GENTLE READER:

Everybody is being childish here, except possibly the baby, whose behavior has not been reported. What we have here is a friendship in danger over a minor point of etiquette—the very reason that Miss Manners keeps telling people how important the observation of small points of etiquette is.

How late were you with your letter? Two weeks? Six months? Is the baby in graduate school yet? The obligation of anyone to whom a birth is announced is to respond with immediate congratulations, on the telephone if that's the way you are being told, or by mail if sent a letter. Friends follow this up with a visit to admire the new baby (you do not have the choice of finding it faulty), bringing a present; if that is impossible, then just send the present.

Quibbling over whether you were called or written is what is childish. You did it, at least in your own mind, and she did it by going out of her way to slight you by explaining that she meant to demonstrate that she had eliminated you from the ranks of close friends. Why don't you both cut it out right now? A valued friendship is at stake. Miss Manners asks you to set the example of being mature by ignoring the slight and making a tardy fuss over the baby if, indeed, it still is a baby.

Expected Announcement

DEAR MISS MANNERS:

I am a prospective father, puzzled as to what to say to relatives and close friends when I call them from the hospital. When the children of my first marriage were born, the announcement was "It's a boy!" or "It's a girl!" Now, thanks to modern science, we have known and told people for a long time that it's going to be a boy. What do I say—"Justin's arrived at last"?

GENTLE READER:

That sounds to Miss Manners as if his flight had been delayed leaving London. Couldn't you say, "The baby's born! We're calling him Justin"? Such announcements are supposed to carry some element of surprise. If you have already given away the name, as well as the gender, you had better skip quickly to a physical description of the baby (which needn't be detailed, or even accurate, as it is well known that newborns change like kaleidoscopes).

Announcements and Presents

DEAR MISS MANNERS:

The birth of my first child is expected any day, and I've just realized that I have a problem with birth announcements.

I was given three surprise showers, and just about everyone I know was at one of them. I want to send birth announcements to all these people, but I don't want them to send another gift. I think writing ''No gifts, please'' is tacky, and my husband thinks thanking them again for the shower gift sounds like we're asking for another one.

GENTLE READER:

''No gifts, please'' is a phrase of which Miss Manners disapproves under any circumstances, but in your case it would be worse than usual, as people would start to wonder if it applied retroactively and they had been had.

Send these people announcements in which you mention the present or future use of their presents—as in ''Daniela looks just adorable in the diaper pins you gave her.''

A Present Confusion

DEAR MISS MANNERS:

We have received a baby announcement from a favorite cousin and her husband, announcing the arrival of their first grandson.

However, the wedding of the cousin's son and his girlfriend is yet to be. We have been invited to the wedding, but will be unable to travel the long distance required for the trip.

Although my husband and I are not accustomed to the above sequence of events, we do want to send a baby gift and/or wedding gift. Please let us know which gift would be most appropriate. Incidentally, the child is already receiving a lot of gifts from both sets of grandparents, but we will follow your advice if you think a baby gift is more appropriate. They are a very young couple trying to establish their first household without a lot of money.

GENTLE READER:

The fun has really gone out of that traditional pastime of counting the months between the wedding and the baby's birth. It is impossible to shock anyone, anymore, no matter how the figures turn out, and besides, in cases such as the one you describe, you have to be able to count backward.

The solution, however, remains the same. It is to treat the wedding and the birth as separate events, no matter how closely they turn out to be related. As you are not planning to attend the wedding, you certainly need not send a present, although it is still, of course, proper and gracious to do so. A baby present is not strictly obligatory, either, but Miss Manners would think you would want to send one to the first grandson of a favorite cousin.

Why don't you send them a photograph album with a card saying "With best wishes for your happiness," and let them figure out whether it is a wedding present or a baby present?

Encouraging Thanks

DEAR MISS MANNERS:

Before the girl across the street was married, her mother came over with her (the mother's) wedding dress of satin and lace, and asked me to make an altar pillow for the wedding. It was beautiful. When the second daughter was married, I made her a pillow, plus one for the ring bearer.

Now the first girl expects her baby in June, and I made a truly beautiful christening outfit—long dress of eyelet with ruffled edge, lace-trimmed slip, and a bonnet. The dress has tiny smocking across the chest. It took me a week.

The girl comes home every day to have lunch with her mother, and I handed her the box as she got out of her car. That was two weeks ago, and I have not heard a word, not even a telephoned thank-you, and I am very hurt.

Would it be proper for me to call the mother and ask her whether I can have the outfit back if the daughter does not like it?

GENTLE READER:

Miss Manners wishes you would. She spends half her life cajoling people into expressing their thanks, and one of her techniques is to assure them that thank-you letters encourage the continued practice of generosity, while silence discourages it.

By being good for three presents without receiving any expression of appreciation, you are undermining Miss Manners' threat. After the first present was ignored, you could have responded to hints or requests for the second by saying, "Why, I always thought you didn't like my work. You never said anything."

Your present suggestion is certainly proper: One never taxes a person directly with her bad manners. Going through her mother, with a pretended assumption that it was your present, not the daughter, that was at fault, is exactly the formula for doing this.

Future Guardians

DEAR MISS MANNERS:

My husband and I recently had a baby, and we picked some close friends to be godparents. The idea of godparents was not for religious reasons—it was because this couple is our age, think like we do, and have a similar life-style. If some unfortunate accident were to occur, we feel they would do a pretty good job of bringing up our little boy.

We haven't mentioned this to our families, because we didn't want to upset them; they have given us the impression that "family" should rear the grandchildren. After my sister got divorced, her life got unstable; as a consequence, my parents are raising her daughter.

Is it proper for us to pick godparents because we want to, and not for religious reasons? Is it proper not to mention it to our families? If we did mention it, what would we say not to offend them? How would we bring it up? Do we need to handle this situation in some legal manner, i.e., a will? If so, what do we need to do?

GENTLE READER:

It is true that godparents are called that because they are supposed to educate the child in the ways of God, but Miss Manners is perfectly agreeable to the idea of having them for the purposes of more general spiritual education, provided you stop using the term "life-style" in reference to what you expect them to pass on to your child.

Neither the church-sanctioned godparent nor the secular one will become the legal guardian of your child after your demise unless you specifically provide for that in a legal will. The way to do it is to hire a lawyer to carry out your instructions. It seems to Miss Manners to be a very sensible idea to have such guardians appointed, rather than grandparents who might be too old for the job at such time as it became necessary, or than a sister of yours too unstable to rear her own child.

Miss Manners advises you against spelling this out for your relatives. They won't take it well. Besides, the fun of making a will lies in the fact that you will not be available for argument when the terms of it are made known.

The Extended Immediate Family

DEAR MISS MANNERS:

My mother and I have a long-standing discussion of who is included in the "immediate family." I say that it only includes my parents, my grandparents, and any brothers or sisters that I might have. But my mother says that it also includes my grandparents' brothers and/or sisters. Who is correct?

Secondly, my mother believes that we have to invite my great-aunt to our daughter's christening. I believe that my mother believes this for two reasons: (1) just because I have no brothers or sisters and my husband has one of each, therefore a relative other than my parents should be invited, and (2) because Mother believes that it is proper etiquette to invite my great-aunt.

One more thing—my great-aunt does live in the area; however, the only time we ever talk to her is when something is going on, so that she can get herself invited.

I should mention that my husband agrees with me that aunts and/or uncles, whether they are parents' or grandparents' brothers or sisters, are not in the immediate family, and therefore we do not have to invite them.

GENTLE READER:

The immediate family consists of whomever you would expect to rally around you if you were suddenly poor and undeserving. One cannot have enough of such people. Do not begrudge your great-aunt her glass of champagne at the christening—your daughter may be very glad to have her in the immediate family one day. (For details of christenings and other birth ceremonies, please see *Review*, Chapter 9.)

Attractive Nuisances

DEAR MISS MANNERS:

Upon becoming a mother recently, I have had the joy of this new role somewhat tarnished by the rudeness of others. As I hold the child for the loving admiration she so deserves, people begin to act quite strangely. Some bend close (which is understandable, for she is not large), but from this proximity, it is next to impossible to prevent further familiarities. One person planted a large wet kiss on the newborn's face, then looked up with the overly cute phrase, "Oh, I don't have any germs." Even more distressing is having people unexpectedly take the child from me to hold for a moment and pass on to another. What is one to do? Grip her tightly and shout "No, no"? I find myself in the unfortunate situation of having to anticipate rudeness in friend and family alike, not to mention the clerk in the produce section.

GENTLE READER:

A baby is a classic example of an attractive nuisance. How you have managed to avoid this discovery in your own relationship with her, Miss Manners cannot imagine. Therefore, your encouraging people to admire your admittedly lovely child puts you somewhat in the position of someone who, having asked people in on a hot day to admire the new pool, complains that they put their dirty feet into it.

You do have the responsibility of protecting your baby's health, and must remove her from even the distant presence of people with germs (saying, "I'm terribly sorry, but babies catch cold so easily"). The responsibility for objecting to unharmful amorous advances is hers. Babies may not be able to run away from unwanted attentions, but they can announce their distaste for them in no uncertain terms, which is a bigger satisfaction than the rest of us generally have. It does seem cheeky of the produce clerk to take liberties, but are you sure you didn't squeeze his produce first?

Superfluous Parents

DEAR MISS MANNERS:

Recently we had our first child, a beautiful, happy, and healthy little girl. At first, we looked forward to taking her out with us wherever we went. But to our astonishment, the sight of this practically perfect infant seems to elicit a strange response from many people. They catch sight of her and approach with rapt looks which we used to think would be followed by suitable expressions of admiration.

Instead, their comments are critical. "She has too many (or not enough) clothes on." "She's too hot (or too cold)." "She shouldn't be using a pacifier." And so on. As if this were not enough, there are also many people who reach out and grab her arms, legs, ears, or whatever they can get. What a shock they would have if a stranger did the same to them!

Of course, many of these persons are considerably older than ourselves, so we have (thus far) controlled the responses we have longed to make. But our daughter's increasing distrust of strangers is swiftly eroding a lifetime practice of respect for our elders. You have been a champion of children's rights to good manners. We appeal to you, therefore, for a suitable response to these intrusions.

GENTLE READER:

Like so many of our rights, this one cannot be enforced without committing another wrong. Being wary of strangers is not a bad lesson for your daughter to learn. Being rude to them, if you and your husband should release your restraint and go in for that sort of thing, is not a good lesson. Adorable children are considered to be the general property of the human race. (Rude children belong strictly to their mothers.) The complaints that you hear are really only dreadful attempts on the part of others to engage in parenting your lovely child. Protect yourself by smiling vaguely at suggestions and then ignoring them, and protect her by drawing her away from others when you can do so in time, saying apologetically, "I'm so sorry, we've taught her not to let strangers touch her."

Early Insults

DEAR MISS MANNERS:

I recently met my wife's employer, and we began talking about our baby. She asked if I had any recent photographs. I said, "No, I do not carry pictures, but I am sure my wife will bring him in soon to see you in person." She replied that she had seen pictures of him as a newborn and to my surprise she then said, "Oh, what an"—pause for the customary compliment—"ugly baby!"

Shocked, I replied, "Isn't it amazing how tactless some people can be"—a remark that went over her head. How should I have responded?

GENTLE READER:

Without proving your point by being tactless. Miss Manners abhors "put-downs" because they add to the total of rudeness in the world, remove the grounds of complaint by putting the complainer on the same level as the offender, and, as you found out, are not particularly effective. Politeness serves so much better. Suppose you had replied, "Really? How kind of you to mention it."

Questioning Parentage

DEAR MISS MANNERS:

I am a Caucasian woman who has been happily married to a Japanese-American man for more than six years. We have been blessed with a daughter, now fourteen months old, and I am expecting our second child. What I need is a snappy comeback to questions regarding my daughter's parentage.

My daughter looks more Asian than Caucasian, with black hair and brown eyes, a sharp contrast to my own blond hair and green eyes. Numerous people seem to think they have the right to ask me outright if I have adopted my little girl. Now that my current pregnancy is evident, the question has taken a new twist, with people asking me if I adopted my little girl, and then was able to get pregnant. Help! What can I say to these people that simultaneously will let them know how rude I think they are, without letting my little girl hear words I don't want her to repeat?

GENTLE READER:

If Miss Manners were not against snappy comebacks, even to counter such extreme rudeness as you cite, she would suggest, "Shhhh! Please don't say that— my husband thinks our daughter looks just like him."

Maternal Names

DEAR MISS MANNERS:

We have granddaughters registered in their mother's maiden name, although the parents are married. (This woman is not a celebrity, famous under her own name.) We just haven't been able to figure out why, and feel they should be registered in the father's name. At this point, the children receive mail in the mother's name, and will probably be sent to school that way. Please, what is your opinion?

GENTLE READER:

Miss Manners' heartfelt opinion is that if you attempt to argue this point with your daughter-in-law, you will never hear the end of it, if you live to be a thousand.

You are going by custom, which gives legitimate children the surname of their father, and illegitimate children that of their mother. Your daughter-in-law, and presumably your son, are going by logic, by which the paternal nomenclature can be shown to be arbitrary, as the children have two parents. Perhaps the realization that no slur was intended on your family will resign you to letting this matter pass without comment. If not, the fact that you will lose a dispute should.

Public Breast-feeding

DEAR MISS MANNERS:

Would you please speak a few words to the '80s women who insist on breast-feeding infants everywhere? Breasts can be seen on buses, in churches, in airports, on trains. They can be seen in sports arenas, department stores—anywhere. The final straw, disgusting without equal, came in a formal, sit-down restaurant. This was no junk-food, cash-and-carry eatery. A woman with a three-year-old that had already irritated everyone within thirty feet suddenly lifted a previously quiet, small infant from a seat beside her and commenced to breast-feed the child, exhibition-style. Dinner for my party was abruptly ended. Agreed, breast-feeding is a natural act. But this one, along with several others that come to mind, couldn't draw a massive crowd of paying spectators. Please, Miss Manners. ask them to give us a break. Even in the '80s, self-respect is still fashionable. Breast-feeding is inappropriate in public places.

GENTLE READER:

Dear, dear. Miss Manners has done this, time and again, only to be viciously attacked by those who think her a beast, determined to find obscene all that is most beautiful in nature, and an accomplice to the starvation of innocent children. Like you, she only wishes to confine all this beauty and nourishment to its proper setting. One can, in public places, find a restroom, which is where we go to perform other perfectly natural, healthy functions that others do not wish to witness.

However, Miss Manners does not want to endure such attacks again, especially from new mothers, who need to conserve their strength for other tasks. Therefore, let it be stated that she is merely reproducing your letter, rather than volunteering her own opinion. She cautions you to be wary when you approach your mailbox.

A Response

DEAR MISS MANNERS:

I have no intention of being so unmannerly as to call you a beast, as you predicted in your advice to nursing mothers, but I do feel compelled to make the following remarks:

In most cultures, historically, and in most parts of the world today, the sight of an infant taking its nourishment is no more a cause of remark than anyone else eating in public. It is an aberration of our culture that one may quite properly display the breast provided one's point is to secure admiration. It is taboo to display the breast if one's purpose is utilitarian. In other words, low-cut evening gowns are fine; feeding an infant is not.

I couldn't resist pointing out this oddity to you. I do agree, however, that one of the aims of good manners is to avoid offending the sensibilities of others, however peculiar those sensibilities may be.

In this area, your recommendation that the mother retire to the restroom is seriously deficient. Many, perhaps most, public restrooms do not, aside from the obvious exception, provide a place to sit down as part of their amenities. Surely you would not insist that a mother feed her baby in an environment in which you would be unwilling to eat a sandwich.

The proper advice should be to recommend nursing discreetly while in public. A shawl, receiving blanket, or poncho can be used as an aid. Proper clothing, properly managed, is often sufficient by itself. It is perfectly possible to nurse without immodest display.

Those who are unintentionally in the presence of a nursing mother should be admonished not to stare at her. Thus they will be less likely to have their sensibilities offended. It is, of course, bad manners to stare at others in any case. If the behavior of the infant should cause a momentary exposure, bystanders should politely ignore such accidents, much as they would ignore any embarrassing episode when the offender has little or no control over the occurrence.

I hope you will see fit to correct the unfortunate recommendation you made. I would be disappointed to learn that Miss Manners herself could make an error and be unwilling to rectify it.

GENTLE READER:

Miss Manners will not disappoint you. Your approach, that of taking amusement from the illogic of etiquette but still understanding the necessity of conforming to its prejudices by combining practicality with discretion, is after her own heart.

Now that she has behaved so admirably, will you allow her one little quibble? That is an objection to the how-would-you-like-it? approach of regulating the behavior of quite different creatures, such as babies. Miss Manners doesn't find that babies much care about interior decoration at feeding time. If she were to judge their desires by her own, she would certainly never agree to such things as holding them up by the ankles to change their underwear or stuffing rubber nipples into their mouths when they are cranky.

Baby Talk

DEAR MISS MANNERS:

Is baby talk harmful?

GENTLE READER:

Baby talk, as an affliction of practically everyone who comes into contact with a baby, even one that doesn't articulate at all yet, is as illogical as it is irresistible. Nevertheless, the household that gives in to it is doing the child a serious disservice. Eventually, he will find out that words such as ''oo'' are not on the college entrance examinations, and he will have to learn a second language.

It is self-evident, Miss Manners would have thought, that the point of child-rearing is to pass on adult civilization to children, rather than vice versa. Why, then, do so many parents learn to talk from their babies, rather than the other way around?

Miss Manners nevertheless understands the feeling that makes adults go all silly when they admire babies. She recommends a compromise in the matter of speech, which is both satisfying to the emotions and beneficial for the infant. That is inappropriate adult talk.

Inappropriate adult talk is when you tell the baby about the project you are working on at the office, ask him what you should serve for dinner tonight, and read him the political news from the newspaper. It is not difficult to learn, because it consists of a steady stream of what is on one's mind, which is a companionable and pleasant thing to do with someone for whom you care. The cuteness quotient is also filled, because of the contrast between the subject matter and the tiny face to whom it is addressed. It accustoms the child to hearing language, pleases him by directing lots of attention to him, and sets the standard of treating him with respect, rather than condescension.

Of course, when the baby is old enough to understand what is being said, you will have to stop asking his advice on the stock market, unless you intend to take it.

Pre-Kindergarten

At Home

Banned Emotions

In an age that believes that the full expression of any emotion is in itself an act of glory—in spite of the daily disasters resulting from the full expression of ugly emotions, some of which would have been fleeting—Miss Manners maintains a list of emotions that ought never to be felt, much less expressed. Children under her jurisdiction soon learn that she does not permit boredom, guilt, depression, or jealousy. She does not deny that such feelings are natural, but believes it to be one of the noble purposes of child-rearing to provide civilized alternatives to these dreary messes.

One banishes boredom by alerting children, through the years, to the curiosities and riches of the world. For the short term, one makes practical suggestions ("You could read a book, you could call a friend, you could play with that new toy you were so anxious to get, you could make something . . .") and then one responds unsympathetically to whining pleas of terminal ennui ("Well, then, it sounds as if you might as well spend the time giving your room a thorough cleaning").

Children must be taught to sift that amorphous substance called guilt to find out what part of it is actually true shame, curable by refraining from disgraceful acts (or by acknowledging them and doing appropriate penance). The rest, that great cloud of nonspecific guilt that hangs over our society, may be safely blown away.

Depression, another national pastime, is a term invoked by functioning people in order to give false dignity to such common feelings as annoyance, sadness, and being out-of-sorts. Miss Manners does not permit that exaggeration.

Jealousy is not, in her mind, an emotion made respectable by admitting it. Miss Manners knows that it is not easy to teach the lesson that one's competition in life is one's own best potential against one's weaknesses, and that the achievements, failures, and honors of others ultimately have very little to do with it. But she thinks this worth the effort. A child naturally finds it easier to focus on the unjustness of the world, as proved by the successes of anyone and everyone else, than to improve himself or herself, but such a tendency should be stopped before it turns into the career of a lifetime.

Now, Miss Manners expects to receive a good deal of nonsense about all this from people who believe that children are emotionally ill unless proven otherwise, and that all training of them should therefore be therapeutic and infinitely tolerant. Miss Manners has never accepted the popular view of life as a psychological problem. She would like to slide away from the argument by turning to a gentler example of an emotion that while not entirely unattractive nevertheless is inconvenient and encumbering, and that should be added to the list of emotions to be expunged. That is embarrassment.

Embarrassment, in its nicest form, is the becomingly modest belief that one is taking up too much social space, and the laudable desire to refrain from annoying others with one's mistakes. But it does not do one any good. One relief for general embarrassment, which also happens to be part of the cure for boredom and for a great many other nasty things, is learning to imagine the feelings of others, which leads to the conclusion that they cannot be much different from one's own. Another is to learn that each individual is responsible for his own behavior, and that the child may therefore be relieved from being embarrassed on behalf of his parents or other socially inept relatives or friends. A parent may be asked to change certain small habits that directly affect the child ("Please don't call me Bunny in front of my friends"), but one who agrees to alter or suppress anything basic is only encouraging the idea of embarrassment by association.

Lastly, there is the embarrassment that comes of making a social mistake. Relief should come from knowing that few people are immune, and that nearly anything can be carried off with an apology or a laugh at one's own expense. To act embarrassed, after one has done something accidental but awful, is worse than the original gaffe—because it causes other people embarrassment.

Creative Sulking

No parent worthy of the name will tolerate a tantrum or an outburst. Swift punishment or the technique of treating the offender as a nonperson for the duration of the fit are the standard ways of dealing with this behavior, which fortifies the steadfast parent in maintaining whatever dictum brought it on. How, then, is a poor child to register his or her strong disagreement, on an emotional level, and in such a way as to drive the parent bananas without provoking stricter injunctions?

By sulking, of course.

Properly done, a sulk is wildly irritating to the parent, but leaves him or her totally unable to pin a punishable offense on the sulker. It is therefore the ideal revenge of a theoretically powerless person on a supposedly powerful one. Miss Manners is fortunate enough to number among her acquaintance an experienced juvenile sulker who was willing to explain the technique for the benefit of any younger sulkers who may be coming along. She has noticed that it bears a resemblance to an adult weapon, known as "acting huffy," useful for registering disapproval without open conflict, but readily admits the superiority of the classic sulk.

The apprentice sulker must be careful not to confuse sulking with the silent treatment, said the expert. There are similarities, of course, but a full refusal to speak is a detectable felony, of less magnitude than overt anger, but just as sure to lead eventually to an overt reaction.

"The reason sulking is so annoying is that it really is perfect behavior," said Miss Manners' source. "You do everything exactly as you are supposed to, but you are still sulking all the while. After all, nobody can say to you, 'Stop being perfect.'" The sulking part consists of "being as quiet as possible, avoiding people's eyes and looking off into space if they catch yours, and keeping your mouth closed. It doesn't work so well with shy children, but in naturally bubbly children, the effect is obvious. When you have to talk, so that nobody can get mad at you for being silent, use as few words as possible. I don't think the mouth actually has to be pursed, as long as it is generally closed. The most anybody can say is 'What's the matter?' The answer is 'Nothing.' You can say it coldly, but I prefer to pretend to try to be cheerful, if you follow me. No matter how many times you are asked what is wrong, you always have to keep insisting, 'Nothing.' Once you agree to discuss your complaint, you are no longer sulking."

Struck with admiration at this useful social tool, Miss Manners inquired whether there were any further details she ought to know. "Yes—don't bother wasting this on brothers and sisters," said the expert. "You can yell at them." What, Miss Manners pursued, if the recipient of the sulk refuses to react, either from not having noticed the quiet perfection, or out of a conscious decision to ignore it? "Sulk louder," said the expert.

Disobedience

DEAR MISS MANNERS:

Is it acceptable to deliberately disobey your mom?

GENTLE READER:

No, it is not. You might grow up to disobey Miss Manners. However, it is conventional practice among children who cannot be taken to task for bad manners to obey their parents, when they disagree with them, with what we may call reluctant grace. This is surprisingly effective.

snow

Ski-lift tag turns suit into ski suit

Every-day play clothes

Best velvet Nutcracker Ballet dress

Outfit to melt a parent's heart

for joggers

Never!...

Grown-up world (also has suit)

Informal

WARDROBES FOR PROPER CHILDREN (and a Few Things That Will Never Be Allowed Out of the Closet).   There are two acceptable styles of clothing for children: those they like, and those their parents like. The deal is that if they wear what their parents like when with the parents' friends, they may wear what they like when among their own friends. Parents can sabotage this arrangement by banning garments they say are vulgar, sure to cause colds, or not worth the money; children can more easily sabotage their parents' choices by outgrowing what they don't like.

Parent gear

Parent Gear

Informal

Peer Gear

Peer Gear

except on Hallowe'en

Just Ask

for dances

Informal

Grown-up world

Showing Off

DEAR MISS MANNERS:

What do you recommend for exhibitionism? I'm not talking about the nasty man in the trench coat, but the nasty child (it happens to be my brother's youngest) who always demands attention and gets destructive until he gets a rise out of us. Outside of killing him, which I have considered, is there anything I can do?

GENTLE READER:

You can't have an exhibition without an audience. Your nephew realizes this, and keeps increasing the drama of the show in hopes of attracting one. Unless that works, however, he will eventually have to close down. If your brother or other family members attend, you can still excuse yourself to go out to the lobby, or the nearest equivalent, until the drama is over.

Clothes Combat

"Do I have to wear my leggings? Nobody else does."

"You know it drives your father crazy to see your hair hanging down like that."

"You call that dressing up? For what?"

Such remarks, once the perennials of the family garden of tussles, are now rarities. The way to get a child to wear a snowsuit, bib-style leggings and all, is to attach lift tags to the zipper and call it a ski suit. The emotional charge any argument over hair length in children used to produce is no longer possible, because the batteries are too weak. And dressing up, these days, seems to be a custom only kept alive artifically by people who are attending parties given by or for those who design dress-up clothes.

Miss Manners hates to see such venerable topics for disagreement disappear. It seems to her that children and parents need to maintain healthy differences of opinion, just to keep them in good argumentative trim, and that if they have no superficial pretexts, they are in danger of finding fundamental ones. Here then, in the hope of reviving the struggle, are Miss Manners' basic rules for fighting out that great generational question of Do I Have to Wear That? or You're Not Going Out Like That!

1. Health considerations. The cause-and-effect relationship between wardrobe and disease is so regularly invoked by adults who believe in punitive medicine ("Of course you have a sore throat—you went out without your mittens last Thursday") that no child gives it the slightest credence. Miss Manners believes parents should have the final say in decreeing what must be worn for health reasons, but that they will obtain this only through subterfuge. The idea is to make the despised item take on glamour—from an association with sports, the arts (loosely defined to include noise), or sophistication—most valued by the child. There is a world of difference between leggings and leg warmers. Remember, no mother ever died of pneumonia from not putting on her fur coat. Incidentally,

the privilege of complaining that a child's clothing will lead directly to illness is a permanent one. Asking one's middle-aged child, "Is that all you wore over here?" is considered a sign of affection.

2. Taste. This is a tricky matter, as our society is unfortunately set up so that young people sometimes get the general fashion news first. You do not want to ban anything you might be wearing next year. The best thing is to permit nothing permanent (such as tattooing) or that cannot be well concealed (such as a shaved head) and fight the rest of the question out on the grounds in section 3.

3. Appropriateness. Clothing being a convention of the society, the argument of wearing what everyone else wears has some validity to it; more, certainly, than in the moral realm, which would be doing what everyone else is doing. One does want to conform, in a general way, to the prevailing standards. (N.B.: This rule may not be invoked to support purchasing expensive fad items.) The prevailing standards are different among adults. A sensible compromise is to allow the child to dress, within reason, as do his peers when he is among them, provided he dresses, when among the parents' peers, within their standards of how a child should look for whatever adult occasions the child may be attending.

There. Miss Manners hopes these rules will enable the generations to take up the conflict again in an orderly manner. She really cannot bear the sight of all those families, sitting about in their identical jeans, sneakers, and T-shirts, too listless to get into the fray. (For more on children's clothes, please see pp. 165–167 and 194–195.)

Manners vs. Snobbery

You would think, given Miss Manners' crusading spirit, that she would have been pleased beyond measure to hear of "etiquette camps."

Indeed, she was, at first. With all her heart, she believes that manners must be taught by parents to their children, fourteen hours a day (nine hours for sleep, and no shouting instructions to them while they're in the bathroom) in order to be effective. But she has also noticed that there is a lot of remedial work to be done, and is heartily grateful for all assistance in this noble effort. Imagine her horror, however, when she found out some of the things that were being taught at etiquette camps. There was one story about three-year-olds having been trained to kiss ladies' hands—possibly the most extreme example of bad manners ever perpetrated upon an innocent child and his helpless victims. Hand kissing is not properly performed at all by Americans, by children, or, literally, by anyone—a mature European gentleman who has been brought up to do so may kiss the air above the hand of a married lady only, but anyone else who tries it is being pretentious and ridiculous. How many three-year-olds, or thirteen-year-olds, in this country know how to greet someone correctly by looking him or her in the eye, shaking hands, and saying clearly and pleasantly, "How do you do?" That is what one ought to learn at camp if one is not learning to make gimp lanyards.

Other children were being taught to order food in French, take afternoon tea, and refrain from drinking the water in finger bowls. These are all useful skills.

May Miss Manners assume that they were already proficient in eating chicken, chewing with their mouths closed, and generally making themselves pleasant during family dinner—remembering to refrain from announcing all their food dislikes? There was a refresher course in how to ride in a limousine, which, in Miss Manners' experience, is one of the least difficult of life's trials. Riding on a public bus so that nobody's feelings or shins are bruised seems to be one of the most difficult.

What upsets Miss Manners most profoundly is that all this perpetuates the public idea that manners are a series of snobbish gestures that the rich, or those who wish to pass for rich, use to intimidate the poor. Miss Manners has met few children in her life whose most urgent need is to be taught to manipulate the symbols of luxury. Properly brought-up children learn such things if and when they are appropriate to their lives. The child whose family has a limousine is routinely taught—if he is taught any manners at all, and the rich are far from setting a good example on that score—to treat it and the driver with consideration. Improperly brought-up children, of whatever income level, will not be served by lessons that compound their basic bad manners with snobbery.

Gamekeepers

When acquiring a child, as when acquiring a car, one never sufficiently considers the parking problem. Yet delightful and welcome as the acquisition may be, one can't spend all one's time running around with it.

However, one can easily spend all one's time worrying that it will be damaged in one's absence. There is simply no question that anyone planning to have a child will at least occasionally require a safe parking place, with a responsible attendant in charge. Why people don't consider that before they take the very first step toward having a child, Miss Manners cannot imagine. Nannies first, and then babies, seem to her the natural order of life.

Nannies come in various guises these days, practically none of them starched, let alone equipped with the desire to devote themselves entirely to the care of some-one else's child, topped only by the desire to take second place to that someone else in the child's affections. The fashion for having hired help bring up the children was never expected to be accompanied by the current fashion for the parent's making all the decisions and getting all the credit.

Intermittent amateur help is much more the rule, which means that the person in temporary charge is likely to be someone else's parent, or someone else's child.

Yes, Miss Manners is aware that we are all at least one of these. She means that it is likely to be the parent of the child's friend, or the child of the parent's friend. Oh, never mind. We're talking about playgroups and babysitters, and they are either people who are minding their own children as well, or who are children who are more or less minding themselves. One hopes.

Among adults, such arrangements are likely to have payment in return service; child sitters, being more practical, demand cash. In either case, accounts must be kept strictly, without the common temptation of feeling that one's acquaintances really like to help one out without thought of recompense. Because the convenience is also a social arrangement for the children, or is disguised as one, it is only too easy to confuse warmly given household daycare services with hospitality, which means that someone's house and time are being used as one would a free public accommodation.

Time must also be specified strictly. The freedom you feel from knowing that you needn't rush home because your child is in the hands of a good sitter depends on that sitter's parents worrying because their child is out too late. Possible delays must be stated in advance, and even emergencies are rationed.

Miss Manners assumes that anyone mature enough to have children also knows about leaving telephone numbers for home emergencies, stating allergies and regulations, and generally outlining reasonable expectations for the period of absence. One does not instruct a sitter to "make" a child do tasks that the parent has been unable to enforce, or leave the preparations for tomorrow's formal luncheon along with a general invitation to eat everything in the refrigerator.

Courtesy rules should also be left. Even tiny children can be told to respect the person in charge, and that person must be allowed to take a firm hand. One screens out child-beaters beforehand.

In adult-run playgroups, courtesy is enforced by that great prompter of civilized bahavior, the certainty of instant retaliation. Parents of children of the same age, whether they met in pre-birth classes or in post-birth playground pickups, are apt to notice the convenience of two-generation friendships—right up to the point where one family's child learns to talk or read, and the other's doesn't. If similar standards of behavior are not observed, things are going to turn nasty quicker than that.

When the parents are trying to conduct their own visits, with the silly expectation that the children will play quietly, this means each polices his own from destroying anything valuable, such as furniture or the other child. When one parent is in charge, the trust that that person can set the discipline is re-inforced by the fact that it is usually that person's house and furniture at stake.

It is a tradition in this country that people who are so soft-hearted as to love children are also soft-headed, and so do not notice when their own interests are being abused. This is why we don't pay teachers, and why women who have been told that child-rearing is the most important task of the society report that being therefore one of the most important persons in the society doesn't cut any ice at cocktail parties.

Miss Manners feels obliged to warn parents that relying too heavily on this assumption, in large matters or small, is not in their interest.

Belligerent Babies

DEAR MISS MANNERS:

I go to an exercise class where we do co-op baby-sitting. One of the children in the group is an absolute terror. He is constantly scratching, biting, and knocking down the other children. He is three, and often walks up to the babies and pushes them over. Some of the children have cried about going to the group because they don't want Tyler to hurt them.

I have a lot of compassion for the mother and her problem child, but I'm sick of it. I go to this class to enjoy myself and find it difficult at times because I wonder if my child is safe. I know how defensive we mothers can be about our children. How can I tell her about my feelings, as well as those of other mothers, in regard to her child?

GENTLE READER:

Politeness does not require a mother to stand by while someone is knocking down her baby, not only doing nothing to prevent it, but trying to work up sympathy for the mother of the offender at the same time. The person who is doing the baby-sitting when the problem occurs—such a moment being anticipatory, rather than after all the babies are lying flattened on the floor—must assume the professional manners of an adult in temporary charge of someone else's child. This means first of all preventing the child from hurting others; second, making it clear to him that such behavior will not be tolerated; and third, informing the parent of this behavior and its unacceptability. The place for tact is in this third step, when you may open by saying, "I don't know whether you are aware of Tyler's difficulty in relating properly to other children, but perhaps you can help us deal with it, because we would hate to have to isolate him from the group," and other such psycho-sympathy as may soften the point while not obscuring it.

Working Mother's Lament

DEAR MISS MANNERS:

My daughter, Kara, is now attending preschool three times a week, and I have gone back to my old job, which I left when I became pregnant with her. She loves school, and is up early on school days, racing around excitedly and eager to be off. I count that as a big plus, because the first week, she cried and clung to me, and I had to stay with her until she got so interested in what the other children were playing that she forgot me.

It's the two days a week she doesn't go that are driving us both crazy. (Next year, she can go five days a week, but although she's more than ready for it now, they don't allow them to at her age.) She comes into my room while I'm getting dressed and cries and begs me not to go. Before she started school, we used to do lots of fun things together like bake and act things out with dolls, and she wants me to stay home and play with her. I tried to find a play group where she would have other children, but couldn't, and my cleaning lady, who is a lovely person but is too busy to do much playing, keeps an eye on her.

Needless to say, I feel terribly guilty about this. My husband points out that we don't really need the money from my working this year, but we will as soon as Kara starts kindergarten, for tuition and lessons and all the extras we both want her to have. I feel lucky that I was able to get my job back, and am afraid to leave again.

Is there a tactful way to show Kara that I would love to stay with her but can't stand these scenes in the morning? By the time I get to work, I just want to go into the ladies' room and cry.

GENTLE READER:

How about saying, "Suppose I cried and carried on and said you didn't love me and pleaded with you to stay home when you want to go off to school"? Better yet, just do it, if you can manage to pull it off in an amusing fashion, some morning when she is eager to be off. A good dose of "See how Mamma feels?" never hurt any child.

In the Office

DEAR MISS MANNERS:

This place is supposed to be an office, but it's really a nursery for wayward kids. Yes, I am an old grouch. Yes, I am unmarried and childless and bitter. But I am sick of trying to concentrate on what I'm doing while some brat squalls nearby, a toddler decides that my shoes are toys, or Sweet Mama stinks the place up because she's too busy talking to her girlfriends and admiring their children to change her own kid's diaper.

All right, I'm exaggerating. But at least once a week, someone brings in a baby. Babies do not belong in offices, under any circumstances. Why can't those people stay home where they belong?

GENTLE READER:

Why, indeed? Miss Manners will do you one better, and suggest that the babies go out and get jobs like decent people, instead of loitering where they don't belong and making trouble for honest working folk.

If that isn't practical, she has another suggestion, based on the assumption that the mothers work for the same reasons you do, and that they take their babies along less for intellectual companionship than because they have no place to leave them. A society that recognized that both working and having children are parts of the normal human condition would insist upon day-care centers in offices, where small children could be supervised out of the way of working people, but nearby enough to draw upon the necessary attentions of their parents. Short of demanding one from management, the people in your office could set up a cooperative one, pooling their money to pay for it. If Miss Manners were there, she could come around asking you to help pay, on the grounds that children are the responsibility of everyone and that this would be in your immediate interest as well, but she doubts that anyone else would have the nerve.

Perhaps children do not belong in offices every day unless all the workers agree to have them there, but they should certainly be taken to visit their families' workplaces when they are first old enough to take in their surroundings. It is reassuring to children to know where their parents are when they disappear, and helpful to both families and the education of the young to allow them to observe productive work. If Miss Manners agreed that babies are not allowed to play with your toes while you are trying to concentrate, would you soften up enough to give them one of your grisly smiles on a day set aside for holiday family visits?

Traveling Troubles

DEAR MISS MANNERS:

Because of a difficult and complicated job situation, which will soon be settled at long last, my husband and I have been crisscrossing the country, taking the kids back and forth with us. We thought this, bad as it was, preferable to parking them for a few months with their grandparents and running the risk of having them think we were deserting them or cared more about our careers than about them.

Have you noticed that women traveling with small children are treated differently by stewardesses, fellow passengers, and so on than men are with the same children? My husband denies this; he claims I'm not "handling" things properly.

When he arrives with the children, he has just as many sad stories as I do—Leah threw up on the plane, Jeremy cried because he'd forgotten his stuffed rabbit, and that kind of thing. But he always adds that the stewardess mopped up, a nice lady told Jeremy a story that distracted him, or a couple of teenaged girls organized pattycake games that distracted the children. With me, it's different—people just glare and turn away. Can you tell me why things are different, how a parent is supposed to behave when a child has trouble traveling, how others are supposed to behave—and maybe make me feel better about this injustice?

GENTLE READER:

A father traveling with a screaming baby is presumed to be a widower who is devoting himself to the welfare of his poor babes, and therefore simple humanity requires that strangers do what they can to ease his burden. A mother traveling with a screaming baby is presumed to be a slovenly person whose husband was driven away by her neglect of discipline and the resulting bad behavior of the children; others naturally try to distance themselves from the mess.

Miss Manners does not feel that she did very well with your request to make you feel better. Let her try to answer your other question, instead.

It is the obligation of a parent to prevent his or her offspring from annoying people, and the pathos that created the annoyance does not, unfortunately, create sympathy or provide an excuse. But you needn't waste any anger on the callousness of people who seem to think that your baby is crying for the sheer pleasure of it, or being sick on purpose. What is required to placate them is the same thing that is needed to comfort your child—namely, relieving the situation that has caused the trouble.

When a child is sick, clean him up; when a child is crying, calm him down. The only differences between doing this in public and in private are that in private, you might allow a fretful child to cry himself out, or you might show him some anger, which you cannot do in front of an audience; and that in private, you would have the luxury of imagining that you claimed the sympathies of all the adult world.

Physician Phobia

DEAR MISS MANNERS:

My son is deathly afraid of his pediatrician, a kindly, gray-haired man who has never hurt him worse than necessary for giving a shot, and even his dentist, who has never hurt him either. I have told him that they love him, and only want to keep him happy and well, but it doesn't seem to help.

GENTLE READER:

That is hardly surprising. Who could believe in the love of a dear friend who sees one only twice a year, on appointment, and usually with a steel instrument in hand? It would probably be less frightening to compare him with your automobile mechanic, who cares for the car, checks it, and sees to it that it gets what it needs to operate safely and comfortably. But then Miss Manners hasn't seen your mechanic.

Blankies

DEAR MISS MANNERS:

Security blankets are all very funny in the comic strips, but having filthy rags around the house and watching your child walk into a room full of guests dragging a tattered old blanket as if he had no nice things is no joke. Is there anything I can do, short of having a tug-of-war with my son in front of everybody, to get him to keep the nasty thing hidden, and maybe eventually even to get rid of it? I don't want to cause him psychological problems, and I know "blankies" are normal, but his is also disgusting.

GENTLE READER:

The principle is the same as if he were fifteen or twenty years older, and had brought home a young lady fitting the same description—that is, one to whom he was wildly attached, but whom you found repulsive. First, you would wickedly encourage him to distribute his affections promiscuously; in the case of the blanket, that means introducing, if you can, a second blanket so that he will have one to use while you have one to throw (holding it at arm's length, pinching your nose shut with the other hand) into the wash. As with a young lady, this will be easier to do at the earliest stages of the attachment, before the emotions become too fixed. Next, you would begin a subtle, if nasty, campaign of propaganda, insinuating that some objects of affection, however useful in satisfying one's private passions, are not quite up to family standards and had best not be displayed to friends. In both cases, the struggle will be a draining one for you and the child, but if you can hang on, the likelihood is that he will outgrow the attachment.

Social Life

Protection on the Playground

The law of the jungle gym is brutal—but does that justify paternalistic intervention? That is the philosophical point that is occupying the minds of all grownups who are sitting mesmerized on playground benches, no matter what the titles of the books lying neglected on their laps or being held as protective shields against sights they cannot bear to witness.

It is universally acknowledged that the big powers are brought in only when grave matters involving safety arise. But safety from what? Most adults would not hesitate to remove a sandbox shovel from its owner who is using it to pat down the heads of playmates. But what about safety from psychological terrorism? And what, Miss Manners demands, about the safety of civilization if one sees it threatened by the ugly laws of intimidation?

There are questions of jurisdiction. What tactics besides retreat are available to the parent of a child being victimized by the child of an isolationist? Does the parent of a neutral have responsibilities when injustices among strangers are observed? There is the crucial matter of diplomacy. How do you stop skirmishes without inflicting the kind of public humiliation that leads to further rebellion?

Some of this may explain why Mamma did not get her brief written when she had a whole afternoon with nothing else to do but sit quietly in the sun, or why Papa does not look rested after being out in the fresh air all day. As havens for adults, playgrounds are vastly overrated. The only real recreational activity they offer for grown-ups is the comfort of finding other grown-ups in the same predicament.

Basic playground rules for parents are:

You do not let small children loose among their peers without explaining such unnatural activities as taking turns, fair play, proper use of playground equipment, and consideration for others.

Physical offenses are halted immediately, with cries of "Watch out," and the snatching away of weapons and victims' bodies.

Psychological warfare is halted by calling to one's own child, "Come here, Serena, I need to talk to you." If she is the offender, she is told in a whisper, "Cut that out or else"; if the victim, she is told, also in a whisper, "We have to go now; we'll come back and play later."

Or less passively, the offender's parent is told, "They seem to be having some trouble playing nicely together. Do you want to explain the rules to them, or shall I?" If no such parent is in sight, the offender is told firmly, "I don't allow Serena to play this way. Either you all play fairly or the game is over."

The idea, throughout, is to hold one's child responsible for his or her behavior without treating other children to the spectacle of the child's being chastised; to hold other parents responsible for their children's behavior without seeming to do anything more disapproving than calling their attention to what they might absentmindedly have failed to observe; and to convey the idea to other children that their abuses of authority over their peers will lose them that position if, for no other reason, only because they will be left with no one to victimize. In other words, the playground is a demonstration area for child etiquette, but not the place where the actual instruction takes place. Neither does any adult reading or resting.

Proper Toys

DEAR MISS MANNERS:

What are Miss Manners' favorite toys? I need some suggestions for proper children.

GENTLE READER:

Miss Manners is very fond of her tea set, especially when there is tea in it. Nevertheless, she does not recommend it for children of either gender who might find the beverage overstimulating.

There are two types of toys: those parents like, and those children request. Occasionally, the two overlap, but if not, it is considered a weakness in parents to get the latter. All their friends will assume, upon seeing the latest hussy that calls itself a doll, or the newest battery-run weapon, that the parent is dominated by the child, and the child is, in turn, at the mercy of television advertising.

Adults, including Miss Manners, like flat-chested dolls, unpainted blocks of wood. the books they had as children, and the electric trains they wanted but didn't get. Toys that did not exist during their own childhoods are charmless for them, and are called fads. A show of enthusiasm, including the willingness to play with—not instead of—the child will occasionally transmit the adult's enthusiasm. There is quite a respectable rationale for this kind of toy, as it does not break or bore as easily as the complicated modern items the child requests.

A suitable compromise is for the parent to buy those things of which he approves and in which he is confident of being able to interest the child, and to tell other relatives who ask what to get about the child's own wishes. A child should also be encouraged to use his own money, allowance, earned income, or cash presents, to buy the latter; it is a wonderful incentive for saving.

Uninvited Guests

DEAR MISS MANNERS:

Am I correct to assume that it is always impolite to invite oneself to another person's home, even if one is a child?

This problem arises with some of our younger neighbors, who phone to ask, "Can I come over to play with Beauregard?" A variation occurs when one of my children invites a same-age friend to come play, and minutes later, both that friend and his or her sibling appear at the door. I can only assume that the parents encourage these calls and uninvited visits, since these same people have come to our door with a child in tow and announced cheerfully, "Our Matilda would love to play with your Beauregard." I do want my children to play with their neighborhood friends, and I do invite those children to play in our home when it is convenient for me. Also, should one accept an invitation if one has no intention of reciprocating? Some children who have visited us more than once have never invited my children to their homes.

(In case you're wondering, other parents and teachers have informed me that my children are well-behaved.) My feelings are hurt when my children are not invited back, but fortunately my children do not seem to mind very much.

In summary, how do I set an example of good manners for my children, protect myself from nervy parents, and protect the friendships and feelings of all the children involved in these matters?

GENTLE READER:

By all means, teach Beauregard to reciprocate invitations, and to refrain from issuing himself invitations to other people's houses. Then all you will have to do is to teach him the higher forms of etiquette, which include refraining from criticizing the manners of one's playmates, and conducting one's social life without keeping strict tabs on what other people are doing for you.

The fact is that the social life of small children is conducted with less rigor than that of adults. Whose yard or house is played in more often is likely to be a matter of whim or convenience, and having children trailing through one's house is not in the same category with full-fledged entertainment of adults. You do not need to dress up for these visits, or sit around and make conversation. You don't even need to have them when they are an annoyance. If a child or parent proposes such a visit, there is no reason that you cannot reply, "Oh, I'm sorry, this is not a good time." The same may be applied to drop-in adults, for that matter.

The Rotten Apple

DEAR MISS MANNERS:

There is a rotten apple in our neighborhood. I feel a little rotten myself, making such a statement about a little child, but there is general agreement among all us mothers that this kid is nothing but trouble. If the trash cans are knocked over, if the kids get out of the yard they were supposed to be playing in, if the neighborhood pets are being tortured, and if you look out the window and see a pile of clothes and a bunch of kids running around naked in the cold, we all know that Warren has been at it.

Some of the mothers have forbidden their children to play with him, but it doesn't do any good. There are a lot of kids on the block, and it's not easy to watch every minute to see who's in the group. Others, and I am one of them, have tried to tell our children why we don't like him, but they can't understand. Either it's too different from what we usually tell them, about their not being "bad," just sometimes doing bad things, or we actually create respect for Warren by making him sound so important that we're afraid of him.

Do you believe in a bad child, and, if so, does a mother have the right to demand that her child not play with him?

GENTLE READER:

Without engaging in ungenerous, psychologically oriented quibbling, Miss Manners will say that she does believe in a bad influence. Any child with an ounce of imagination will come up with a terrible plan of action once in a while, but to accumulate a consistent record bodes no good. Miss Manners darkly suspects Warren's parents of not having taught him manners, and she hopes you appreciate the depth of that as an insult.

A parent certainly has the right to regulate who comes inside her own house or yard, but to extend the right to placing a geographically accessible child outside the bounds of decent society is a mistake. As you have noted, it can only render him glamorous. A more effective attitude is to show your distaste for him, while letting on that you understand that your child is not as discriminating. The reason you give for not having him in the house or on excursions or other treats you may plan is that you find him unbearable. (Miss Manners does not care to be accused here of cruelty toward Warren. It can only do him good to discover that the popularity that results from breaking rules also ostracizes him from greater domains.) A child may enjoy seeing his parents obviously threatened by a mere playmate, but he will take less delight in being pitied for such an alliance.

Television Addiction

DEAR MISS MANNERS:

I sometimes invite children from my four-year-old's nursery school over to play with her in the afternoon. These children are literally addicted to television. They demand that I turn on the cartoons at three o'clock, which, as you may not know, is when two hours of cartoon fun starts. When I refuse, they mope and ask to be taken home.

I was brought up to believe it is bad manners to watch TV when company is present. Furthermore, I see no value in preschool children's sitting like lumps for half the afternoon. I invite other children over so that my daughter will play. If I wanted her to sit watching sugar commercials, I wouldn't bother inviting other children; she could do that alone. In my position, would Miss Manners stick to her guns, or would Miss Manners graciously give her guests what they want?

GENTLE READER:

Stick to her guns? Miss Manners would bring out the heavy artillery. It is the privilege of the hostess (or the hostess's mommy, if the hostess is not of age) to set the terms of the invitation. The guest (or her deputy) can then accept or refuse, but cannot demand to change the terms. If you invite guests for poker, they are not allowed to demand to be allowed to play soccer instead.

Perhaps you should make your invitations somewhat more clear by saying, "Daniela would love to have Rosalinda over to play this afternoon, but you know, we don't allow the television to be on, so if she really can't miss her cartoons, perhaps it's not a good idea." If you think there is an element of shame intended here for the parent who has not imposed any such rules and has therefore nurtured a child who prefers passive to active entertainment, you are correct. This is because Miss Manners hopes you will be a good example to passive parents.

Sensible Sharing

DEAR MISS MANNERS:

Are there exceptions to the rules about sharing toys? We have always tried to teach the children to share with their playmates, but it seems particularly hard on them when it's an extra-special toy—because it's new or because it's the favorite animal they go to bed with—or when they take something to the playground and don't get much time with it because everyone else wants a turn.

GENTLE READER:

Miss Manners admires you for teaching sharing, but let's not overdo it. You don't want them to grow up to share their husbands or wives, do you?

Guests in the house are permitted to play with available toys. Fragile or sacred toys are simply put out of sight. On the playground, sharing is required on the equipment that is there, but only encouraged for toys individuals have brought with them. An owner may reclaim his property when he likes, but generosity is suggested with the not-always-true inducement of its eventually being reciprocal.

Go Out and Play

DEAR MISS MANNERS:

Do you have any suggestions for amusing children during school vacations, when the mother (me) does not have time off from her household chores?

GENTLE READER:

Small children may be persuaded that being allowed to help with household chores is a tremendous treat. Those too old to fall for that are old enough to be asked, "Do you want to find something to do, or do you want me to find you something?"

Split-Level Entertainment

DEAR MISS MANNERS:

We often have social events which children attend, and I desperately need to know how to handle (manage) my child, as well as others, when we are either guests or I am the hostess. For example, when we were at a friend's house, the hostess's child was crawling all over my child and myself. The hostess sat and enjoyed the conversation while I felt like a baby-sitter. To make it worse, her child had a horrible cold at the time. I'm afraid I might say or do something that might offend a guest or a hostess.

GENTLE READER:

You are speaking of two-tiered entertainment, a convenient form for people with small children, but one that requires planning. It would be nice if the children would play quietly on the rug, like kittens with a ball of yarn, but it is unlikely.

As a hostess, you must plan entertainment for all of your guests, and the conversation that engrosses the grown-up ones is not sufficient for the children. Designate a play area, close enough to the adults if the children need constant supervision, but far enough away to keep their activities separate. If a child comes to an adult with a problem, then, it is clearly seen as an interruption with a definite ending, and not part of the normal activity of the occasion. A calm "If everything is all right now, dear, why don't you go back and play with the other children?" is not out of order.

As a guest, this is more difficult to arrange if the hostess has neglected to do so. Some gentle prompting might be in order, such as bringing toys that can be shared, or saying, "Would Dora show Katy her swings? We can see them from here, can't we?" Naturally, any explanation involves the plea that you don't want your child interrupting all the interesting things your hostess is saying.

The cold is a different matter. Etiquette never requires a parent to expose her child to illness. "Oh, dear, poor Dora. I'm afraid we'd better go home and let her get some rest so she'll be well enough to play with you very soon" is a sample exit line.

Interrupted Overnight

DEAR MISS MANNERS:

My daughter keeps begging me to let her stay overnight with a friend, but she is so young that I know she's going to get homesick and we'll have to come and get her in the middle of the night, as we did last year when she stayed over at her cousin's. It's embarrassing to the hosts, who can't help thinking that they didn't do enough to make her feel at home. At what age is this kind of visiting appropriate, and how do we prepare her for it?

GENTLE READER:

It is appropriate at the age at which the child who has begged to be allowed to go is no longer panicky about spending the night away from home. You find out what age that is for an individual child just as you are doing—by experimenting every once in a while, and being prepared to make midnight trips. When you do this, apologize to the hosts, but don't waste any embarrassment on the incident. Everyone sympathizes with the effort of a small child to be more daring and independent than she really feels, and derives kindly amusement from the surrender. Such a child should know that her parents, although inconvenienced, are always ready to supply reassurance and rescue.

Preparation for such an event includes explaining the guest's obligations, as well as telling her what to expect and how to call you exactly at the time you have managed to get to sleep. The chief duty is to remember that one has two generations of hosts, and to greet, fall in with the plans of, and thank the parents of the house and to leave it as one found it, bed made, furniture intact, and towels folded. This includes remembering to take home one's hairbrush, fuzzy animal, and sleeping bag and other luggage. Leaving at midnight is forgivable, but returning two hours later for one's blankie is not. (For more advanced houseguest techniques, please see pp. 179–180, and *Houseguests*, Chapter 7.)

Premature Romance

DEAR MISS MANNERS:

Our six-year-old daughter hugs and kisses her "boyfriend" with great frequency and gusto. As I recall, I did the same thing when I was six years old, and my mother told me I shouldn't do it. I feel I should tell my daughter the same thing, but I cannot decide what the appropriate "reason" is. Any suggestions?

GENTLE READER:

Aren't you fortunate that Miss Manners is not a psychoanalyst, and has not the slightest interest in discussing your daughter's psychosexual development—or yours either, for that matter.

We do not hug and kiss others, with great frequency and gusto, in social circumstances, because it is not done. Isn't that enough of a reason? If you want something stronger, how about "because it isn't quite nice"? You will get into great trouble with your child if you lead her to believe that logic is a requirement for all manners (what is the logic of saying "Good morning" on a rainy day?), but just between you and Miss Manners, people get very annoyed after a while at being hugged and kissed publicly, no matter how much enthusiasm they may show at the beginning. Even an adult male in love will rebel if, for example, his wife goes after him in such a fashion in public indefinitely, and a presumably six-year-old boy is going to be less judicious about how he signifies his wish that she stop.

If Miss Manners were in the therapy business, she would wonder why you call this boy your daughter's "boyfriend," thus superimposing adult expectations on what probably started as an innocent attachment. As she is not in such a trade, she will simply tell you to cut it out.

A Time and a Place

DEAR MISS MANNERS:
Why do children always ask embarrassingly specific questions about sex when they are in public places (on the bus, etc.)? And how do I cope with this?
GENTLE READER:
Why? Now that is an example of a childish question that need not be answered at all.

However, such questions as "What do 'soft core' and 'hard core' mean and what's the difference?" asked in a clear young voice by an alert child reading the signs while riding through the business district on a packed bus, do need to be answered. They are properly answered in two parts, only the second of which actually addresses the question. The first part consists of "I'll tell you later," and is designed to disappoint a suddenly silent and attentive busload of passengers.

The Entrance: greetings rather than grabbings

Planned and supervised entertainment ... or

natural, spontaneous, creative activity

Two Styles of Children's Birthday Parties: *Bearable and Unbearable*

Birthday Parties

Why should people who don't drink, flirt, or make conversation wish to give parties? Nevertheless, most children Miss Manners knows give parties at least once a year.

Presumably, they do it to get presents. But if that were the only reason, Miss Manners would propose a solution suggested for a similar problem by a charitable institution courting weary philanthropists. "Have an evening on us," the invitation said, promising that in exchange for a contribution, the organization would refrain from giving a ball, but would allow the contributor to refuse all other invitations for the evening with the excuse that he was devoting the evening to the charity.

Even aside from greed, however, children need to give and attend birthday parties because these horrible events teach them civilized social behavior, although not always so's you'd recognize it. The principle of community fun through the performance of individual duty and the restraint of unacceptable urges is a difficult one to grasp, and a great many people go through life without getting very good at it.

The obligations start with the guest list. The old rule of thumb—invite as many guests as your child is years old—is as reliable a guarantor of sanity as ever. "But it's my birthday and my party!" shrieks the host in a refrain that will be repeated throughout the event. "Why can't I ask only the people I like?" The parent must

137

then explain why the child must also invite people whose feelings would be hurt, whose parties he attended, whose parents are intimate friends of the host's parents, and so on. Just why is that? A lecture on social duty follows, which if boring enough will convince the child to drop the question and the protest.

The next lesson is at the expense of the host, who must be given the moral forcibly enough to remember it when he is a guest. That is the consequence, in emotional wear and tear on the host, of guests' neglecting to reply to invitations immediately. A child who suspects that no one may attend, or that the people he especially wants will not, is a very forlorn child, indeed.

Then comes the necessity of learning to disguise greed. An astute child may understand why it is necessary to perform the courtesy of saying "Hello" to someone who has not yet handed over his offering, but the need for social niceties once the present has changed hands may not be so clear. Many rehearsals are necessary to perfect the unnatural technique of seeming surprised and pleased at each and every present, no matter how paltry, redundant, and unappealing. A list of stock remarks—such as "That doesn't matter—I wanted another one" and "Wow!"— is handy, along with instruction in the appropriate facial expressions.

"Seeing to it that everybody has a good time" is another despised activity that the host must perform. His natural instinct is to go after the lions and shun the wallflowers, like everyone else, if not to ignore everyone in pursuit of his own pleasure. Looking after the needs and wishes of others is a high price for being host, even counting all the loot. If not for the convention that the birthday child gets the first piece of cake, and that it can be the part with his name or the sugar roses on it, Miss Manners fears that a great many people would be lost to social intercourse at this point.

The toughest test of all is the concept that the birthday child should probably not win the games, but certainly must not, even if he does win, go off with the prizes. Some people cannot bring themselves to impose this standard, running the risk that their children will grow up to take home Caribbean vacation tickets and new cars from the charity balls of which they are the chairmen.

Compared to that, the job of seeing guests to the door ought to be child's play. But it isn't, because the children are playing then, and don't want to be interrupted. The departure of guests only means that there are fewer in the game, even if the game is now that of racing around under tables until the first lamp is broken. Nevertheless, the host must be available at the door to receive the second-hand thanks ("Say thank you to Abel for the lovely time, dear," followed by a growled "Thanks") of his guests.

One might point out to him that this is a good way of keeping track of who left his favors and prizes behind, so that these may be sent on the next day to their proper owners. One might try. But by that time, one might also, having shut the door on the last guest, consider that the host has learned enough for one day, and that it is time for the host's parents to have a good Scotch.

Where are these people when their children are invited to the parties of others? The only proper answer to that is: standing over the child after marching him from the mailbox to his desk, and not budging until they have made him produce a reply to the invitation.

Extra Guests

DEAR MISS MANNERS:

Last year, I sent invitations to my daughter's second birthday party, in care of the children's parents, of course. I did expect that, given the tender ages involved, some mothers would stay to help oversee their offspring. To my complete astonishment and dismay, not only did mothers stay, but fathers did, and, in some cases, siblings of as much as ten years the guests' senior and infant siblings.

What this amounts to is a party on three or four fronts—an early-afternoon cocktail party for the adults, attempts to entertain older, more easily bored children, and refereeing and entertaining a roomful of toddlers.

This year, I very much want it understood that it is just my daughter's friends who are invited, and I would like to ask several of my mother-friends to stay and help. I thought when the invitation had only the child's name that etiquette would dictate that the parent ask if other children or fathers could attend. But apparently I am alone in this assumption.

GENTLE READER:

Miss Manners is trying hard to equate this with the etiquette violations of adults who bring uninvited dates to other people's parties, but she can't. Those extra guests are not there because they thought it would be fun to crash a two-year-old's birthday party. They are there because they believe they are needed to keep the guest they brought behaving in a presentable fashion.

The families of toddlers can usually stand being separated from them for two hours on a weekend afternoon—but only if they are secure that no disasters, social or otherwise, will occur in their absence. You may ask them, on the invitation, to drop off Arabella at four and pick her up at six, or tell them at the door, "Don't worry about Arabella; she'll be fine. You can pick her up at six."

By that time, Miss Manners promises, you will be very happy to see these people. (For birthday parties for older children, please see *Parties*, Chapter 4.)

Written Thanks

DEAR MISS MANNERS:

I would like to know if it's necessary to write a thank-you note for presents my son receives at his birthday party. He will be four. It seems ridiculous to me, but some of my friends do this.

GENTLE READER:

Miss Manners presumes you have taught this child to thank each guest with enthusiasm as the present is given. If so, you must be exhausted, and you may skip your written thanks and save any strength left for teaching the child to write thank-you letters when he becomes literate.

Consolation Prizes

DEAR MISS MANNERS:

My neighbors held a birthday party for the gentleman's six-year-old daughter at a local ice cream parlor. All the children met at the child's grandmother's house, and were ferried to the party and then returned to the grandmother's house for cake before being picked up by their parents. One boy, whose parent seems to have misunderstood the time, arrived at the end of the party, so the grandmother gave him the birthday girl's party hat as a consolation prize. The adults were quite incensed by this, and the birthday girl was not so keen on the situation, herself. The general feeling was that it was the young boy's tough luck. But if the grandmother's handling was not appropriate, how should one handle such a situation?

GENTLE READER:

"Tough luck" is really a charming attitude to take toward a small child guest who was disappointed through no fault of his own. Miss Manners congratulates the adults on their sense of justice (as opposed to mercy) and the effective way they were able to reinforce such feelings on the part of the six-year-old hostess.

Many parents do use birthday parties as opportunities to teach their children greed, selfishness, and other of the qualities they wish to pass on, and they are remarkably successful. Miss Manners prefers to think of them as occasions for teaching that one's very happiness creates the obligation to look out for others. More specifically, it means explaining to the birthday child that being her own guest of honor does not excuse her from the sacred duty of a host to look after her guests, even at immediate personal sacrifice.

Attention Needs a Center

DEAR MISS MANNERS:

Few people seem to consider the feelings of children who are left out when attention and presents are given to their brothers and sisters. For instance, when I visit a newborn baby, bringing a present which it, of course, cannot appreciate, I always bring something for the older children in the family, too. I am undecided, however, about whether I should have my daughter bring a present for a birthday child's sibling when she attends a party. Others don't do this, and it might make them feel bad. What would you think of this as a custom?

GENTLE READER:

That it would be a very expensive one, emotionally as well as financially. Miss Manners is entirely in favor of remembering to give some attention to the brothers and sisters of a newborn or a birthday celebrant—indeed, it is basic good manners not to neglect anyone in a household one is visiting. But the full fuss and the presents are for the celebrant. Anyone who grows up expecting to be the bride at every wedding and the corpse at every funeral is going to have a difficult life.

The Fundamental Duty

Christmas and birthdays are the days we write our thank-you letters. We are all primed for the job, because we have just been graciously thanking everyone in sight for the lovely presents, haven't we?

Why Miss Manners is addressing this to children, and in the first person plural, too, she doesn't know. The fruit punch must have gotten to her. Or perhaps the habit of referring to herself in the third person has finally taken its toll. In any case, it is the parents who do the real work when children write thank-you notes, and Miss Manners always feels the impulse to congratulate the mother of the bride when she receives a well-written letter from the mere bride herself.

Getting children to say "Please" and "Thank you," directly and in writing, is one of the chief tasks of child-rearing. It is a simple matter, requiring about ten years of constant vigilance, but those who give up on it might as well—and generally do—concede failure on the entire enterprise of civilizing their young. The task should begin at birth, and the basic technique varies only slightly through the years. (Miss Manners does not really expect the infant to thank the obstetrician for his efforts, although that would be nice; it is the parent who must be sure to associate the habit with parenthood from the very beginning.)

Babies, when they express desire for something, should be routinely told, "Say 'Please,'" and, when they get something, "Say 'Thank you.'" This should be done cheerfully and entirely without rancor, to establish the idea that the words are there to add to the pleasantness of life. To emphasize the point, the parent holds on to the cookie or toy or his own keys just a fraction of a moment longer than the child expects, so that the formula is heard just before the desire is gratified.

The first variation on this occurs when the child is old enough to feel the first stirrings of social consciousness, which always turn out to be connected with the desire not to be taken for someone his own age. In deference to these feelings, the parent may switch from "Say 'Thank you'" to "What do you say?" This indicates that the child has progressed from the stage of rote learning to being able to produce the answer after some research into his store of accumulated knowledge. The next step is for the parent to say nothing at all, but give the child a look that says, "Do you want to do it voluntarily, or shall we give them a little demonstration here of bringing you up?"

The written letter to an unseen benefactor is a more abstract concept, but it, too, begins early. Christmas afternoon and the lull after the birthday-party guests go home are the proper times. This not only teaches nonprocrastination, but produces relative quiet in the house just when the grown-ups' temples are pounding unbearably. An illiterate toddler is made to sit down, while its parent takes up the pen. "What shall we tell Aunt Mindy about the snowsuit?" is the opener designed to instill the unnatural habit of thinking of the merits of a present in terms that can safely be transmitted to its giver. The correct form is "Natalie has asked me to write you," followed by the dictation, preserving the child's (parentally approved) language. Miss Manners doesn't approve of parents' pretending to be

Dear Mrs. Perfect,

What a super idea the bird-watching glasses are! I just love them. We don't have many birds here at Christmastime, but I will use them lots in the spring, and in the meantime, I have been practicing focusing them and have seen lots of interesting things around the neighborhood.

Love,
Lauren

A CHILD'S LETTER OF THANKS *must abide by certain rules: It must be written the day the present is received or, if that is before the birthday or Christmas, the holiday on which it is opened. It must not start with "Thank you for the...." It must include some favorable mention of the item, and must avoid mentioning that the child already has one.*

their children, but no one will ever believe that the child participated in a truly adult letter. Older children must write their own letters, although the parent is responsible for making literary suggestions and imposing severe deadlines on the job until the child no longer lives at home.

At that point, the psychological struggle reverses itself, and it is the parent whose social delicacies are foremost, rather than the child's. ''I don't care how busy you are—how do you expect me to face my friends when they ask if you ever received their wedding presents because they 'just want to know if they got lost in the mail'?'' is the formula then.

Children's Paper

DEAR MISS MANNERS:

All right, all right, I hear you about the thank-you letters. Now tell me what is the proper stationery for children. Do I let them use my good paper with our address on it? It's expensive, and they always mess up the first time. If I have to buy them their own paper, what is right for children? Personally, I hate the bright-colored papers and cute things with funny pictures that people are always giving me, but don't know if it is worth it to have their names put on paper that isn't going to be cheap, either.

GENTLE READER:

Paper with a child's name or initial on it is a charming idea, but only after they have used up all the childish paper not suitable for adults that their parents have in their desks. The good house paper of the family is used for the official correspondence of children if and when they have any—applications for jobs or schools. It may also interest you to know that all children are required to do rough drafts of parent-supervised letters, such as thank-yous and answers to invitations. In their private correspondence, to pen pals, relatives to whom they can complain about their parents, and notes to be confiscated during school, they are allowed to spell at their own risk.

Calling Cards

DEAR MISS MANNERS:

I am wondering what is the proper use of hand-lettered-style calling cards for little girls and boys. I would love to order some for my daughter, but how are they properly used? My husband says that if I don't know how to use them then I shouldn't order them. (Men!) Are they used only as thank-you cards?

GENTLE READER:

Little boys and girls do not properly have calling cards, not even if they are in the habit of paying formal morning calls or sending flowers to their hostesses, the chief uses of such cards. What you may order for your daughter is letter paper with her name on it, to be used for letters, which is the proper form, anyway, for thanking people. Miss Manners did not mean to sound so snippy. Actually, she is delighted that you are teaching your daughter to write letters, and hopes that pretty paper will encourage her to do so.

Elementary

School

Educating the System

Our educational system has gotten so thoroughly into enrichment and emotional development that conscientious parents may get a little tired of hearing what a wonderful school day their children have had seeing movies or discussing their feelings.

The crisis usually comes when a parent discovers that these same children are totally innocent of such things as multiplication tables, how the United States government works, and English grammar. Personally, Miss Manners thinks that the parents of America should offer the school systems a bargain: You teach them English, history, mathematics, and science, and we will take them to the movies and museums and to sample foreign food, and will look after their souls.

Schools first started doing parental tasks because they thought parents were neglecting them; and now there are parents desperately trying to make up for the neglect of academic subjects on the part of teachers. The neglect, on both parts, is rarely mere callousness. On the contrary, it is often connected with the idealistic belief that the object of anyone entrusted with a child is to make that child happy, and that the happiest child is one free of constraint. Miss Manners loathes that theory, and doesn't notice that it has much of a record of success. It is her belief that happiness is a by-product, and that the happy child is one who has been carefully trained to use his abilities to take on challenges and overcome them.

The happiness theory is full of self-defeating characteristics. It directs the child's attention back into himself, instead of taking the natural self-absorption with which we were all born, and which we are in no danger of losing, and turning it outward, so that the ability to take delight in a varied and curious world may be developed. It also coddles our natural laziness, so that energies that could be put into growth are put into finding excuses and examining reasons for the lack of it.

The parent who is doing remedial academic work, like the teacher doing parental work, is at a disadvantage. Home time, when duties and homework are done, is supposed to be leisure time. The trick, then, is to demonstrate to the child that learning is one of the great joys of life. As an educator of Miss Manners' acquaintance puts it, "Life is full of wonderful passions that come and go over the years, but the only one that will never let you down is reading."

That is not to say that the parent should adopt the school's misplaced emphasis on field trips and dramatizations, and away from what are inevitably now called "dull, dry facts." As a matter of fact, children adore dry facts, and if you don't make them learn historical dates, they will memorize timetables or batting averages. It is adults, whose memories are going, who are rightly afraid of being tripped up by smarty little kids if they admit that facts are a necessary framework for supporting thought.

The excursions are all very well, but they are more often in real danger of being dull and dry. A child who is taken through a museum without preparation will show enthusiasm for only the cafeteria and souvenir shop, and one who is fed history through unexplained movies will retain only the irrelevancies. An interesting briefing beforehand, an idea of what to look for, and a debriefing, in which the child can shine by showing what he has learned (it is particular fun, as we all know, to catch filmmakers in historical error), are what make excursions fun.

While children soak up facts easily, they should not be asked to take in opinions without a struggle. Family discussions in which the facts are discussed so that the conclusion is open for argument are tremendously entertaining. You do not, for example, deliver a lecture on the benefits of democracy. You let the child argue them, or argue against them, in the role of the framers of the Constitution, or in that of, say, George III. Part of the pleasure is in making people think within the terms of the discipline—no anachronistic thinking allowed in historical discussions, for example.

After all, not only is the active use of the mind one of life's greatest forms of recreation, but testing one's parents, and occasionally outarguing them with a case so solid that they must yield, is surely one of the greatest pleasures of family life.

Educating Parents

Many parents who have a tough time getting through school would find that if they could only master Basic Deportment, the rest would be a breeze. Disapproving teachers, the nightly burden of homework, shame over less-than-perfect grades, the embarrassment of reciting poorly in front of others—all these problems can be lessened, if not erased, if only parents could learn to behave like little grown-ups.

The children, of course, would still have all these difficulties. That is the nature of things, and the memory of difficult school years gives a person a rich feeling of satisfaction all through life at having grown beyond their reach. But parents can escape them and benefit their children at the same time.

Take the matter of reciting, which is the name given to discussing new subject matter until one's ignorance is apparent to all. Most parents, when their children report having learned something at school, feel as if they have been called upon in class. Instead of listening to the children's newly acquired knowledge, as politeness demands, they take the mention of the topic as a direction to tell everything they know about the subject, thus not only squelching the child's pride, but eventually often getting themselves into that awful situation when the child reports that the teacher's version differs convincingly from theirs.

If a wife comes home from work and tells the family at dinner what happened that day, is she immediately cut off by everyone else present with lectures based on everyone else's knowledge, however vague, of her field? Yet a child who meekly volunteers something like ''We studied the Declaration of Independence today'' will find he has irrevocably surrendered the floor to grown-ups who consider this an opening to tell everything they know, and a great deal that they have forgotten, on this subject or anything remotely related to it. The simple courtesy of replying, ''Oh, really? What did you discuss?'' and then listening, with an occasional question or comment indicating that the material is important and that the child may have acquired something interesting to say on it, is almost unheard-of.

Then there is the homework. If the parent takes over responsibility for homework's being done, which is not the same thing as supplying modest help on request, the parent has relieved the child of a difficult burden and taken it upon himself. Husbands and wives do not generally write each other's professional reports. However much they may advise and contribute, they usually assume that the person with the responsibility also has the competence. This may not always be true in the case of a child, but proof that a thirty-five-year-old can turn in a better paper than an eight-year-old does not do much to advance the purpose of education. The motive, of course, is to help the child capture the greatest rewards of his situation. A parent who is willing to do homework is therefore under an obligation to keep it up through graduate school.

It is another common rudeness for parents to criticize grades automatically, even if they are good ones. A child who brings home a 96 is rarely congratulated; he or she is told, ''Next time, see if you can make it 100.''

Showing interest in, respect for, and attention to the occupations of loved ones, from their triumphs to their personal problems, is one of the constant duties family members owe to one another, and the child's career of schooling should be considered to be of top-ranking importance in this respect. But something happens to people who take a decent interest in the gainful employment of adult relatives—sympathizing with ups and downs, supplying confidence when the going is rough and recognition when it has not been sufficiently bestowed officially—when it comes to their children. It is made clear that those children must achieve the academic excellence that their parents surely achieved themselves.

It gives children a lot to live up to, of course, when they find that their parents already know everything they can learn, can perform better at their tasks, and would never settle for anything short of perfection. It also gives them the idea that, given the statistical possibilities, it is hardly worth their while to try.

Talking with Teachers

Parent-teacher conferences are enormously educational, teachers of Miss Manners' acquaintance have confided to her. What the children haven't already volunteered about the parents' shortcomings, the parents will usually demonstrate themselves.

There are the ones that use the conference as an opportunity to quarrel with each other, and the ones who, long divorced and reunited only on these occasions, use it to flirt with each other. Some parents turn childish and tongue-tied, and others childish and imperious. What the parents expect to have done for them is usually spelled out—the teachers should perform the parental functions of instilling honesty, discipline, and kindness; while the children should take over the parents' unfulfilled ambitions.

Miss Manners is against this sort of exercise, at least on the child's time. Why submit yourself to be graded when you don't have to? All the parent need do is accept the traditional parent-teacher bargain of ''You don't believe everything the child tells you about me, and I won't believe everything the child tells me about you,'' and spend the time exchanging useful observations about the child.

These include interests, work habits, pressures, problems, and practical suggestions on both sides as to how these may be put into the service of educating the child. They do not include general philosophical or psychological analyses by either parent or teacher. Nor is it their business to analyze each other. There is altogether too much of that kind of thing going around, and a little straight reporting on both sides—''She doesn't understand the homework,'' ''He can't keep still in class''—is more helpful than all the vague talk about complexes and inadequacies.

All parents know that the reason educators are paid so little, in spite of our all believing that the job of educating the young is the most important task of society, is that teachers are rewarded enough by being allowed to spend their workdays with cute children and their nights and weekends reading their adorable papers. Nevertheless, she thinks it a matter of elementary manners to treat a teacher with some respect for the profession, which involves not circumventing, or helping the child to circumvent, the rules and requirements of the classroom. Teaching is cursed with being one of the jobs, like moviemaking or being president, that every layman is certain he could do better than the professionals.

Acting on the unchecked reports of usually unreliable sources, i.e., small children, is a mistake. The most honorable children have a lively sense of the arbitrary in human events, which does not correspond to the adult concept of cause and effect. The statement "He started it" may be correct as far as it goes, but it presupposes a void before that action. And every child firmly believes that teachers have unshakable personal likes and dislikes among their pupils, of completely undiscernible origins. Try telling a child who says the teacher hates him, or loves someone else, that a teacher's heart is there for the taking by any child who shows interest and industry. An "unfair" teacher, in Miss Manners' observation, is generally one who refuses to waive standards on the appeal of a child who counts on having winning ways.

As much as Miss Manners admires family loyalty, she thinks it in the best interest of children for their parents to be frank about them in private conferences. Unless the parent has been doing the homework and writing the papers and therefore is really attending the conference in the hope of persuading the teacher that his work deserves better marks—don't think it doesn't happen—there is not much point in defending the child from a teacher's criticisms. The other side of this is that there is not any use in a teacher's offering a criticism without some hope for its being corrected.

"I have to keep reminding myself," said a teacher of Miss Manners' acquaintance, "that the parents are probably not going to trade the child in for another one, so there's no use in pointing out that he is impossible."

Perhaps if parents promise to behave themselves, the teachers will let them off easily, and not send home notes requiring them to produce bunny costumes, five dollars, three empty milk containers, or themselves by ten forty-five tomorrow morning.

Classroom Rules

DEAR MISS MANNERS:

I am just starting out on a teaching career, somewhat intimidated by what experienced teachers tell me of today's discipline problems, and the lack of cooperation from parents, either in training kids or in punishing them when misbehavior is reported. My first class will be second-graders in an urban public school. My hope is that if I get them young enough, and show enough authority (keeping my qualms to myself), I will set the proper tone and they will pick it up. Can you suggest some rules for classroom decorum? I want to be fair. But if there is trouble, how do I find out who is really responsible, without turning the children into tattletales, and getting them into deeper trouble with their peers?

GENTLE READER:

According to a wise school director of Miss Manners' acquaintance, a teacher rules through force of personality. Here are some of her suggestions for law enforcement:

· All feet belong on the floor at all times.
· Personal remarks are never allowed, not even compliments. If you can tell

the teacher she is pretty, you could presume it all right to mention that a class-mate is ugly. If it is acceptable to point out that a child has nice new shoes, it would seem reasonable to point out that he also has crossed eyes.
· Do not debate family values, as in "My mother says you should hit back." School rules prevail.
· You are not allowed to say everything you think; the idea is to learn to think things through first, to sift out what is offensive, irrelevant, or otherwise in-appropriate.
· The idea that a free society permits anything should be squelched immediately, and a lesson be given instead in the meaning of law in a democracy.
· When you have permission to leave, leave quietly.

As for crime detection, Miss Manners is told that it is not necessary to use in-formants because children can easily be persuaded to incriminate themselves. The exercise of letting them do so also serves as protection to the tipster.

First, you round up the suspects and give them a general lecture on the necessity for obeying rules, fairness, and so on—slowly and painfully closing in on the par-ticular infraction. You then question small groups, suggesting that you know a great deal more about what happened than you are ready to share. The weakest of the wrongdoer's cohorts—they always have cohorts—will crack, and start to blurt out what happened. Before the others can turn on him, you say, "Isn't that brave of him?"—thus reshaping his reputation from that of a squirt whom it is safe to attack later to something of a leader himself. The actual leader will have been powerless to keep his troops in line, and will be a leader no longer.

Miss Manners hopes this will be of use to you as a teacher. If not, she can think of several other lines of work in which you might try it out.

The Treatment

DEAR MISS MANNERS:
How can you tell when a child is really sick, if there's nothing obviously wrong, or when he just doesn't want to go to school?
GENTLE READER:
Miss Manners is not in the medical business, so you will have to allow her to deal only with the etiquette aspects of the situation, and turn the rest over to a doctor.

It is well known that hurt tummies are epidemic on weekdays. It is rude to question the veracity of a child, and risky because if he really does turn out to be ill, you will feel pretty terrible yourself for having done so. The procedure, then, is to treat him with such care that only a person who isn't up to snuff can bear it. Serve only safe and uninteresting meals, propose appropriate trips to the doctor, speak of medicines and unspeakable remedies, and prescribe rest for the mind as well as for the body, including canceling the closest desirable engagement.

This generally discourages the malingerers. However, if the child really turns out to be sick, the procedure must be reversed, and attempts made to tempt him with interesting food, amuse him, make the remedies palatable, and speak happily of what fun we will have as soon as he feels better.

If you find this contradictory, allow Miss Manners to remind you that medicine is an art, not a science, and the true test for any cure is whether it works.

Notes from Home

DEAR MISS MANNERS:

Is there a correct form for writing notes to your child's school—explaining absences, giving permission to participate in special events, and so on? I've been dashing these off on bits of scratch paper from the kitchen, as my son generally forgets to mention that he needs a note until he's halfway out the door, but his homework this week has to do with writing business letters, and I'm suddenly embarrassed to think that the teacher knows he comes from a household that doesn't know how to do that.

GENTLE READER:

The key thing about a parent's note is that it look as if it could not possibly have been written by a child. Miss Manners trusts she does not have to go into the reason for that.

It needn't be a full-fledged letter on letterhead paper, but it should be written on something—a blank note card, for instance—that looks as if an adult bought it for that purpose. That does not include the backs of shopping lists and the margins of newspaper pages. It is a good idea to be able to spell the teacher's name, but it is possible to leave off a salutation, as if you were assuming that the letter needed to be read by more than one authority. But the letter must be properly signed, with the parent's full name. This is an added protection, as few children believe that their parents do not sign themselves Mommy or Melanie's Mother. And it is just as well, no matter how upright you have trained your children to be, to put the full date on the note.

Names on Notes

DEAR MISS MANNERS:

My oldest son requires notes from school if he's late, sick, or goes home with a friend in the afternoon, and for numerous other activities. He and I have different last names, as his father and I are divorced and I married again. My other children have the same last name as I do, so when they go to the school there will be no problem about how I sign the notes to the teacher—it will be obvious that I am their mother. But how do I sign the notes to my oldest's teacher so she knows I'm his mother? With my previous married name? With both my first and second husbands' names?

GENTLE READER:

Sign whatever you wish. A grown woman who is interested in the whereabouts and illnesses of a child is assumed to be his mother unless proven otherwise.

MRS. THEODORE BISHOP RIGHT
421 FAR HORIZON LANE
SEAPORT, CONNECTICUT

Dear Mrs. Books,

Orville complained so severely of a stomach ache yesterday that I had to keep him out of school to take him to the doctor. Fortunately nothing seems to be wrong.

He tells me that he missed tests in Participatory Democracy, Exploring Our World, and English Grammaronomics. I would appreciate it if you would let me know directly how he can make these up.

Yours truly,

Daffodil Right

A PARENT'S LETTER *explaining a child's absence from school may be written on any plain paper, as long as it is clean. Daffodil Right is only using this paper (proper to a married woman's household business), because she found it in the attic, untouched from the first Mrs. Right's trousseau. The address is outdated, but Daffodil Right figures that the teacher is lucky to get at least one note that isn't written on the back of an old shopping list.*

Presents for Teachers

DEAR MISS MANNERS:

What is a suitable present for a fourth-grader to give to his teacher at Christmas? We don't have much money, and can't compete with the expensive items other parents send, but don't want to place our son at a disadvantage.

GENTLE READER:

The most suitable of all would be to work with the administration to effect a rule prohibiting material expressions of affection. The bottles of awful perfume and odd handkerchiefs that are the usual tokens of such occasions do not do much for the admittedly deplorable standard of living most teachers are forced to endure, and are a pointless burden on parents. The way for a child to show his gratitude for what his teacher has done for him is to express it, in person or, better, in a letter that demonstrates that she or he has taught him how to write well. The way for a parent to express gratitude is to tell both the teacher and her supervisor what a marvelous job she is doing, and to support raises for teachers at every opportunity.

Valentine Massacres

The classic Valentine's Day procedure has passed from use in many schools merely for the flimsy reason that it was unbearably cruel, wreaking havoc with the emotions by destroying most children while falsely aggrandizing a few.

For those who remember it with fond nostalgia, for any schools that retain it, and in the hopes of retaining some of its advantages, if any, Miss Manners will review the form.

A large cardboard carton, covered with silver foil and construction-paper red hearts, the latter with creases bisecting them vertically because folding was the only way to prevent lopsidedness, was placed conspicuously in the schoolroom. Through a roughly carved slot on the top, children pushed Valentines they had addressed to their classmates. At the appropriate time, a ceremony was held, in which the teacher or a favored classmate with a smug expression at being thus elevated beyond the reach of the judgment of the masses presided, opening the box, and calling out the names of the recipients. It thus became public who had received how many, and who got none at all, but as a double check, the protocol called for a social period afterward, in which those who had many Valentines could go around the room asking those with none how many they had received.

Miss Manners needn't spell out the social effect of all this on the various little psyches, but perhaps she should explain why anyone, outside of the disgustingly popular children who we all trust shortly went on to bad ends, remembers it fondly. It is partly that pleasure is enhanced by contrast, and although Miss Manners cannot approve of people who derive that contrast from the misery of others— which is, of course, what those Valentine-laden children were doing—she finds the contrast one makes between one's present life and one's own past perfectly adapted to this use. To have achieved such thorough and hopeless confirmation of one's social doom at an early age is helpful, because nothing in adult life can ever be that bad. Another reason is that many of the Valentine victims looked elsewhere for consolation, and can trace the beginning of a lifetime's love affair with books or the birth of the creative imagination to the search for consolation when the first-choice elementary-school goal, that of being popular, was confirmed as hopeless.

It was a rough tactic nevertheless, and sensitive adults, i.e., those who had Valentineless children, worked to change the tradition. In some schools, rules were added to make it mandatory for each child to address at least one Valentine to every child in the class, and in others, the custom was eliminated altogether, in favor of having children make Valentines for their parents in arts and crafts period.

Now, Valentine's Day happens to be Miss Manners' favorite holiday. She can get stirred up for the Fourth of July if the picnic is properly packed, and she has even mastered the art of coloring eggs and turning the insides of jack-o'-lanterns into breads and pies. Valentine's Day has the most opportunities for charming little courtesies, however, and yet—or because of that—is now the most neglected of the holidays. What can we do to revive it?

Let us encourage the proper written expression of affection, in all its forms. The improper ones are the nasty or obscene Valentines that Miss Manners refuses even to discuss, and the imprudent Valentines in which unrequited crushes are exposed to those who have no scruples about crushing them. The Valentine is the only form of mail that may properly be sent anonymously. We do not even read anonymous letters in daily life (do we?), and we certainly don't believe what we have read in them or allow it to annoy us. But the anonymous Valentine either contains obvious cues, which gives it an added playfulness, or it remains mysterious, in which case it gives one the pleasant feeling of being more widely adored than one had imagined.

Parents who write little love notes or cards to their children, and who provide the encouragement and scissors-and-paper-lace to receive them in return, will soon understand Miss Manners' affection for the holiday. The traditional present from a grown gentleman to a grown lady was a pair of gloves or, in more recent times, a heart-shaped puffy satin box full of chocolates, and Miss Manners would consider it a mere extension of the custom if this traffic flowed in both directions. In any case, it is a rare thing now for children to be discreet witnesses to their parents' romantic attachment for each other, and all the more important in that circumstances have made such a situation all too rare. We live in a time when even the offspring of obviously happy couples are worried, and when the most ordinary and polite parental disagreement produces the dread in a child that he is going to hear the announcement of which so many friends have told him.

Could we not also have, in some less harsh way than before, an exchange of Valentines among children? If the publicity of the traditional method was too damaging, and mandated universality renders it all meaningless, what about allowing a discreet exchange in school, with a small preparatory lecture about keeping them nice and remembering minor friendship as well as the major?

Of course, Miss Manners knows that the minute school is out, the more vulnerable children will be pounced upon and asked the dreaded question. She cherishes the hope that these children will learn to get away quickly, and thus be safely home earlier to begin the compensatory activities that will ensure them future acclaim, which is, after all, only the adult version of popularity.

New in School

DEAR MISS MANNERS:

I have to go to a new school, right in the middle of the semester, because my father's office moved away, and I won't know anybody. What do I do if nobody talks to me?

GENTLE READER:

The automatic adult answer would be ''Talk to them,'' but Miss Manners has an easier way. Look calm, happy, and curious about your surroundings, but say nothing. If you look anxious, this won't work, so practice in front of a mirror by relaxing your face, and smiling slightly (nothing goofy or maniacal) as if you were enjoying everything, but were too busy thinking about it all to bother commenting. Everybody always wants to be friends with people who already look contented; those who look badly in need of a friend do not attract them. Miss Manners is sorry, but that is the way it is.

A note of caution: If the first people who speak to you try to get you to be mean to others—don't. Wait until you make your own decisions about people before you even think about picking sides.

Impolite Lice

DEAR MISS MANNERS:

My daughter, who goes to a very exclusive private school, brought home a note that there are lice in the school; that is, several of the children were found to have lice in their hair. I find this outrageous, and am even thinking of taking her out of the school. It is hardly what I would expect for a school with a fine reputation. The immediate problem is that I have told her to keep her head and her things—comb, scarves, and such—away from all the other children, but she says she can't tell them they can't borrow her comb because they have lice. I understand that she doesn't want to insult the other children, but it seems to me the problem is more important. Do you have any suggestions?

GENTLE READER:

Rest assured that lice are found in the very best schools these days. This does not make them fun, because they do the same things in expensive hair that they used to do elsewhere, which is crawl around and lay eggs. The difference is that they are no longer unfashionable, and may be borne openly as are other afflictions of the rich, such as gout. Tell your daughter that she need not say to her friends that she will not lend them her comb because they might give her lice. Tell her to say that she is refusing it because she doesn't want to give them lice. This is not only more polite, but infinitely more effective.

Car Pools

Telephones are busy in the fall, with anxious and cajoling voices setting up their most significant networks of relationships for the season. These are the human ties that will determine how, and sometimes if, they will get through the year. Miss Manners is referring, of course, to the arranging of the car pool.

Specifically, she is referring to the children's car pool to and from school, with side trips to related institutions, such as ballet school, the orthodontist, and the hospital emergency room. Such car pooling is second only to marriage in the un-realistic expectations it inspires and the corresponding bitterness. And it's not second by much. People expect it to work, and make their own plans on their nondriving days, confident that their children will be picked up by others. There are few times that an adult can be so unfeeling about the illness of a child as when that adult realizes that therefore that child's parent is not going to drive.

Sick leave, as well as vacations, business trips, and malfunctioning automo-biles, must therefore be built into the car-pooling contract. There should be a substitute driver always on standby duty. This is, naturally, impossible, since all the participating adults are overbooked by definition of being parents. It helps to draw as many people as possible into the situation—not only both fathers and mothers, but all adults under the roof. Two weeks as the live-in lover to a per-son with school-age children and you are eligible for the draft. While allowances must be made for individuals' schedules (such as the fact that everybody can drive in the morning and nobody in the afternoon), it is no fair fathers' claiming it's all the mothers' problem, and then leaving the mothers-with-jobs and the mothers-without-jobs all to claim that the others are expecting too much of them.

Nothing, as Miss Manners is well aware, will make car-pooling children bearable. But there are a few suggestions to alleviate the torture:

- Each driver may set his or her own rules to accommodate such adult idiosyn-crasies as not being able to stand choruses of "A Hundred Bottles of Beer on the Wall."
- Passengers planning to go home with friends after school must notify the car pool rather than letting it sit there and wait.
- All fights must be verbal.
- Promptness is preferable to presentability. If one must finish putting on one's shoes or chewing one's breakfast in the car to avoid keeping the car pool waiting, so be it.
- Passengers are requested not to exhibit to one another two-day-old lunch items or what they have under their knee bandages.
- Equipment that makes sudden, startling noises, such as band instruments and dolls that say "I WANT ANOTHER DRINK OF WATER!" are banned.
- Choice seats must be rotated.
- Items of which passengers wish to dispose inconspicuously, such as vitamins, bubble gum, or undesirable lunch ingredients, may not be buried in the back seats of cars.

- Distances that will be traveled to pick up forgotten items should be codified. It could be announced, for example, that the car pool will return within one block of the pickup point to retrieve a forgotten lunchbox, two blocks for a costume needed for a play, and three blocks for homework.
- The driver is allowed to relish privately all information about the private lives of the other drivers, as information overheard when these people's children expose the details to the other children—but must regard it as privileged conversation, which may not be repeated (except to the driver's spouse). (For more on the family car, please see pp. 57–59.)

After School

The Lone Homemaker

DEAR MISS MANNERS:

There are hardly any stay-at-home mothers in my neighborhood, and I notice that the women who are most anxious to get out to work every morning are the ones who see me as a kind of all-purpose mother of their own. They think nothing of asking me to make extra trips with their children (I do most of the car-pool driving as it is), having a child over in the afternoon because they're going to be late, letting in the plumber and telling him what's wrong, and receiving their packages, which I then get to deliver at night.

Then there are my children's ideas of my capacity. They have made it known that I am available for baking cookies, making costumes, going on field trips, finding and delivering crates, boxes, and other necessities, and calling other mothers to ask them to do things they all tell me they're too busy to do.

I chose my way of life, and in a way, I'm glad my children know they can always depend on me. But first of all, I can't do everything, and second, I'm tired of everybody's thinking that my contribution is automatic, and not much deserving of praise, because after all, "I'm home," and probably have nothing better to do anyway. How can I take some sort of stand without seeming mean to my own children, and rude to my neighbors?

GENTLE READER:

Miss Manners fails to see how anyone can get through any sort of life without learning how to say a polite no. She understands and applauds your desire to be a good mother and a good neighbor, but goodness never means simply acceding to everyone else's ideas of what you ought to be doing (for them). Adult virtue includes being able to decide what you can do, in terms of the importance you assign a task and the cost to you of performing it.

The way to say no is to say it—with a small apology, but no excuse or explanation. "No, I'm so sorry, I can't take Lauren this afternoon," "I'm sorry, dear, but I can't bake tonight," and "Oh, dear, I'm afraid I won't be able to see your plumber." The answer to "Why not?" is "Because I'm afraid I simply can't." A few of these, and your children will get the idea that they have to check with you before volunteering you; and your neighbors may understand that you have as busy a schedule as anyone's.

Once you stop letting people impose upon you, and stop feeling imposed upon (which may be harder), you may feel differently about these tasks. Wasn't one of the reasons you chose to stay at home so that you could be involved with your children more? Enlisting their help, in baking or sewing for school, is a pleasant way of being together. And as for your neighbors—that, too, could be mutual. Could you ask a neighbor for whom you do at-home favors to pick up some groceries for you on the way home, or do errands near her office, or take the children on a weekend when you and your husband want to go out? Polite people do help those who need it. But they learn to take as graciously as they give.

Privacy

The moral indignation with which children assert their rights to privacy from their parents is awesome. Fortunately, they are rarely troubled at that time with memories of how grateful they once were to have these same intruders peek into the state of their diapers.

Parents do remember, however, and it sometimes hampers them in the granting of increasing rights. Miss Manners is a great believer in privacy within the family— for everyone—but she recognizes that diplomatic genius is sometimes required to deal with conflicting and confusing claims. She has therefore decided to undertake the job.

First, there must be the recognition that everyone old enough to have a secret is entitled to have some place to keep it. There is such a thing as an innocent secret. Those who believe that only the guilty have anything to hide from their relatives deserve to go through life without ever receiving birthday surprises. Miss Manners finds the whole matter of searching for contraband quite distasteful and forbids it among adults, who simply have to collect their evidence against one another without violating the law of privacy that applies to desks, files, drawers locked and unlocked, and purses and wallets.

The conflict arises in regard to children only when it touches on possible crucial matters of health. The Diplomatic Pouch Rule ("We're not allowed to search your pouch, and if we don't find drugs we're in deep trouble—but if we do, too bad'') as applied to children must at least be decently disguised: ''I was only cleaning your room, trying to get into all the corners, and you can only imagine my shock when . . . ''

Even then, one can only produce incriminating objects. A diary is an extension of the writer's mind, as letters are of the sender's; Miss Manners admits of no circumstances under which these may be read by others. For small children only, one may read the envelopes for purposes of remarks such as ''I see you got what looks like a birthday invitation. Don't forget to answer it right away, and let me know when you need to get a present.'' Telephone calls are also scrutiny-free. It is legitimate to say ''Tell whoever it is to call back after dinner'' or ''You'll have to wind up because I need the phone now,'' but not ''What did Sean want?'' or ''Who was that you were giggling with?''

Then there is the trickier matter of privacy on the outside concerning what family members legitimately observe at home. Children are more likely to understand that, as their temptation is as great to regale their friends with funny stories about Mommy and Daddy as ever the parents' is to speak of them. A fair deal would be something like this:

''I will check with you on what cute stories I tell about your little mishaps and sayings, and throw out the ones that most offend you, provided that you clear things with me before reporting them in Show and Tell or to my friends' children.''

Evidence of bad behavior is always a family secret, which even the victims of it are enjoined from reporting for the amusement or sympathy of their friends. Extreme emotions, including falling in love and weeping fits, are property of the person to whom they happen, not news to be disseminated without permission. Questions from outsiders about what other family members think of them should not be answered. Facts pertaining to money, people's whereabouts, and such may be labeled secret by family agreement. Miss Manners does not believe the clever child will have trouble negotiating such privacy. He need only report what he has learned from the examples given by his friends in health and hygiene class.

Allowances

It is not quite nice to notice the fact that people close to you have no money, and use the fact to mess in their lives, order them about, get them to perform menial services for you, and generally make them feel that the financial advantage puts you in charge.

Yet that is what most people do to their children all the time.

Mind you, Miss Manners does not dispute the right of parents to mess in their children's lives, order them about, make them perform menial services, and establish that the parents are thoroughly in charge. She just doesn't like their citing the money advantage to do so.

Children tend to be born penniless, but lacking in the desire to remain so in order to enjoy the simple pleasures of life. It is therefore customary, when they reach the age of indiscretion (financial indiscretion begins with an awareness of money as the basis for trade, and it seldom ends), to give them a pittance, also known as an allowance.

It is customary to make the following speech on the occasion of the first allowance, in the hope of calming the eager squealing of the recipient: "We are not rich people, but as a member of the family, you are entitled to share in the assets we do have, as well as in the responsibilities. This is yours to use as you see fit, with the exception that you may not use it to go against the rules of the house—buying candy for times when you know you're not allowed to have candy, for instance. We will not ask, otherwise, how you have spent this money—it's yours, and you don't have to account for it. On the other hand, don't ask for advances if you've squandered it. This is it, and it's up to you to budget it so that you can buy what you want." (Rich people use the same opening, as nobody feels really rich these days. Super-rich people may open with "We have been more fortunate than most, but that doesn't mean we don't have an awareness of the difficult economics of our time . . .")

You may notice that this is an extremely tiresome speech, full of concepts that six-year-olds with their chubby little hands out cannot possibly understand. That is to get them used to the ideas that (1) solemn, ceremonial occasions are properly marked by pompous speeches, and (2) money is not only fun. They will find this out for themselves by spending everything immediately on things that don't work, pleading in vain for loans, and perhaps, ultimately, facing the dreary prospect of deferring pleasures in order to save up for bigger ones. The size of the allowance should be geared to this—just enough to buy small treats, but not enough for middle-sized ones unless two or three weeks' allowance is saved.

Miss Manners does not believe in paying children for chores in their own households—hence that clever association between assets and responsibilities. In her mind, it is an ugly idea that a child should contribute his part to his own household for wages, while the parents do the greater work for free.

Children who want extra money may be able to do chores or appropriate small jobs for others, but should be required to contribute their efforts at home simply because it is their home, and because they naturally share also in its myriad benefits.

The alert child will therefore make a speech of his or her own, at appropriately spaced intervals, in which he cites not only the rising cost of living, but also his own increasing share in the responsibilities of the concern from which his money comes. That, my dear little ones, is what Mamma and Papa do when they find themselves running short.

Pets

DEAR MISS MANNERS:

We have a spaniel dog that my brother, mother, and I take good care of. We feed him and take him for walks, and let him come with us wherever we go in the house we live in. But the dog becomes "my" dog when it comes to taking him out into the garden at night before I turn in. Out in the cold and dark of night. I refused to do it after several nights. Couldn't we walk him more during the day when it is more agreeable?

GENTLE READER:

Parents sometimes forget how frightening the dark can be to children, and Miss Manners will remind yours, and endorse your request to take an earlier turn with the dog, if you will cooperate on the chief point your parents are trying to make.

That is that the privilege of having a living creature in your care—as your parents have you and your brother, and you have the dog—"is not like having a toy." You are supposed to take care of your toys, Miss Manners hopes, but if you are tired or sick or away from home, you might be allowed to neglect this task.

With a living creature, you are never excused—no, not even with the best excuse in the world—but must either see to its needs yourself or arrange for someone else to do so. That is what your parents are teaching you by saying it is "your" dog. Even if they agree to take the dog out at night, it will be your responsibility to remind them. Even better, you could propose to your brother that you take the dog out together, and, in return, that you take one of his turns at feeding or washing.

Training the Dog

DEAR MISS MANNERS:

My dog never says thank you when I give him his food. Could you tell me how to teach him how to say thank you?

GENTLE READER:

A great educator of Miss Manners' acquaintance used to say "Good morning" to a statue of Artemus Ward every morning, as her route to school took her around a circle named in his honor. The children she had with her were wont to ask why. "Because if I do it often enough, eventually he is going to respond," she replied.

Smile when you give your dog his food, pause, and then say, "You're welcome." This was undoubtedly the way your parents trained you.

Braces

Perhaps because her bite is worse than her admittedly formidable bark, Miss Manners is in sympathy with people who wear braces on their teeth. However, the sympathy ends abruptly the minute they reach into their mouths at the dinner table to extract construction materials. Head braces with dried dribble on them, which look as if they had done years of duty in the mouths of cab horses; tiny round rubber bands, left around in pairs like the tooth marks of vampires; retainers cunningly made of pink plastic to resemble disembodied palates—Miss Manners is not oblivious to the suffering associated with these, but does not think they do much, when left lying around, for the smiles of others.

The etiquette of braces begins before this equipment is issued. It begins with knowing that when the first child in a class to get braces appears, you do not make remarks about train tracks, Jaws, and Metal Mouth. That child is likely to be the first person out of braces, too, when his tormentors are themselves locked firmly in. Braces can be, however, a subject of polite conversation at the appropriate age levels. "How long have you had them?" and "How long do you have to have them?" are standard and inoffensive conversation openers among the braced as weather, the economy, and the general decline of civilization are among their presumably straightened-out elders. It is also permissible to discuss the reason for your braces—underbite, overbite, buck teeth, gaps. This is a bit more personal, but has become unremarkable, in the way that naming the causes of marriage breakups is among adults.

But the observation "You're not supposed to eat that" has the same unacceptability as the same phrase does to overweight adults. Only the most privileged relationship (parent to minor child) justifies this. Everyone else is expected just to watch as someone with braces bites into a caramel: That person has already heard the theory from his dentist, and will undoubtedly discover the truth of it for himself after this little experiment.

For authorized eating, the rule is to do whatever is necessary to enable others to enjoy their meals. This means that rubber bands, head gear, and retainers are removed in privacy before one appears at the table, and reinstalled in privacy afterward. In the meantime, they are kept in their cases, not parked next to someone's dinner plate.

The chief problem, then, is transferring the food from the plate to the digestive tract. When one has braces, it tends to make a stopover on the front teeth. Any cleaning up that can be done by the tongue with the mouth closed is legitimate. A quick scrape with the thumbnail in the mouth isn't legitimate, but if Miss Manners doesn't see you do it (the napkin goes up to the mouth with four fingers visibly holding it, so that it appears the lips are merely being wiped), it doesn't count against you. Serious picking with tools must be conducted away from the table. This is a nuisance, but it does give one the pleasure of having a second helping when everybody else's meal is over.

The most important rule is that social embarrassment over the fact of the braces is not permitted. Houseguests should bring their head gear, and their hosts are honor-bound not to notice that the guests have drooled on the pillows. And refusing to smile for two and a half years does nothing at all for one's social standing.

Teaching Taste in Clothing

In ordered times, a mother taught her daughter to shop for her own clothes by investing her with authority to choose what she wished, and then marching her into Mamma's favorite store and announcing, "My daughter loves navy blue. She would like to see something in a good wool coat that will last."

Miss Manners doesn't see anything wrong with this system, except that the store no longer exists, and no child will stand for it. (The daughters all hated navy blue, even then, but were too timid to say so.) But the basic rule is the same—teach the child to ask for what you yourself like. It works in the beginning, and it works in the end (no one who has been taught in youth to examine the inside seams of clothing with a scornful, little-old-lady eye will be able to resist doing so indefinitely), provided you allow some rebellion in the middle. This is known as teaching good taste. Good taste means what Mamma likes.

Children must be taught, while they are still young enough to be caught and dressed, that there are different styles of clothing for different occasions. This is apparently a very difficult notion to master, the word having gotten around that blue jeans are symbolic of a virtuous soul.

It is also wise to teach them that there are clothes not suitable to children—girls do not wear black, except velvet-trimmed dresses; boys do not wear dinner jackets, not even to weddings. This creates an incentive to grow up, although it cannot be taught by parents who believe that the outfits they despised in college physical education classes are now perfect for them to wear everywhere.

A child who is too old to be forcibly dressed is allowed partial approval on whatever is bought for him. This is less because of deference to his feelings than because otherwise you will go mad trying to argue him into wearing what you select. Argument is avoided by offering a choice between or among alternatives acceptable to the parent. A parent who asks, "What do you want to wear today?" has only himself to blame for the result; a parent who asks, "Do you want to wear the blue shirt or the green shirt?" will have the child fooled, possibly long enough for the child to acquire tolerable taste.

This loose partnership between parent and child continues until the child can be trusted to handle a clothing allowance. If that is ever to happen, it is only because the preceding period is filled with propaganda concerning quality, value, and fashion. The first topic will fall upon deaf ears, as children really don't care if their clothes last—the ones they loved were all taken away from them because they were outgrown, anyway—and can't believe anything ever wears out.

Value includes wearing hand-me-downs for unimportant items, so that there will be enough money to buy more interesting clothes they covet. That is the chief lesson of the allowance, and cannot really be learned until the money is all spent and something else is needed or wanted. Fashion mostly means that a vain attempt is made to show the children how fleeting their tastes actually are—remember last season when you were dying to have this brand or that look, and now you won't wear it?

Clothing allowance permission should require the child's making an inventory of what is already in the wardrobe and what will be needed for the various occasions he attends—school, birthday parties, going out with parents, sports, and so on. (For more on children's clothes, please see pp. 120–121 and 194–195.)

The etiquette aspect of all this, in case you were wondering—Miss Manners does have a tendency to wander—is that a child must learn the social interpretation of clothing, and the limits of proper use.

To wear something obviously inappropriate—sports clothes to church, party clothes to school—is to inform everyone present that you disdain the activity. To fail to understand the difference between being daring, in one's appearance, and shocking, is to mix up pleasing with defying them.

The latter may, of course, be what the child wishes to do. The clothing allowance allows him to buy what he needs to do that, while the other house rules bar him from doing so when the parents are affected—that is, on almost any occasion except when the child is among similarly dressed peers. The realization that one has spent all one's clothing allowance and that one still has nothing enjoyable to wear for most occasions of one's life is an important step toward giving in to good taste.

Breakage

DEAR MISS MANNERS:

Once, when I was about nine, I was upstairs in my room practicing to be a caveman when I grew up, throwing spears at my stuffed Dalmatian (who eventually sustained a fatal neck wound) and, in a moment of ineptitude, speared the window instead. The cost of the new glass came from a combination of allowance and extra household chores, and I learned something about replacing windows by supervising my father when he put in the new one. But what about the etiquette of damage to property outside the family—the neighbor who gets a fly ball through a large plate glass window? Is it the same as for adult damage—two offers to make the damage good, followed by a nosegay if both are refused? (The nosegay would probably take the form of offering to mop up or do other chores in the damaged house.)

GENTLE READER:

Not exactly. When a child hits a fly ball through someone else's window, there are two damaged parties who need to be satisfied. One is the property owner, who is all too likely to consider that children are unlikely to have enough money to buy windows, and may be more of a nuisance than a help in doing chores. Depending on whether that person played softball as a child, he is therefore apt to extract only a friendly promise to play farther away from his house, or to satisfy himself with a snarl at parents who are so careless as to have children who have accidents.

The other damaged party therefore consists of the parents, who should be less easy to placate. It's not their window, but it's their child. In addition to salvaging their own neighborhood reputation, they must teach the child that someone has to pay for damage, no matter how excusable, and that the perpetrator is the appropriate one. They must therefore insist and direct the sort of restitution you describe your parents having required, in the hope that the child does not, in fact, grow up to be a caveman.

Letters from Camp

Children who are away from home for the summer generally want to take up letter writing—because they miss their dear families, because they are anxious

1324 NEW HOPE ROAD
BAY RIDGE, CONNECTICUT 06228

Dear Mr. Skrill,

I feel terrible about having broken your birdbath during baseball practice. Please let us know how much it costs. My father says he will advance me the money, and I can pay it back out of my allowance over the next few years.

If you need any chores done, I would be happy to do them to show how sorry I am. I am usually very careful.

Your neighbor,
Lauren Right

A CHILD'S LETTER OF APOLOGY *does not properly ask whether the child must pay for replacing the item, which would make the adult-victim feel stingy (unless he is too angry to care), but announces the intention of doing so, endorsed by a parent. The child has been allowed to use the good house paper (after having submitted a rough draft for parental inspection) to impress all concerned with the solemnity of the occasion.*

to share their new experiences and impressions, and because many camps have a policy of not giving them dinner until they have produced letters home. It is an art at which children are not notably proficient, Miss Manners has concluded after studying the most recent anthologies of Collected Thank-You Letters of American Children.

"Dear Aunt Lucy, Thank you for the book. It was neat. I got a lot of neat things. Well, I have to go now. Your friend, Joshua."

Somebody should tell friend Joshua that while this may have gotten past his exhausted mother, there is no chance that Aunt Lucy will tie a satin ribbon around it and carefully place it in an ivory box against the day he becomes a great man and she may dispose of it at an auction house to her material advantage.

Miss Manners considers that sufficient incentive for raising the state of the art. The letter from camp is an excellent learning opportunity, containing, as it does, so many of the emotional essentials of life. The purpose of such letters is to complain, brag, beg, and alarm. The desired effect on the parents who receive it is to reassure them of the mutually exclusive facts that the child is having a marvelous time and misses them terribly; also, a really skillful letter should produce tangible results, in the way of packages of sweets. For example, serious complaints about the camp disturb the parents' satisfaction in having done the right thing, and should not be made unless the child finds the situation hopeless and wants to be fetched home. (Of course, by the time the frantic parents arrive, the child will have gotten a part in the play and life will look different.) But mild complaints, humorously phrased, instill a desire to pack off little compensations. Although parents are the only people to whom one can brag undisguisedly, a prudent child might want to employ general social disguises for self-congratulation, thus taking time to indicate steady improvement on difficult tasks, rather than trumpeting only full-blown triumphs. It depends on how many times the child wants to be rewarded.

Begging is more effective when it is immersed in what appears to be sentiment. Alarms should be sounded only in the interest of suspense, and not, unless there is an emergency, to provoke action. Here is a poor and, Miss Manners fears, common letter from camp:

"Dear Folks, They are making us write letters. Everybody is mean here, and I hate it. I can swim better than anyone else. Send me some candy and money, because what they have here for meals is garbage. We're going to raid the girls' cabin tomorrow night."

Compare Miss Manners' version:

"Dear Mommy and Daddy, I'm learning a lot here, but not how to identify what is what they call food. I miss you. I'm working hard for the swim competition and I think I have a good chance. Most of the other kids have pocket money they buy candy and stuff with, but what I miss is homemade cookies. This afternoon I fell off a horse."

Now, children, Miss Manners asks you: Which letter will get the better response? (For more on letter-writing, please see pp. 211–212 and 230–231.)

An Uplifting Question

DEAR MISS MANNERS:

We love to take elevator rides, but the mean manager won't let us. It is the only building around with elevators. How can we take elevator rides? Thank you for answering our letter.

GENTLE READER:

Thank you, sweet little children, for asking so nicely. Now stop tying up the elevator, will you?

Social Life

Social Acting

Are you giving your children acting lessons? Why not? Don't you want to be supported in your old age by at least one movie star? Why else are you putting all that money and exasperation into having their little teeth straightened?

Truthfully, Miss Manners does not mean to encourage you to put your children on the stage, Mrs. Worthington. There is quite enough of that sort of thing going around. But it is wrong for a parent to allow a child to go out into the world unarmed with the skill of acting, as in "acting like a lady," "acting like a gentleman," or, at a minimum, "acting like a human being." This does not come naturally. Conveying an emotion from one's heart to one's audience is a technique that must be learned.

There are exceptions, the observation of which is what misleads parents into believing that children can perfectly well express their feelings and that a lack of satisfactory expression indicates that the feeling is also lacking. The child did not have to learn to make its feeling of hunger, pain, or anger intelligible, they note, and so a failure to express pleasure can mean only one thing.

Indeed, that is not true. For every time that you observe a child's face light up on opening a coveted present, you can find ten instances of its saying "Uh," with no expression, when given or offered something it wants. "Would you like to go to the game with me and pig out afterward?" the parent inquires. "Uh," says the child; and the crestfallen parent puts it down to a lack of interest or enthusiasm. That is not necessarily what it is. It is much more likely that the child was never taught to say "Why, I'd love to!" in the proper tone of voice and with the appropriate accompanying expression.

This is the first and simplest acting job for which the child must be prepared: projecting his actual feelings. If you are pleased, you must act pleased.

The second course in acting involves demonstrating general, basic feelings, rather than the less attractive immediate ones. If you don't actually like the present, you act pleased anyway, because you like the principle of being given presents, and hope to encourage the practice, because you may do better next time.

The third level is still further removed from the immediate feelings, because it involves acting out a wish to please others, on the off-chance that this will inspire them at some future time to try to please you. In other words, this is acting pleased when not actually being given a present.

Let us now try some acting exercises.

1. Acting pleased to see someone. (On level one, this means conveying actual pleasure in seeing someone; on level two, it means acting glad to see someone one likes but is not thrilled to see at this particular moment; on level three, it is acting pleased to see someone one doesn't like.) Expression: bright eyes. Dialogue: "How do you do?" or "Hello" or "Hi." "How are you?" "Yes, school's fine this year." And so on.

2. Acting grateful for a present or the offer of one. Expression: wide eyes, huge smile with mouth dropped open to indicate surprise. Dialogue: "I love it" or "Oh, I'd love to" or "Wow—that's terrific."

3. Acting out the idea that you would like to have a pleasure, such as a party invitation or even a visit that might lead to something more tangible, repeated. Expression: eyes shining with reflection of happiness, mouth closed but curved in smile of satisfaction. Dialogue: "I had a wonderful time" or "It was really good to see you" or "I hope I'll see you again soon."

A child who can master all that will not only lead an enriched life, but will discover some way to be able to give his or her parents a luxurious old age.

Best Friends

"Best friends" is a classification of human social relationships that Miss Manners has long tried in vain to discourage small children from declaring. Nothing good can come of a partnership in which both people recognize the obligations and neither the duties.

Your best friend, under elementary-school conditions, should be someone who is always available to you but not a nuisance when you want to play with someone else. A best friend should rejoice in your triumphs but does not have successes that overshadow them. A best friend should commiserate with you but not bore you with recitals of woe. A best friend should confer distinction on you but cooperate in seeming disassociated from you when there is only embarrassment to be shared. A best friend should tell you all the gossip about everyone but never be tempted to repeat your confidences. Miss Manners knows of several marriages that were established with these expectations.

"Why," she keeps asking little children, "do you have to be 'best friends'? Why can't you just be friends? That way you can have other friends, too, and no one is hurt."

"Because," they always say, "it's different." Miss Manners tries to remember not to argue with little children.

There is such a thing as "best friendship" between grown-ups, and even occasionally grown-ups of opposite genders. And yes, Miss Manners will permit you to have your opposite-gender "best friend" stand up for you, as they say, at your wedding. But what most grown-ups mean when they speak of such best friends is not true "best friendship." Better, perhaps, but not best. When a gentleman says his wife is his best friend, or a lady says that a gentleman and she are nothing but the best of friends, they are talking about something else.

Your best friend is someone who delights you by confessing to having fallen happily in love with someone you haven't yet met. See the difference?

The duties of "best friends," in both grown-ups' and children's versions, must be mutual. The chronically cheerful and the chronically morose can seldom sustain a best friendship, with one always listening to the other's rejoicings and the other only hearing complaints.

Specifically, a best friend must:

· Admire unreservedly your grades, trophies, new toys, family car, guppies, and room.
· Entertain a warm respect for your parents, but maintain a bias in your favor when a conflict exists.
· Tell you when your clothes are seriously awry if you are in a position to fix them, and deny that there was ever anything the matter if you are not.
· Tie you to a tree when you announce that you are going to tell your teacher what you think of him.
· Work at your parties, filling silences and flattering wall flowers, instead of having a good time.
· Tell you first of any major steps he or she is taking, but allow you to go around announcing yours without getting in with the story first.
· Treat your misfortunes as serious instances of bad luck, not the result of character flaws.
· Treat your successes as the just reward of character and ability.
· Enjoy your successes more than your misfortunes.
· Consider that any addition to your life that seems to please you is wonderful —including a new friend to shoot marbles with.

The Eternal Triangle

DEAR MISS MANNERS:

I'm in third grade. I have two best friends that always are fighting. If I play with one, she will tell me not to play with the other. One will get mad and say that I like the other one better, but I like them both the same. What should I do?

GENTLE READER:

Let both of them know, right now, that you do not agree that being a friend requires you to take on the feuds of your friends. Practice saying "I'm sorry—I like you, but I also like Jeremy." It will come in very handy later in life.

Persistent Friends

DEAR MISS MANNERS:

My sister's best friend's sister is crazy about my sister. My sister isn't particularly fond of her. She (the best friend's sister) sticks to her like glue and has invited herself over to our house several times. She hasn't caught on to the subtle hints my sister has sent her. My sister isn't too awfully good at giving false excuses, but is afraid of hurting her feelings. Both of us just can't figure out what to do. What do you suggest?

GENTLE READER:

False excuses do not work on glue. Besides, they create just as big a mess. What your sister must say to the unwanted guest is "I'm sorry, but this time Samantha and I just want to visit alone. I'll invite you some other time." "Some other time," as all adults know, is a time that never arrives, but it is saved from the classification of "false" by being under the kinder and more useful category of "vague."

Sidewalk Socializing

DEAR MISS MANNERS:

Every day after school, my friend and I walk home. Occasionally, a friend of hers will stop by and talk to her. I am new in the area and I don't know most of her other friends, so I usually just stand by until they finish. When my friend and the other girl say goodbye to each other, should I also say goodbye? I usually don't, because I figure the other girl was talking to my friend and not me, so she says goodbye just to my friend. What should I really do or say?

GENTLE READER:

The rule about sidewalk socializing is that introductions are not necessary when greetings are merely exchanged in passing, but are when people stop and engage in chatter—chatter being something between inquiries on how things are going, and the actual exchange of information.

That doesn't help much if you are the third party, standing there like a dummy trying to look invisible while others are having a full-fledged visit on the street corner. Your choice then is either to treat it as if it were, in fact, a prolonged greeting, in which case you stand there with a vague look and dreamy half-smile indicating that you are in a state of contented suspension, and merely nod when the person departs; or to intervene, stick out your hand, and say, "I'm Alison Piffle," and join the conversation, after which you would also join in full goodbyes. Either is proper, but Miss Manners recommends to you the latter, as you are new in the area, and may well find that your youth could pass waiting for those you do know to perform their social duties.

Shyness

DEAR MISS MANNERS:

I have a very big problem. I am a junior high school student who is very shy. I have gone to the guidance counselors, but nothing seems to help. My family is very poor and I cannot afford to go to a shrink. My best friend borrows money from me occasionally (she is not using me) and I from her. But I always pay her back. She never pays me back. I cannot ask her for it, because I feel stupid. You know it's kind of hard saying, ''Hey, do you have my money?'' She's making me broke, and I don't know what to do.

GENTLE READER:

Never mind the shrinks. All nice people turn shy at about the time they realize there are other people in the world (a revelation that tends to occur in about the fourth grade). Eventually, the wear and tear of the world rubs some of this off, and they turn into charming people. Those who were brazen in junior high school rarely do.

This is not to say that Miss Manners is recommending only time as a cure for your shyness, or for your more immediate financial problem. Time takes so long, doesn't it? The cure for shyness is to accept calmly the fact that you are shy, and to learn to act the part of someone who is not shy. Miss Manners has very high standards of acting, and does not suggest that you plunge in with some crude imitation of the nearest popularity king or queen. Study the facial expressions and mannerisms of people whom you consider to be also shy, and then observe those of people who are not. When you begin to have a feeling for the difference, start subtly imitating those of the nonshy. If nothing else, this should take your attention away from yourself and focus it on others, which is, in itself, a cure for shyness.

The financial problem is even easier to solve. As each of you borrows from the other, you need only keep secret accountings of the exchanges. If you have come out three dollars behind, you do not ask for ''your'' three dollars; you simply tell your friend that you need three dollars and ask to borrow it. Isn't that what your self-confident friend would do?

🌹 PARTIES

The Slumber Party

DEAR MISS MANNERS:

I am planning to give my daughter a slumber party for her tenth birthday. Can you please enlighten me as to the proper activities and foods to serve at a slumber (pajama) party. All persons scheduled for invitations are in the age range of nine to thirteen.

GENTLE READER:

You have chosen one of the most complicated forms of human socialization to honor your daughter's birthday. Compared to the pubescent slumber party, the sit-down dinner for forty with service *à la Russe* is child's play. The difficulty is that for the children to think it a success, there must seem to be a state of relative lawlessness, while actual lawlessness is disastrous, socially as well as for the sofa cushions. Thus, the menu should seem to the guests to feature nutritional chaos, but should not make anyone sick, including a parent to whom it is later described. Chicken to be eaten with the fingers, corn on the cob, fruit juice served in wine-glasses, and sandwiches in cookie-cutter shapes are the sort of thing that will usually pass. Snacks of whole nuts that have to be attacked with nutcrackers are less likely than the contents of cellophane bags to mess up your bathroom.

The chief entertainment will be staying up late and giggling, but you can curtail the duration by carefully wearing out the guests beforehand. This group is too old for active indoor games and too young for real conversation, so you might take them skating, send them outdoors to play basketball, or dump them in a supervised pool somewhere. Television watching is neither novel nor exhausting enough.

You can add to the excitement of staying up late by talking about bedtime earlier than usual—"You have about an hour to play, and then start getting ready for bed," followed by the hopeless question, at normal bedtime, of "Is everybody ready for bed?" No one will be, and there will be a chorus of protests to which you can reluctantly accede by saying, "Well, all right, but just for a little while, okay?" All this emphasis on time, done without much authority in the voice, is what gives young people the ridiculous idea that staying up late is, in itself, fun.

As hostess, you should generally give the impression of someone who has rules but is swayable, partly because of the specialness of the occasion and partly because the guests are so winning and charming. A wheedled concession is more valued than one achieved through parental neglect.

You should also be clumsily underfoot, appearing periodically with an excuse for the intrusion—a tray of glasses of milk, a pile of towels to be distributed—and an apologetic look acknowledging that you feel them entitled to privacy and know that it is an intrusion. The reason for these checkups is not so much the protection of your property as the protection of the guests' feelings. Two or more of the following things are likely to happen:

· Someone needs to go to the bathroom but is embarrassed to ask where it is, or to ask whether there is another one if the one she knows about is apparently permanently occupied.
· A game of telling or demanding embarrassing truths about individuals present is wreaking psychological havoc among the less sturdy guests.
· Shyness has put someone together with something to which she is allergic, and the results are beginning to appear.
· Someone has lost her dental appliance.
· Someone has lost the stone from her ring.
· Someone has caught her hair in her chain necklace.
· The guests have suggested a pillow fight, and the hostess has been warned not to allow it.

At any of these times, an intruding mother is a welcome sight. (For birthday parties for younger children, please see Chapter 3.)

Planning a Party

DEAR MISS MANNERS:
My mother and father will not let me have parties at home. They say we live too far out in the country, although I have many friends who live in my area. My friends agree that we could have a good time without a lot of people coming. On my eleventh birthday, I had a party in town, at a restaurant that holds parties. But I still want to have a party at home. What should I do? What should I tell my parents—that it's not fair?

GENTLE READER:
Better tell them more than that—enough to convince them that you could hold a party that was fair to them, and to the family property. Instead of going to your parents with a complaint, go to them with a plan—how many people you would invite (including character recommendations on each), what you would do to prepare, how you would keep the guests entertained, how you would react if one of them got out of hand, and how you would clean up afterward. Miss Manners assures you that a child with an eager look and a list is practically irresistible. A child with that old whine about things not being fair is not.

Ladyhood

DEAR MISS MANNERS:
I am a nine-year-old girl. My friend (?) across the street is eleven. I have lived here for four years, and I've always invited her to my birthday parties. She has always included me in hers, too. That is, until yesterday. She had a party without me! I know because I saw three girls troop into her house with wrapped presents under their arms. (I don't know who they were because I couldn't find my binoculars. I'm sure they don't live around here, though.)

I am wondering what I should do about this situation. My mom says ignore it, act as if nothing happened, and, above all, "Be a lady," as Miss Manners would wish. Actually, I want to punch this kid in the nose and inform her she'll never darken my doorway again . . . at least not on my birthday. What do you suggest?

GENTLE READER:
It is not incompatible with being a lady "as Miss Manners would wish" to want to punch this kid in the nose. Doing it, however, is. In fact, Miss Manners cannot think of a more succinct definition of a lady than "someone who wants to punch another person in the nose, but doesn't."

You may ask why not. The obvious answer is that blood ruins white gloves. But there are deeper reasons, as well. Those have to do with the effectiveness of the gesture. Yes, it may make you feel better for a moment, although if your target is two years older than you are, you will not be feeling good for long. But the gesture will not produce the results you really want. It will not get you invited to subsequent parties. It will not make the hostess feel bad; on the contrary, it will convince her that her judgment in excluding you was even wiser than she had thought.

Consider, instead, the likely results of your acting like a lady: You see her in the neighborhood, and give her a friendly wave. (''Whew,'' she thinks, ''she doesn't know that I gave a party.'') ''I forgot to wish you a happy birthday this year!'' you say cheerily. ''I hope you had a wonderful birthday.'' (''Oh, oh,'' she realizes with a sinking feeling, ''she knows.'') At the first reasonable opportunity, you say enthusiastically, ''I hope you'll come to my party—it wouldn't seem like a birthday without you.'' (''I shouldn't have done it,'' she thinks in a paroxysm of guilt. ''I'd better invite her soon.'') See how easy that is? You have made her feel terrible and remorseful—and all by behaving like a perfect lady!

Now Miss Manners asks you to listen to a small lecture on the rights and obligations of friendship. The fact is, no matter how much you resent it—and hasn't Miss Manners helped you express that resentment effectively?—that your friend has a perfect right to give a party without you. No person can reasonably expect to be included in all of the social activities of another person. Even the closest of married couples have social engagements, whether lunch with one friend or a gathering of colleagues, for example, in which they see people separately. Certainly, when one gives parties, one cannot always have the same guest list. Your friend may have wanted to have all people of her age this time, or her school class, or some other category into which you did not fit.

Because you are neighbors, this exclusion was obvious to you. Under such accidental circumstances—and your friend cannot be expected to hire another house to spare your feelings—the proper thing to do is to ignore what you were not meant to observe. A lady finds, as she sails through life, that she can spare herself a great deal of anguish by not taking notice of unpleasant occurrences that were not intended for her notice.

The Combined Party

DEAR MISS MANNERS:

My friend and I are having a combined party to celebrate our birthdays. Most of the people invited will be friends of both of us. However, some of them will know only one of us. How can we let them know that they're not expected to bring gifts for both of us?

GENTLE READER:

Send separate invitations—''Please come to my birthday party, which I am celebrating with Jessica Piffle . . .'' Some will get the idea; others may ask and should be told, ''Oh, no, we're not expecting presents from each other's friends''; and still others will buy you each token presents, for which you merely thank them. You should both open presents together, but in a chaotic matter, no alternating, for example—because an orderly fashion would make it clear how many presents each of you got. Protests of "I didn't know I was supposed to get you [Jessica] anything" should be answered with a warm smile and "Oh, no, we were just so glad you could come."

Houseguests in Training

There is no such thing as a natural-born houseguest. Anybody who always feels like eating and sleeping at the exact times proposed by others, and whose favorite recreations inevitably happen to be the very things that are suggested to them, should probably live in an institution, where such conditions exist.

Children must therefore be trained to be houseguests before they can be sent off alone to stay with relatives, or whoever else is willing to have them. The fun and adventure to be had in short-term solo visiting, not to mention the pleasure of an occasional absence from home, is immediately apparent to the smallest recipient of such an invitation, so it is only fair to pack children off with the skills of making themselves tolerable in another house.

Basically, they should be instructed as follows:

You will be playing a game in which the object, for both houseguest and host, is to make the other person state his desires while you conceal your own. As a houseguest, you will be presented with apparently unlimited choices, but if you take advantage of this opportunity to declare a definite want, you will lose—that is, you will be deemed a nuisance, or spoiled. What you must do is to force the host to state what he is really willing to make available, and then choose. See if you can tell who is winning the following match.

Host: "What do you want for breakfast?"

Houseguest: "Oh, I don't know."

Host: "What do you usually have? What would you really like best?"

Houseguest: "Lemonade, Sugar Stix, and hot chocolate with whipped cream."

Host: "Oh. Well, I suppose I can get some if that's what you're used to."

Now suppose the houseguest's second move had been, instead, "Oh, I like everything, and also it's fun to try something new."

The host is then forced to go again, and tries something like "Well, there are eggs and cereal, or I could make you some French toast."

Does the houseguest then make a choice? Not if he is good at the game. He says, "They all sound good. What kind of cereal?"

Cornered, the host replies, "Fortified Health Chex."

Not cornered, the houseguest comes back with "And I also just love French toast." He wins.

The clever child will soon see how to play this game when the opening is "What time do you like to get up in the morning?" ("If I'm tired, I sleep late sometimes, but otherwise almost any time—what time do you get up?") or "Is there anything special you'd like to do?" ("Mainly just visit—but there are probably lots of things to do in this town I don't even know about.")

It is not that the houseguest is forbidden to express his true tastes and habits.

All he has to do is make them approximate one of the multiple choices that he has forced his host to offer. (An exception is allergies, or other dire health matters. You don't need to wait to be offered these—you may have all you wish, provided you announce them upon acceptance of the invitations. After that, the rest is easy. Make your bed, call collect when you telephone home, pitch in with whatever chores the host does unless twice told to desist, pretend to be more interested in museum exhibits than museum shops, and write a thank-you letter immediately upon returning home.

Remember: What you practice at Grandma's cottage today will be perfect by the time you grow up to meet people who own ski chalets. (For younger and older houseguests, please see pp. 133–134 and *Houseguests*, Chapter 7.)

Secondary

The Sub-Culture

Peers of the Realm

Peer pressure seems to Miss Manners to be an affliction that strikes only the ignoble. The peers of any realm she cares to inhabit accept prevailing standards on matters of social custom, but refuse to abdicate to any such rule on moral issues. She is therefore astounded when she hears such traditional wails as ''I'm the only kid on the block who has to go to bed this early,'' ''Everybody I know is getting tattooed,'' and ''I had to take a drink because I would have been the only one not doing it'' being seriously entertained as arguments by the people to whom they are addressed.

Mind you, she is not shocked at hearing these arguments made. Little minds and wills need exercise, and putting forth what seem to be irrefutable claims based on universal laws of human behavior is perfectly natural. The ridiculous part is to let anyone win with a case like that. The proper answers to these pleas are ''Why, you poor thing—it's tough to be the only child in the world with such awful parents'' and, as a parent of Miss Manners' acquaintance put it, ''You're a peer, too, you know, so why didn't you do the right thing and start some peer pressure in the other direction?''

Failure to use these retorts seems to stem from parental confusion about when society properly makes the rules and when individuals, or the individuals under

Reclining Brood   The Nursery Slouch   Jr. High   Slump

POSTURE PICTURES. *All dreadful, except for baby at bottom, so to speak, who is considerately sleeping so that visitors can see his face, and young people at right, who are beginning to assume a human stance.*

whose immediate rule they are, do so. As many parents get themselves into trouble by saying "I expect you to behave appropriately" ("Okay—but everybody's going topless because it's hot out") as by saying "You must always be honest" ("But that's how I got into trouble; it was true that my teacher has bad breath"). The fact is that making general statements of principle to smart alecks, also called children, is a risky business. Practically any such statement must be qualified. Qualifications, in matters of social conformity, often have to do with reasons of finance, ethics, health, or taste.

You don't drive to school, even if every other student does, if your family can't afford an extra car; you don't cheat on tests, even though you swear it is expected that answers will be traded, if your family has any sense of honor; you don't eat sweets for breakfast or skip the meal entirely even if no other parents impose rules, because yours consider it bad for your health; and you don't dye your hair pink, even though that is in style in your class, if you are also expected to get along with people to whom that would be provocative.

Parents who are hopeful of rearing young lawyers, which seems like a clever investment, may allow discussion and arguments in connection with these decisions. That is all very well, if they have the strength, but then they, as judges, must also have the strength to hold out against the argument that community standards prevail over all other considerations.

Occasionally, enterprising parents band together and discover that there are no such people as those described to all of them by their respective children—those ideal parents with the endless tolerance and money. The jig is then up for their

Super-Coil   Bonsai Slouch   A Human Stance

children. It still seems to Miss Manners to be conceding the erroneous point that indeed, peer pressure is a force in determining matters properly belonging to individual circumstances or consciences. Information about what Everybody Else is doing on such issues is, if correctly reported, of great interest to Miss Manners, who has a lively curiosity about the varieties of human behavior. What it should have to do with her or hers, she cannot imagine.

The Reason for It All

DEAR MISS MANNERS:

HELP! Please help me explain to my teenage son why manners are important, especially table manners. Sometimes I can hardly sit through a meal with him, and he feels all my explanations of why table manners are important are ridiculous. His younger sister and brother watch him very carefully, and are now beginning to pick up his poor table habits.

GENTLE READER:

Miss Manners has asked dear Somerset Maugham to come to her assistance, and offers you the following quotation from his book *The Narrow Corner*:

"Many people are indulgent to the vices they practice, and have small patience with those they have no mind to; some, broader minded, can accept them all in a comprehensive toleration, a toleration, however, that is more often theoretical than practical; but few can suffer manners different from their own without distaste. It is seldom that a man is shocked by the thought that someone has seduced another's wife, and it may be that he preserves his equanimity when he knows that another has cheated at cards or forged a cheque (though this is not easy when you are yourself the victim), but it is hard for him to make a bosom friend of one who drops his aitches, and almost impossible if he scoops up gravy with his knife.''

You are welcome to translate this into a more simple form if you think it necessary. Teenagers have a difficult time understanding the fact that they will be judged more on their manners—which include not only table manners, but all conventional practices, such as choice of clothes, speech, and forms of behavior—than their character. They point out, quite rightly, that there is a ridiculous emphasis on the superficial in this. Miss Manners advises against arguing that this method should prevail—a losing proposition by any decent person's standards—and for teaching merely that it does prevail.

Manners are the folk customs of any given society. Those who violate them are almost certain to arouse extreme distaste in those who obey them. This is as true of subculture manners, such as those of American teenagers, as of anyone else. The only misunderstanding you really have with the child is that he is operating in a society of those—other teenagers—who probably don't know, either, what the proper use of a fork and knife is, but who would be outraged to see anyone mishandling video toys, for example.

Therefore, the point to make is that he will soon want the goodwill of people who do know table manners: a girlfriend or her parents, a college recruiter, a prospective employer. And right now, he needs the approval of someone crucial in his life, to whom this also makes a difference, namely you. If this sounds as if it all gets back, in the end, to ''Do it because I say so,'' so be it. That, too, is an important lesson in life. (For rules of table manners, please see *Mealtime*, Chapter 8, and *Review*, Chapter 9.)

Of Noble Appearance

DEAR MISS MANNERS:

I am not such a terrible fellow. I am generous with my time and attention to people, kind to animals, I tell some good jokes, I avoid mean ones. But I'm not a saint.

One of my worst sins, it seems, to some people, is my poor grooming. I wear old clothes a lot, my hair looks like a bird's nest not infrequently, and somehow that suits me fine.

Now, Miss Manners, maybe that disqualifies me from the possibility of being your friend. That would sadden me a bit. But I would be all right. But suppose one of your family members invited me for lunch. Would you not refrain from heaping abuse on me, without a trace of humor?

I was caught in a similar situation recently and felt trapped. If I got up and left, I feared I'd hurt my friend. If I stayed, I'd have to accept those immoderate outbursts from my friend's father, and I did so. It was easiest to accept it without any back talk and leave when it seemed to be most natural—which was *very* shortly after we finished eating. I had little appetite.

Well, Miss Manners, I stuck it out. My friend understands perfectly, and apologized for his father's behavior. But I wish I had left right away. Would that seem to you, O great arbiter of propriety, to be an acceptable alternative?

If you think my hair is tangled, you should see how tangled what's underneath is.

GENTLE READER:

If your question consisted solely of the surface inquiry, Miss Manners would have no trouble agreeing with you that it is rude to criticize guests at one's table. She would also rule that you made the correct choice originally, in treating it as an excess of parental emotion, rather than making it the occasion of an open break.

But then there is that other question lurking in your letter—would a person of refinement not believe that appearances go for nothing, and what counts is only a noble heart? Only slightly beneath that thought does she detect that you are actually bragging about your appearance, and using it to defy general social standards, in hope of provoking people whom you can then label superficial.

Miss Manners cannot allow all this to pass by her without registering a protest. The way you choose to look is a symbolic rendition of how you feel. That is why costume and makeup are important elements of characterization in the theater.

Note that Miss Manners has limited her criticism to the areas in which you have a choice. The quality of your features is not a matter of choice; whether you comb your hair is. If you have old clothes because you cannot afford others, it is not held against you; if you select old clothes to wear when more of an effort is expected, you have signaled to your hosts that you do not think them worth that exertion. When people defy such trivial and easily accomplished conventions as dress and grooming, Miss Manners has her suspicions about the nobility of heart to which they lay claim.

Fighting Nails

DEAR MISS MANNERS:

My husband and I have a thirteen-year-old "typical teenager," who is very concerned about appearance. However, she enjoys having very long fingernails, always manicured and polished. I object to their length because of their appearance being that of an older woman—a harlot, I should say. Being a nurse, I also consider them a carrier of bacteria. None of her friends have such talons, and her nails are a topic of conversation (and envy) among them. My husband does not support me in my effort to trim the situation. Any suggestions?

GENTLE READER:

Miss Manners' first suggestion was to find something more significant to fight about. It is not her impression that growing fingernails is the worst behavior that typical teenagers can invent, if pressed. After thinking it over, Miss Manners decided to discard this suggestion. Why force the child to think up something else that will annoy you?

If Miss Manners must side, she will state that long nails, especially if red, are considered vulgar, in grown-up women. In thirteen-year-olds, they are considered to be an amusing sign of mild rebellion.

It was Miss Manners' dear mother who first pointed out to her the harm of complete parental tolerance. During the 1960s, when many parents not only condoned but imitated their children's attempts to rebel, the poor children were driven mad trying to find something that would work the age-old trick of shocking their elders. She predicted that many would find nothing left to them but to indulge in extreme forms of religion and chastity, if they wanted to earn the disapproval of their parents. It is with this in mind that Miss Manners has decided that there would be little harm in your fighting your daughter over the ludicrous question of the length of her fingernails. It should keep you both happily occupied until maturity.

The Jerk

DEAR MISS MANNERS:

What are we supposed to say when Daughter brings home a jerk? Sorry, but there is no other way to put it. Sharon proudly displayed, for her father and me, a disheveled, pimply, inarticulate young creep (the word we would have thought she would use for such a creature), who is at the bottom of their class. Ever since, she has been saying eagerly, "What do you think of Kevin?"

We see this as a no-win question. If we say we think he's just wonderful, we seem to give our approval of, at the least, her taste, and, at the most, this awful relationship that we hope will die as soon as she opens her eyes. But if we say what we really think, we drive her into his arms. We know that much. What do you suggest?

GENTLE READER:

A couple of Miss Manners' acquaintance recommends "Well, dear, we're sure he must have qualities we can't see," delivered in just the right tone to suggest the ones they can.

Punching the Time Clock

DEAR MISS MANNERS:

How do I enforce my sixteen-year-old daughter's curfew without embarrassing her in front of her friends? She knows when she's supposed to be in (the time varies, depending on homework, whether it's a Saturday or Sunday night, etc.), but says "a few minutes one way or the other" don't matter—it's always "the other," and sometimes up to forty minutes—and she can't let people know that she's such a baby that her parents don't trust her if she's not there exactly. Also, sometimes she gets in on time, but brings her friends with her, and then, when the evening drags on, claims she doesn't know how to get them to go, and would "die of embarrassment" if we did.

We don't want to be inflexible, but frankly, it's hard on us. We worry about kids' driving, about her getting enough sleep, and so on.

GENTLE READER:

Miss Manners hopes that she doesn't detect an apologetic tone when you speak of worrying about your child, or seeming inflexible. It is certainly the parents' prerogative to worry; and inflexibility, Miss Manners believes, is easier on everyone concerned than the eternal hassle that comes of arguing the circumstances of each evening as a special case.

A gentleman of Miss Manners' acquaintance recommends the system his parents used, which he plans to use for his daughter, sometime after she quits wearing diapers:

The curfew is set, and so is an alarm clock near the parents' bed. It is the child's task, when she comes in, to turn this off so that the parents can sleep peacefully through the night. If this is not done, everyone knows when they will get hysterical, start telephoning the police, or appear downstairs saying, "I'm afraid it's rather late now." (No fair turning off the alarm if the child's friends are still in the house.) Given the choice between obedience and embarrassment, the child is extremely likely to decide on the former.

Disposable Income

DEAR MISS MANNERS:

Through no fault of my own, my teenager has a professional modeling career. I had sent her to a charm school to learn posture and neatness, but the school put her in the way of some jobs, and she is now making more money than seems right for a young girl. I wanted to put it away for her to have when she is grown-up, because I am told that child modeling does not necessarily lead to a career as an adult, and she may not be able to make that kind of money at least for a long, long time. But she argues that it is her money, she works hard for it, and has the right to spend it. She spends it on sweaters, makeup, and stuff like that. I can't say it is bad for her, but it is so much more than she needs, and more than any of her friends, who I think are beginning to find her show-offy. What do you think is right?

GENTLE READER:

It's time that your daughter, and you, too, learned the lesson, that there are some things money cannot buy, and independence for teenagers is one of them. Miss Manners sympathizes with her only to the extent that it is difficult to work without getting any reward. Why don't you allow her to take from her earnings a weekly amount that would generously supplement her allowance but not raise her spending power to the ridiculous? Then put the rest into an account, keeping her informed of the increasing amount and the year in which you will consider that she is grown enough to handle it herself.

Business Manners for the Young

DEAR MISS MANNERS:

One lady I baby-sit for always underpays me. I'm sick and tired of being cheated by this woman. Baby-sitting is a hard job and demands a lot of patience. People are always cheating me out of hard-earned money. I think I speak for a lot of baby-sitters who are just fed up! Please tell me the polite way of asking for two dollars an hour.

GENTLE READER:

Allow Miss Manners to teach you a principle that will stand you in good stead throughout your life. It is that good business manners are different from social manners. It is not by definition rude to insist on being paid properly for one's work, at a rate stated when you take the job.

What you must say is, "I'm sorry, but the rate is now two dollars an hour, and so you owe me ten dollars, not eight dollars." If there is any further question, you may say, "Well, then, I won't be able to sit for you, because that is my fee." The politeness is in the way you say it—firmly but pleasantly, as if you are conveying information, not making accusations.

Unacceptable Present

DEAR MISS MANNERS:

If a nice young boy named David appears at your daughter's birthday party with a gift of white pajamas with blue polka dots, what is the mother's appropriate response?

1. Sigh and faint.
2. Shout, "Oh, my God!"
3. Ridicule the boy.
4. Throw them in his face.
5. Shout, "Oh, how she needs them!"
6. Smile and say, "I know you know she didn't need a fig leaf. This is a joke."
7. Quietly respect the intent of a boy who hadn't made a religion of cheap perfume.

Now, this hasn't happened to me, but it happened to my mother, and she was quiet. I kept them. I was eighteen.

GENTLE READER:

Eighteen? Good grief. You wouldn't like to make that eight, would you? No, Miss Manners supposes not. And to think that people accuse Miss Manners of making up the questions she answers! If she did, you may be sure that she would have made the age in this one such that the mother could reply, "Why, David, dear, did your mother choose this sweet little playsuit for Rosebud?"

Back to grim reality. A young lady of eighteen may not accept clothing, certainly not pajamas, from a young gentleman. But she may play what Miss Manners believes interrogating squads call "good guy, bad guy," by saying, "I think they're cute, but my mother would never let me keep them." If the mother is standing by, she has to take this all on herself, saying, "Now, I know I'm going to disappoint Rosalinda, but David, dear, she simply cannot accept this, however innocently you meant it." David, who really meant to brag in the locker room that Rosy was wearing his pajamas, will have no choice but to keep quiet and accept this.

Refreshments for Young Ladies

DEAR MISS MANNERS:

A bunch of us have a group house at a local seaside resort, and last weekend we ran into a rather touchy and puzzling situation.

It so happens that this guy in the house is seeing a seventeen-year-old girl at the beach. Saturday afternoon, the girl visited him on the beach, and none of us knew what beverage to offer, the drinking age at this resort being twenty. She certainly didn't need the diet sodas that all of the women in the house tend to swill, and truthfully, we were too embarrassed to offer milk (growing bodies do need their calcium, though). So the thirsty young thing went refreshmentless. What is one to do?

GENTLE READER:

My, you are all having a good time thinking about the needs of this growing young body, aren't you? Miss Manners cannot precisely identify the lasciviousness in your apparent quest for etiquette, but she is quite sure that if one of your friends had been visited by his seventeen-year-old daughter, the question would not exist.

Every house that has a supply of liquor also has some sort of soda, too, and often juice, if only to use in mixing cocktails. It is a rare crowd in which everyone chooses liquor at refreshment time—what with problems of dieting, driving home, following medical orders, and so on. The adult women in your group do not generally drink liquor, if Miss Manners correctly understands your statement about swilling women. Stop acting like a silly teenager, and fetch your guest something decent to drink on a hot day. Oh, while you're up, Miss Manners would like a Mimosa.

Social Life

Dances

Show Miss Manners a grown-up who has happy memories of teenage years, with their endless round of merry-making and dancing the night away, and Miss Manners will show you a person who has either no heart or no memory. Dances for the young were surely not intended to be lighthearted. That is probably why nature always ensures that the couple who enjoy them most—the most popular girl in the prettiest dress matched with the most popular boy in the best car—always come to reluctant early parenthood, poverty, and piggishness of appearance.

Those who hope to lead pleasanter lives must endure the ritual of young social agony. To those who have missed out, for lack of invitations, Miss Manners offers the comfort that they are getting off easily, and that confessed unpopularity in childhood is an endearing trait in an adult. If the dance is to be attended in pairs, the rules for ordinary dating apply: The gentleman makes a specific offer for the occasion, with some warning ("May I take you to the dance a week from Saturday?" not "What are you doing tomorrow night?"), and the lady can accept or refuse. The difference between a private date and a public dance is that if she plans to show up with whoever asks her next, the wording of the refusal had better be ambiguous, such as "I'm so sorry, but I already have plans for that evening."

192

More than in general dating, the custom prevails of having the gentleman call for the lady. He also assumes responsibility for her being pleasantly occupied for the evening, claims at least the first and last dances, and fetches food and drink or accompanies her to get it. The return responsibility is that the young lady undertakes to occupy herself for much of that time, even if she is reduced to engaging the chaperons in animated conversation. Miss Manners misses the dear barbaric days when ladies had dance cards on ribbons at their wrists and could schedule their evenings. If juggling one's admirers didn't tax the strength, then inventing names taxed the imagination.

The request for a dance is correctly worded "May I have this dance?" Miss Manners would advise a young gentleman not to adopt the alternate wording "Do you want to dance?" that suggests the answer, which Miss Manners hopes would remain unspoken, "Yes, but not with you."

Acceptable answers to the former, correctly worded offer are: (1) "Why, yes, how delightful." (2) "I'm so sorry, I promised this dance already." (3) "I'm just too tired to dance now." One cannot hop up on the floor with someone else after offering the third excuse, but there is nothing to prevent one's taking another companion for a bit of refreshing air or punch during that time. Unless cutting in is against the local custom, the procedure is for a young gentleman to tap an engaged young gentleman on the shoulder and spirit away his partner; the second young gentleman is not allowed to offer to tap the first on the nose for his trouble. It is a long-established custom on the part of young ladies to encourage cutting in by delivering a soft look over an alien shoulder to the prospective cut-inner. Waves of distress, however concealed from the cause of that distress, are not permissible.

You will notice that proper behavior encourages opportunities for disaster by having the participants mix and socialize, rather than stay safely anchored to the secure date, however dreary. Like all social customs, this has a purpose. It makes adult social life seem simple and carefree.

Declining a Dance

DEAR MISS MANNERS:

I was at an informal dance several weeks ago. When approached by a young man and asked if I cared to dance, I answered yes, and we proceeded to the dance floor. When the dance ended, a slower and softer song began, and my partner assumed that I would continue to dance with him to this new music. However, dancing intimately, as is expected with such music, with a near-total stranger makes me extremely uncomfortable.

I smiled at my partner, shook my head, and left the dance floor, surprising and (unfortunately) offending the gentleman. Ought one to sacrifice one's comfort to avoid hurting feelings, or is there a better way to handle this problem?

GENTLE READER:

What do you mean, "dancing intimately"? Not since we all got over the shock of the invention of the waltz some years ago has Miss Manners heard anyone assume that there was anything inherently indecent about the conventions of ballroom dancing.

Leaning against one another to music, with more hand motion than foot, is another matter. It has always seemed to Miss Manners that an important step has been skipped between that and the hands-off dancing of recent years. However, the ballroom rules still apply.

You are not obligated to dance more than the one dance you accepted with the gentleman, but he—do consider his position—has an obligation not to leave you stranded. It may be that he was seized with a desire to dance with you through eternity, but there are gentlemen with no such seizures who nevertheless find themselves doing so because they do not know how to say, "Let me take you back to your friends."

In any case, all you need do to get out of the second dance is to smile and say, "I must find my partner for this dance," or "I think I'll sit this one out," or just "Excuse me," and be off.

High School Dress

DEAR MISS MANNERS:

Recently, at my high school, there has been a slight disagreement concerning the definition of casual, semiformal, and formal dress. Would you please give the final word on what these three terms refer to? Also, what is considered proper dress for the following occasions: a high school dance in which there will be mostly dancing and not much sitting; and a banquet during which awards will be given and, of course, dinner will be served?

GENTLE READER:

Recently, in the world, there has been a slight disagreement concerning the definition of casual, semiformal, and formal dress, so why should your high school be any different? The general definition of all three these days seems to be what Miss Manners would lump together under the heading of dishabille. Look it up. If there is a French teacher handy, try *déshabillé*.

Miss Manners would be a fool to attempt to "give the final word" on such a shifty matter, and yet she does not want to retreat into blather about "prevailing community standards," that being the last refuge of people who can't make up their minds. Let us make up a reasonable set of standards for a high school community, and then stand back and watch the fun as everybody goes into tailspins disagreeing with it.

"Formal," Miss Manners supposes, means black tie for the boys and long dresses for the girls. (She says this tentatively because to her, but to practically no one else, that is "informal" while "formal" is white tie. Never mind—that is her problem and needn't concern you.) You will probably expect Miss Manners to approve of this for school dances, but she does not. First of all, it puts a financial strain on most students; and, higher on her warped scale of values, it is inappropriate for gentlemen under the age of eighteen to wear evening dress.

"Semiformal," a term Miss Manners loathes because it suggests a humorous contrast between the top half of a costume and the bottom, probably means suits and ties for the boys and dresses for the girls. This is what Miss Manners recommends for both dances and banquets at high school. It gives the girls quite a range of choice in the elaborateness of their outfits and the boys extremely little, which is the proper order of things.

What "casual" means to high schoolers Miss Manners trembles to think. A definition that would suit her, as appropriate for classroom and related activities, would be sport shirts or sweaters and trousers for both genders. With the one exception of the name of the school, these should be wordless. That means no statements of one's political or romantic proclivities on the chest, and no stranger's name on the backside. (For more on children's clothes, please see pp. 120–121 and 165–167.)

Practicing for Proms

DEAR MISS MANNERS:

I am a fifteen-year-old girl and even though my junior prom isn't until next year, I'll be serving at the upcoming prom at my school. (Serving consists of serving punch and cookies and doing other odd jobs.) Would it be proper for the servers to wear long dresses, even though we aren't juniors or dates of juniors? We do get to dance and socialize.

Also, if next year I decide to take a non-junior to my prom, who pays for the tickets, dinner, and his tux, and who drives? We have a new Cadillac and I'd like to drive that, but my mother says it's tradition for the boy to pay for everything and drive, too. But I feel it's my prom, so I should pay for everything, and if not, at least split the costs with my date.

GENTLE READER:

Perhaps you could sell the Cadillac and split the money. Perhaps we can work out something simpler.

It is traditional for a host or hostess to meet certain expenses connected with an invitation, and as there were always more occasions when a boy was host on a date, people, including your mother, came to think that the gender was the factor in this, rather than the role. If you invited a boy to a prom and to dinner beforehand, you should not pay for his clothes, any more than you would expect him to buy you a dress because he invited you out. In the matter of driving, considerations of safety, along with the role of boy as host, have made his doing so customary, but if your parents don't mind your driving, Miss Manners doesn't, especially if it is their Cadillac.

As for this year, you don't want to dress as a waitress because you will be socializing as well, and you don't want to assume the dress of a junior when you are not one. It just so happens, though, that the proper dress of a sophomore at a junior prom is indistinguishable from the proper dress of a junior at a junior prom.

The Best Method

DEAR MISS MANNERS:

What is the best way for a girl to ask a boy for a date?

GENTLE READER:

What is the best way for a boy to ask a girl for a date? In such a way that it can be refused without insult.

Note that Miss Manners did not say without heartbreak, or without discouragement. These may be inevitable, but they may be suffered in private, without the humiliation of their being shared. If you consider the difference between a negative response to "Are you free on next Tuesday to go roller-skating?" and one to "Would you like to go out sometime?" you will understand what Miss Manners means.

Returning Hospitality

DEAR MISS MANNERS:

I can still recall the pain of not being allowed to accept an invitation to a "perfectly fabulous" party in high school because my mother pointed out to me that I had no intention of ever returning the invitation, hence should not impose on my host's hospitality. (Well, he *was* a drip.) "But, Mother, everybody is going, and I'm sure they're not going to bother to invite him back, either." "Well, those people have no character" was the immediate rejoinder.

I'm not sure I would be quite so rigid in following this rule were Ronald Reagan to invite me to a soirée, and I hope he and Nancy would understand if I only followed up a charming evening with a sincere thank-you note. But now I'm beginning to understand why she said what she did. After years of being the office party-giver (on my own time and money), with a return rate (on either thank-you notes or invitations) that would be merely embarrassing to recount were it not so painful to me, I have finally seen the light and had to shift my social intentions in other directions. The only thing is, I keep getting comments like "You don't have those great parties like you used to, do you?" (this from a girl who has never even asked me to join her for a Dutch-treat lunch with her other buddies) or, "You should join the entertainment committee, because you really know how to throw parties" (that remark from a person who, with husband, dined at our house several times and even furnished her cottage with our giveaways).

Another "fabulous party-giver" has picked up my mantle and her complaint is the same. I'd like to tell her she'll end up feeling as used as I've felt, but I don't like to pass on my sour attitude, because her answer would be the same as mine would have been: "I love people and I'm glad to see them have a good time." Are there people in this world who invite such abuse? (Or does Miss Manners address herself to such analysis?) How does one adjust to being a giver and never a givee?

GENTLE READER:

God bless your mother for teaching you that accepting an invitation, like accepting a present, is only proper within the system of mutuality that is called friendship. And yet Miss Manners has heard of such as she abused for robbing childish society of its spontaneity by insisting that getting be paired with giving.

One cannot, of course, always repay in kind. Perhaps some of your high school friends could not reciprocate because family circumstances made entertaining impossible; perhaps your office colleagues have also, for reasons of time or money, been unable to match your parties. But no excuse about time or money will justify omitting a letter of thanks to someone who has invested his time and money in entertaining you. And that is just the beginning. Other ways for someone who has received hospitality to show that he reciprocates the warm feelings that prompted it include sending small, thoughtful presents, such as home-baked food, extending an invitation to a manageable event, even if, as you suggest, it must be on a Dutch-treat basis.

We cannot pardon any of your guests who have made no efforts at all, probably because their mothers allowed them to be carefree accepters without the inhibition of considering the feelings of the givers. Such people grow up thinking of party givers as professional entertainers, as if they were owners of restaurants or night clubs. They probably feel equally free to cancel out at the last moment, to bring additional guests without notice, and to criticize your hospitality to others. One does wonder why even the most generous person would find satisfaction indefinitely in giving such people good times. Miss Manners does not blame you for turning your talents to more worthy people; nor would she blame you if you replied to their rude complaints that you had tired of being always a host and never a guest. The reaction will be that you are petty and calculating, and probably your mother will be blamed for having taught you manners. You might console yourself by remembering that she also taught you not to make the mistake of socializing with people you find to be drips.

Things Mother
Never Mentioned

Teenage Romance

This society fully subscribes to the notion that the emotions of small children can be of great importance and serious intensity. It is also aware that pregnancies among the youngest teenagers must be the result of approximately the same activity that produces pregnancy in adults. What it cannot believe in is the existence of ordinary but painful lovelorn problems among the pubescent. The idea of their suffering from tender feelings about one another is too funny to contemplate. Junior high schools are therefore full of pupils who have been duly warned about the dire consequences of everything except the one danger they realistically fear most, which is dying of embarrassment. If no one else is brave enough to tell small teenagers how to behave when they are in love, Miss Manners will have to call it all etiquette and do it herself.

The rules are very strict, and the social consequences of disobeying them are severe, so pay attention. In an adult population, it can safely be assumed that everyone is or has been susceptible to falling in love, and therefore a sort of Geneva Convention exists about which atrocities are acceptable and which are not. It is not always respected, of course. In the very young community, however, it doesn't exist. Therefore the object of unrequited love may well have no sympathy at all for the emotional state of the lover and will use the knowledge of those feelings to gain something he or she does want—a quick laugh, material for bragging, information for annoying someone else, or any other such unpleasant goal. Hence the rigid rules for the lovelorn, for whom not being loved in return is the least offensive possibility and being held up to public ridicule by the adored one only too likely.

Rule one is that you never engage in discussions, even among sworn friends who offer like revelations, about whom you "like." It is not easy for a child steadfastly to maintain that he or she believes that the word "like" is being used to designate very ordinary sociability. ("Do you like Kristin?" "Well, sure, I guess so, don't you?" "No, I mean do you *like* her?" "I like her all right; I like a lot of people," and so on.) There's no use saying you hate the person—that is rightly interpreted as being identical to a declaration of love.

Rough handling and dirty teasing are also rightly understood as a declaration of love, but the object of them should relentlessly treat them as hostile behavior. Teaching people that nasty wooing is unacceptable is a skill that cannot be learned too soon.

It is also useful later in life to learn the habit of resisting impulses to telephone, write, or give presents to someone you love. (While this is practical for keeping such impulses under reasonable control in adulthood, Miss Manners hopes you will then be able to relax it and produce charming attentions to grateful recipients.) In adolescence, especially early adolescence, it is an essential survival skill. Do you want your love notes passed around the class? Your presents scorned? The frequency and duration of your calls exaggerated for comic effect by the household of the receiver until that person can hardly bear to hear your name?

All you have to do then is to follow your warm impulses unstintingly, without calculating what you are getting in return. It's a rough ordeal, and Miss Manners can only promise you that if you get through it with disciplined dignity, things will ease up. If not, the consolation is that you will have a good fund of comically pathetic anecdotes with which to attract adult admirers later.

Separated Sweethearts

DEAR MISS MANNERS:

My boyfriend moved away a month ago. He now lives in the East, and I live in the West. We have been going together for six and a half months. We decided not to break up just because he was moving. I talk to him every Saturday. We plan to get married if everything works out, when we are old enough. We are both fifteen years old. I will be sixteen in a couple of months. We are more mature for our age than most people.

I know what you are thinking. "We are too young to get this serious." But we already thought of that, and we know what we are doing. He wants me to go out there next summer and I also want to go. He said he will pay the way. The problem is our parents. His parents like me very much and are glad we got together, but they might not like me going out there because I will have to stay at their house, and they might not approve. Now, my mother most likely won't let me go. I'm going to wait a few months to ask her, and pray that she will let me. We love each other very much, and I would like your opinion of this.

GENTLE READER:

Miss Manners is going to take you at your word about being mature. It is certainly mature to worry about your parents' reaction, as you are doing, so she will join you at it.

Conducting a long-distance romance is not easy at any age, but it is possible. Miss Manners trusts that you are, or are becoming, a good letter writer as well as telephoner. If you and your beau do not make it a habit to share the facts and concerns of your separate lives, you will find that you have little to talk about when you see each other. The exception is that you do not share information about other dates or crushes you may have. Now, do not be shocked. Miss Manners knows that you can't bear to look at another boy, and would not be able to bear it if you thought he looked at another girl, but she hopes that when the temptation to do so comes, you will both give in to it. That way, neither of you will come to feel, should you sustain your love and actually get married when the time comes, that you have never really looked around, and have missed out on the pleasures of playing the field. At any rate, any new beaux should be described as just friends.

Now, as to getting together. No, you cannot do so without both of your parents' permission. Miss Manners would encourage the parents to grant it, because the summer would be a good test of whether you want to continue your association, and it would be—you might point out to them—under parental supervision. If your beau can talk his parents into inviting you, with a letter directed at your mother, your mother may be more agreeable about letting you accept. You'd be surprised at how persuasive such details of etiquette are. By the way, you can then practice your letter-writing skills by writing home frequently to your mother, telling her what a wholesome summer you are having.

The Fifth Wheel

DEAR MISS MANNERS:

I have two friends of the same age as me, thirteen, who are "going together." Since I am close with both, it doesn't bother them or me when they hug or kiss in front of me. When they do this, they are otherwise alone. (My friends are pretty average kids, not superb in manners.) I usually turn around or walk away or look at the wall and exclaim, "Oh, what interesting paint!" I just wondered what the proper etiquette would be, especially since their relationship amuses me, though I try not to show it.

GENTLE READER:

You are not succeeding in not showing it, but you are practicing the proper form of etiquette. It is extremely rude for two people to become exclusively absorbed in each other in front of a third person, no matter what the activity or degree of friendship with the extra person, and humorously calling attention to this snub is the right approach. Miss Manners hopes you will remember this when you are going with someone, and the admittedly huge temptation to show off this fact seizes you.

A Presumptuous Crush

DEAR MISS MANNERS:

I have some neighbors who have a small boy who obviously has a crush on me. I take that as a compliment but every day he comes around asking me to ride bikes, play Frisbee, etc. So! I do ''play'' some of the time, but it really gets annoying. He's the follow-you-everywhere type, so it's hard to give an excuse. Help! Should I keep up our game of keepaway, or move to Ireland?

GENTLE READER:

If the young gentleman really intends to follow you everywhere, it would not be a good idea to move to Ireland. What would you do with him there?

Crushes do involve some obligation on the part of the crushee, but not to the extent the crusher requires, which is usually endless. You must cultivate the ability to say firmly but politely, ''I'm sorry, Jeremy, but I'm busy now,'' and you may invoke this as often as you like. Miss Manners feels obliged to warn you that this will make the crush even stronger, but as it will be less of a nuisance to you, you will be able to enjoy the compliment more.

Transitions

Educating One's Elders

Back when the world was orderly, adults possessed all the desirable social attributes and practical skills, and children were eager to acquire them. There were powerful incentives for children to be polite, in their wish to imitate the civilized behavior of those in control, and in their anxiety to learn how to control things themselves.

Now that youthful behavior is inexplicably admired by the elders of the society, and a major skill—the ability to understand and use computers—is more often found in the young than the old, what is to make children polite? Only, Miss Manners is afraid, the same sense of charitable kindness and pity, of noblesse oblige, that traditionally required adults to be good to children.

Here, then, is a plea to children whose parents apply to them in the hope of learning computer skills or some other area of youthful wisdom, such as teenage slang or hair-feathering: Be patient and tolerant. Basic teaching skills, when the learning is voluntary, require great amounts of courtesy. (Adults, too, will profit from knowing this, if they should be so fortunate as to be in possession of knowledge their children want.)

The first is a respectful attitude, in the face of the obvious fact that one person is knowledgeable and the other isn't. We pretend that that is simply an accident, easily rectified, and that the ignorant person possesses the ability to master the material with diligent application. Remarks such as "Don't you even know that?" or "Maybe you'd better not try" or especially "How can you be so clumsy (stupid, dense)?" are therefore not allowed.

As in so many issues of manners, the appropriate phrases "You're doing fine," "This just takes practice," and "Don't be discouraged" emphasize politeness at the expense of literal truth.

Officially, therefore, there is no such thing as a dumb question. The ability to listen respectfully to a—well, to an idiotic interrogative—and to respond to it with apparent thoughtfulness is one of the severest tests of a good teacher.

Allowing the adult to make his own mistakes is another hardship on the clever child. The temptation to take it away and say "Here, let me do it" is overpowering, but must be resisted. How else are adults ever going to grow to be self-sufficient?

And the teacher must steel himself to bear repetition—repetition of questions, of mistakes, of self-doubts.

The bright child will suspect that this course of instruction accustoms the instructor to many virtues—respect, generosity of praise, toleration, patience—that characterize the better form of etiquette. (There are nastier forms of etiquette, such as sweetly encouraging people to make fools of themselves, but those are in the postgraduate program, after you have mastered the niceties.) Indeed, the best teaching, as the best teachers are tiresomely fond of saying, teaches the teacher most.

If that is not sufficient incentive to undertake the education of one's elders with sensitivity for their feelings, Miss Manners will add a threat. At the rate things are going, present children will one day find themselves at the mercy of their own children. So if they don't make the most of their superiority now, the chance will be lost forever.

Graduation Presents

DEAR MISS MANNERS:

My grandnephew, who does not otherwise favor me with his attention except on Christmas, has sent me an announcement of his graduation from high school. It is not even an invitation, although I live four hundred miles away from him and can no longer travel easily. Am I right in suspecting that this is a more or less blatant appeal for a gift?

GENTLE READER:

How clever you are. Your nephew is one of countless teenagers, all over the country, who have devoted years to studying, straining their eyes, and risking their health staying up nights in hopes of cudgeling their great-aunts out of a fountain pen, tie, or dictionary at the end of a mere few years. If you do send him a present, it may encourage him to repeat this audacity by attending college, from which he can expect another graduation. Do not think he will stop at that. Perhaps he will marry, in the hope of extracting another tribute from you, and breed children, at the rate of one fuzzy sleeper or bootie set each. Unchecked greed will never stop on its own. He will encourage his very children to have children.

The Director, Faculty, and Graduating Class

of the

Elizabeth Borden School

request the pleasure of your company

at

Commencement Exercises

Sunday, the tenth of June

at three o'clock

on the Lawn

AN INVITATION TO A GRADUATION, *provided by the school. The child encloses his card. In the likelihood that he doesn't have one, since he rarely pays formal calls or sends flowers to hostesses to apologize for his party behavior, he may buy blank cards and write his name on them.*

Meanness doesn't seem to know any boundaries, either. Is there anyone out there whose first reaction, upon opening an announcement of graduation, wedding, or birth, is "Why, how nice!" rather than "Do we have to get them something?"

No, you do not have to get him anything. It might have been nice had you felt like doing so, but it is not obligatory. It would also be nice if you simply wrote him a letter expressing congratulations on an event he was proud of and wanted to announce to you, but you don't have to do that either. You may, if you prefer, sit by yourself and muse bitterly on the lengths people will go to in order to make other people pay tribute to them.

The Graduation Reception

DEAR MISS MANNERS:

My daughter lacked two credits to finish high school, and decided to acquire them by taking a summer-school course and a correspondence course. The high school that she attended honors these credits and has issued her diploma as an honor graduate. Since she did not graduate with the rest of her class or have the conventional method of announcements and graduation exercises, it is my wish to give her some type of reception to honor her completion of high school. I would like to have this in our home, but as we have many relatives and friends, space is a problem. I thought of an open-house type of occasion, where people could come and go during a period of several hours.

Would this be in good taste, and if not, what could I do to honor her completion of high school? If I give some type of reception, how do I word the invitations, and could you please describe the type of invitations I would require?

GENTLE READER:

Certainly you may honor your daughter at a reception (a word Miss Manners prefers to the ambiguous "open house," but the idea is the same), and a lovely thought it is, too. Just, please, do Miss Manners a favor and refrain from finding cute little cards printed with cap and gown or cocktail glass or whatever.

On your own good writing paper, or an informal card (with your and your husband's name and possibly your address), simply write down what your guests need to know, including the information that it is "to celebrate Esmeralda's graduation." On letter paper, you simply put it into a sentence ("Please join us ..."). On a card the information can stand alone.

Applying Oneself

DEAR MISS MANNERS:

I am applying to several schools, and they all ask for some version of my life story, to be told in my own words, telling them about my interests and about why I am applying to their particular school. The truth is that my chief interest and my reason for applying are the same: I would like to get away from home. My

Heather Right
1324 New Hope Road
Bay Ridge, Connecticut 06228

March 15, 1985

Mr. Cuthbert Burbage
President
CBK Productions
Hollywood, California 90074

Dear Mr. Burbage:

My stepbrother, Gregory Awful, suggested I write to you
about my hope of getting a summer job in the field that
interests me most, the cinematic arts. He said that although he
only sees you occasionally, at what I gather is a literary men's
pub, he feels that he knows enough about you to be confident
that you are always kind and helpful to young people.

Although my chief ambition is in literary intrpretation
(acting), I would be glad of any opportunity to observe the
communications business. I can do any kind of office work,
including computer programming. The Supervisor of Volunteers at
Merciful God Hospital, where I worked last summer, can provide a
recommendation. According to her calculations, I saved the
hospital $25,000 when I reviewed and computerized the billing
system.

I will call your office Monday morning, a week from today,
at ten o'clock your time. If that is inconvenient, perhaps your
secretary could tell me exactly when to call back. Having
always worked for experience, rather than money, I am on a
strict budget.

I hope you don't mind my adding that I think you make the
only truly artistic films in Hollywood, and that I am also a
great fan of your wife's, as is my stepbrother, Gregory.

Yours very truly,

Heather Right

Heather Right

A STUDENT'S LETTER SEEKING SUMMER EMPLOYMENT. *It is written on blank paper to suggest
that if the student gets the job, she will not steal enough office letterhead to write personal
letters to all of her friends for the rest of her life, as many as possible on company time.*

parents and I don't get along, and now they are having a trial separation and I don't want to live through it with either one of them. I don't know that this is anybody's business, but I want to get accepted at at least one of these schools, and don't know what to put down. Do they expect you to be perfectly frank with them?

GENTLE READER:

Of course not. They are looking for people who are smart. Your interests are one academic subject, one sport, preferably a team one played at the school, and one cultural activity, preferably with no drug associations. Your reason for choosing each school is that you heard of its fine reputation in each of these fields.

Impressive Interviews

"Do you have a social conscience?" the young applicant was asked by his college interviewer.

"I didn't understand the question," he confessed afterward in the privacy of his home. "If it means do I want to make the world a better place, that's silly—who doesn't? But was he really asking whether I was worth educating, or whether I would be likely to make trouble once I got there?"

Miss Manners will not join the chorus of protest at the cynicism of wanting to give a person in authority the answer he wants to hear. The ability to sift complicated material for what is, under the circumstances, the right answer is surely one of the signs that one is educable. She assumes that the intelligent college application, while honest, is filled out with the purpose of getting into the college, not of unburdening the soul. The latter is what college dormitories are for.

The college application, written and oral, is a version of the job interview. The assignment is not, as it would seem, to tell an institution what you are like, but to tell it how well you would be able to do what it wants people to do. The aim of every college, the behavior of its alumni on homecoming weekend notwithstanding, is to pass on the knowledge and the culture of the civilization to receptive people, in the hope that they will eventually make their own contributions to it. (To civilization, not to the college. That comes later.) The chief way of telling is, of course, how you have managed at these tasks so far. If you haven't put much effort into that in the twelve, or at least four, years prior to the college application, there's not much you can do about it now.

If you have, you can still foul things up now. It doesn't seem quite fair to Miss Manners that what we shall call talk-show skills should be a factor in college admission, any more than she believes it right that authors should have to be glib on television to bring their books to the attention of the public. But so it is, and the clever student will learn how to present himself appealingly. Here, then, are a few quick rules for college interviews:

· Dress like a graduate teaching assistant. It is true that educators and their representatives are supposed to be able to look at a high school student and envision a scholar, but it's hard. If you dress like an undergraduate, you only help a little, and if you dress like a member of the faculty, you seem pretentious.

· Use the manners of a ten-year-old in an old-fashioned dancing class. You don't have to get punch for the interviewer, but "Sir" or "Ma'am," rising when an adult does, and sitting still, looking the interviewer straight in the eye, will be interpreted as respect for education.

· Use the speaking delivery of a kindergartener in Show and Tell, although not necessarily the vocabulary, grammar, and plot lines. Eagerness and enthusiasm in discussing your interests are as important as the nature of the interests. It gives rise to the vain hope that you will look awake in class.

· Display the solidity of a member of the board of trustees. It is not reasonable that someone in the stage of seeking higher education should seem to have an orderly sense of the universe, and confidence that he will fill a useful place in it, but it is nevertheless reassuring to college administrators. They think it will save wear and tear on the buildings.

You will notice that none of these represents the normal behavior of a college student. They figure you will pick that up soon enough.

Collegiate

Writing Home

Knowing what Miss Manners thinks of people who can spend a weekend in someone else's house and not write a letter afterward, you can imagine what she thinks of those who spend seventeen or eighteen years in the same house and then go off to college and never write. Although the offense is greater, the penalty is less because the student is going to be invited back. Parents can be as offended as anyone with a display of bad manners but they lack the recourse of saying, "You can tell what kind of people he must come from."

Miss Manners is not suggesting that a thank-you note is needed for the simple task of child-rearing. Nor is she suggesting that it is necessary to send one's parents a running commentary of everything that happens to a young man or woman away from home—they deserve better than that. But no child should be allowed to depart his native city for school without an understanding with his parents about how often they expect bulletins. Miss Manners recommends that a sizable percentage of these be in the form of letters, rather than collect calls, not only because of the expense but to give the parents a chance to see if the education is taking. (It is not, however, up to them to issue grades. Parents who return letters with spelling mistakes circled do not deserve to get any.)

Every once in a while, each child is expected to write a letter that contains no mention of money or services he would like to receive from home. The ones that do must never open with these requests. It is not necessary to trouble parents with the new eating habits and hours a child tries out on his first extended sojourn away from home. However, if there are natural consequences, the child is obligated to notify the parents before the college infirmary does. Miss Manners is sympathetic with the wish of every devoted son and daughter to help parents live happily in a fool's paradise. Nevertheless, unconcealable trouble is best stated first by the student—with the opening of "Don't worry, but . . ." that stops every parent's heart —before the dean, a friend who has a child in the same class, or the evening news tells them what the matter is.

Surprisingly, there are also students who neglect to inform their parents of the approach of prizes and honors. That is not only inconsiderate, but it seems to contradict the very achievement involved. Nobody with any brains would neglect to report success where it is most appreciated. A student is required to invite parents to all ceremonies or parents' days, and it is no good saying that the student has made the decision not to attend. The choice is the parents'. A student who really wants to avoid this writes, "I'll feel terrible if you don't stay with me. I'll arrange to borrow sleeping bags for you, and I hope the noise won't bother you."

School holidays are presumed to be for the express purpose of visiting home. That doesn't mean that one always has to go home, of course—only that the failure to do so must be properly and regretfully excused. A model letter from a child who is not going home is: "I've been looking forward to being home and seeing you so much that I hate to have to wait until Christmas. But it does seem silly to have you spend all that money for just four days, when most of it would be used up traveling, anyway. So I thought, since I've been studying so much that I have neglected getting any exercise, that I'd just do a little skiing near here, and then get back to work. I certainly will miss having Thanksgiving dinner—which I would have missed, anyway, since I can't get away until Thursday—and I'll be thinking of you then."

Outfitting for College

DEAR MISS MANNERS:

No doubt you are familiar with those lists, provided in most infant magazines, which describe in great detail the proper layette for baby. Well, baby is now seventeen and has been admitted to one of those frightfully old and well-known schools in the Northeast. Yes, Harvard, to be exact! Pardon me a moment while I attempt to bring my astonishment (and pride) under control.

Perhaps you might provide us with a layette list, telling us what is really in, behind those ivy-covered walls. How many tiny undershirts will he need? What about Levi's? And his Louisiana State Bird T-shirt, the one with the huge mosquito on the front? A tuxedo? Sheets? Towels?

Friends have suggested that he make the necessary purchases when he arrives up North, but this child has great taste (if you know what I mean). Bankrupt City is not what we have in mind. Therefore I would appreciate having your list while there is still time to do some shopping here.

We are trusting you, Miss Manners, to tell us the entire terrible truth. But please keep in mind that the child's father is a civil servant and his mother will be going back to work as a high school teacher to help meet the extra demands on an already shaky budget.

GENTLE READER:

If you will cast your mind back some seventeen years, you will recall that baby's layette, cunning as it seemed when you assembled it, was of amazingly short-term use. Those wee sweet undershirts were too hot for him in the summer, unnecessary under soft warm clothes in winter, not dressy enough for visitors, and too much trouble for the at-home look. He never even got a chance to wet or spit up on them all before he had outgrown them.

The same general principle applies to college wardrobes. All hometown clothes are inappropriate at college. This is not the school's fault. Harvard, for example, tolerates two quite different looks: pressed, and unpressed. Whichever you, your son, or Miss Manners thinks appropriate for him now, he will develop a yearning for the other by mid-September. Therefore, your friends are correct. Did they mention giving him a check instead of a charge account?

The Fresh Start

DEAR MISS MANNERS:

I am going off to college in another state, and I plan to make a fresh start in several respects. I'm going to use my real name—my parents put a blight on me by calling me Cookie, and, as I have been in the same school complex since kindergarten, I have never been able to get rid of it entirely. Then, also, although he doesn't know it yet, I'm planning to ditch my boyfriend. This is long overdue, and it just seems that it will be easier when we are two hundred miles apart than when he comes hanging around my house and I see him in the halls at school all the time. It's more than just him—I want a whole new type of friends. My policy here was just to go around with whoever asked me, and I think it's time I did some choosing for myself.

My problem is that everyone keeps saying what fun it will be to visit me at college. The heck it will be. Not if I see them first. I tried to talk to my mother about this, and she got all upset and said she hoped I wasn't going to be a snob, that those friends were good enough for me once, and so on. Do you think it's awful to do this? Actually, that's not my question, because I plan to do it anyway. My question is how.

GENTLE READER:

Carefully. One cannot be too careful with people who know too much about one. For example, Miss Manners, while sympathizing with your hope of acquiring a set of people more to your taste, would not provoke them by stating this as a policy. The most you can do along these lines is to tell your beau that you do not think it wise to recognize a commitment during the separation. After that, you tell

Dear Joshua,

You're so sweet to write me right away like that. I'm sorry that I was so tied up getting settled in the dormitory, meeting new people and getting the right start in my classes that I haven't had a chance before to reply.

College is a lot different than I had imagined. For one thing, it's a lot more time consuming, and I'm afraid I better not try to go away for a weekend. Thank you for asking me, though. I'll see you when I'm home for Thanksgiving, or if I'm too busy with the family, at Christmas vacation for sure.

Of course, I still like you. Didn't we practically go together all through high school, which is longer than most people stay married these days? I'll always think of you as one of my very good friends.

Yours,
Heather

A LETTER WRITTEN TO DISCOURAGE *last week's beloved from thinking that he would be welcome this week, or remembered next week. Heather borrowed the paper from a genuine princess (daughter of a genuine pretender) she discovered living down the corridor in her dormitory, from whom she also got the idea that she could do better in college than she did in high school.*

him, and your friends, that they should wait to visit until you settle in, so you will have time for them. Then you tell them you will see them anyway at Thanksgiving, or Christmas. By that time, the natural drifting apart will be clear to all.

Nevertheless, someone will show up, and probably divulge something, or otherwise embarrass you in front of your new friends. The consequences will not be as bad as you fear, because this will also have happened to everyone else at college. But nevertheless, you do have the obligation to be kind and unpatronizing to your old friends in the new setting. Got that, Cookie? (For new names in college, please see *Review*, Chapter 9.)

The Send-off

DEAR MISS MANNERS:

Must a college freshman sit still for an embarrassing send-off from his family?

GENTLE READER:

The embarrassing send-off is a sacred ritual marking the transition from the parental roof to the collegiate one, and should not be neglected. If possible, it should be conducted at the college itself, in front of all the victim's new classmates, but the home version will do if it is sufficiently soppy to make a lasting impression. Miss Manners advises going heavy on the admonitions ("Now you won't forget to . . . take your vitamins, write every day, bundle up warm . . ." etc.) and the bathos ("Imagine—our little bunny a college student. Why it seems only yesterday that . . .")

The point is not only, as children believe, to allow the parents to get a return on their tuition with a good sentimental wallow. It is also to impress the child with the fact that he will never fully be able to separate himself from his background, and that this consists of people who take an uncomfortably eager interest in his welfare. This warns him not to get too reckless with his new independence, but it also serves to bolster him emotionally. The exasperating burden of an affectionate family can be used equally as a point of common commiseration with one's new friends and as a secret source of comfort in difficulties with them.

Classroom Decorum

DEAR MISS MANNERS:

I am a college professor, and what bothers me more than the apathy and laziness of some students is their classroom manners. Particularly, I am referring to those who chew gum in class, those who sit and blow and/or pop the bubbles in front of the teacher, who is trying to lecture and concentrate on getting a message across to those who do care and are in class to learn.

One day, after having had it happen many times, I asked a young lady to please refrain from blowing bubbles and to keep the gum in her mouth. When it happened again, I asked her to please remove herself from the room and deposit the gum in the trash can, or, better yet, to remove it before entering the classroom.

She acted insulted and as if her inalienable rights had been violated. I had not embarrassed her, but had asked her quietly.

Please say something to remind millions of students that this is very rude and annoying to the teacher. The same goes for chewing candy and drinking pop while the professor is trying to keep their undivided attention.

If they find the lectures boring, they needn't bother to come to class. Even sleeping is better than these annoying mannerisms. Perhaps I speak for many other professors.

I've thought about using the tactic that an old high school teacher once used. Those who are caught chewing gum in class will have to buy a package of peanuts for everyone in class. But this would not work, and would be rather childish. Just a gentle reminder from you may cause them to think of the rights of others. At least it's worth a try.

GENTLE READER:

Miss Manners will certainly endorse and help teach the rule that classroom decorum, for students of any age, requires sitting still with the appearance of paying rapt attention and refraining from activities, such as eating, drinking, and gum-chewing, that may distract others. (College students, unlike young pupils, may claim that they can concentrate best with their eyes closed.)

Through the high school level, it should be established that the teacher has the right to impose such restrictions as part of the instructions. On the college level, it should be established that attendance of classes is a privilege that may be haughtily withdrawn by the professor if, like a judge or a sea captain, he finds his not unreasonable standards of behavior violated. That should end the nonsense about inalienable rights. Your student has the alienable right to behave as she wishes after you have thrown her out of class.

Rules for Roommates

Considering the seriousness of the decision of young people to live together, and the consequences it is bound to have, Miss Manners is astonished that choices are made so easily, with little regard to the participants' own deepest beliefs and standards.

She is referring, of course, to college roommates. Much misery can come from ill-assorted couples who have not even the ability to walk out on each other, and Miss Manners, ever interested in promoting harmony so as to put less of a strain on good manners than they must already bear, wishes people—and colleges—would be more careful about whom they take up with.

If only they would settle the chief issues of compatibility beforehand, there would not be such unseemly squabbling. Miss Manners, who tries not to push her way into peaceful households, even if they are not quite to her taste, interferes only when she hears the terrible accusation of rudeness being sounded. It is not rude to keep a disgusting household if those who run it are happy (and do not try

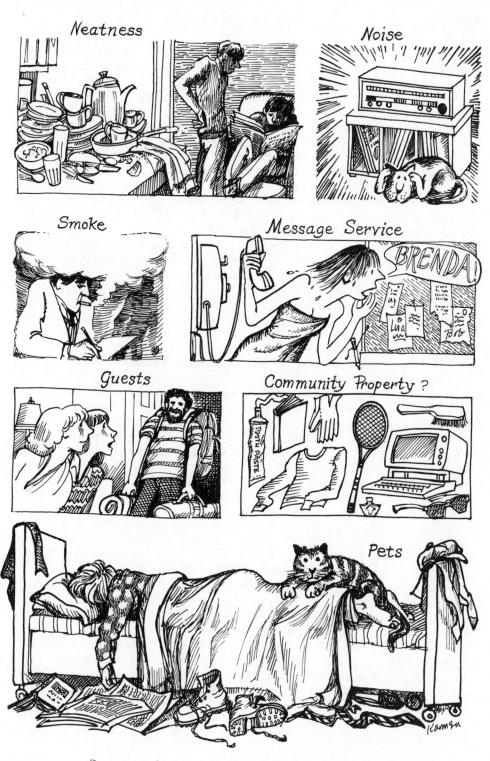

Suggested Areas of Contention in Shared Quarters

to corrupt small children by allowing them to believe that carryout food is properly served from cartons); it is only disgusting. But that is another matter.

The issues that must be settled include:

- Neatness. The general state of things must be agreed upon before the chores for keeping it that way are divided. (If it is to be a sloppy household, who must spread the Sunday paper out so that it covers the floors of two rooms?)
- Noise. One category of this is oddly called, by those who enjoy it, "music." Another is called "How was I to know you'd been up all night and were sleeping late?" What kind, how much, and when must be negotiated.
- Smoke. If, where, and what about the guests?
- Message service. Does this include creative replies such as turning your back on a roommate and telling the caller, "I don't see her"? Does it include breaking the news to no-longer-welcome suitors?
- Guests, especially of the regular, long-term, and intimate variety. In stricter times, when opportunities for such romance were rarer, it was considered to take precedence over mundane desires, such as the wish to spend an evening in one's own room studying. Miss Manners knows some late-blooming gentlemen with racy roommates who lived for four years in college libraries, and only visited their rooms if they had good excuses. Nowadays, the same rule is in effect as under parental roofs: only if you are so discreet that nobody else is made uncomfortable.
- Community property. Whose is what, and what is available to whom, including food and discarded admirers.

If these things are settled beforehand, roommates will at least be able to agree on what they are quarreling about. In case of a fundamental disagreement, Miss Manners decrees that the decision go in favor of whoever is most like her—quiet, nonsmoking, neat, and well behaved. She would not go so far as to say that such a person is less offensive than a noisy, messy one—she herself drove an entire college dormitory crazy once, until her annoying habit of making her bed every morning was sympathetically diagnosed by a psychology major as an unfortunate case of compulsiveness—but virtue should have some rewards.

Roommates are not generally among them.

Dormitory Interruptions

DEAR MISS MANNERS:
    I live in a dormitory and having a lot of friends just goes with the territory. But I do like being warned before people stop by. When my friends, usually male, ask to come over, I tell them to call before they come. Most do, but there are those insistent few who knock at my door unexpectedly. They always seem to come at the wrong time. I either have other company, am sleeping, or just don't feel like being sociable at the time. How can I stop this behavior without being rude?

GENTLE READER:

Put a sign on your door that says "PAPER DUE—Jot down your name, and I'll call you when I come up for air." This is bound to be true—everyone always has a paper due at college—and the request for the name indicates that you don't want friendly faces popping in. If the rebuffed visitor complains of having heard merry voices behind your door, he may be told, "Yes, they came over to talk about work." That, too, is bound to be true. No social encounter of college students, however intended, is complete without work's being mentioned, even if it's only "I shouldn't be here—I have a paper due."

Visits Home

DEAR MISS MANNERS:

When a daughter returns home for term breaks from college (or any other place where she has been mistress of her own abode), is it good manners for her to strew her belongings all over her room and all over the house? This strewing consists of clothing and other components of her daily life. When she is asked to be a better housekeeper for the duration of her visit, there is a certain surliness, even anger, in her response. What to do? I mention mothers and daughters because, in my situation at least, sons have not acted this way and Father seems not to mind this strewing.

GENTLE READER:

Miss Manners is not quite sure what it is, but something in the tone of your letter suggests that you do not expect her to come out on your daughter's side. Indeed, Miss Manners does not favor strewing, as you call it, and believes that the housekeeping standards set by the mistress of a house, and its master, too, if he takes an interest, should be observed by everyone staying there. What she fails to understand here is why you did not enforce these standards when your daughter was too small to fight back. In that case, respect for the maternal turf, if not the habits of a lifetime, should have prevented the current problem from arising.

Miss Manners is aware, however, that the most blameless parents, administering the strictest standards, do not always succeed in passing on their good habits to their children. Even dear Queen Victoria herself was forced to become aware of this unfortunate reality. Presuming, therefore, that you did your best but that your daughter, once out on her own, fell into bad ways, the question becomes whether you can exact temporary reform while she is in your house.

You should certainly try. A reasonable appeal to an adult child would be that if she is willing to respect your territory, you will respect hers—that is, you will refrain from criticizing or cleaning up when you are visiting her, and will even politely attempt to strew your clothes around her territory, if that is pleasing to her. If this does not succeed, you have only the choice left to any hosts about any guests: to decide whether the pleasure of the visit outweighs the annoyances it creates. In this case, Miss Manners imagines you will decide that blood is thicker than the other mess. (For more on adult children visiting home, please see pp. 244–247.)

Social Oblivion

DEAR MISS MANNERS:

Several months ago, I hosted a party. During the course of the evening, one individual had too much to drink and spent a very audible ten minutes in the bathroom paying penance.

This episode halted conversation among my other guests with a rapidity which made my palms damp. When I inquired if I could be of any assistance, another guest was requested, and their departure soon followed.

In the days and months that followed, this person neither apologized nor alluded to this incident and, largely as a result of this, faded from my circle of friends. My feeling at the time was that someone who was unable to handle himself better in a social situation was more a liability than an asset.

My questions are: Was an apology from this guest appropriate? Was I ridiculously stuffy or unreasonable to expect one? Was it, in fact, my obligation to inquire about his condition? Most of all, Miss Manners, I don't want to be a hopeless prig about all of this.

GENTLE READER:

In that case, you must be a little more charitable in your assumptions. As little enthusiasm as Miss Manners has for aligning herself with that person making a mess in your bathroom, she is bound to point out that his was not the only inadvertent social error of the evening.

In these crude days of blurting out everything, so to speak, people have gotten out of the habit of practicing social oblivion. When someone leaves the room at a party, it is the obligation of all to maintain the social fiction that no one is speculating about where he is going or what he is doing. Sitting around in silence listening to someone throw up is not in the best of taste. Only if the person's behavior becomes visibly dramatic may you say, ''I'm afraid you're not well—would you like to lie down? Or may I have someone see you home?''

It would have been gracious of him to apologize later for having been indisposed, but remember that he does not have as clear a recollection as you do of what went on, and is probably hoping against hope that no one actually did notice. If you had wanted to rub it in at the time, you could have called him the next day and said, ''I hope you're feeling better now,'' which would have made him feel terrible.

The polite thing now is to treat it as a minor social accident long since forgotten. If you really want to be gracious, you will invite him again with no reference at all to what happened, which will relieve him considerably. Miss Manners' guess is that he will then behave perfectly. If not, at least you will know that last time was no accident.

Bringing Friends

''Can I bring home a friend from college?'' is a request that used to gladden parents' hearts. It was taken as a sign of the child's pride in the home and desire to bring together the two most important milieux in his life.

That, of course, was when parents knew that the friend would be of the same general gender as the child. "Of course, we're always delighted to see any little friend of yours" is the automatic reaction still of a few parents who have not caught on to the possibilities.

Let us first deal, then, with the obvious issue concerning a friend who turns out to be not quite the sort of playmate the parent had in mind. The rule there is that families do not fight (hopeless) battles on moral issues when guests are present. For the child, that means observing the appearance of respecting the parents' rules of behavior and not brandishing the ugly truth that the parent can no longer control the child's behavior outside the family house, and is therefore weak enough to be challenged inside, as well. Miss Manners does not care if such a conflict is dignified by being called "an assertion of values"; she calls it rudeness. For the parent, Miss Manners recommends a poem by dear Sappho, to the effect of (Miss Manners' Greek is a bit weak today) : If you are squeamish, don't prod the rubble on the beach.

Does everybody understand the practical application of this? It means that we all go to bed where we are supposed to, and if a guest gets lost in a strange house on the way back from the bathroom during the night, the hosts, being officially asleep, remain oblivious.

Now, let us get on to the important rules of entertaining the child's houseguest. The child is the chief host, not a fellow guest, even though he may arrive and depart at the same time and should also write a nice letter afterward. This means that he offers his services in the work of hospitality—shopping, cooking, cleaning up—and supervises the guest's entertainment.

The child has the responsibility of explaining to the guest those of the house rules that affect him ("My parents go to bed early, so let's turn the volume down"), in order to allow the parents to play the role of gracious hosts who would not dream of interferring with their guests' wishes.

Parents do not take official notice of whether or not their child's guest makes his bed. That means that they don't make it themselves, but they don't comment on it either. After the guest has left, however, they may break down far enough to say to their own child, "I certainly hope you make your bed when you visit his house —it makes such a terrible impression on parents when you don't." The child is not allowed to take up the contradiction of how they knew, when a polite host never violates the privacy of the occupied guest room.

The parent is allowed to pump the guest for information on his own child only if it can pass disguised as general conversation. The parent who has had a diplomatic career or been in military intelligence will understand how this is done. "Stephen tells me you know Jessica. We haven't met her yet, but she sounds so enterprising. What kind of a dancing job does she have? Stephen must have told us, but he meets so many nice girls that we sometimes get them mixed up." But the parent is not allowed to let out any information without approval. "Ellen, is Stephen's friend Jessica a friend of yours, too?"

Finally, the parents must usually do most of the work in keeping up the pretense that they, being ultimately in charge, are the guest's real hosts—greeting him, asking if he needs anything, making conversation with him, and seeing him off. They are only barred from issuing invitations to visit again, because they are not really in a position to judge whether the visit was a success—and that is probably just as well.

Being the Guest

DEAR MISS MANNERS:

My boyfriend lives in a distant city. His mother invited me to stay in their home for the weekend, during which my boyfriend's birthday would be celebrated. I accepted.

An older friend thinks that Miss Manners would say that my boyfriend's mother should have discussed the invitation with my mother before extending it to me. Though I think he is a bit old-fashioned, even he is unsure whether Miss Manners would further require that I stay with a female friend of my boyfriend's family, or whether it is permissible for me to stay in the home of my boyfriend. I am a college senior. As a modern woman, I have no wish to be shackled by the outmoded customs of an older generation. But I want to avoid unpleasantness with my father, who thinks my staying in my boyfriend's home is ''chasing him.'' And I do want to do what is socially correct by Miss Manners' sensible standards. Please advise.

GENTLE READER:

Oh, dear. If only you had omitted that dreadful sentence about not wishing to be shackled by the outmoded customs of an older generation. You see—well, Miss Manners does not know quite how to tell you this, as she does not wish to shock you, but you are behaving properly. There is no need to insult tradition, especially when it is on your side.

It was perfectly correct for your friend's mother to invite you; she, of course, assumes that you will discuss the invitation with your mother. (Please don't tell your hostess or Miss Manners if you have not.) With such a chaperon as the boy's mother, you may certainly pay a proper visit. What you are actually doing is visiting an older woman friend who happens to have a son you like. Modern, indeed! The most sheltered Victorian girl would have known enough to put it to her papa that way. ''Chasing'' is when such a lady is unaware that you will be visiting her until you show up on her doorstep.

Far Better Too Formal

''Do you mind if I call you Sophie?''

Well, yes, Mrs. Spurgeon minds very much. In the first place, her given name is Sophronia, and nobody but her sainted parents and the late Mr. Spurgeon ever called her Sophie, and then only in moments of extreme tenderness. In the second place, the questioner is someone one-third her age whom she has just met, and who did not think it necessary to supply a surname of his own, if, indeed, he has one. How can she refuse? The young man has a friendly, interested look on his face when putting the question, and obviously expects a positive answer. At that, she is amazed he bothered to ask—many people have just jumped in and done it.

The young man's intentions are flattering. He wishes to show that he accepts her as an equal, in spite of the age difference, and that he wishes to be on comfortable, informal, sociable terms with her. Galling as she finds such patronizing assumptions, she reminds herself that he truly means well. So she mumbles an assent; and he keeps calling her Sophie, and she tries not to shudder visibly every time he does it.

Now—has this young man succeeded in his kind desire to make this lady feel comfortable with him?

Let us try another approach. The young man shows by flatteringly respectful attention that he is pleased to have the privilege of knowing a lady whom he keeps addressing as Mrs. Spurgeon. As the relationship progresses (we shall say that she is a corporation president who could throw a lot of business his way, or a social leader who could give him entrée to people he wants to know, or a motherly soul who could serve him as a valuable adviser and a comfort, or perhaps just one terrific old sexpot), she one day turns to him, putting a gentle hand on his, and says, "Oh, please call me Sophronia."

Later, in a moment of passion of whatever kind—it could be that the stock she advised him to buy suddenly zoomed, or it could be whatever else you imagine— he takes the third step and says soulfully, "Oh, Sophie!"—just as the dear departed Mr. Spurgeon used to do.

What has happened here is not only that our young man has succeeded, from the beginning, in making the lady feel comfortable with him and disposed toward friendship, but that he himself has had the new experience of enjoying the development of true intimacy.

Instant intimacy, which is what is assumed when people open their acquaintanceships with first names and personal confidences, precludes this development. It is very much in vogue with the young, and Miss Manners thinks they are thus depriving themselves of great pleasures, in addition to offending those who use a different system, in the very act of attempting to ingratiate themselves.

Miss Manners, too, recognizes that they mean well. (Meaning well does not count all that much in the world of etiquette, but it counts some.) She has also watched the evolution of manners long enough to understand that we may go over completely to the newer system and that surnames will drop off vestigially from lack of use.

She rather hopes not. The thrill of progressing to being on a firstname basis, whether it is with a lady or a boss who has finally admitted you to the ranks, or an individual who is both, will be lost. Fortunately this has not yet happened, and the young person who wishes to be courteous to anyone who, through age, rank, or preference, uses the older system would be well advised to take a chance of erring on the side of formality. That way one doesn't run the risk of having someone strike a true blow for her own comfort by drawing herself up to her full dignity and saying, "Oh, please call me Mrs. Spurgeon."

First Names

DEAR MISS MANNERS:

My niece and I are arguing about how to address friends of family:

A former neighbor of hers, a lady schoolteacher, permitted her to call her by her first name when she reached her eighteenth birthday. Now she allows herself to address all the people she gets in contact with by their first names, which embarrasses me. Would you please comment on the argument?

GENTLE READER:

You are going to have a hard time believing this, and Miss Manners has a hard time saying it, but we live in a world where there are people who are insulted by not being called by their first names, right along with people who are insulted by being called by their first names. The former often say it makes them feel old, as if there were anything wrong with that. If you want your niece to be polite in such a chaotic world, you need only encourage her to inquire of older individuals their preferences, and to follow those preferences.

Handling Career Advice

DEAR MISS MANNERS:

What is the correct thing for a young man of college age to say to his grandmother when she continually tells him he must go to law school and become rich, when all he wants to do is devote himself to the arts? The grandmother in question is a strong, opinionated woman of good character and generous ways. The young man is artistically talented and warmhearted, but it is getting to the point where he is seriously considering not talking to his grandmother if she continues in her entreaties.

GENTLE READER:

It is not a good idea to sever relations with a generous grandmother—no, Miss Manners meant to say a well-meaning grandmother whose only intention is to offer guidance for what she considers a successful life. Of course, it isn't necessary, either, to accept such advice. The answer to all questions about plans is ''Well, I hope that whatever I do, you'll be proud of me someday.'' The answer to remarks about becoming rich is ''You may be sure, Grandmamma, that whatever I have, I'll see to it that you are never in want.''

Undergraduate Romance

The Prerequisite Heartbreak

What a marvelous, carefree time college is. There is nothing to do but read and write, all in beautiful and dignified surroundings, in the company of unattached and attractive people of one's own age, interests, and abilities.

It is too bad that such an idyllic existence is confined to the reveries of those who are not matriculated. Not content with this ironic discovery, and recognizing that it is not quite nice to take amusement in finding that youth has its troubles, too, Miss Manners has long puzzled about why clouds of human suffering should hang over such pretty institutions.

It was long ago, as a student herself, that Miss Manners first noticed a pattern to undergraduate romance. Just about every young person, she observed, had a passion for some other young person, who treated the admirer with callous cruelty. In turn each of these victims of love commanded the passions of another person, known as the Creep, who was treated, in turn, disdainfully. Thus, an endless chain of misery was formed.

Why anyone would want to live that way, Miss Manners could not imagine. Why was unrequited love such a powerful force, and why was anyone with a passion for oneself considered contemptible? Miss Manners would have thought that someone's being madly in love with one's own dear self would be a most alluring demonstration of good taste.

And so it is, in the mature. After people have attained full emotional growth, which is unfortunately never for a great proportion of the population, they can actually enjoy being truly loved. When you hear of someone who can't be happy if allowed to become secure about a partner's affections, you know that such a stage has not yet been reached. Miss Manners is always suspicious of the concept of ''being taken for granted,'' used to explain the demise of a romance. It either means that the person subscribes to the heinous idea that it is not necessary to be mannerly to those who are committed to one, or that someone is unable to sustain interest in anyone who does not provide the cheap excitement of uncertainty. To the real grown-up, knowing that one can rely on another person's love is one of the greatest joys of life.

Miss Manners does not expect such wisdom to appear in, say, the first third of life. It is quite reasonable then, she believes, to be interested in finding out, in a variety of ways, how one measures up in the society. Grades and careers are one way of doing this. Another is considered to be the ability to attract someone worth attracting. What makes all that trouble is deciding who is in that category.

In elementary and secondary schools, the children are notoriously incapable of judging one another individually. The whole class agrees that this or that child is the most beautiful, much to the amazement of parents, who notice that this person may be quite homely and a truly good-looking child goes unnoticed. That is because the very young recognize only self-confidence, and render group judgements based on accepting people at their own high or low evaluation.

In the late teens, there tend to be more distinctions based on objective standards or individual preferences. Still, the idea often hangs on that only a person who thinks he or she is too good for you is good enough. Conversely, on the Groucho Marx principle of not wanting to join a club that would accept members like him, there is the feeling that a person who loves you can't be worth loving.

Miss Manners tries hard to sympathize with this state of affairs as a necessary part of social development. She understands that the state of life devoted to ''How am I doing?'' is a necessary prelude to the more interesting (to her, anyway) state of ''What do I want to accomplish?'' She cannot, however, help wanting to alleviate gloom and despair when she sees it. And there is an awful lot of it to be seen in the love lives of young adults.

For one's own relief, she advises examining the state of one's affections in terms of the pattern she has described. Does the loved one have any quality to offer other than that paradoxically compelling one of rejection? Admittedly, this is not an easy cure, but it might help along the development of the maturity that leads to romantic happiness. A sure cure is only promised to those with the nerve to reverse the process and begin acting superior to the one who has been doing it to one. If everyone did that, the entire chain would be flipped.

That piece of advice, which Miss Manners doesn't expect anyone but the most daring to try, uses up Miss Manners' sympathy, and she has none left for the meanness with which people in the same state treat their own admirers. There, a realization of the pattern also helps; it is possible that a perfectly nice person has the misfortune to admire you. Believe that or not, however, it is necessary to be polite to those so afflicted. (It is not necessary to return the affections; the gift of romantic love cannot ever presume to create an obligation in kind.) They may, upon mature reflection, turn out to be not so completely devoid of taste as you had supposed, or to have nice friends.

The History Major's Lament

DEAR MISS MANNERS:

Hey, how ya doin'? I really need your help! You see, I'm a student at the university, and I need to know all about the social graces. This is where you come in.

My problem is my major field of study. You see, most of the people at the university major in business. But I'm not.

Situation: I'm at a serious social function (free beer, but you have to bring your own cup) and I get involved in a conversation with a girl. Almost every time, the girl will ask me what my major is. Well, I signed the Honor Code and I'm not going to lie. So I say, "I'm majoring in history." Without fail, the girl says, "Oh, that's neat. Excuse me for a minute while I go get some more beer." Yes, Miss Manners, you guessed it. The girl never comes back. I usually see her later on with a business or pre-med student.

Why do girls not like history majors? Is there something socially unacceptable about them? If so, should I just respond to that question with something like "I'm undecided, but I'm thinking about business"? Please give me some advice that I can use, Miss Manners. If possible, I want to remain a history major, but socializing is an important part of one's college days.

Also, I don't want to paint a totally one-sided view. Sometimes, a girl will stay past the "I'm a history major" part. But when I ask her what she's majoring in, she's usually into something both anti-Republican and gross, like dental hygiene. Then, I'm the one who says, "That sounds really interesting, but excuse me while I go get some more beer." Is there any hope?

GENTLE READER:

Miss Manners thinks history and dental hygiene both eminently respectable professions, but notices that what they have in common is that, unlike business and medicine, they do not provide the slightest hope of making the practitioner rich. How ya doin'? Please excuse Miss Manners while she goes to get some more mimosa tea.

Dating Rules

DEAR MISS MANNERS:

What are the rules of college dating these days? We brought up our daughter to respect herself, but are uncertain what to tell her about how to behave at college, when she meets young men. When we were dating, which was in the stone age, of course, my husband had to call me by Tuesday if he wanted to go out on Saturday, came to get me even though my campus was a long bus ride away, paid for the movies and food, and took me back to the door. Our daughter hasn't been dating yet, except for school dances, because she goes to an all-girl school, but she is very sweet-looking and will probably have lots of opportunities to go out. She says that nowadays, the girls don't expect to be picked up or even asked out formally, they just gather together somehow, and everybody pays his own way. Of course, we don't know, being older even than most parents in her class, but we don't like the sound of it. If you tell me that is the custom now for nice young people, we will try to accept it.

GENTLE READER:

Let's not accept all modern customs without a struggle, shall we? That wouldn't be any fun.

Indeed, at many colleges there is little formal dating and more of the amorphous activity that you describe. It seems perfectly harmless to Miss Manners, if somewhat less exciting than the form of your courting days. The one-couple, prearranged outing does still exist, but who provides transportation and who pays the bills no longer goes by a single rule. Going Dutch and considering convenience rather than gallantry in making the arrangements is more common than not. Only a belle would have the nerve to demand the traditional services, which are now considered shocking (Miss Manners adores living in an age where it is possible to shock people simply by doing what one's mother told one to do), but which would probably make her popularity legendary. At any rate, when your daughter gets to her college, she can find out what the custom is there, and, if she doesn't like it, negotiate a better deal if she can.

Faculty-Student Liaison

DEAR MISS MANNERS:

I am a graduate student nearing the end of my education at the institution I am presently attending. I have developed a special affection for a particular instructor, which appears to be mutual.

While student-faculty fraternization is common, so is nasty gossip. What are appropriate and uncompromising activities we could share before graduation? May I visit his home? Lunch or dinner in a well-lit place? On campus or off? Movies, plays, museums? Locally, or out of town? I understand the need to keep our behavior in good taste, but I need guidance as to the specifics.

GENTLE READER:

Fraternization is getting to be a popular subject on campus not only for gossip, but for legislation. Do your friend a professional favor, and incidentally add some piquancy to your budding romance, by being extremely discreet while you remain a student.

No school has wanted to prevent students and teachers from intellectual exchanges, even in informal circumstances. It is extracurricular activities that are under suspicion. You might bear in mind that campuses are remarkable places for transmitting news. The more you try to hide, the more likely it is that you will be seen and juicily discussed—and no one will think you are meeting in Bermuda to go over your thesis. But you might go to his house to do so. Just carry a lot of books. Museums and meals—yes, those could be related to your work. Movies and plays are not places to discuss anything. You will be overheard occasionally in any public place, so you might learn to flirt in the jargon of your field, which could be a lot of fun.

Consider this all a challenge. Young people today have few opportunities to discover how thrilling romance could be when the very possibility of it was considered naughty.

Of Porch Lights and Passion

DEAR MISS MANNERS:

I was puzzled what to do about the porch light on the departure of some guests Sunday, and wonder how you would have handled this situation.

My guests included a young woman whom I have known since she was a young child and for whom I have much affection. The occasion, in part, was to effect my first introduction to a young man with whom she is evidently in love, as he is with her.

We had a very pleasant evening, and I approved of and liked the young man. I was touched that from time to time he reached over and squeezed my young friend's hand as an expression of affection, and grateful that evidences of their mutual affection were contained within proper bounds on this occasion.

The two young people came and left in separate cars, as he lives in town and she in the country, not far from my house, with her father. They were the last to leave, and of course I turned on the porch light. As I cleared glasses and emptied ashtrays afterward, I became aware that I had not heard their cars start up and realized they were having some long good-night kisses in my driveway, which was rather well lighted by the porch light.

I felt that turning out the light, while it would give them more privacy, might appear unfriendly or even disapproving, which I was not. Would it have been more or less polite to turn out the light?

GENTLE READER:

Miss Manners is hardly the one ever to say "What does it matter?" but she does have the feeling that your young friends would probably have remained cheerfully oblivious to your electrical activities, whatever they were. By your account, they behaved well in your house and officially departed. They are then out of your jurisdiction, and you can take no official notice of them. That is to say that any peeping must be done from a darkened room, and you are not allowed to tease them later about what you saw.

Miss Manners' instinct would be to leave the light on, presumably as usual, to disguise the fact that you did not go to bed before this late show began. If, however, you believe that the lack of privacy—which does not seem to have bothered them—will attract an audience of neighbors, you might turn the light off.

They are not likely to know whether this is your habit when guests have gone and you have finished cleaning up, and Miss Manners is of the opinion that they are not likely to transfer their emotions of the moment to worrying about that.

Proper Love Letters

DEAR MISS MANNERS:

I am currently engaged in a long-distance relationship. The object of my affection, in fact, resides in Great Britain. I am at a loss as to the proper behavior when the other is an ocean apart.

Even with such technological advances as Concordes and telephones, a letter takes five days to cross the Atlantic, and phone calls can quickly become prohibitively expensive.

Surely this problem has been encountered before: Men have gone off to war or traveled around the world, thereby reducing the love affair to only the written word. What does one do when the other develops writer's block? How can one disagree with the other, when, by the time a letter reaches its destination, the sender may either have forgotten or else be in a seething rage? What are some remedies against pining away over the length of time between visits?

GENTLE READER:

Pining away is exactly what you are supposed to be doing. It is, in fact, the official occupation of separated lovers, and should be mentioned in all letters, even if one has to interrupt one's account of a marvelous all-night party in order to insert it. Make that "especially if." That does not, however, mean that it should be a full-time occupation, except in the case of lovers separated because one is fighting a war or otherwise enduring hardship, while the other is living in more or less normal circumstances. When both are in a temptation-ridden environment, pining away is described in love letters as the bittersweet accompaniment to an otherwise full and cheerful life. "The ball was dazzling and full of fascinating people, but I ached to think how much more I would have enjoyed it with you," for example.

Why? First, because you need some substance in the letters, to set off the mushy parts, and also because if your letters are truly eventful and interesting, your lover may quote them in conversation, thus establishing you as a presence in his life, among those whom he sees more often. Also, unrelieved mush makes you sound like a drip. If your lover has in his mind only one picture of you, and that one melancholy, he will soon forget what you look like.

The second chief reason is that an absent lover should know that the most stalwart of sweethearts does have, within easy reach, the antidote to neglect. That is a very good reason for his not developing writer's block. Each lover must have the sense that the other is leading an interesting life, in spite of the sacrifice both are making, and that it would be well to reward that sacrifice as much as possible.

That is not to say that you threaten the lover with a replacement, even in the relatively subtle manner of describing a likely one without acknowledging your interest. One never admits to the slightest infidelity, even of the spirit. You don't know what comfort the other person has at hand.

You are right that you cannot safely conduct a quarrel by letter. Accusations that would take six minutes to hurl back and forth orally can occupy weeks by mail, and what is more, foolish statements in writing cannot be denied. The way to make a complaint by mail is to be hurt, not angry.

A Clean Break

DEAR MISS MANNERS:

You have addressed the problem of the proper way to break off a relationship from the female's point of view—with her not returning messages and the male being mature enough to get the hint. But would you now address it from the male standpoint? How should a man tactfully break off a relationship without hurting the woman or putting her through the idea that she is being rejected?

This situation can apply to a casual dating relationship, where the man believes things aren't meshing, and she says she is being "dropped." It also applies to an established, serious relationship. What if she doesn't want to let go, and continues to phone and follow the man when he goes out to socialize? It would be helpful to know how to handle this without being harsh or rude.

GENTLE READER:

You have set four standards which you are asking Miss Manners to employ in an explanation of how a gentleman may end a relationship that the lady doesn't wish to end. All of these are commendable, and at least two are impossible.

Miss Manners will agree that you should not be rude, will endeavor to help you avoid being harsh, and will strive to keep you from hurting the lady more than is strictly necessary. Will you then agree to drop entirely the requirement of not giving the lady the idea that she is being rejected? If she doesn't get that idea, after all, the entire exercise will have been futile.

Miss Manners values kindness as much as you do, but the fact is that rejections are sometimes necessary and always painful. She assures you, however, that the prognosis for recovery of a broken heart is extremely good. But as recovery does not begin until the patient acknowledges that the heart is irrevocably broken, the breaker has an obligation to accomplish his work quickly and cleanly.

What constitutes filthy behavior, on the part of the breaker, is to draw out the pain by allowing the patient to believe that the rupture can be bandaged, or that talk therapy will effect a cure. In other words (and we need some other words, before someone demands to see Miss Manners' license for dispensing medical confusion), you must not succumb to discussions about what went wrong, temporary reconciliations, and other such cruelties that the patients demand in the mistaken name of human decency. They are not in a position to know what is best for them.

Miss Manners presumes you have stopped asking the lady for the pleasure of her company. In a casual relationship, it is not necessary to give a reason. In a serious one it is, but the vaguer the reason the better. If you stick with "It just wasn't working out for me" or some such variation of your "not meshing" statement, you can add polite phrases about what a wonderful person you think she is. But if you attempt to give real reasons, you will end up dispensing insults. (Anyway, reasons, one way or the other, have little to do with falling in or out of love. They always come after the fact.)

The next step is the response when the lady persists. This, too, must be firm and unopen to discussion or debate. Every time she calls, you must say that you are too busy to talk; when she follows you socially, you must keep excusing yourself from her company and engage yourself with others.

This may take a while, and Miss Manners hopes you keep the patience to repeat your rejections in conventional phrases and polite tones, until the lady finally gives up. But if she then accuses you of dropping her, for heaven's sake, don't deny it and drag all three of us through this painful routine all over again.

The Chaperon's Jurisdiction

DEAR MISS MANNERS:

Our son, age twenty-five, has been going to school out West and is very serious about a lovely girl of about twenty-one who has never been East. They plan to visit us this summer.

They are not living together. She lives with her parents, whom we have met and who are lovely people. Our son would like to settle in the East and I believe he is trying to sell her on New England.

I will write to the girl's mother, extending an invitation to the daughter to visit. My question is: To what extent am I expected to chaperon their activities?

Obviously, they are both of age and heaven knows what they have been up to prior to this. But I fear that under my auspices, the girl's reputation may be in danger, because I know that the first thing they are going to want to do is take off to Cape Cod for a few days. I would probably not be able to prevent this outing from occurring, but what is her mother going to think of me?

Incidentally, we have no friends on the Cape with whom they could "stay."

GENTLE READER:

Miss Manners is delighted to see again the respectable term "chaperon" and pleased that you understand the concept so well. Chaperons, even in their days of glory, were almost never able to enforce morality; what they did was to force immorality to be discreet. This is no small contribution. When a society abandons its ideals just because most people can't live up to them, behavior gets very ugly indeed.

The simple fact that you are the resident hostess constitutes full chaperonage when the young lady is in your house. It would be unwise and even impolite to attempt to supervise their activities. Such nosiness would imply that you think they are up to—heaven knows what, as we call it.

However, you cannot extend your sanction to their travels unless you go with them. Whatever happens, Miss Manners doubts that the other mother will consider it your doing, but you may clear yourself by writing, "We are so happy that we are to have Kristin here until the 15th. The young people speak of going to the Cape after that." If Mamma doesn't like that, she will at least know where to register her complaint.

Invoking Mother's Manners

DEAR MISS MANNERS:
Is there a polite way to tell a young man his table manners are disgusting, and still retain a relationship?

I am no model of perfection at the dinner table, but recently I accepted a dinner invitation with a very tall, blond, handsome motorcycle racer, and I was revolted. He shoveled the food in, talked with his mouth full, and used his index finger for a knife. My mother would have shot him, and I bet his would have, too.

Otherwise, this is a pretty classy guy. He dresses well, speaks well, is very gentlemanly, but eating with him is downright embarrassing! This seems to be a common problem. A lot of my girlfriends also complain that their guys learned their manners in a trough.

I want to go out with that man again, but not until he takes a few lessons in proper table manners. I think he'll call again. How can I tell him my feelings without destroying his ego?

GENTLE READER:
How can you tell someone he is a pig without making him feel you have criticized him? Ah, another easy question!

You can't, of course. But you can foist the criticism off on an innocent person: "My mother would just adore you, and I'd love to have you meet her. There's just one thing, though. She's terribly finicky about table manners. Can I just warn you about some of the things she's strict about?" You will notice that this depends on your knowing the gentleman fairly well, and on your being confident that he would make an effort to please you. And you have just met. Can you get to know him better on dates that do not involve dinner? If he takes you out for a spin on his motorcycle, surely he will keep his hands on the handlebars and not be able to use them to pick his teeth.

Comments Both Useless and Rude

DEAR MISS MANNERS:
I have a cousin and I must admit that if she weren't a relative, I'd ask her out. Besides being very nice, she's extremely pretty and after seeing her the last six summers in a bikini, I can attest to a spectacular figure. I unfortunately see her quite infrequently, mainly at large family gatherings.

I saw her last weekend, for the first time since last summer, and I'm embarrassed to say I didn't recognize her from across the room at first, which I guess is understandable because, incredibly, she must be about forty pounds heavier than during the summer. I really felt sorry for her because she was wearing jeans and it was very obvious that her abdomen was bulging way out, and her hips and thighs had gotten very heavy and were layered with fat.

I must say that several of my relatives quietly mentioned to me that wasn't it a shame my cousin had gained so much weight.

I've always thought it bad manners to discuss weight, and even worse manners to tell people they should go on a diet. However, in this case, I'm not sure. I will be stopping to see my cousin to drop off a book at my convenience, and I just feel I should tactfully bring up the weight subject. I just think it's a shame that someone as young and attractive as she is suddenly gains so much weight. What is your opinion on what I should do?

GENTLE READER:

Whew. Do you know what Miss Manners thought your problem was going to be after she had read your opening paragraph? There will be a slight pause while she draws her little lace handkerchief across her forehead.

One reason that discussing another person's weight is bad manners is that it is of no practical use. Miss Manners assures you that it is impossible that you and others have noticed your cousin's sudden forty-pound weight gain but that she herself has not and would say, "Oh, for heaven's sake, I didn't realize that. Thank you for letting me know. Why I'll just run upstairs right now and throw away that box of chocolates I was going to use for a midnight snack. You'll see—I'll be back in that little old bikini in no time."

All you would be telling her is that people are noticing how awful they think she looks. How were you going to do it tactfully—by saying, "Gee, you're really rounding out nicely now"? The only possible approach Miss Manners can suggest is to complain of a weight gain of your own and announce that you are going on a special diet, giving her the opportunity to volunteer to join you on it. You could launch this by offering to take her out to a sparse dinner. And then Miss Manners would be stuck with the question she thought she was going to get in the first place.

Commencement and Reunions

Proper Pomp and Circumstance

No matter how much she is enjoying herself, a debutante must always remember to say that she had not wanted any fuss, but is going along with it for the sake of her parents. There is not a word of truth in this, but it sounds good.

What young people generally ignore is that it really is true about college graduations. The graduates are welcome to enjoy the festivities, and many do, but it is the parents for whom these occasions are really held, and it behooves the graduates to go along to humor them. This not only means attending graduation if one was reluctant to do so, but treating it seriously. And, as at debuts, the true pleasure of letting loose with the whoopee afterward is its contrast to the stuffiness of the ceremonial part. Miss Manners considers it a dreadful shame to go through a graduation in an informal, rather slapdash manner. It's not fair to the parents, and it takes the edge off what the graduates are supposed to do after delivering them to their hotels. What is the fun in tossing all decorum aside if there wasn't any decorum to begin with?

The graduate who behaves properly agrees to send invitations or announcements to those relatives his parents think should get them. After that, he may invite friends of his own. (One sends out the school's formal card, with one's own card enclosed—classmates with friends in common may use one invitation with all their cards enclosed.)

The academic gown is a wonderful garment that can hide a multitude of sins, such as blue jeans and T-shirts, and Miss Manners does not speculate about clothes she cannot see. But the outside should not be used as a billboard. Aside from the vulgarity of people wearing bumper stickers, it is disheartening to see four years of education reduced to one slogan, however worthy the sentiment.

One uses one's full name for the occasion, submitting it to be written on the diploma and in the program, and to be pronounced when the individual diploma is given. And, yes, the person who reads the names should be able to pronounce them. We don't care if he uses crib sheets, but mistakes suggest a certain callousness on the part of the administration, not to mention an inability to do research or read.

In recent years, Miss Manners has noticed the spread of social kissing to the graduation platform. This must be stopped. The symbol of welcome into the company of educated men and women is a handshake, not a kissy-poo.

All those making speeches should remember the importance of stuffiness. When the distinguished speakers horse around, call one another by first name, and indulge in kidding, like a bunch of television anchor people, it gives the unfortunate impression that they share television's standards of scholarship. Levity is allowed —heavy jokes, especially ones in Latin—but not silliness.

Student speakers are allowed somewhat more leeway—they may make one or two funny references understood only by their classmates, so that a great buzz of ''What'd he say?'' goes around the audience—but only if they are properly over-earnest in the theses of their speeches.

After the recessional march, where, unlike the processional, waving is allowed and those who have babies may carry them, the graduates must pose patiently for the cameras of all their relatives. They must then walk them around the campus, telling prematurely nostalgic, pointless stories to which no one will pay attention. This is the most crucial part of the ceremony, and cannot be omitted. Any faculty members they encounter are obligated to smile and pretend that they know them, even to the extent of muttering words of praise—about an unknown member of a four-thousand-person graduating class—to the accompanying relatives.

After a full day of this, with the visitors safely tucked away, the graduates are allowed to act their age. By that time, they will have earned that right.

Letters from the Lettered

DEAR MISS MANNERS:

Very shortly I shall be receiving a master's degree. I have earned my degree during the past few years, working part-time, and I would like to let family and friends know that what was begun is now finished.

My problem is just how to announce the accomplishment. I feel it needs to be somewhat formal, because a few years ago my husband received a degree he earned through studies at home. His brother made a comment to the effect that congratulations via cards and gifts were not warranted because it was not the big event his graduation was. Indeed, none came from parents or siblings.

I do not wish to be treated like that. I would like a tasteful recognition for what has been at times a sacrifice for husband and children and a lot of hard work.

GENTLE READER:

How, exactly, do you wish to be treated? Why don't you set the figure and ask Miss Manners to go out like a bill collector and get it for you? Your education is not complete until you learn that you cannot demand a return from others for the work or sacrifices that you undertook. Your brother-in-law's attitude is merely the reverse side of the base coin you trade in by treating an important occasion in your life as a tollbooth for others. The way to let people know that you have received your degree is to write them letters telling them so. Perhaps if you pretend that you do so solely from the pleasure of sharing your satisfaction, you will inspire in others the desire to give pleasure by the tangible means that so appeal to you.

Rules for Reunions

The purpose of attending a college reunion is to demonstrate that you have learned something since you left. What you wish to demonstrate having learned— professional or romantic success or perhaps just competency—depends, of course, on what your classmates thought you least likely to succeed at.

Some of you may not have found time to study for the reunion in the last five, ten, or fifty years, however, and so Miss Manners is going to cram you with some last-minute information. She will include a few facts for those who are not actually at the reunion for credit, but who, as spouses or children of classmates, or as graduating seniors of the institution, are voluntarily or involuntarily auditing the event.

The first principle is that the rules of bragging in polite society apply at college reunions. Anxious as you may be to replace your undergraduate reputation with the improved version you have since devoted yourself to developing, it cannot be done instantly. Information that is pulled out of one is not only more socially acceptable than the kind that is announced or displayed, but is more readily believed.

To show that you are now rich and important, for example, you do not show up flashing expensive things. (The proper dress for the occasion is a refined version of whatever the school's faculty of your age group tends to wear.) You describe yourself as "working for" an organization of which you are the president, for example; you explain the position, when questioned, as "managerial" or "administrative"; and you only admit to the title on the third round. Or you arrange to be harassed by calls from your office requesting decisions during this little holiday, or to look fretted to distraction after checking the financial pages of the local paper.

To seem newly attractive to those who refused to date you in college, it is best to have an accomplice in the person of a tender and solicitous spouse. Recently acquired spouses, especially for those a few decades out, used to be considered particularly good for this purpose. But nowadays, to appear with an original spouse who seems still in love with you is more impressive.

Bringing a date to a college reunion is a big mistake. Perhaps you have forgotten what a dormitory critique is like. If you don't have a spouse, it is better to have passionate telephone calls.

The other chief principle has to do with how to treat others. Warily. You don't know whose fortunes have changed, especially if the others are following Miss Manners' rules, and the class butt may be your boss's hero.

Temptations to confess your old secret estimation of others should be resisted. Sentences beginning with "You probably never knew this, but I thought you were . . ." should not be started. If they inadvertently are begun, they should be finished with ". . . a terrific guy, and I'm delighted to see you looking so well." Miss Manners doesn't know which is worse—confessing an old crush (with the implication that it seems silly now) or confessing an old animosity (with the implication that you now forgive the offensive quality or think the person has outgrown it). You realize, of course, that the worst thing you can do is to re-create your collegiate behavior. But, then, that is the fun of college reunions, isn't it?

A word to those who may be having less fun:

It is the duty of spouse and children to support whatever claims are made or postures taken—and some of them will be strange—and to bathe the reunioner in a glow of love and admiration from those who obviously know him or her now. The spouse, after all, probably has a college too; and the children may want to get into the institution themselves someday.

As for the graduating seniors who may be forced to witness the foolishness of alumni revisiting their old haunts—which may be those seniors' living quarters—restraint is required. Yes, it is irresistibly comic to see middle-aged people pretending to have been the same age once as oneself, but it is wise to resist laughing in their faces. Miss Manners will be glad to tell them why if they will come back and ask in five or ten years.

Postgraduate

Coming of Age

Maturity Test

Having long fought the idea that etiquette is the refuge of the fainthearted—a sort of wishy-washy code of honor for those too timid to look after their own interests—Miss Manners must now point out one area in which heavy doses of the virtue of tolerance are required. That is in the ability of the grown-up child to recognize and nevertheless forgive past transgressions on the part of his relatives.

Psychotherapy has made the blaming of parents into a national sport. The sweetness of knowing that one is not responsible for one's own problems is offset, however, it would seem to Miss Manners, by the drudgery of sour reminiscing. How much pleasanter it would be, not to mention more gracious, to forgive and get on with one's life.

Miss Manners was once privy to a not entirely lighthearted conversation between two elderly sisters, in which one gave a complete airing to her grievances. These at first seemed reasonable, if not unusual, being along the lines of you-always-knew-that-if-you-cried-Mamma-would-take-your-side. Miss Manners' sympathies for the self-declared victim were just getting fired up when they were abruptly interrupted by the perpetrator of these crimes, who said gently, "Yes, it's true. I was a brat. But that was sixty years ago." Just as abruptly, Miss Manners changed sides.

Rule one, then, is that there is a statute of limitations in family complaints, and that hoary grudges are not permitted. If Miss Manners did not believe in the possibility of improvement upon human nature, she would long ago have been driven to despair and probably have taken an overdose of bonbons. Whatever the hardships of one's childhood might have been, dwelling on them later can only make adulthood a hardship as well.

Rule two, or perhaps it should be one, has to do with reevaluating the past in terms of the additional knowledge one has as an adult about the complications and conflicts of life. Given the circumstances of your parents, would you perhaps have done, or at least sympathized with, the things that you now condemn? Hindsight arrogance is a characteristic of the uneducated. Anyone with the least knowledge of history must pick up enough perspective to understand how different circumstances produce different ideas of what is best.

Miss Manners always assumes, unless it is proven otherwise, that people, and especially parents, do try to do their best. Monsters there may be, but they are very few. Miss Manners always advises young novelists and actors to put themselves into the consciousness of all villainous characters; if no self-justification can be produced, then you have a most unlifelike character there. It is an exercise in the use of the mind, as well as in kindness, for the child to consider what his parents' problems and motivations might have been, before censuring their behavior.

The ability, in fact, to enter into another person's point of view is a requirement of true maturity. Teaching a child to do so should be one of the chief objects of child-rearing. If you heard, throughout your childhood, a chorus of ''How would you like it if someone did that to you?'' and ''Consider how that makes Aunt Barbara feel'' and ''See? You don't like it when it happens to you, do you?'' then you were being taught that concept.

Not only one's manners benefit from this skill. If you want to manipulate another person's behavior, whether it is to make him want to give you a raise, to inspire him to fall madly in love with you, or to change his will on your behalf, putting yourself in his place and then acting upon empathetic knowledge of what he would like is essential.

As you can use this for fulfilling your selfish desires, it seems only fair to use it as well for spreading happiness. ''I understand how you feel,'' convincingly spoken, is one of the most soothing declarations one person can make to another. From child to parent or sibling, offered retrospectively, it is a major kindness.

''You know, I never realized, when I was little, how much the financial problems you never mentioned to me must have burdened you when I thought you just weren't paying enough attention to me.'' ''It couldn't have been easy, bringing up children alone; whatever faults I may have accused you of, you did an amazing job.'' ''What a trial I must have been as a kid—it's a wonder you didn't just smother me in my crib.'' ''You know, we had our differences when we were little, but I finally learned to appreciate you.''

This kind of statement is hard to choke out when one is filled with a sense of ancient injustice. But until one can manage something of the kind, even if it is only the acknowledgment that one still doesn't like one's parent or sibling—accompanied by the decision to be gracious to him now nevertheless—one cannot consider that childhood and childishness have been left behind.

Post-Kindergarten Society

Kindergarten is an excellent institution, in its way, and Miss Manners can think of few better solutions to such problems as keeping five-year-olds off the streets and producing handmade pot holders. But she does not see why she, having reached what we shall call a certain age, must continue to be subjected to its rules and practices in what ought to be a larger, if not more sophisticated, society.

In kindergarten, nobody has a last name, and few even have full use of their given names. Everyone has a simple nickname, and must always be telling everyone else what it is. We make quite a point, then, of addressing them correctly, and of helping others to do the same to us, as in "Hi, I'm Cindy." Naturally, nobody has titles—even many of the teachers have ceased to be "Miss Twinkles" and become "Hi, I'm Pam."

In kindergarten, we all wear simple, durable play clothes that are practical, mostly in bright colors, and sporty. We dress up only as a big joke. And those of us learning to read like to have signs across the fronts of our shirts and our possessions marked with their names—lunch bags that say LUNCH BAG, and so on.

In kindergarten, we are not expected to go very long without juice and cookies, and so we can eat at our desks and wherever we wander, and we always have simple snacks available for breaks. We prefer to drink from heavy mugs marked with our names or pictures of our favorite cartoon characters.

In kindergarten, we have Show and Tell, in which we are assured that nothing is too trivial or too personal to command the attention of all, who must treat any revelation, no matter how pointless, with rapt attention. We are assured that if we blurt out everything that is on our minds, we will feel better.

We may also have general conversation in kindergarten, but it should be about things that everyone understands, such as sports or television programs or how we feel about our food.

In kindergarten, exercise is very important, and anyone who does not want to play is cajoled into doing so.

In kindergarten, creativity is important, and so we praise and accept anybody's efforts and consider them all equally worthy.

In kindergarten, we must all learn to work together and to share in the rewards, and anybody who wants to go off alone or who piles up more than his or her share must be gently led back to the group to let everyone else participate and catch up.

Most of all, we must learn, in kindergarten, to like and accept everyone else. Not only do we not want loners here, but we want to show everyone that if you make an effort, you can like anyone at all, and all of them more or less equally. We assume that dislikes are only a matter of prejudices and misunderstandings, and that any people if placed together in pleasant circumstances can get along as well as any other people.

In kindergarten, if we discover anyone who simply cannot learn and flourish within these standards, we suggest a little outside help, because we know it must be a sign of emotional problems.

Miss Manners does not quarrel with any of these rules, under which kindergartens have flourished for some time now. She only pleads that, having put in her time, she be promoted into a society where formality, distinctions, subtleties, individuality, standards, and eccentricities are permitted.

Empty Nesting

It seems so callous of children to grow up and leave the family home without family problems. For those parents who fail to amuse themselves with such modern devices as midlife crises, law school, or breaking up quarter-of-a-century marriages, we have therefore invented a new problem. It is called "empty nesting."

Miss Manners is not without tremendous sympathy for those so afflicted. She is resolutely in favor of adding generations onto families, rather than spinning off individuals—provided, of course, this takes place in enormous houses with porches, and that she is the eldest and gets to boss everyone else around. But as young people seem to be on to this scheme, and as the suitable houses have mostly been made into condominiums, there are quite a few empty nests in the forest.

Much of the literature on the subject takes the optimistic approach of focusing on the gains—bathrooms, closet space, the chance to get a word in edgewise at mealtime, and so on. The tone is that of articles addressed to young working women assuring them that a dateless Saturday night is a fortunate opportunity for self-improvement. Miss Manners rather doubts that any of this fools anyone. To those used to heading a complicated household, the prospect of a simpler one, however filled with opportunity, is disconcerting.

Miss Manners cannot tell your adult children to stay home. She can, however, and will tell everyone how to behave in regard to that home, after they go. Is that a comfort?

It is certainly emotionally consoling, to both parent and child, to consider that the parental household is, in many ways, a home permanently available to those who have been nurtured in it. "This will always be your home; it is here whenever you need or want to come here" is the traditional speech, so grating to whatever family the child has acquired on his own.

The exceptions occur first to the people who still use the place as a house, not to the departed ones, who can afford to be more sentimental. No child can really understand and forgive the selfishness that prompts his parents to dismantle a shrine to his high school years, to be visited by the former owner faithfully at least once a year, simply to turn it into a study or guest room for their own convenience. However, since the children don't care to decorate their sophisticated new homes that way, they therefore swallow their indignation if their old rooms are cleaned out. The parental offer of hospitality is not considered violated unless there is no place at all for a returning child to stay. There need not be a place for yearbooks, old volleyballs, and dried prom flowers. If there is family attic space available, the parents can try to live up to the child's expectations of devotion by pretending to be unable to part with any of his primary-school arithmetic workbooks, but many perfectly adoring parents are content with one graduation photograph and one crayoned drawing per grown-up child. "Come and get all this junk if you want it, otherwise I'm throwing it out" is a perfectly proper remark for a loving parent to make to a child who lives elsewhere. Time limits are even advisable.

Whatever the adjustment in quarters, it will serve to make the point that the child is, if not a guest in his parents' house, not a resident, either. The more guestlike courtesies the child performs, the greater his welcome.

Having told children since they were small that no, they are not equal to their parents and not entitled to say "If you do it, why can't I?" Miss Manners finds it difficult to get them into the habit of treating their parents as they would wish to be treated. A grown-up child who would be outraged to have his parents descend upon him without notice, refusing him the dignity of privacy or control over his own schedule, nevertheless fails to consider that his parents might occasionally make plans that would be disrupted by unannounced visits.

Only when one scrupulously asks if it would be convenient to drop in, for an hour to pore through the attic, a week to save money between apartments, or a month to recover from a bad romance, is one told, "Darling, you don't have to ask. This is your home, and it will always be. Come whenever you want; the door is always open."

Miss Manners highly approves of this statement—but not of those who take it literally.

Grown-up Children at Home

Through no fault of their own, more families seem to be together these days. College students have less money with which to practice the traditional summer pastime of hanging around away from home, doing nothing. People on their first jobs have less with which to establish sovereign (no regular laundry days) domiciles. For such reasons, not to mention those of affection, great hulks of children who might otherwise have vacated the premises so fast that the wind would have knocked their parents over, are staying in, or returning to, their original homes.

Actually, why isn't affection being mentioned? Why doesn't the grown-up child say "This is the happiest place I know," rather than "I'm broke," when explaining his presence? Didn't anyone ever teach him manners? No wonder he's broke.

Even if manners have always prevailed in the household, certain adjustments are required when the little ones become bigger than the big ones. Miss Manners is far from suggesting that etiquette is based on deference to power, although it does make some logical sense and is not unknown in the branch of the field called diplomacy. Socially, however, chivalry introduced the quixotic concept of the strong yielding to the weak.

Now we have something of a mixture of the two. In family terms, that means that children yield to their parents because the parents are financially and otherwise stronger than they, until they are able to yield to the parents because the parents are more fragile than they. Both are called "respect." We are talking here about deference of manner. Any child with spunk will long since have learned how to toddle respectfully around parental authority.

As the nature of the authority changes, so do the daily rules of etiquette to be practiced by both parent and child. The parent has much the harder task, in that he or she must scrupulously maintain the fiction that the child is now a responsible human being. The child's job is to trade one sort of accountability for another. In return for freedom from being continually brought up, he must portray himself convincingly as one who has been properly brought up.

The polite and independent person always wishes to do his share. Miss Manners is not prepared to make general rules about financial contributions by grown-up children (except to say that the proper term is "contributing" or "helping out," not paying rent), but contributions of work to the upkeep of the household are obligatory. Anybody who expects to be waited on should also expect to be scolded.

Mutual respect is to be shown in use of common items, such as cars or television sets—adult children are expected to take into consideration the preferences of those with whom they live.

Information about general plans ("I'll be quite late tonight—don't expect me for breakfast") should be volunteered, so that rigorous questioning becomes unjustified. Of course, all guests are cleared in advance with other members of the household. The object, in sum, is to show that the child in need of guidance has been replaced—by someone his parents no longer recognize.

Going Home Again

DEAR MISS MANNERS:

I would dearly like to know what etiquette applies to the occasions when family members who now live apart come to stay with one another. My youngest son, now seventeen, brought this up at dinner last night, observing that one older sibling and wife rushed him all over San Francisco from treat to treat, without asking whether he wanted to go or not, while another sibling's husband immediately set him to work digging up a sidewalk. (This is perfectly true.) He said he did not really object to either, but would like to know what his proper role should be: guest or low man still in the pecking order.

When children come home for more than a day (with spouses and sometimes grandchildren), who does what work? Are they back to making their own bed and doing their own washing? Do they automatically help, offer to help, or not help with the meals? If they are guests, and Granny can't quite cope with all this since she can't run as fast as she used to, can Granny conscript the grandchildren? Some guidelines would be much appreciated.

GENTLE READER:

There are two systems of behavior suitable for former members of the same household when they visit one another. (Miss Manners is not counting formerly married couples who still visit. Good for them, but she would prefer not to be asked over at the same time.)

System one is that those who formerly lived in the household they are visiting, and who can therefore be presumed to know the routine and where the soap is, do as much as they can without interfering with present plans. They certainly are back to bed-making, washing, and doing auxiliary kitchen chores. What's more, they are in charge of directing their spouses and children toward helpful behavior. This does not apply to siblings visiting one another's adult households or parents visiting their children's, as the visitors have never resided in these houses. They go on guest behavior—bed-making, cleaning up their own messes, and offering to help elsewhere, but accepting no for an answer. The hosts are also, then, on these rules, which means that it is all right to ask if the guest would like to go dancing or strip the wallpaper, but peremptory assignments of either are not made.

System two is generational. It means that a visitor of a younger generation pitches in, but one of the same or an older generation than the hosts asks first about tasks other than cleaning up after himself.

You may choose either system with equal propriety, as the results are identical.

Avoiding Kissing Kin

DEAR MISS MANNERS:

How can I evade being kissed by an elderly woman whom duty requires that I visit frequently?

I am not really the kissing sort, and everything I have tried—quickly engaging her in conversation or handing her something I have brought for her—fails. It's always a kiss on the cheek upon arrival and departure. I don't want to hurt her feelings, yet I detest being kissed by her. Miss Manners, I would be ever so grateful if you could solve this dilemma for me!

GENTLE READER:

How bad can a kiss on the cheek from an elderly lady be? Never mind, Miss Manners does not really want to know. Her business is only to answer your questions. At the beginning of your friendship, presuming that you were then old enough to defend yourself, you could have stuck out a hand for a handshake that would have punched her in the stomach had she tried to get closer. Now, however, it is too late for that. The only remaining subterfuge that presents itself to Miss Manners is for you to put both hands in front of you when next you meet and scream out "Don't kiss me! I think I'm coming down with something, and I don't want to give it to you." Perhaps if you do this every time you meet, she will get out of the habit of kissing you.

The price will probably be having to discuss your health, what you are doing wrong in your life to bring illness upon you (punitive medicine being a popular concept in this country), and possible remedies. If her kisses are really that bad, the trade will surely be worthwhile.

Too Personal Inquiries

DEAR MISS MANNERS:

I am a twenty-nine-year-old single woman. I have a career and a full life. I have not, however, yet found a suitable mate. In general, I am quite happy, but at times my lack of an intimate relationship can be terribly lonely and frustrating. I do get tired of coming home to an empty house.

But these are very personal and private feelings which I keep to myself. I try to go cheerfully along, and only rarely burden my best friend with my inner torments.

However, nearly all my attached friends, relatives, and even acquaintances regularly inquire how my love life is. I have been alone for several years, and the constant questions and comments about my lack of a boyfriend are becoming painful. These people mean well; the tone often leans toward actual pity.

But I don't presume to inquire how their marriage is working out, or if a child or a divorce is in their future plans.

I find their questions rude. Don't they know that if an engagement occurs, I will announce it? Really! These questions have been coming from friends, friends of friends, parents of friends, aunts, great-aunts, and grandmothers. Please, Miss Manners, what is the most polite solution to these tiresome remarks?

GENTLE READER:

Meaning well doesn't cut much ice with Miss Manners when people are that thoughtlessly rude. Inquiries into the state of your private life would be out of bounds even if you were conducting a raging romance; that it is also inconsiderate of your feelings, because you are not, is merely salt on the wound.

You have anticipated Miss Manners' answers: first, that the most effective reply would be ''Planning a divorce yet?''; second, that she will not permit you to say this; and third, that they must be reminded that the lack of a public announcement can safely be interpreted to mean that there is nothing the public—which includes your grandmother and those others, when courtship is concerned—needs to know.

Practice saying, ''I have nothing to announce—when I do, you may be sure you will be the first to hear it.'' To elderly relatives, you say this with an affectionate pat on the arm; to remote acquaintances, with a cool smile. Should anyone persist by asking, ''Does that mean something is in the works?'' you must merely produce a cooler, forced smile (serious expression except for curled lips) and repeat, ''It means that I have nothing public to announce.''

Grown-up Dress

In Monetary Terms

Full of sympathy when distraught people complain to her of the immense difficulty of introducing friends to one another because it requires the trick of remembering their names, Miss Manners is turning suspicious. Some of the same people go around demanding to be introduced to their friends' clothing.

"Is that a Perry Ellis blouse? Your skirt looks like Ralph Lauren; is it? What's the jacket?"

Miss Manners is appalled. Time was when one did not even introduce friends unless one was sure in advance that the introduction would be agreeable to them. She is quite sure that she doesn't want to meet anybody else's clothes, and she certainly doesn't want to launch her own on independent social careers.

A lady's clothing is presumed to be hers. It ceases to be the manufacturer's—Miss Manners was going to say when she has paid for it, but with the popularity of credit cards, she had better say once the lady walks out the shop door with it, provided no plastic tags set off alarms. It is not quite nice for the lady to remember too clearly who made her clothes, where she bought them, or how much she paid. These facts are not considered polite conversation, any more than are the provenance, subsequent history, and cost of the food being consumed at the dinner table, or of the real estate serving as the site for the dinner.

One hardly hears anything else these days, as Miss Manners is only too wearily aware. Her objection is not that everyone is interested in money—if one finds oneself among people who claim not to be, one should always keep one's hand lightly resting on one's wallet—but that no one seems to know how to discuss it properly. Well-behaved people do not discuss what they paid for their shoes; they talk about the state of the economy. They use the price of their shoes as an example of how expensive shoddy workmanship is these days, or what imports are doing to the American market—or something. If they feel called upon to explain why, then, they have invested so much more than is necessary to be decently shod, in order to display shoes with bits of old stable hardware caught in them, the reason would be that they have a hard time finding comfortable shoes, or that the old ones had worn out and these were in the nearest shop. Wearing things out is, of course, an aristocratic tradition, the maxim being "Buy something good that will last." The other adage is "Don't embarrass people with your wealth—let them pay for everything."

Miss Manners is not saying that she approves of this. But the underlying attitudes about money for which these ideas are clumsily striving are proper ones, though directly contradictory. The first is that nice people always worry about money only on behalf of those less fortunate than themselves, even if it means bravely saying that something will turn up in the job market, and they are only glad that they have marketable skills and are concerned about those who don't. The second is that nice people never act as if the price of even small things—especially small things—doesn't matter to them, much less as if they gloried in spending unnecessary money. Without discussing amounts, they must nevertheless not seem to reject the general notion that everyone is grateful for a bargain.

Taken together, these do not, Miss Manners admits, make much sense. But it is still more sensible than going around talking to pieces of clothing.

A Lady's Hair

DEAR MISS MANNERS:

I have very straight dark-brown hair which falls two-thirds of the way to my waist.

My husband adores it long, and I enjoy it, too, but I wonder just how much longer I can wear it this way and not look like I'm imitating a teenager. I've tried various ways to pull it back and up, but am not very talented at it. My experience with hairdressers has always been that they want to cut long hair, not style it. Also, my hair doesn't hold waves or curls.

Most people say I look younger, and I consider myself attractive but not a ravishing beauty. My husband and I have a black-tie affair coming up and I'm in a quandary as to how to wear my hair.

GENTLE READER:

One could make a case for its being none of Miss Manners' business how you wear your hair, as long as you behave properly. One could, but Miss Manners won't. She considers the voluntary aspects of one's appearance a visual expression of manners. If your husband were to wear jeans when black tie was specified, for example, it would obviously be a provocative violation of etiquette. So she is flattered that you consulted her on this matter.

Fashion has retained the essence of the old-fashioned custom of a lady's putting up her hair on reaching maturity (a state happily anticipated, as so it should be), by frequently assuring women that short hair is more flattering and more appropriate than long to anyone over twenty-five. Actually, long hair put up achieves the same effect, only (in the opinion of such romantics as your husband and Miss Manners) better. As you will learn from looking at nineteenth-century fashion plates or paintings, the basic ''bun'' can be adapted to any type of hair or face, and a slightly slipshod look is considered part of the charm. It is as appropriate for daytime as for evening, when fancy combs or flowers may be added. Besides, when your husband begins to look forward to watching the ritual of your slowly taking down your hair at night, for his eyes alone, daytime fashions will seem less important to you both.

Summer Dress for Ladies' Legs

DEAR MISS MANNERS:

I am curious as to the rules of summer dress. I have good, well-tanned legs, and in hot weather I prefer not to wear hosiery. After I attended a wedding last year without hose (I was wearing sandals), my mother gave me a lecture as though I were a small child. I cannot understand why, as I keep my legs clean and neat, I was comfortable, and those of us who were not wearing nylons were much more congenial than those who were sweltering in them. I also find it hard to believe that with the wedding itself going on, anyone paid that much attention to my feet.

I have just returned from college, and my mother again has objected to my wardrobe's orientation to bare legs. What should I do?

GENTLE READER:

The rule about summer dress for ladies' legs is that you may go without stockings if you don't get caught. While you are correct in saying that the chances of your being noticed at a wedding were small, the fact remains that you did get caught, didn't you?

Miss Manners is, in principle, opposed to increasing informality of dress and quite impervious to arguments about comfort. Nevertheless, even she has noticed how hot it can get. She is prepared to offer you a deal. If you will wear stockings to formal occasions, she will persuade your mother not to inspect your feet every time you leave the house. The only formal summer occasions are weddings and funerals. The Fourth of July is definitely informal, and dances don't count because neither your mother nor Miss Manners can tell what you are wearing under a long dress.

The Unpainted Lady

DEAR MISS MANNERS:

I am a young professional woman who wears no makeup, because it's not my style and I think it's yucky (as do most of my friends, particularly men). My mother suggests, and I tend to agree, that I should wear makeup for my upcoming role as bridesmaid.

Am I right to feel so obligated? Are there professional or social circumstances under which a woman really ought to wear makeup, and why? Does one wear it because it is part of a uniform, or because one is to spare spectators the sight of pale lips, short lashes, and blemished skin?

GENTLE READER:

Like the gentle reader who wondered timidly if it would be wrong to add a few personal words to a purchased greeting card, you have left Miss Manners shaking her head and muttering about what the world has come to. She has long acknowledged that the rule about no nice lady's painting is defunct, but not that it has been reversed, so that a lady must paint. No, you need not wear makeup. If anybody questions you on this, just tell them that you went to a lot of trouble and expense to achieve the latest "natural look," and are pleased to hear that you have succeeded.

Old-fashioned Immodesty

DEAR MISS MANNERS:

Having watched a delightful old movie with Loretta Young and Ronald Colman, we were stumped by the young people asking why Miss Young wore almost-shoulder-length white gloves when in evening dress. Those of my age saw nothing odd in it, but the young people were truly curious as to the reason for such attire. Certainly it was not for modesty, for the dresses worn were extremely low-cut.

We do not mean to imply that your age is such that you would have worn such gloves, but think that you probably will know the reason, if anyone does.

GENTLE READER:

Miss Manners is hurt that you think she would not have worn such gloves. You never know when you will insult people, do you?

The reason for the gloves is immodesty, a principle that young people, brought up to run about half-naked, do not understand. The idea is, the lower the dress, the higher the gloves. Miss Young very properly did not want to put on an extremely low-cut dress only to have people stare at her bare elbows.

Adult Romance

(More Things Mother Never Mentioned)

Shocking Assumptions

It has been such a long time since Miss Manners has enjoyed the thrill of being shocked. It saddens her to think that there are young people coming along who have never experienced that delicious little chill produced by the discovery that the sins of others are even beyond what one has naturally and uncharitably attributed to them. The time was when almost any subject would do. Rising prices were a traditional favorite ("So flimsily made—and you won't believe what they're asking for it!"), as were changing fashions ("Can you believe that anyone would actually be seen on the street in such a thing!"). The element of disbelief, or at least feigned disbelief, was essential. That is why it is virtually impossible to be shocked these days. The answer to both sample statements is now a bored "Sure, I believe it."

Nevertheless, Miss Manners has decided to be good and shocked once more, if only for old times' sake. She has chosen the topic of sex, because it was always the one that worked the best. You young ones can have no idea of the shocked satisfaction millions of people used to derive from the simple exercise of counting off the normal human gestation period from the dates of their friends' weddings. (Aha—Miss Manners shocked you there, didn't she, you sweet, nonjudgmental thing you; you can't believe that civilized people would ever do this, can you?)

253

It is true that the element of disbelief is now missing from this calculation and, indeed, from any statement about the juxtaposition of human bodies. Miss Manners finds those who still try to evoke some shock on these matters—she still gets the occasional indignant letter demanding to know if Miss So-and-So, recent history enclosed, is "entitled" to wear white at her wedding—unbearably tiresome.

Miss Manners has elected to be shocked by the prevailing standards, rather than by the violations of previous standards. In other words, it is not the change in what people do that shocks her—behavior has changed a great deal less than the naive suppose—but the change in what they think they ought to do. Respectable young people of both sexes have been led to believe that such patterns of behavior as picking up strangers in bars or other public places and consummating a new acquaintanceship on the first date are *de rigueur*. Miss Manners often hears from those who wish to deviate from those standards without being rude—plaintive little requests of "How can I politely tell a strange man to go away?" or "How can I not spend the night with a girl I've taken to dinner, without hurting her feelings?"

Miss Manners does not deny that there always has been naughtiness and sudden passion in the lives of some highly respectable people. How insufferable they would be if there weren't. And she hopes that when the erotic lightning bolt strikes, they will find her a sympathetic and indulgent confidante. It is something quite different to maintain that the forms of behavior to which the inflamed emotions may lead should be set forth as models for normal social life. Miss Manners finds the idea that this has happened, to the extent of intimidating dissenters into apologizing for maintaining their standards of decorum, reprehensible.

In fact, she is deeply, deeply shocked by it.

Avoiding the Solicitations of Strangers

DEAR MISS MANNERS:

I am a student in my early twenties and I have to study a great deal. To do this, I must spend a lot of time alone, either in libraries, cafés, or other odd spots. Unfortunately, while I always begin alone, it is very difficult to stay that way.

"Gentlemen" whom I do not know, and have no wish to know, keep trying to make my acquaintance. It isn't as if I were in a bar, or even giving the slightest bit of encouragement. I certainly do not dress provocatively or make eye contact. I have even stopped smiling at people!

Yet some of these "gentlemen" persist in making nuisances of themselves. How should I deal with them, Miss Manners? I want to be polite, but I also want to be effective. Please don't tell me to change my study place: I have already done so several times, yet it keeps on happening. Besides, this occurs when I'm not studying, too.

GENTLE READER:

You see? This is exactly why Miss Manners opposed, from the beginning, the relaxation of society's rules about accosting strangers, and the increasing acceptance of the pickup for people of moderate respectability. She has heard nothing to convince her that the advantages to lonely people outweigh the dangers of such molestation as you describe, and a lot worse.

You will be happy to learn that Miss Manners has never endorsed the idea that it is proper for a gentleman to make overtures to a lady to whom he has not been introduced. You are at liberty to make individual exceptions, if you wish, and those who enjoy it can do it all the time to their hearts' content as far as Miss Manners is concerned, but you are also free to treat it as an outrage. The idea of needing to be polite to strange men soliciting one's attention is preposterous. Please stop making excuses about your choice of public places or of clothing. Miss Manners refuses to concede that going anywhere short of a brothel, or wearing anything except a T-shirt extending a general invitation to the public, robs you of your right to be treated as a respectable lady who does not pick her acquaintances from the street.

A man who makes any personal remark or suggestion to you should be given a cold stare, followed by a cold shoulder. If this does not discourage him, say "I beg your pardon!" (an expression whose only true use is such an occasion) in a voice loud enough to attract the attention of others, who will be able to see, from your expression, that you are being annoyed. If that does not work, you must inform him that if he does not leave you alone, you will invoke the aid of the nearest person of authority—the librarian, a policeman.

That, my dear, is the way people in polite society deal with such "gentlemen."

When a Lady Pays

DEAR MISS MANNERS:

My upbringing and social experience have taught me that when asked to dinner by a young man, the responsibility for paying the check is solely his.

I encountered a situation quite to the contrary when a casual acquaintance invited me to dine and requested that I please bring along two friends to serve as dates for two of his chums. Being the free spirits we are, my friends and I accepted the invitation (may I add, these gentlemen were a few years older than our twenty years).

When the inevitable check arrived after the meal, the boys willingly took out their credit cards. My date remarked that when boys pay for girls, they deserve something sexual in return. I was appalled by his lack of taste, and told him my friends and I would not be dessert!

Our dates paid, and we all went our separate ways. The next morning, I received a phone call from the young man, who reprimanded me for not offering to pay. Nevertheless, his remarks were as tasteless as his after-dinner comment. Were we wrong?

GENTLE READER:

Yes, indeed. The question of who pays the check is somewhat up for grabs these days, but the tradition of how to react to insult remains the same, and you have violated it.

Suggesting that a lady barters her favors for meals, or anything else, is, and always will be, an extreme insult. The proper way for you and your friends to react to such provocation was to fling down a sum of money covering the cost of your meals. One never accepts hospitality from people who insult one. The question of sharing checks is by no means as clear. Under many circumstances, it is now proper for a lady to pay her share or even the entire check. But even without the insult, no lady would have argued against doing so when it was clearly expected.

Social Freedom

DEAR MISS MANNERS:

I thought you could enlighten me as to how to react (or how I should have reacted) to a situation that happened last night.

I went to a party with a man I'd met a couple of weeks ago. I was upstairs, talking to some people, and he was downstairs. After a while, I went downstairs to see how he was doing, and I walked in just to see him taking down a woman's phone number and telling her he was off on Mondays and Tuesdays. I stood there for a moment, not knowing what to do, and then went back upstairs. But they both knew I saw and heard what had transacted.

What I felt like doing was making a scene, grabbing the phone number, tearing it up, and telling her and him to drop dead. But I played cool. When he came back upstairs, I held back nasty comments and went on to have a pleasant night. I like him a lot and was looking forward to getting to know him. But I found what he did very nervy, and it changed how I feel about him.

So my question is, how should I have reacted to catching him taking her phone number? And when I hear from him next, should I bring up the subject and state my displeasure? What do you think of a man who would do that? I would like to see him again, but if he does that kind of thing a lot, then I won't bother. I would like to let him know how I felt about him doing that when he was my date, but I guess I want to say it in a way to avoid future uncomfortable situations, and not chase him away at the same time.

GENTLE READER:

Miss Manners is happy to tell you that you acted correctly. Tearing up the telephone number and telling the young man to drop dead probably would not have led to the goal you state of getting to know him better.

Technically, he did not commit a crime, but was the victim of an accident. The bond of datehood doesn't prohibit a person from initiating a new relationship during the course of a bespoken evening. ("Go out with him anyway; you'll meet his friends," as Miss Manners' dear mother used to say.) The faux pas is courting one lady in front of another, but he did not intend to do that. Had you known that he instead telephoned the host the next day to inquire who that devastating woman was, you would not, Miss Manners dares say, have felt much better.

Let us therefore give him the benefit of the doubt—perhaps she had told him that she knew the name of a wonderful paperhanger and he was jotting down her phone number in order to be able to telephone her and get the details—and suppose that he will take care that such an accident does not recur. The question you then face is whether you can handle a nonexclusive relationship with him until such time, if ever, as you both decide you cannot bear not belonging to each other.

And the answer (Miss Manners will kindly supply it for you) is that you must. The desire to limit another person's social freedom is never attractive, and is tolerated only when that person has a desire opposite in direction and equal in intensity. A premature desire of this kind is a disaster. Or rather, as Miss Manners knows perfectly well that we would all like to be able to cherish complete freedom while binding others to strict fidelity, the expression of such a desire is a disaster.

Steps in the Mating Dance

How does one conduct a courtship backward? What are the steps for proceeding from the greatest intimacy to opening an acquaintanceship that one hopes will lead to friendship and then romance?

It took Miss Manners a long time to understand the question. When people first started asking her what to do after they spent the night together, she thought they had confused her area of expertise and were consulting her about what makes a nutritious breakfast.

Sometimes it would be spelled out to her that the social event was what is known as a one-night stand, and that the question was what was required afterward. Most of those who made the inquiry were feeling aggrieved because nothing had happened afterward. Then she would have to spell out what the term "one-night stand" meant and explain that no, dear, she could not chastise a participant for not calling and sending flowers the next day, because those gestures had to do with another, unrelated social form called courtship.

The surprise was that the two forms are sometimes related, at least sequentially. Some people apparently do call the next day, voluntarily, but are then stymied as to how to proceed from there to begin the courtship. My, my, isn't modern life full of surprises? Now that Miss Manners understands the question, she is perfectly willing to address it. The answer is that there are stages of courtship that cannot be skipped if any sort of romance is to ensue. Getting to know something about another person's background, opinions, and tastes is essential, in addition to memorizing the features so as to be able to recognize the face by daylight.

Drawing out the thrill and uncertainty of discovering that a person you find attractive also finds you attractive has generally been considered one of the most rewarding aspects of courtship, and that, of course, is lost if there is no intermediate step between the exchange of glances between strangers and the exchange of everything else, except possibly surnames, between strangers. It does seem to Miss Manners a shame to remove the suspense from the drama of life.

Be that as it may, it does not serve as an excuse for removing the civilities as well. In courtship, these consist of:

1. Establishing what seems like disinterested interest in the other person. That is, one shows a lively attention to discovering the other's attributes but with no

sense that one is going to appropriate them. You would be, for example, fascinated by the other person's field of endeavor, but not the least curious about how much disposable income this might provide to anyone who teamed up with that person.

2. Indicating an interest that you seem to be fighting, because your life is in good order and, rather than hoping to improve it through an alliance, you are afraid that an alliance might disrupt it.

3. Allowing yourself to be won over, in spite of yourself, because of the other person's overwhelming attractiveness.

There will be those who disdain this sequence as being baroque, which indeed it is, and demand to know why they cannot simply state their needs at the beginning and skip these preliminaries.

Well, you tried that, didn't you? The fact is that no one is pleased to find that he or she has simply filled a minimal, uncomplicated need. We want to have all those individual interior complications examined, admired, and adored, along with our outsides. So one must, however incongruously, refrain from using the ultimate intimacy as an excuse for assuming other intimacies, which have not been duly earned. By being pleasantly aloof in other respects, one encourages others to pursue emotional intimacy through the time-honored steps of courtship.

Anybody who remembers when movies were routinely shown continuously, and it was necessary to be able to see a finale and then dismiss it from one's mind and start at the beginning as if fresh, will understand what Miss Manners means.

Thanks for Romance

DEAR MISS MANNERS:
My fiancé is in the nasty habit of saying "Thank you" after we have physically expressed our love (I'm trying to be dainty here). This seems somehow cold and mercenary to me. He is otherwise a perfect gentleman, but this misuse (?) of "Thank you" makes me cringe.

Although "Thank you" is all too underused these days, I wonder if this is a correct usage. If so, should my response be "You're welcome," or "Thank *you*!"?

Please, Miss Manners, please help me. I feel as though I've just handed him his dry cleaning, rather than demonstrated my undying love.
GENTLE READER:
"You're welcome" is certainly one correct answer to "Thank you," and "Thank *you*" is all right, too. So is "Oh, it was nothing, really," although Miss Manners does not particularly recommend that in this instance.

She is somewhat disturbed by your mentioning, in your case against the appropriateness of your fiancé's politeness, that you find it mercenary. Are you suggesting that he is thanking you for giving him free what he might otherwise have to pay for? Surely not. Cannot you assume, as Miss Manners certainly does, that his statement is a brief version of "Thank you for enriching my life and entrusting to me the great bounty of your love"? If not, the fact that what ought to be a tender moment is one that you associate with dry cleaning, to put it equally daintily, is, although not an etiquette problem, a problem that Miss Manners strongly suggests you resolve between the two of you before proceeding any further.

Romantic Roommates

DEAR MISS MANNERS:

Is there a delicate, socially acceptable way to announce to one's parents, friends, and other interested parties the fact that one is "living with" someone of the opposite sex? Being very perceptive, Miss Manners probably noticed that parents were the first group mentioned, and understandably constitute the stickiest part of the problem. For example, one tires of hearing how hard it is for loving parents to reach their wayward son, no matter how late (or early) they call his apartment. And as you can well imagine, the situation will certainly deteriorate even further when one's apartment is given up in the name of economic common sense.

GENTLE READER:

The delicate way is to take advantage of the bewilderment of your parents at the absence of the conventional standards with which they are familiar. The more your parents protest that they don't know what the world is coming to, the more you can confound them by proving that, indeed, they do not. Here is a sample of how it goes:

"No, of course you haven't been able to get me—I'm in the middle of moving, and I'm so sorry I hadn't yet given you my new number. You remember Adelina Sturgeon? It's her apartment, and we've decided to split the rent."

"What? You are going to live with that—that woman? I can't believe that a son of mine would do any such immoral thing."

"Father, what are you saying? Surely you don't think there's anything wrong?"

"Wrong? Nothing wrong about living in sin?"

"Mother, you shock me. People don't think quite so much about sex nowadays as they did when you used to assume that everyone was using every opportunity to sneak around the rigid rules. I assure you, nobody thinks it's improper anymore to have roommates—even a large group of them—of opposite sexes. Besides, Adelina is such a good friend, and we'd be going out together a lot anyway. Do let me bring her by; I'm sure you'll love her."

And so on. Notice that Miss Manners has not required you to lie to your parents. After this, telling your friends should be child's play.

A Proper Proposal

DEAR MISS MANNERS:

I plan to ask my boyfriend to marry me soon. Please tell me, does this fit into your rules of etiquette? Am I being too pushy? We have known each other for the past three years, and I feel it's about time we start talking seriously. We are both in our twenties and have full-time jobs. How do you feel about this?

GENTLE READER:

Miss Manners accepts it entirely and hopes that the gentleman will do the same. Contrary to popular belief, passed down through the obfuscations of mothers and grandmothers, ladies have always initiated marriage proposals or had others do so on their behalf. Traditionally, a lady would say, "My father says that people are beginning to talk about us, and we shouldn't see each other anymore." Miss Manners' favorite example of a parent's doing this is in *War and Peace*, when Prince Vasily, impatient because Pierre says nothing when left alone with the prince's daughter, bursts in on them, simply announcing, "My wife just told me everything," and begins embracing and congratulating the young man.

Miss Manners only hopes that ladies who perform the service for themselves these days will observe the proprieties of proposals that gentlemen have long been expected to follow. The proper form for a proposal of marriage is not "It's about time we started talking seriously." It is not "Why aren't you willing to make a permanent commitment?" It is not "I don't care, but it would mean a lot to my parents if we got married, and I just want them to stop hassling me." It is not "My biological clock is ticking away." It is not "Aren't you ever going to be ready to take responsibility?"

The proper form for a proposal of marriage is "I love you so madly, I can't live without you. Will you marry me?" Miss Manners would not go so far as to say that this works every time. But at least it does not inspire the response of "Will you quit crowding me?"

The Child Marries

The Ritual of the Guest List

A wedding invitation is beautiful and formal notification of the desire to share a solemn and joyous occasion, sent by people who have been saying "Do we have to ask them?" to people whose first response is "How much do you think we have to spend on them?" The making of a wedding guest list is therefore a momentous ritual. It is also usually the occasion of the first breakdown of pleasantness between two groups of people who have been trying to pretend that it is perfectly natural, and even wonderful, to find that you are about to become related to a bunch of strangers selected through inexplicable whim.

The first matter to be fought out is the size of the wedding. Weddings come in three sizes: private, small, and large. No one ever says, "We thought we'd like to have a medium-sized wedding."

A private wedding is designed to exclude certain near relatives who can be told, "We didn't want any fuss—just our parents," in the hope that they will not find out that thirty-five people attended, some of them not so closely related as they.

A small wedding is one everyone describes during the planning stage as "seventy-five at the absolute maximum, I don't care what the cut-off is, we just can't have any more." It is attended by one hundred fifty guests.

A large wedding is described as "Well, so what? We're really going to do it up right, and have all the people who mean something in our lives." The list grows from two hundred to five hundred because of such suggestions as "What about the Whittlesmiths—those people you met on the cruise that time? They're good for a pair of silver candlesticks, at least."

Whatever the number is, it is then divided evenly between the two families, with the bride's family secretly reserving the right to throw in a few extras, a privilege strictly denied, in both meanings of the word, to the bridegroom's family. The bride also persuades the bridegroom to put their mutual friends on his list.

The Wedding Party

THE CONTEMPORARY FAMILY WEDDING PARTY,
*Including the Bridegroom's Former Stepsisters
and the Bride's Grandfather's New Friend*

*The object of a wedding invitation list is to include the relations and friends of both families,
however irregular the connections, rather than to identify conventional bridal family roles
and then dismiss all who do not qualify. The way to shorten such a list is to insist firmly that
guests may not have guest lists of their own. Grandpapa's friend has been included because she
takes such an interest in the bride and will probably soon be her step-grandmother, though
several years younger than the bride; Uncle Montgomery has been told he may not bring the
lady he met at Club Med last week, no matter how nice she is.*

Each side then figures out how to fill its quota. Miss Manners' guidelines for the
task are:

Cut-offs by category (no second cousins, nobody under twelve) are easier than
by individuals. They do not preclude grumbling, but it is more general ("If she
hates children so much, why is she getting married?") and therefore less offensive
than the specific ("Of course, he's always hated Daniela since that time she told
on him in the playground").

Anybody who writes "and family" or "and guest" on a wedding invitation
deserves whatever she gets.

A bride's or bridegroom's antipathy toward the other's relatives or parents'
close friends carries no weight whatsoever.

Statements such as "Let's go ahead and ask them—they'd be hurt if we didn't,
and they live three thousand miles away and aren't well and are having financial
troubles, so there isn't a chance in the world they'll come" never turn out to be
true. These people will mortgage their cat, charter an airplane, and get there.

One should never yield to the plea to be allowed to bring a date. A wedding reception is not a night club, to which one brings one's own guests. If a couple cannot spend one afternoon or evening apart, why don't they get married themselves, because—

One cannot invite one member of an engaged or married couple without the other, no matter how many grudges one has against that person. (For the purposes of social harmony, Miss Manners usually assumes that people who share a household are secretly engaged or married.)

Following these rules, one should be able to make up the guest list without having to call off the occasion to which they are invited. It is, after all, the sharing of confidences between the bridal couple about which of their own relatives are likely to make fools of themselves at the wedding that is the true first step toward creating a new family. (For other ceremonial occasions, please see *Review*, Chapter 9.)

Singles at the Wedding

DEAR MISS MANNERS:

My cousin intends to be married soon. He and his fiancée plan to invite only married cousins, rather than all cousins, to the wedding. I am single, as are most of my brothers and sisters. This arrangement would, therefore, exclude most of my parents' children. This offends them and me. Would you please comment on this rather unusual form of discrimination.

GENTLE READER:

Having just advocated keeping wedding guest lists down to size by using apparently arbitrary categories, Miss Manners finds herself in an awkward position. She has gone on record as saying that it is less offensive to exclude certain people if one can find a rule to fit them (no third cousins once removed) than to ban certain eligible individuals. But this is ridiculous.

If no single people are to be admitted to the wedding, the bride and bridegroom would be ineligible. Besides, weddings are famous for being charming opportunities to begin acquaintanceships that blossom into other weddings, so it seems a particular hardship to exclude the single people; the married people can always use the extra time to straighten up their households. However, Miss Manners was not consulted, in this instance, by bride, bridegroom, or their parents, and neither, she gathers, were you. The proper behavior for all of us, therefore, is to sniff among ourselves about how badly this was handled, and yet show no indication of displeasure nor register any complaint.

Miss Manners doesn't know about you, but she can face this task with perfect equanimity.

Pairing Off

DEAR MISS MANNERS:

My brother's fiancée has asked my sister and me to be in their wedding. I am really excited.

My little brother, eleven, also is included in the wedding. There's only one problem. There will be five ushers and five bridesmaids, so one of the bridesmaids has to pair up with my little brother. My mom said I should be the one, since I'm the youngest in the party (the next youngest is twenty-two). I am five feet five inches without heels and my brother is four feet eight. Wouldn't it look funny for the girl to be a head taller than the boy?

GENTLE READER:

No. Miss Manners assures you that the sight of you walking next to your brother the length of the church aisle will not bring down the house.

The answer to your real question is that the pairing of bridesmaids and ushers is not a step toward romantic bonding, even for the duration of the wedding. Walking with your brother does not link you to him more than blood has already done; and doing so with an unrelated usher would not have given you a leg up, so to speak, in acquiring his company for the reception or anything else you may have in mind.

Congratulatory Offerings

DEAR MISS MANNERS:

For the past twenty-five years, our family has enjoyed a companionable relationship with a small group of other families whose children are now all married, our daughter being the last to do so.

As was their preference, the marriage ceremonies of our friends were formal ceremonies which included the mailing out of formal wedding invitations. Whether or not we attended, for reason of liking the marrying couple, it was our custom to send the brides wedding gifts.

About a year ago, our family moved to another part of the country, and our daughter, who is going to graduate school, is in still another part of the country. Recently, by prearrangement, while visiting us she married a young man with whom she was attending college. As was our preference, the wedding was the ultimate in informality, the civil ceremony performed by a magistrate in our courthouse. Afterward, the young couple returned to college.

In any event, while our closest friends have since visited us and expressed interest in our absent daughter's marriage (seen photos of the ceremony, etc.), to my knowledge they have not written her any congratulatory notes, let alone sent gifts.

Our question is, Miss Manners, is it usually strictly a matter of etiquette that such tokens of good wishes are usually to be offered only where wedding announcements or invitations have been issued? While our friends are not acquainted with the groom, they are fond of our daughter.

GENTLE READER:

For years, Miss Manners has been railing against the crass manner in which both bridal families and wedding guests have come to treat the matter of wedding presents. Sweet little girls in white turn mad with greed, calculating the transference of their shopping lists to people who are supposed to be their friends, and supposed well-wishers demand to know whether or not they have to come across, and for how much.

Miss Manners finds all of this revolting. A wedding invitation is not a bill for a present due, but a request to share an important occasion. One sends a wedding present as an offering of affection to people one cares about, not because one has received notice.

If you care enough about certain people to accept their wedding invitations, you should want to present a tangible expression of your feeling. Similarly, if you care about people whose marriages you have been told about, in formal or informal announcements, you should also make the gesture.

For people who don't really care, the announcement of a marriage or a refused wedding invitation requires only a note wishing the couple happiness.

But, then, as you have the good taste not to think of weddings as present-engendering occasions, you haven't noticed whether or not your friends sent anything, have you?

An Heirloom Present

DEAR MISS MANNERS:

I own a pair of beautiful gold antique bracelets, valued at six hundred dollars each. I planned to give one to my soon-to-be daughter-in-law as a personal wedding gift. Inside the bracelets is a date, 1880, and initials of a long-gone relative. My question, considering that the initials do not match the bride's, is whether it would be proper to give this gift. Also, if you say it would be fitting and proper, would it be tacky of me to suggest to her that the bracelet is of some value, and not just junk jewelry?

GENTLE READER:

There is no more charming present a bride can receive from her new family than something that has been treasured in that family for many years—especially six-hundred-dollar gold bracelets that have been treasured, etc. You are quite right that your prospective daughter-in-law must understand what it is that she is getting. The non-tacky way of doing this is with a small presentation speech that goes, ''My dear, I hope you don't think this too old-fashioned to wear. It was given to my Great-Great-Aunt Flora when she was a bride, and I hope that someday you will give it to your son's wife, if he should be so fortunate as to have as lovely a bride as my son chose.''

If she doesn't understand the value after that, Miss Manners must advise you to suggest that your son find himself a bride who is a little quicker mentally.

The Mother's Demeanor

DEAR MISS MANNERS:

My problem concerns the proper way to greet the parents of a newly wedded bride or groom. I was aware that one congratulates the lucky groom and wishes the best of luck to the blushing bride. But what of the parents?

This question was raised in light of an occurrence at my cousin's wedding. In the receiving line after the ceremony, I was so filled with joy that I congratulated

Dear Mrs Awful,

That was a lovely wedding you and your husband gave Lisa. My wife and I remember it with pleasure, even after all these months.

We hesitate to bother Lisa, knowing how busy she must be setting up housekeeping, and wonder if we could trouble you to check on a small matter. Several weeks before the wedding, we ordered four dozen crystal wine goblets to be sent to her. Having heard nothing since, we assume that the store lost the order, which distresses us greatly, as we had so hoped to please your charming daughter with this trifle. Before we register a very severe complaint with the inexcusably negligent shopkeeper, we would appreciate if you would find out if Lisa has any clue as to what might have gone wrong.

Yours very sincerely,

Cuthbert Burbage

A LETTER THAT SHOULD NEVER BE RECEIVED, *because the necessity for writing it should not exist. It is, however, the classic remedy for an all-too-common problem, as Mr. Burbage explained when Mrs. Burbage declined to appease their joint anger by writing it. "Well, I'm not afraid, even if you are," he replied, producing this on his own writing paper.*

my aunt—the mother of the bride—on the wedding. She gave me a quite unpleasant look and replied, "Why congratulate me? It's not my wedding!" I was dumbfounded. I later regretted not having a snappy comment to save face (mine).

My dear Miss Manners, was I incorrect? Or was my aunt oversensitive? I am anxiously awaiting your reply, as I am soon to go to another wedding and wish to avoid such unpleasantness in the future.

GENTLE READER:

Please convey Miss Manners' congratulations to your aunt. They are not offered on her daughter's wedding—indeed, the rule about wishing the bride happiness, rather than offering her congratulations, applies to her family as well—but because she has succeeded in creating an emotional disturbance on a happy occasion and suggesting that she is not satisfied with the match her daughter made. Anyone can marry off a daughter, but a mother who manages these feats in the brief time of a receiving line is to be congratulated.

Sharing Correspondence Duties

DEAR MISS MANNERS:

My future mother-in-law delivered a lecture last night on the "proper" way to thank people for their wedding gifts: totally the bride's responsibility, period.

I am not a great traditionalist—have been even described as a bit of a rebel at times—but I certainly hate to upset her social order. Yet I have no interest in, and see little sense in, my handling all the correspondence. First, all these presents are arriving from out of town, often from people I have never met and my fiancé has known his whole life. Second, we both work full-time and my available time for this activity is as limited as (if not more so than) his. I feel the bride (or wife) in the sole role as social secretary is a bit of an anachronism for me. Any comments?

GENTLE READER:

Miss Manners agrees with you about the issues, although she cannot identify with you politically. You see, Miss Manners is such an old-fashioned slip of a girl that she goes back beyond the tradition of the wife's handling all the social life because the husband had to earn a living, all the way to when both ladies and gentlemen devoted themselves to social duties because neither of them would dream of earning a living. (If you hear of such an opening nowadays, please let Miss Manners know.)

While she sees nothing wrong with dividing letter-writing duties, she does object to offending in-laws so early in the marriage. What will you do for entertainment later?

Here is a brilliant solution. You write to his family's friends, and have him write to yours.

A Child Too Well Reared

DEAR MISS MANNERS:

Have you ever heard of a bride-to-be being reproved for writing her thank-you notes too soon?

My daughter had a shower on a Saturday evening and wrote and mailed the thank-yous the very next day. Some of the guests received their notes on Monday. Her fiancé gently chided her for being so prompt. Having never seen such a question raised before and not being able to find an answer, I hope you can come to our rescue. She has written each thank-you on the day a gift was received, but is now holding the notes for fear of being chided again.

GENTLE READER:

Is it too late to put a stop to this wedding? That child of yours is a treasure and Miss Manners does not want her marrying someone who does not appreciate her.

If only he realized how lucky he is. Her promptness is not only a sign of efficiency that could fill the rest of his life with ease and pleasure, but her politeness —and what is it but the most flattering politeness to appear to be so enraptured with a present that you cannot stop yourself from showing immediate gratitude?— is a rare graciousness that will be the crowning touch to a well-organized household.

The immediate benefit to him, if he but knew it, is that he will never encounter his own mother in a state of anger or despair, passing on the complaints of her friends that Charlotte hasn't thanked anybody, along with the request that he "make her" do so. The long-range benefits are beyond description.

Now that Miss Manners has given vent to her astonishment, she feels obliged to admit that yes, she did hear once before of a similar case, in which the bride had been advised that it was "wrong" to write thank-you letters for wedding presents until after the wedding. As Miss Manners suspected, this outrageous misinformation was traceable to a source who invented it from wishful thinking because she had planned to write these letters on paper marked with her married name, and knew she couldn't use that before the wedding.

The Duties of Wedding Guests

Even if the best man did forget the wedding ring, the marriage would still be legal and it would give the couple a charming and amusing story to repeat on anniversaries for the rest of their lives. But there are other duties, on the part of members of the wedding party, the bridal family, and certain guests, that are much more likely to be forgotten, and the omission of which is more damaging.

It is, for example, the obligation of the bridegroom's youngest brother to dip into the deserted champagne glasses at the reception. This distracts the bridegroom's parents from criticizing the social arrangements made by the bride's parents, making them feel suddenly vulnerable themselves.

If a former beau of the bride's has been invited, he has the duty of looking darkly discontent. He is allowed to check out all the bridesmaids, but must maintain a distracted expression, suggesting that he is unsatisfactorily seeking consolation— for example, he may hold a dancing partner tightly, but only if he stares off moodily above her head. This is intended to add some needed spice to the otherwise insipid concept of the happy ending.

The flower girl, or the most junior bridesmaid, is supposed to run up to the bride and say, ''You're so beautiful! You look like a princess in a story! When I grow up I want to have a wedding just like this!'' She is allowed to run around and repeat the sentiment to other guests, provided that someone is alerted to cuff her when it gets tiresome.

The maid of honor's chief duty is before the ceremony, when she is stationed in the bride's room to say soothing things such as ''Well, then, let's call it off right now. So what? It's better than tying yourself to him for the rest of your life if that's really the way you feel about him.'' If the bride shows signs of agreeing, the maid of honor is charged with saying, ''Okay, you explain it to your mother, and I'll take him out of here and buy him a drink and see if I can make him feel it's all for the best.'' The maid of honor is also required to go around the reception saying politely to each of the guests, ''Oh, I don't know—when I meet the right man, I guess.''

The bride's grandfather's girlfriend is supposed to reply to all inquiries by describing herself as ''a very old friend of the family's'' even if she is younger than the bride and has never seen any of them before.

All people there in a professional capacity must steadfastly refrain from comparing the wedding with any wedding other than that of the bride's or bridegroom's parents, and then only if those marriages are still intact.

The woman whom everybody knows the bridegroom proposed to first should pretend that that happened when they were both toddlers, and that they have more or less grown up together as brother and sister ever since. This stimulates conversation by driving the most popular remark underground, where it belongs, and gives her a glamorous air of magnanimity.

The bride's mother's husband must retain a genial expression and a fast reflex for stepping back if anyone tries to give him the father-of-the-bride kidding act when the original father is nearby, even if the bride doesn't recognize the latter on sight.

All grandmothers must wear whatever flower arrangements are pinned on them, or an absence of such, with equal grace.

Miss Manners promises everyone that if these duties are taken seriously, such trifles as the wedding ring can safely be allowed to take care of themselves.

Preserving Wedding Myths

DEAR MISS MANNERS:

My fiancée and I have been living together for almost two years, and everybody knows it. Everybody, that is, except my grandmother and my two spinster aunts who live with her.

My mother has gone to unbelievable lengths to keep them from finding out—including insisting on a big fairy-tale wedding, complete with little girls throwing rose petals, that nobody else really wanted. However, we're all going along with it, determined to have the best time we can at this very expensive shindig. My friends have been told to keep their mouths shut, and my bride has promised to blush when I look at her and squeal if I touch her. I have the feeling that in spite of all this, someone is going to let the cat out of the bag. Any suggestions?

GENTLE READER:

Leave the reception as early as possible. When a bridal couple stays endlessly at a wedding reception, it is not only a nuisance to guests who are too polite to leave before they do, but a dead giveaway that a fancy party with all their friends is the most novel pastime they can think of at the moment.

In the Family Way

DEAR MISS MANNERS:

I am getting married in two months, and I am almost three months pregnant. Is it proper to wear a white wedding gown and still plan a big wedding? My future in-laws are very upset and want us to cancel the wedding and reception. Should I do as they want and go to a justice of the peace, or go ahead with the big wedding?

GENTLE READER:

A wedding is a solemn public event, and why so many people persist in believing that it is license for them to speculate, giggle, and pass judgment on the intimate relations of the principals is something Miss Manners simply cannot understand, even when she does it herself.

The white wedding dress, as Miss Manners has said until she is going gray, is symbolically associated with a first wedding and was never intended to advertise the physical condition of the body inside of it.

Eliminating the truth-in-packaging aspect of this situation, you are left with two problems: a fashion problem and a family-relations problem.

The heavily pregnant figure, which may be quite beautiful in its way, becomes comic in the sort of wedding dress where the bulk is intended to be at the hemline. It is precisely because this draws attention to the private aspects of marriage that it detracts from the public form of the wedding. At five months, however, you should easily be able to find a wedding dress whose focal point is not what we might call in fashion parlance "belly interest."

The family problem is more weighty. Marriage is the joining of two families, and to do so in a way that one of the families does not like, for whatever reason, may not be worth whatever enjoyment the other family or the principals may have in making a social occasion of it.

The Far-Flung Family

DEAR MISS MANNERS:

For some years now, sociologists and such have been bemoaning the demise of the nuclear family. I have never concerned myself with such matters, until recently, but have now come to understand the perils of moving from one's birthplace prior to marriage. My fiancé and I are trying very hard to get married, but, regrettably, the logistics seem to be only slightly less than those for the Normandy invasion.

The problems center around his and my demographics and our familial geographics. We live in city A, but met in city B, where he grew up. His siblings are still in city B, as are a few (but not many) of his/my/our friends.

His parents now live in city C, along with a couple of distant relatives and a few friends. My parents and siblings live in city D, where I grew up, but almost none of my friends still live there, although their parents do. Most of my relatives also live in city D, and, of course, that is where my parents' friends live.

His/my/our other friends live in cities E through H, including one of the non-contiguous states. For the most part, each of these cities is at least eight hundred miles from each of the other cities. The exception is cities B and D, which are half that distance from one another.

Now for the other half of the problem. One set of parents is elderly and retired, and traveling anywhere is a problem, both financially and physically. The other set of parents is divorced and not on speaking terms.

My fiancé and I are in our thirties and have been living together for several years, in part because every time the subject of marriage has come up, we have given up in the face of what it would take to get our families together for a wedding. I'm not kidding!

Since I've been self-supporting for ten years, I don't think that my father expects to pay for the wedding, but my fiancé and I cannot afford to pay for even a relatively small wedding, what with the cost of flowers, a hall, catering, a band, a special gown or suit, invitations, announcements, postage, booze, etc. In addition, I work and really don't have the time to make all the arrangements, especially for a wedding in another city. Our living room is too small to accommodate all of the immediate family. What do you recommend?

We had thought about eloping and telling our parents afterward. It would save everyone the inconvenience that would surely result, no matter what city was chosen. It would mean that none of them would have to go trudging cross-country. We feel certain that no matter what the degree of hardship involved, all four parents would insist on attending if they knew in advance of the "elopement." On the other hand, some or all four might feel hurt if they are not invited to attend. As much as we might like to have some sort of small wedding, we are afraid it would turn out to be a horror, rather than a pleasant memory for all. Whatever we decide to do, our friends will understand, but our parents probably will not.

I realize it would take the wisdom of Solomon to solve this one, but if you have any suggestions, they would be appreciated. In these days of divorce, mobility, and marriage at a later age, is it any wonder that cohabitation is so appealing?

GENTLE READER:

After listening to your woes, Miss Manners is tempted to agree that you had better forget the whole thing—if it were not for all those people, in cities A through H, murmuring, "They seem so right for each other—why do you suppose they don't get married?"

Here are your choices:

1. Cite tradition, and be married from your parents' home (city D), imposing a hardship on his parents and the citizens of A, B, C, E, F, G, and H.

2. Cite modern custom, and be married in your own home, city A, offending B through H.

3. Take the show on the road, and either repeat your vows everywhere, or be married secretly and hold a wedding reception in each city, offending no one except your own budget.

4. Elope with no advance notice. (Actually, that is redundant: There is no such thing, as you suggest, as inviting people to an elopement.)

It is up to you, but Miss Manners, in your position, would go for number 4. That way, you favor none of these sensitive people, but if they are all offended, well, at least you haven't wrecked your finances, so you will have enough to start a new life in city I.

What Would Father Have Wanted?

DEAR MISS MANNERS:

A very dear relative of mine has all her plans made for a big church wedding. The invitations are back from the printer, and since her mother is dead, her father's name is of course on the invitations. Now the tragic part. Her father died very suddenly last weekend, and the poor girl doesn't know what she is going to do.

Knowing her father as well as I did, I know he would want all the plans to go ahead as though nothing were changed. If the girl decides to go ahead with the big wedding, what should we do about the invitations? What is the proper thing to do?

GENTLE READER:

Knowing the bride's father not at all, Miss Manners is certain that he would not want the bereaved to go merrily on their festive courses, taking no notice of the fact of his death except for the unfortunate detail of having to send out or throw out formal invitations issued by someone now in his grave. Miss Manners also assures you that many, if not all, of the guests will take the same view, which will put a decided damper on all this blithe gaiety.

The thing to throw out is the wedding plans. The daughter may still marry when planned if she does it quietly, but if she still wants a big wedding, she must wait a decent interval. The out-of-date wedding invitations may be used as scratch paper for the new plans.

🌹 PARENTS' DUTIES

The Forgotten Parents

The chief duty of the bridegroom's family is to pretend to be crazy about the bride. Some find this as difficult a task to sustain as all the planning, financing, and execution of the bride's family's duties put together. Nevertheless, it must be borne constantly in mind, as the bridegroom's parents are run through a routine not of their own making. They have few tasks, but constantly repeating how lovely everything is—the bride's grandmother, the wedding silver, the bridesmaids' dresses, the striped tent on the lawn, the wedding breakfast, the promises about when thank-you letters will be written—is essential.

Miss Manners sympathizes with those who thus find themselves compelled to endorse things they abhor—raised-print invitations, eccentric clothes calling themselves formal, and so on. But this is not an occasion on which the most nearly perfect form of etiquette predominates, unfortunately. The truly correct thing is to go along as much as possible with the decrees of the bridal family, and hope that a lifetime's instilling of values in the bridegroom will enable him to reeducate the bride as soon as the first blinding raptures have subsided.

The first of these jobs is to tell the bride, or to write to her, of her fiancé's parents' overwhelming happiness at welcoming her into the family. From the moment of being informed of the engagement, they are barred from discussing, in front of their son, whether her hair is dyed and why she talks so funny.

They must then call on her parents. "Call on," in these days when one's children marry outside of their parents' circles, can be a telephone call or a letter to another city, although for engagements of more than a weekend, it is polite to plan a trip to see what the young man is getting himself into. If the young lady has more than one set of parents, as also happens these days, the ones with whom she is or was resident are the most important, but it is proper to visit nonresident parents, as well.

All the while, the bridegroom's parents should be madly declaring how lovely they find everything and everybody.

They may, if they wish, give a party to introduce the bride to their friends, but no parties—repeat, none—are obligatory on the part of the gentleman's family.

The next job is to supply full and correct names and addresses to fill that part of the guest list that is allotted to them. Meanwhile, they should keep saying how lovely they think the choice of wedding size and all other arrangements to be.

Miss Manners thinks it barbaric for a bride to attempt to costume anyone not in the wedding party. But the mother of the bridegroom, if told to wear her dress short or long, pink or gray, to match or complement that of the bride's mother, should remember what she thinks of the bride's and her mother's taste: She thinks it perfectly lovely. So are the flowers that they send her as a badge.

It has become increasingly common for the bridegroom's parents to give a rehearsal dinner the night before the wedding, but it is not traditionally obligatory. Neither is paying for any part of the wedding. Generosity is nice, but may be resisted, if demanded, on historical grounds.

They are expected to go to their allotted places at the ceremony and the reception, murmuring about how lovely it all is. Then, as a reward, they may go home, take off their shoes, and say to each other, "Did you *see* those people?"

Blackmailing the Bridegroom's Parents

DEAR MISS MANNERS:

Help! My son is getting married in California in two months. His fiancée and her parents, after months of deliberation, called us to advise us of their plans which they have been making there and which are, frankly, quite elaborate. We have had little, if any, say, but rather have been told, after the fact, what has been planned and how much it is going to cost. It adds up, so far, to about six thousand dollars. This is without our plane fare, the stay in California, and the wedding gift we plan to give the children.

Neither family is in a position to put on a costly wedding, and we advised them of our position at the start. However, the most recent call from the mother of the bride gave every indication that they expect monetary help. The costs are too much for us to handle in this short a period of time. Had we been given a year to plan, as in the case of most weddings, we would have been glad to foot the whole bill.

How do we tell these people? The message apparently was not heeded before. If we do not contribute our "share," I am sure that our son will feel the brunt of their displeasure. We'd like the wedding to be a happy occasion for the children, but so far it has been giving us ulcers.

GENTLE READER:

Allow Miss Manners to recite to you the rules of etiquette that apply to this situation:

1. It is the duty of the bride's family to plan the wedding, and consulting the bridegroom's family is merely a courtesy.

2. The mandatory proper share to be contributed by the bridegroom's family consists only of the bridegroom.

Your standing on this formality would not, Miss Manners admits, do much for the happiness that is your stated aim. What you might do instead, after firmly repeating your regret that your circumstances do not permit you to do more, is to offer to pay the costs of a modest wedding in your hometown (which will not be accepted) or to take over one of the wedding bills, such as liquor or flowers (which will be).

If it were Miss Manners' son, she would stand back and allow him to discover now whether the family into which he is marrying is the sort that turns vindictive after unsuccessful blackmail.

The Slighted Family

DEAR MISS MANNERS:

My son is twenty years old and plans on marrying soon. He insists that the plans are none of my business but his, his girl's, and her family's. The wedding is one-sided. The girl is having her older sisters as maid of honor and bridesmaids. My son is having his friends and her brother for the best man and ushers.

He has made no effort to include us in his plans. I have two daughters, eighteen and sixteen, who weren't even considered to be in the wedding and an older son in the army who wasn't even notified and asked to be best man. To top it all off, we, the family of the groom-to-be, were sent invitations as if we were friends or far-off relatives.

On the day of their wedding, the ceremony is at three o'clock and the reception is at six o'clock. As mother of the groom and under these circumstances, am I supposed to entertain them after the ceremony until the reception?

I always thought a wedding is shared by not just the bride and groom, but also both the families. Isn't the best man supposed to be the groom's brother, and aren't his sisters supposed to be included as bridesmaids? Is it proper for the groom's family to be sent an invitation? I thought I was automatically in the wedding and its plans. On the day of the wedding, do I enter the church with everyone else who has received an invitation, or am I supposed to be properly seated, and where would my daughters be seated? Aren't we supposed to be together?

As far as dress, I heard the bride's mother has first choice as to color and style, but whenever I bring this matter up, my son tells me it's the bride's show and her family's and what they wear is their business.

I am hurt and angry, not only because of his attitude, but because of my lack of knowledge as to what is proper and what I am supposed to do as the groom's mother. I am widowed. I do not drive, and therefore it is impossible for me to go over to the bride's family and confront them with all this. They have made no attempt to get in touch with me to include me or my daughters in their plans. Please advise me what are my duties and how I should handle all this.

GENTLE READER:

Please do not think Miss Manners unsympathetic if she is forced to tell you that by the strict laws of etiquette, the bride's family is correct. You know, and Miss Manners knows, that they are also being heartless. But when people wish to be mean to one another on ceremonial occasions—and that does seem to bring out the worst in everyone—etiquette is often used as the weapon.

Traditionally, weddings were not shared by both families. The bride's family did everything, and the bridegroom's family, and for that matter the bridegroom himself, had nothing to do but to show up on time.

Only in the last few decades did anyone notice that it took two to have a wedding. Such customs as having the bridegroom's family entertain the wedding party the night before the wedding, which is a sensible idea and takes the pressure off the wedding hosts, and having the mothers of the bridal couple coordinate their wedding clothes, which Miss Manners thinks is a silly idea, are of quite recent origin. Including the bridegroom's siblings in the wedding party is not even a new custom; those who are close to these people may, and others may not.

Your duty, therefore, is only to attend the wedding, dressed as you think proper, and to sit wherever they put you. Nothing more. Indeed, Miss Manners would advise you to combat the exclusionist attitude you correctly sense by stand-offishness, rather than by confronting anyone, least of all over the subject of etiquette. The tactic of clubbing others in the name of propriety is self-defeating, as your son and his bride may yet live to learn. Concede the wedding gracefully; perhaps they will someday turn to you to learn about the more complex rules of behavior that are required for a happy family life.

Dressing Up Mommies

DEAR MISS MANNERS:

My daughter says the mother of the bride has to wear pink, and the groom's mother blue. I have never heard of this before. Is it true?

GENTLE READER:

Miss Manners has never heard of this, either, and what is more, she never wants to hear of it again.

While we are at it, let us abolish forever the idea that the bridal couple's parents are to be told what is proper to wear to a wedding by the little snippets whose wedding day it happens to be. Let them pick on their own friends, the bridesmaids and groomsmen, and leave the elder generation to exercise their own judgment.

The Old Rules Still Apply

DEAR MISS MANNERS:

What do the respective parents of the prospective bride and groom do when the latter finally state that they are going to be married in August and they have been living together in Wyoming for a couple years? We dare not question why they are waiting until August to tie the knot. Should we have a quiet dinner in a fine restaurant, just the four of us? I am sure you will be receiving more questions like this, since these are the 1980s, after all.

Should we call on one another? Should we have a tea? What? The couple are both fine, bright people. However, they do not carry on traditions which we did in 1955. Should we go to the wedding? Please help.

GENTLE READER:

Miss Manners is not sure how much you carried on in 1955, but to her, marriage is still marriage, no matter what has been going on in Wyoming beforehand.

It is, therefore, still appropriate that you have a ceremonial family dinner with the young couple, that the parents of the prospective bridegroom call upon you, that you give an engagement tea and perform whatever celebrations you would consider fitting upon the approaching union of fine, bright people. Of course you go to the wedding.

The Mother's Name

DEAR MISS MANNERS:

Since my divorce, I have continued to use the title "Mrs." with my first name and my married last name, as in "Mrs. Jane Doe." Occasionally, I use my former husband's full name, as in "Mrs. John Doe."

My former husband objects to the use of his name, on the basis that he is now remarried and his wife uses the name Mrs. John Doe. Although I am not overly sympathetic to his objections, the situation is complicated by the impending marriage of our daughter. I want to issue the invitations in the names of Mr. and Mrs. John Doe. He feels that this would be confusing, inappropriate, and an insult to his current wife. As he is financing the affair, I am forced to take his thoughts into consideration.

I have been told that my use of the title "Mrs." is improper under any circumstances—is that correct? Also, what names would be appropriate to list on my daughter's wedding invitations?

GENTLE READER:

By traditional standards, a lady has the right to continue to use her married name (Mrs. John Doe) after a divorce if she was blameless in the divorce, it was entirely her husband's fault, and if she plans to continue her life as if she were still bound by marriage. To invoke such a rule today, you would have to be crazy.

Let us try another old-fashioned rule, though, just as venerable but a trifle less provocative. That is to use the title of Mrs. with your maiden name, followed by your married surname: Mrs. Smith Doe. This is impeccably correct. What is not correct, although it is widely practiced, is the use of Mrs. with a woman's first name, as Mrs. Jane Doe.

The joint wedding invitations should be issued from Mrs. Smith Doe and Mr. John Doe, unless, of course, you wish to begin a melee that would dominate not only the wedding, but your family life for generations to come.

❧ STEPPARENTS

Step-Weddings

DEAR MISS MANNERS:

My stepson will be married this fall, and his bride has shared her distress with me about potential problems, to which I add my own share of hesitancy.

1. Where should the mother of the groom be seated during the church ceremony?
2. Where should his father and I be seated?
3. Should I, his stepmother, wear a suit and hat rather than a party dress?
4. Must I invite our son's mother to the rehearsal dinner, even though I will be serving the meal in our home, the former home of the mother?

5. Where should the mother be seated at the bridal table at the reception/dinner?

6. Must I invite the mother of the groom to the shower I will be giving the bride? The shower will also be held in my home.

My personal feelings toward his mother are that since I obviously can't do anything about her, she is a fact of life, undesirable as she may be. She is his mother, and I wouldn't want to be the one to keep her from enjoying her own son's wedding. But I really and honestly do not think I can handle entertaining her in my, formerly her, home.

In our opinion, the seating in the church ceremony matters little. We would gladly give up the first pew to the mother and her parents, and we then would sit anywhere else. However, the bride's wish is that my husband sit between his ex-wife and me. That makes me cringe; it upsets him; and it would be a confusing statement to the other guests. To me, that would be in the worst of taste. Please help us!

GENTLE READER:

Miss Manners believes it her duty to take the point of view of those who solicit her advice, rather than to wander off with unrequested sympathy for the villains in their stories. But asking her to condone barring a mother from an event connected to her son's wedding on the grounds of the pain at having to entertain her felt by a wife who is in possession of her husband and home is too much. Also under the category of too much is the notion that a whim of the bride's should dictate seating against all tradition and common sense. If the two of you will please get a grip on yourselves on these two issues, Miss Manners will resume her natural graciousness and give your problems full attention.

1. The mother of the bridegroom, and her immediate relatives if she wishes, sit in the first pew on the right.

2. You and your husband sit behind them, unless you think your presence will provoke her to violence, in which case you let your husband sit there and take a less conspicuous position yourself.

3. Both a dressy suit and an afternoon (party) dress, with hat, are suitable for a wedding, so you may wear either. Contrary to popular opinion, there is no special costume for mothers or stepmothers, and those who distinguish themselves by wearing long dresses during the day, as if they were superannuated bridesmaids, are not acting in what we shall gently call the best of taste.

4. The immediate family is invited to the rehearsal dinner, and you cannot get more immediate than being the bridegroom's mother. If you don't want her in your house—or if it would be painful for her to be a guest in her former home—then hold the thing somewhere else.

5. The parents do not sit at the bridal table, which is for the bridal couple and their attendants. It is customary to have a parents' table, at which the clergyman or clergywoman with spouse and special relatives or friends (grandparents, godparents, and such) sit, but there is no reason not to have two such tables to keep unfriendly parents and stepparents separated.

6. You should not be giving a bridal shower; friends, not immediate relatives of the bridal couple, do that. But if you do it anyway, remember what you promised Miss Manners about your house.

Personalized Ceremonies

DEAR MISS MANNERS:

I am in my late twenties and am about to enter my second marriage. My family lives in another state, and will be traveling here for the wedding, as this is now my home, and my fiancé and I are providing most of the financing for the wedding.

My parents were divorced about ten years ago, and my father married the Other Woman, whom I'll call O. There is still a lot of tension between my mother and O., yet I know that they will be civil to each other for the sake of my wedding.

The problem is that we are planning a part of the ceremony in which we acknowledge our families and say something special about them and the way we feel about their roles in our growth, and that sort of thing.

I like O. well enough, and I don't blame her for my parents' split; nonetheless, I don't feel special about her, and I don't consider her family. On the other hand, I feel awkward about having her and my father sit apart, partly because everyone would wonder why they weren't sitting together. Can you suggest a course of action that would solve the etiquette problem and still allow me to be true to my feelings about my family?

GENTLE READER:

Yes, but you won't follow it.

Miss Manners does not believe that a public ceremony is the place to discuss the roles of individual family members in your growth, in however edited and favorable a manner. (If you were to do it thoroughly and honestly, you would probably have to admit that your first husband played a large role, for better or worse, in your growth.) Why can't you write long, sentimental letters to each of your parents, expressing your gratitude? Or if you wish to do it in front of your and their friends, you could put it all into toasts at the wedding reception. It seems to Miss Manners that the promises that you and your bridegroom make to each other in the ceremony are quite enough in the way of publicly announced intimacy for that part of the occasion.

Knowing that you are going to go ahead anyway with your plan, Miss Manners will now assure you that it is quite common and natural for a bride to focus on her original parents, rather than on subsequent additions. It is civilized of your mother and stepmother to call a truce during your wedding, and no violation of anyone's rights for you to treat your mother as the sole mother present, and your father as the sole father. No one will think, if your parents sit together, that they are rekindling their relationship at the expense of his wife. Nor would it be improper for your original parents to sit apart, your father with his second wife, and for you nevertheless to single them out where they are.

All right? Now, how many parents does your fiancé have?

Sabotaging One's Stepmother

DEAR MISS MANNERS:

My parents are divorced, and both have remarried. I live with my father and stepmother because Dad got custody of us kids after the divorce. I don't like my stepmother. She's only nine years older than I, and if she hadn't married Dad, I probably could have gotten Mom and Dad together again.

Dad says I should acknowledge her birthday and their wedding anniversary, but I don't want to, and know it hurts when I don't. Should I listen to Dad?

Also, I'll be getting married soon and have some questions. My mother and step-mother are not friendly and my mother's side of the family is giving me a bridal shower. Should my stepmother be invited? Does she have to be invited to any of the showers? Should my stepmother have last choice on color of her dress for the wedding? Does she get a corsage and can it be not as nice as my mother's and mother-in-law's corsage?

GENTLE READER:

Miss Manners finds her heart suddenly going out to your mother-in-law-to-be and your husband-to-be, to the extent that she is tempted to give you all the wrong answers and let you demonstrate to them your approach to family life.

However, there are ethics, even in the etiquette business, so here is a straight answer. Behave yourself. Whether you like her or not, give your stepmother the full honor of her position as your father's wife. Whom you think you are serving with your miserable plans for petty rudenesses, Miss Manners cannot imagine. That you believe you might have arranged your parents' lives better for them than they did themselves, or that you can still make the point by sabotage, is an affront to their dignity.

The scheme about the not-nice flowers is surely the most insidious idea Miss Manners has ever heard from a tender young bride. Keep it up and you will prob-ably fail your blood test.

Fathers and Other Strangers

DEAR MISS MANNERS:

My parents have been divorced for seventeen years, since I was ten years old. Five of those years, my brother and I were totally ignored by my father—no com-munication whatsoever. Then we heard from him about twice a year. Mother is still single; Dad is married for the third time. My parents do speak to each other.

I have decided that an uncle, not my father, will escort me down the aisle. I would also like to mention that my father did not ask about the wedding plans, or offer at any time financial or other help at all. My fiancé and I are paying the entire expense.

Do I have to invite my father to the church and/or the reception? If I do, should he dress as a guest (suit) or should he wear a tuxedo, as my fiancé's father will do? When pictures are taken, should they be with my mom or dad? What about the uncle who is giving me away? Family would know the difference, but everybody else may think he is my dad because he is wearing the tuxedo.

Must I invite my dad's third wife if I invite him? I hesitate because she is unpredictable—at my brother's wedding, she was telling guests that she was the mother of the groom. If I invite my dad, should I include him at the table with my mom, the priest, my fiancé's parents, etc., or should I have the uncle and his wife there?

I would like my wedding day to be as worry-free as possible, and I'll feel more at ease knowing I did the proper thing for all concerned.

GENTLE READER:

Actually, you have only one etiquette problem here, and that is whether to invite your father to your wedding. He is already out of the bridal party, and therefore should dress and be treated as a guest. The notion that those outside the bridal party, however closely related or cherished, are distinguished by costume or other forms of star treatment is erroneous. Wedding photographs are not, contrary to popular opinion, part of the ceremony. If you want pictures of the bridal party, your father will not be in them. The only reason to have him photographed is if you want a memento of his being there; forcing your mother to pose with him seems artificial and silly.

As your father has shown little interest in you, and his wife is a known trouble-maker, it would be understandable if you assumed that they wish to continue to be omitted from your life. If, however, you feel that the tie requires you to treat him as a father, in spite of his behavior, you must do so in a generous manner, including the wife. This in no way cuts into the role of your uncle, who is in the bridal party and should be treated accordingly. It is nobler to be forgiving, but Miss Manners promises not to call you improper for failing to invite someone you hardly know.

Bipartisan Parties

DEAR MISS MANNERS:

I must confess that I have done a less than admirable job of raising my father and his two wives. This was evidenced several years ago, during my older sister's wedding. All three adults said they would bite the bullet and agree to get along. Unfortunately, they continually reminded my sister of this sacrifice, until she was a complete wreck—a mental state best reserved for her wedding and mate selection.

The wedding was a rather tense affair. My mother's relatives boycotted because my father attended. My mother literally cried for eight weeks prior to the festivities, over this and because she feared my stepmother would be more elegantly dressed.

My younger sister and I bore the brunt of everyone's discomfort, since no one wanted to "burden" my older sister. My father told us that we each were entitled to a college education and the wedding of our choice, but he certainly hoped we would have the decency to elope. My younger sister and I made a pact that we would either never marry, or else exclude the parents from the wedding.

Now, six years later, I have fallen deeply in love with a man who recently proposed to me in a most romantic way. I have accepted. I do harbor some reservations —not about my intended, but about the three unruly adults who, if anything, have gotten worse through the years. I have refrained from breaking the news to them for obvious reasons. My fiancé and I plan to have a small wedding, followed by a reception for our relatives and friends. An extremely undignified (but fun) blast will follow the respectable one.

I don't particularly relish coping with either my mother's fits or my step-mother's imitation of the Snow Queen. Whatever his faults, my father is capable of behaving well in public. The only solution I have come up with is to invite all my relatives and let them decide whether they can tolerate the others. Since I am nearly thirty-two, I don't feel any pressing need for my father to give me away to a man I already live with. I also prefer not to turn wedding duties over to my mother. I prefer to have them attend as guests.

GENTLE READER:

Congratulations! This is not upon your being married—Miss Manners never congratulates brides; traditionally, they are offered best wishes, while the bride-groom is congratulated—but upon the round of partying Miss Manners has in store for you.

You will have three, not two, wedding receptions. It would be nice if you could manage two ceremonies to go with them—say, religious and civil—but if you cannot, you may still take advantage of customs permitting the festivities to be reasonably prolonged. There will be one party for each side of your family, at either or both of which the presumably better-behaved family you are marrying into will also be present. The third party, if you still feel up to it after planning the other two, is what you call the blast. Miss Manners trusts you to do that one without her help.

Naturally, each side of your family will think the party to which they are not invited is the better one. To confuse them, you might have one immediately after the ceremony, which seems more significant, but the other one be more elaborate —a seated dinner, for example. Or you could hold one of them in that parent's hometown, within a week after the ceremony, and call that the real reception, as opposed to a small gathering of your friends on the day.

The other possibility is to trust everyone, as you suggest, and let your sisters bear the brunt of any problems, claiming that the elder owes you, and that you will now owe the younger.

Miss Manners is glad that tradition does not forbid her to wish the bride good luck.

🌹 MARRYING AGAIN

Second Wedding Obligations

DEAR MISS MANNERS:

Please inform me what a parent's financial obligations are for a daughter's second marriage. It is her second, his third. A large church wedding is being planned in England. (He is British.) We are being informed, but not consulted, as to plans, and are alarmed at possible costs.

GENTLE READER:

You are obviously not the hosts at this wedding, as parents generally are for a first wedding and may be, if they choose, for subsequent ones. There is therefore no more admission charge for you than there is for any of the other guests.

The Second Time Around

DEAR MISS MANNERS:

My daughter is getting married for the second time in three years, and wishes to send out invitations. My question is: Is it appropriate to send wedding invitations to family and friends the second time around?

GENTLE READER:

As long as it is appropriate to get married, it is appropriate to invite family and friends to the wedding. Twice in three years does not seem to Miss Manners to be excessive by today's standards.

However, if your daughter is planning to keep going at this rate—and perhaps even now—you should make allowances for the fact that people will not make quite the same fuss as they would if the event were unique. Presents are by no means as conventionally given for second marriages as for first, for example.

It is also considered polite to vary the event somewhat, to keep the spectators interested, and also to remove from them obvious opportunities for satirical comparison. This is one reason for the "quieter" second wedding, and also a reason why that very custom is often ignored by people who had simple first weddings and wish to do it up thoroughly at the next opportunity.

"Quieter" does not refer to the noise level, and hence the supposed amount of merriment, or even to the number of guests. It means that you save on engraving costs by inviting people by individual letters ("Hortense is being married to Arno Smiles on Saturday the twenty-seventh and we do hope you can be with us") and you put the wedding costume money into a stunning dress or suit that a real person might wear in real life. And then you give a wonderful reception and enjoy yourselves. After all, it could turn out to be the last such chance.

Quelling Remarriage Objections

DEAR MISS MANNERS:

I am remarrying my ex-husband. Since our first wedding was informal and hasty, we would like to celebrate this ceremony of mature commitment in grand style. The church is delighted to open its doors to us, and many friends have hinted that they would like to be there. We want to have a basically traditional, if simple, wedding.

The problem? Invitations and relatives. How do I inform the proper relatives of our wish to share this day with them, and not appear to be asking for gifts to be given by those who fulfilled that obligation at the time of our first wedding? My ex-husband wants formal invitations to go to his family. My mother feels after-wedding announcements would be more appropriate.

I, myself, would like to throw etiquette out of the window, along with the relatives who would be offended by my gesture of welcome. But, then, Miss Manners would possibly fling herself out of the window as well.

GENTLE READER:

Oh, dear, no. It is kind of you to be concerned about Miss Manners, but put yourself at ease. She would so much rather go in by those church doors that were thrown open with delight than out through the window.

A remarriage such as you are planning has—to Miss Manners and, she would venture, to most people—a peculiar charm, not untinged with a certain reflective humor on the general subjects of love and maturity. Of course, it should be festive, but there is no reason to throw etiquette out the window. (Would you, in fact, be kind enough to close that window? It seems to be creating an emotional draft.)

Miss Manners has long since acknowledged the propriety of people who are old enough to know what they are doing celebrating their marriages as thoroughly as presumed innocents do theirs. She may counsel a more sophisticated format for such weddings than the rituals and dress intended for extreme youth, but she is not outraged when a sentimental attachment to such forms overcomes stylistic considerations. By all means, have your traditional wedding. Your well-wishers will be full of kindly smiles, anyway, and it would take a great deal of churlishness to criticize the charming blend of romance and realism that this occasion represents.

Now, as to that pesky matter of presents. How many times has Miss Manners said that wedding presents are not obligatory, and that for the bridal couple or the guests to consider a wedding invitation as a solicitation for dry goods is in disgusting taste?

The correct posture for any bride is to be pleasantly overwhelmed when she receives a present, because the consumer aspect of getting married had been the furthest thing from her mind. If you have relatives who think of weddings in terms of commerce, that is their problem.

However, if you want to be particularly gracious, Miss Manners has an idea for you. To those who attended your first wedding, you might send, in addition to the invitation, an informal letter in the tenderly amusing spirit of the occasion, mentioning that you remember their presence at your previous wedding and want especially to have them with you on this even more important—because it is to be the final—occasion.

Unfriendly Relations

Rearing In-Laws

DEAR MISS MANNERS:

I don't like mother-in-law jokes and I don't want to be one. But you haven't seen the way my son's wife keeps house, if you can call it that. She is really a sweet girl, and I have tried to be a mother to her, because she doesn't have one of her own, only an elderly teenager who comes through once a year to empty the liquor cabinet and show off some new wrinkled old boyfriend. This fine lady never taught poor Susan anything. The house is filthy, half the time they eat carry-out food, and her clothes are held together by safety pins. My son is one of those easygoing men who doesn't notice a thing. He's perfectly happy to live that way, although he knows better. So I don't want to interfere in their lives and am not one of those people who says things like "When are you going to give me grandchildren?" which I know is none of my business. Can't you just tell me a way I can help make up for that upbringing, before they have my grandchildren, so they won't be brought up that way, too?

GENTLE READER:

Sorry. Children-in-law, no matter what age or shape or state of cleanliness when wed, are, by polite convention, presumed to be grown-up. You cannot, therefore, contribute to the upbringing of your daughter-in-law. Grandmothers, however, are allowed to invite their grandchildren to visit them for as often and long as is feasible, for the purpose, among others, of showing them what a proper household is, if they have never seen one. It is not considered fair to point this out in words, but an observant child may, after about twenty years' exposure, notice it for himself. If not—well, your son didn't, either, even after the benefit of your upbringing, and, by your own admission, he is happy.

In-Laws' Criticism

DEAR MISS MANNERS:

I have been happily married for more than five years. Our only problem is my husband's parents, especially his mother. First of all, they simply don't like me, and don't try to make any secret of it, either. I have tried to make our relationship work, I have tried everything to help bring about a change in their attitude toward me, but it has all been in vain. They resent me terribly. I'm a good citizen of the community, I love my husband and family, I work hard, and I also keep myself in good physical condition.

My in-laws treat me as if I'm not to be trusted or befriended. My father-in-law belittles everything I do and say. My sister-in-law is especially hostile toward me. She measures and weighs everything I do and say, just waiting for a slipup so that she can lay into me. My mother-in-law speaks to my husband in a manner that suggests that she feels he committed high treason by getting married and leaving the family circle. She often tells him that his younger twenty-two-year-old sister, who has never had a steady boyfriend or lived away from home, is in no rush to find a boyfriend or to get married, plus ''We take care of all of her financial needs.'' She tells my husband ,''If you had not gotten married, we would do the same for you.'' His mother waves that fact in my husband's face all the time. I think it's a very mean and unfeeling thing for her to say. First of all, my husband and I could care less what they give or buy his sister, and second of all, we can more than afford to take care of our own wants and needs.

She calls us on the phone several times a week, sometimes to ask us what we feel are very invading questions, and if we refuse to answer them she gets very defensive. If my husband and I go out for the evening, she will call all night until we get home and then ask, ''Where have you been? I've been so worried. I've been calling all night. You should call us before you go out and let us know where you are going and what time you'll be home, so you won't have me so worried.'' Needless to say, we have little privacy. We live several miles away from my in-laws, but they insist we drop by to visit whenever they want us to, even if it's inconvenient. If we don't comply, she gets very upset. If we don't go along with her advice, she gets frustrated and angry.

She is always telling us about how much she has sacrificed and done for her children, and is hurt by the lack of appreciation and thanks. This is simply not true. My husband is a very kind and devoted son, and I think she takes gross advantage of him. We have tried discussing these problems but to no avail—she either starts crying and claims that we're causing her great stress, or sulks.

I come from a very loving and accepting family, and I'm simply not used to this type of interaction within a family. My folks live several hundred miles away and have no knowledge of the problems that I have with my in-laws—I have never mentioned it to them, because I don't want to embarrass my husband. As far as my family is concerned, my in-laws are lovely people; they have said nothing but kind things about them to me. My mother-in-law, on the other hand, says nothing but awful things to me about my family. She says terrible things about me and my family to her family and friends, too. I find this whole situation very stressful, and my husband does, too, even though he grew up in it. How do we appropriately handle this in an effective way?

GENTLE READER:

Please remember that you sent this question to an etiquette adviser, and not a human-relations counselor. Miss Manners hopes to give you cause to be grateful that you made that choice. The etiquette credo is that one must behave well, even under difficult circumstances, but that one is not responsible if this does not inspire good behavior in others. The satisfaction in one's own manners should give one the strength to endure the lack of it in others.

A daughter- (or son-) in law's primary etiquette obligations are to speak with respect, even if not so addressed; to refrain from criticizing the in-laws outside of the family; to appear on state and emergency occasions; and not to interfere in direct communication between in-laws and their child. Unreasonable requests beyond this, such as signing out for the evening or constant visiting, may be politely ignored.

It is also an obligation of a daughter- or son-in-law to offer and show, or simulate, affection; but if this is rejected, it need not be pressed. If you follow the other rules scrupulously, not telling her or anyone else what an old bat she is, not counting up how many bogus emergencies she calls, and not telling your husband what he would say to her if he really loved you, you will have quite enough to do to make anyone feel virtuous, no matter how spurned.

In-Laws' Advice

DEAR MISS MANNERS:

My sister-in-law drops into town from time to time, with or without husband and children, for a visit to her family. While here, she calls and invites herself to dinner. (The last time, she announced midway through the evening that she wanted to spend the night, due to her fear of night driving.) From the time she arrives until she leaves, the woman criticizes me relentlessly.

"Why do you quarter your potatoes so carefully? You're going to mash them anyway, just cut them and throw them into the pot." "I noticed you have velour towels. But why spend that much money on linens; terry cloth is more absorbent, and I've never spent more than two dollars on a towel." "You're going to feed your dogs that chicken? Put it in the fridge, and eat it in your next meal." "Why use butter? Margarine is so much cheaper. You can't really tell the difference in taste." "You should gain some weight, you're getting too skinny." (I'm a seven, and I work to stay a seven. I like being a seven, my husband likes me a seven. She's an eighteen.) And on she goes, reciting a litany against our life-style for the entire visit. She argues with and cuts down my brother and their children in front of us. She seems to delight in their obvious humiliation and embarrassment. By the time she leaves, we are frustrated and angry.

She is an outcast from the family—no one wants to be around her. I refuse to be drawn into an argument with her—yet I feel, as do others, as if I'm continually baited. I also don't want to be estranged from my brother's affection. My dad spoke to him once about her, and it only caused resentment. So the problem remains—how do we handle this woman who attacks us in our home, and attacks other family members as well, during reunions in our parents' home? We are running out of cheeks to turn. Please help.

GENTLE READER:

Many families are blessed with at least one person who knows exactly how life should be lived, down to the smallest detail, and is willing to share this knowledge without waiting for the ignorant and the timid to solicit advice. Be thankful that your family is not blessed with two such people, because their expertise is bound to conflict and the family turf becomes a battleground.

Miss Manners applauds your desire to endure, rather than exile, this fountain of knowledge, for the sake of maintaining cordial relations with your blood relatives under her immediate supervision. It will not be easy.

Here is a two-step method Miss Manners recommends for frustrating these spreaders of wisdom. (And you figured that Miss Manners was the one like that in her family, didn't you? Not nice. Miss Manners gives only *solicited* advice.) First, ask the person for advice on everything. "What is the best way to cut up potatoes?" "Tell me the relative merits of different kinds of towels." "What do you think the dog would like for dinner?" And so on. You must ask before she volunteers, and you must offer no arguments—just listen, or pretend to listen, in silence. Then ignore the advice. Don't say you are not going to follow it, but don't. If challenged reply, "Yes, I'm still thinking about that. Why was it again you thought margarine was better?" This is one of Miss Manners' favorite faultlessly polite and cheerful ways to drive others into the madhouse.

Discarded In-Laws

DEAR MISS MANNERS:

Within the past six years, all four of my sons have married, with, unfortunately, three of the four marriages ending in divorce. When my eldest son left his wife, I responded—foolishly, I now realize—by taking the side of my discarded daughter-in-law. I behaved badly in several ways: by scorning my son in his hour of need, by alienating my son's then companion, now wife, by refusing to publicly acknowledge my son's second marriage. In short, I acted as if I were the party aggrieved.

Now that my second son is going through a divorce, I find myself headed in the same disastrous direction, albeit from the opposite perspective. In this case, my son was the one abandoned. Although I had regarded his spouse as my favorite daughter-in-law, I promptly cut off all communication with her, and spoke ill of her to my son, his siblings, my husband, and anyone else within earshot. I covered over their wedding pictures and terminated my association with her family, although I had held them in fond esteem. I realize that again, I am personalizing the tragedy as if it were my own. My son wishes that I simply would let the matter drop. My husband agrees, telling me that I have no business acting as if my children's marriages somehow reflect on their upbringing and parentage.

Now the former daughter-in-law has sent me a gift—an heirloom from her family that she claims she wants me to have as a token of her feelings for me. I don't know what to do, Miss Manners. If I accept the gift and acknowledge its receipt, I will feel like a fool. If I send it back or do something even more rash, I know that my son will never forgive me. I feel myself in the grip of emotions more powerful than I can control, and though I wish to do the right thing, I worry that I will expose myself to either my own self-condemnation or my family's opprobrium.

GENTLE READER:

Miss Manners sympathizes with the problem, but disagrees with the diagnosis. She doesn't at all think that you are inserting yourself into the drama of others, possibly from vanity at the reflection on your parenting.

You are reacting correctly by the standards of another time, when divorce was considered to be an irrevocable blight on the lives of those who were its victims. Miss Manners doesn't know whether she considers it better or worse that people now are supposed to pick themselves up relatively easily and go on with their lives, but so it is. A broken marriage of today is customarily treated as if it were a broken engagement of yesterday—too bad it didn't work out, but better to have found out sooner than later.

If you cannot, or do not wish to, modernize your feelings on this matter, you must nevertheless modernize your behavior, eliminating the grand gestures of condemnation and vengeance. But you have the right to demand that your family modernize their expectations, too, and allow you to associate or not with former spouses and their relatives, as your feelings dictate. Your ex-daughter-in-law is trying to indicate that she still loves you. You may return either her love or her present, but not by making a political stance out of either. "Thank you, but I don't feel I can accept this" will do.

Sorry, Wrong Name

DEAR MISS MANNERS:

I have been living with my boyfriend for more than a year now. I went up to meet his family at Christmas. The whole time I was there (a thousand miles away from my home), his whole family called me his ex-wife's name. His mother told me how much he favored the ex-wife, how nice the ex-wife was, and that she couldn't have asked for a daughter-in-law any better.

This woman, I'll call her Cindy, evidently still calls Fred's mother all the time, and his mother surely made no bones about telling me this, either. The grandmother still had a picture of her and my boyfriend sitting out bigger than a balloon.

The mother and the grandmother also came to visit us and called me Cindy again the whole time they were here. It makes me furious! Freddie corrects them, sometimes. He said his grandmother is just old, and doesn't remember. She had also sent us a card addressed to "Freddie and Cathy" (not even the ex-wife's name).

His mother has no excuse. My family never calls him anything but his name. I might also mention my family is so good to him. He knows when his family calls me Cindy how it bothers me. He just acts like it's no big deal to him.

Please tell me a tactful way of making them remember. I have corrected them so many times that it seems like they couldn't forget.

GENTLE READER:

The tactful way is to stop visiting them until they begin to realize that they are being shut out of an important part of Fred's life. After a while, they will say, "Where's Cindy?" to which Fred can reply, "Why, don't you remember— she moved away after the divorce." They will then say, "No, Cathy—how come you don't bring her around anymore?" and Fred can reply, "Cathy? Who's Cathy?" After a suitable pause, he can clap his hand to his mouth in astonishment and say, "You mean Connie? I'd love to bring Connie—why don't you invite her? Here, let me write down her name for you."

You will notice, Connie, Cathy, Cindy, whatever your name is, that this dialogue requires the active participation of Fred, and that it also requires that his family show some interest and sensitivity about his living arrangements. Without these, you cannot accomplish your objective, as you have already noticed. Miss Manners agrees with you that the grandmother is a doubtful case, but there is little question that the mother's attitude is to make you unwelcome, and if that persists, maintaining your distance is all the more desirable.

The Family Fruitcake

DEAR MISS MANNERS:

When I married my husband three years ago, he was a widower with two boys, nine and thirteen, and I had two boys, eight and thirteen. Blending these adolescents into a homogeneous family has not been easy. Now the main problem is my husband's ex-mother-in-law, his boys' maternal grandmother. Florence, in my opinion, is a fruitcake. This is also the opinion of my husband, her living daughter, and my husband's family.

When we first met, she was extremely effusive to me. You would think I was the answer to all her prayers. "The boys are so lucky to have you, etc., etc." However, behind my back, she has done nothing except discredit me. She accuses me of neglect and abuse, and whenever my stepsons visit her in the summer, they report to me that she spends most of their visit asking very personal questions about me and my past and constantly puts down my own sons, to the point where my stepsons come back feeling so superior the younger one barely speaks to his stepbrothers for days.

But the real "straw that broke . . . ." came when we paid a visit to her new home, which she had been gushing that she wanted to show me. When we got there, I was greeted by an eleven-by-fourteen picture of her daughter and an eleven-by-fourteen picture beside it of my husband—both their college graduation pictures. At this point, I felt my heart drop a beat, but I never lost my poise.

She then ushered us into the family room, sat me in a chair (she refused to let me sit beside my husband, where I wanted to sit) which I noticed faced a fireplace mantel with family pictures of my husband and her daughter and the boys. On the wall was another such collage, including wedding pictures. During the evening, she referred to my "husband" three times, not meaning my present husband, but my sons' father. The clincher was when she took us into our bedroom for the night. She had dug out of her daughter's wedding album an eleven-by-fourteen picture of my husband and her daughter in a passionate kiss, and had propped this picture up on the dresser. She said, "There are extra blankets in the closet, but you probably won't need them—Eileen always said Rick was her armstrong heater." The last time all this happened, I told myself she had probably had all those pictures sitting around for ten or fifteen years and just didn't see any reason to move them. But this is a new house.

I want nothing to do with this woman, other than the boys' obligatory visits to their grandmother in the summer. She is a menace, obviously intent on undermining my marriage and role in her grandsons' lives. She has written she plans to visit us. May I—have I earned the right—choose to not allow her to visit in my home? How can I diplomatically accomplish this?

GENTLE READER:

After due consideration of the tender feelings of a bereaved mother unable to adjust to seeing another, however worthy, in her late daughter's place, Miss Manners has concluded that you are right: Florence is a fruitcake. The graduation and wedding pictures can easily be excused, but the sexy one—and the sexy remark—cannot be.

Fortunately, neither you nor your husband is related to her. Your stepsons are and you have a duty to allow them to maintain the contact, although Miss Manners assures you that the entertainment value, for teenage boys, of being quizzed about their stepmother is close to nil, and you will increasingly find them distancing themselves from her.

The way to refuse any guest-proposed invitation is to say, "I'm so sorry, but that isn't a convenient time for us," and to say it as often as necessary, never yielding to temptation to add supporting evidence or a supplementary argument that can be refuted. Why is it a bad time for you? "Because it's just not a good time for us to handle a visit—we're so very sorry."

Renewing Awkward Relations

DEAR MISS MANNERS:

Almost twelve years ago, my son, who is exceptionally talented and attractive, married a young lady whom I will call Mary, while they were both in college. At first, I was quite taken with her, and since she apparently made my son content, I was appreciative of her efforts. They both entered the same respected profession and did quite well.

After seven years of marriage, my son confessed that his happiness had been feigned for all that time, and that he was leaving Mary because he had finally found a lovely woman who filled his needs and encouraged his potential. Unfortunately, this woman was Mary's friend, and at the time, Mary was midterm in the pregnancy of their first child. Naturally, there were some inappropriate responses to this awkward situation, mostly from ill-bred busybodies. Because of the circumstances and the relationship with my son, I found it necessary to avoid Mary and my future grandchild.

Well, Miss Manners, today my granddaughter is almost five years old, and is a lovely little girl. My son has been remarried for over four years, and has presented me with two other heirs. However, Mary has continued her career, raised the child, and remained single, and we all live within the same city. I find myself longing for my firstborn grandchild. What would etiquette prescribe in this situation? My son does not see the child but twice in any year, and even that causes embarrassment for his new family.

I would not make great demands on Mary. I, also, am a busy career woman, and therefore would only request the child for several hours on holidays and special events. Also my sixty-fifth birthday will be soon, and I wish all my grandchildren present for a special portrait.

GENTLE READER:

Miss Manners hardly yields to anyone in her cool mastery of etiquette under stress, but she is awed by your characterizing the desertion of a pregnant wife for her friend as "an awkward situation" on which comments are "inappropriate," and of a father's avoidance of his four-year-old as a maneuver to avoid causing "embarrassment for his new family."

She is well aware, however, that you did not ask her to make inappropriate comments, either, or appropriate ones for that matter, on you or your son. She only mentions it at all, in the course of addressing the problem you pose, because it is possible that Mary's reaction to your overtures will be colored by just such prejudices.

In theory, your desire for a relationship with your granddaughter should be considered separately from the relationship of the child to her father, as you, too, are a blood relative and ought to be able to pursue your connections independently. You cannot, however, maintain much of a relationship with a minor child against the wishes of its mother and guardian. You can try, by writing the child or otherwise approaching her (cynical people do it through lavish presents), but your chances of success are not good without the mother's support.

Miss Manners therefore suggests that you simply voice your wish to her, putting as much pathos into your feelings as possible and probably omitting your delight that your son "finally found a lovely woman who filled his needs and encouraged his potential." Mary may just be gracious enough to overlook the past. On the other hand, don't hold the telephone too close to your ear.

The Uncle's Uhm . . .

DEAR MISS MANNERS:

My question concerns guests and hosts/hostesses who live in vacation spots year-round, and have taken up a new way of living. I am leaving out the feelings of young people, as they seem better able to cope than we of the older generation. For four years now, I have been in love with a wonderful gentleman whom I moved in with. We have not married because of financial, legal, and other reasons for keeping out complications. We are not alone in this arrangement; it is common here in Florida. We feel married—he refers to me as his wife and to me he is my husband—but there is just not a "white piece of paper." I moved into his house and made it our home.

The problem is relatives who want to come and spend a week in the sun. How do the relatives, who know there is no marriage, treat the woman that Uncle is living with? We have just had such a visit and it was very difficult for all people involved. I tried to act as hostess and arranged entertainment plus meals plus private time for everyone. They were more interested in visiting with neighbors and leaving opened mayonnaise jars, dirty dishes, or whatever for me to pick up. It all finally came to a head and a lot was said. My feeling was that our values are different. I thought they had come to see their uncle. To them, it was "different life-styles based on different life experiences." Also they said that they had acted as they had before, and did not know there were new "ground rules." If you can understand their reasoning, try to make me understand, as I am confused.

As a guest, I try to be polite and respect my host and hostess. Being that I am not married, do they feel that this is not my home, and that I should not feel it is?

GENTLE READER:

The ground rules are the same as always—guests are indeed expected to be polite and respect the host and hostess. If they want to show disapproval of your living arrangements, they need only to refrain from visiting you.

Frankly, it sounds to Miss Manners as if your "values," the current but curious term for marriage or lack of it, have nothing to do with it. Your guests are simply breaking the rules in the same old way they, by their own admission, always have done. If Uncle never minded their wandering about and leaving a mess, but you do, you must set the terms you consider acceptable—politely, of course. If anything, it is worse for hosts to be inhospitable than guests to be rude. Tell them when you have something planned for them, and ask them when they have plans outside the house. Apologize to them for not having a maid, explaining that therefore they will unfortunately have to put back jars they took from the refrigerator. Miss Manners thinks you will find that the question of values will not trouble you nearly so much once the mess in the sink disappears.

Unkind Appraisals

Dear Miss Manners:

My husband and I became engaged while he was on a university assistantship. My engagement ring contains two pavé diamonds, at his insistence. My husband has little inherited wealth; his cousin, however, has a lot. His cousin's wife, coincidentally, wears an engagement ring containing several one-carat stones. One evening, after a family dinner hosted by this cousin, his wife turned to me and exclaimed, "Is that your engagement ring? It has diamonds, hasn't it? But . . . where are they?"

I realize this is a sad situation to be concerned with, but felt my husband and his family had been the intended recipients of her remarks. Although she inquires about the authenticity and price, and insists on examining all my jewelry customarily, this was the only moment in which I sensed her to have shown shrewder than usual insight into the gentle art of making enemies, for, after rigorous scrutiny of the ring, she professed to have been unable to locate the stone without optical assistance, and we parted in search of a magnifying glass, which remained as undiscovered as the diamonds for the rest of the evening.

Must I resort to literary revenge in yet another scathing exposé of the middle class, or could you suggest a more agreeable way to approach this situation?

Gentle Reader:

Let us not blame the entire middle class for this. Miss Manners, for one, is weary of hearing the middle class picked on, especially by its own members.

However, she is not averse to picking on someone of your husband's cousin's wife's kind. What is more, she is willing to tell you exactly how to do it, eschewing cheap generalizations and rudeness. It is one of Miss Manners' basic tenets that there is nothing wrong with defending oneself from the bad manners of others, provided one does not use the same approach in doing so.

Here goes. You may alter the details, if you wish, to fit the facts of your life.

"Ah, you asked about my engagement ring. You can't imagine how much pleasure it brings me—let me tell you the story. You remember that Charles was still on his university assistantship when we became engaged. We were so young and so poor that we knew we should have waited to get married, but we were so much in love, we couldn't, and, as it turned out, those years of struggle are so precious to us. Anyway, I've never much cared for flashy jewelry, and I never dreamed he would be so foolish as to buy me an engagement ring, but Charles is so romantic that he absolutely insisted, and he wanted it to have diamonds in it. Even now, my eyes fill up when I think what he must have sacrificed to get it. I wouldn't trade it for all the queen's crown jewels.

"By the way, that's a very impressive ring you have. Were you ever a jeweler or pawnbroker or anything professional like that? You have such an exact eye for appraising things. How you must be amused by a sentimental idiot like me."

Putting One's Foot Down (Politely)

DEAR MISS MANNERS:

My husband's mother lives alone near us. Though we have our differences, I respect her and enjoy her company very much. I don't know how aware of this my stepmother-in-law is, but whenever we see each other, which is not too frequently because of distance, she indulges in very rude comments against my mother-in-law.

So far, the only way I can think of to respond is silence. This is not very gratifying, neither does it seem to be doing anything to stifle this malicious talk. What do you suggest?

GENTLE READER:

Fortunately, etiquette recognizes situations in which it is necessary to be (1) respectful, (2) polite (actually, there are no situations in which etiquette permits a breach of manners, but read on), and (3) able to convey to another person that you will not tolerate her behavior.

This is such a time. Honor requires you not to let these insults pass. Your reply should be: "I am extremely fond of my mother-in-law, and I won't listen to a word against her." After letting that sink in for a moment, add, "I have never heard her speak unkindly of you."

Houseguests, Relative and Non

Surviving Family Visits

Never ask visiting relatives to make themselves at home. In Miss Manners' experience it is only when members of different branches of a family are made to feel like nervous guests in one another's homes that there is any chance that family ties will survive family visits. The expression "Make yourself at home" was invented for houseguests who drive their hosts crazy by tracking them down at their gardening to ask, "Is it all right if I get myself a glass of water?" or sitting immobile in the living room for two hours until the hosts get up, not getting breakfast or reading the paper for fear of doing something wrong. Relatives who behave like that are trying to pick a fight.

Why, Miss Manners can hear her gentle readers musing, should people who are bound by the casual ties of blood or marriage, as well as by the sacred bonds of hospitality, be spoiling for fights? Why? Because they were allowed to start out feeling at home, and nobody took the trouble to make them feel ill at ease until it was too late. A person can have only one home (Miss Manners assumes that her readers are not too literal-minded to recognize that the home can encompass a town house, weekend place, country retreat, yacht, and porch hammock; or it can consist of a corner of a closet or basement that has eluded parental inspection). Within that territory, the resident is entitled to have things as he or she likes them, a style generally referred to by its designer as "right." The major choices are: neat or messy; dirty or clean; formal or informal; and matched or eclectic, but there are infinite minute variations, from deciding whether the books should be arranged by subject or by author down to that dreadful perennial about which way the toilet paper should unravel.

Do you begin to see the problem? A person who feels at home in a household set up by someone else is seized with an irresistible urge to set things right. This is called "helping." It is natural to feel this way about the houses of people with whom one has previously shared a home. Parents visiting their married children are notorious offenders, but grown children visiting either their parents or adult siblings can be just as bad. Conflicts are more common between in-laws because blood relatives have shared experience of "how things should be done." The advocates of neat and clean tend to be the oppressors, because the dirty-mess proponents are generally too cowed to defend themselves. (However, Miss Manners has heard of one mother-in-law who was outraged that milk cartons were not allowed on the table of her son's household, and who attributed this quirk to the daughter-in-law's snobbishness.)

The solution to such conflict works only if practiced immediately upon the establishment of a new household. When relatives arrive, they should be treated as honored guests. The routine of the house should be explained to them, along with the rhetorical hope that it will suit their convenience. Their needs should be supplied, and offers of help accepted only for limited tasks conducted under supervision. A guest should dry dishes, for example, while a host washes, but should not be allowed to put them away. That is an invitation to rearrange the cupboards.

Any such help should be accepted with exaggerated gratitude, it being so far beyond the guest's obligations. Suggestions and advice should be met with muted sorrow: "Oh, dear, and we tried so hard to make everything look nice for you," or "Do you think so? And we were so proud of this room," or "I guess we'll never be up to your standards— this way suits us so well and we've been happy with it." Firmness in this approach should discourage any nesting-in, but will also establish patterns of behavior which might make it agreeable to invite these people again.

Rules for Adults

DEAR MISS MANNERS:

Are grandparents expected to obey the rules of the house? Our grandparents live on the West Coast, and we consider ourselves lucky to see them once a year. We have small children, so I enforce the rule strictly that one eats or drinks *only* in the kitchen or at the dining-room table. Gran'pa, however, loves to wander around with his coffee cup or his dessert or whatever. More often than not, I find these plates just left in the playroom, and while we have had a few spills, we have, thankfully, never had any broken dishes. I have asked Gran'pa not to do this and I have explained the reasons why. But he just laughs and says, "Are these rules for adults, too?" or "Don't adults get any special privileges?"

As far as I'm concerned, adults are there to set an example. Gran'pa is my father-in-law, but I would feel just the same if he were my dad. With each passing visit, I get more uptight, not only because I've asked politely and reminded, but because the children are now approaching an age where they will remark, "If Gran'pa can do it, why can't we?" Am I too inflexible? Should I make light of the whole thing? How do I teach my children that different families have different rules and we should be sensitive to them when we are guests, even if they are not always spoken?

GENTLE READER:

Your question, about whether grandparents should obey the rules of the house, is an extremely difficult one. Therefore, Miss Manners will answer the questions within your question, instead.

From Gran'pa: "Are these rules for adults, too? Don't adults get special privileges?"

Answer: "Gran'pa, dear, we are so happy to have you here—we see far too little of you. Of course, make yourself comfortable, and have your coffee where you like. You understand, of course, that we don't let Samantha and Tyrone eat outside the kitchen or dining room. You have special privileges, Gran'pa dear—we'd just appreciate it if you didn't encourage the children to think they do, too, at least not until they are grandparents themselves."

From the children (someday): "If Gran'pa can do it, why can't we?"

Answer. "Gran'pa is your grandfather, and besides, he is a guest in our house. You are right that it is one of the rules of this house not to trail food around, and we expect you to obey this; Mamma and Papa do, too. But it's another rule of the house that we do not try to bring up our elders or our honored guests. Gran'pa wants to do things the way he's used to, and was doing long before even we were born, and it is not up to us to correct him. We are trying to teach you to do as we think best, and naturally, that is what we do, ourselves. But it is not for us, or for you, to decide what is best for Gran'pa. Respecting Gran'pa is one of the most important rules of this house. Now, will you please go into the kitchen with that? You know I can't bear to have crumbs all over the house!"

Parents as Guests

DEAR MISS MANNERS:

Could you give some tips or advice on having parents as guests? My husband's parents and sister are from the East Coast and do not agree with the way we expect them to behave when they visit us. I would like your advice on how to handle such situations as their not being satisfied with what I cook for them, wanting to do something other than what we have planned, being careless with our possessions, taking over in the kitchen, bringing their own food with them, monopolizing our TV, and being loud and boisterous.

They argue that when we visit them, we are permitted to do what we want. What they don't seem to realize is that we go along with their ways, so there are no problems. But when they come here, I expect them to adjust to our ways, and they don't agree. They feel they should be able to do what they want and we should treat them as family, not "guests."

GENTLE READER:

It seems foolish to volunteer for the losing side in mid-battle, but Miss Manners wishes to inform you, first, that she is with you, and second, that we will lose. You are correct that the proper order of things is for the guests to conform to the standards of the household, rather than the other way around. Guests do have the privilege of immunity from reprimand, but are on their honor not to abuse it.

What your relatives are really asking is that they be granted the status of guests, without your having the hosts' recourse of not inviting back people who have violated this status by doing things they know you don't like. This is the basis for Miss Manners' feeling of hopelessness. You do not, of course, wish to begin a family feud over such petty violations as you cite, and yet you cannot politely criticize and correct your guests, your elders, and your in-laws. There is much to be said, therefore, for putting up with their visits and rejoicing at their conclusion. The rewards of doing this are consciousness of virtue and a renewed pleasure in the basic household.

However, if you really can't bear it, and feel yourself going over the brink at the sight of them eating their own food—a reaction that Miss Manners would find completely understandable, though unfortunate—you might try their suggestion of treating them as family. Family rules, as you know if you live in peace with your husband and perhaps a child or two, do not mean that everyone can do whatever he likes and no one else has anything to say about it. They mean that compromises must be worked out to indulge foibles, while refraining from annoying others.

In this case, you could tell your in-laws in advance that you enjoy planning their stay, but would find it helpful to know if there is anything they would like to do (including scheduling periods for doing nothing or following impulses), and anything they would especially like to eat (or avoid). It would be flattering to suggest that they bring a particular food specialty that you can plan into your menu. Miss Manners would give in on the television, hoping to keep them occupied while she repossesses the kitchen. As for such characteristics as carelessness and boisterousness, you have to assume that these are not special guest behavior, but their general standard, which you cannot change. It would be wrong on many grounds to criticize them—the only ground on which to accomplish your goals is a plea that they indulge your household eccentricities, regardless of whether they endorse them.

Good luck. Miss Manners still recommends temporary martyrdom. If you air your grievances, your husband's loyalties will be at best divided; if you maintain a sweet submission, he will see their behavior through your eyes.

Drop-in Relations

DEAR MISS MANNERS:

What in the world would you do if a relative drove up to your home, complete with bag and baggage, to spend a few days? This relative did not call, did not make prior arrangements, and could not care less what our plans were.

I found it difficult to say to someone who traveled one hundred miles that we had other plans. Should we have left her to fend for herself? How do you tactfully say to her that she should have called? This—having to entertain a guest who was so rude—ruined three days.

GENTLE READER:

Miss Manners would dash up to this relative with open arms and exclaim, ''Why, what a wonderful surprise! Why didn't you tell me you were coming? I'm heart-broken that you'll be in town, and I will hardly have a chance to see you! If only I had known, I would have been able to entertain you properly. Oh, dear, this is awful! I'm so glad to see you, and now I have to go rushing off! It just isn't fair. You mustn't tease me like this.''

Miss Manners would then go rushing off. If she were feeling generous, she might say, ''Make yourself as comfortable as you can—I'm just wretched that I have to tear myself away,'' and leave the visitor to fend for herself. If Miss Manners were not feeling generous, she might say, ''I'm going to insist that you go to a hotel, because I know I can't do right by you.'' Each time during the weekend that she saw this relative, she would repeat the entire speech, with a chorus of moaning, ''Oh, why didn't you let me know?''

Grudging Hospitality

DEAR MISS MANNERS:

How far does hospitality go with out-of-state guests?

Twice, my sister-in-law and her family stayed with us for a weekend, and both times she insisted that I let her do her laundry at my house. I find this boldness to be unnerving, not to mention the added expense of running less than half a load of clothes in my washer and dryer. She also took the liberty (that is, without permission) of washing her car during their last visit. She maintains that we are ''family,'' and therefore I should not deny her these favors. I feel that she is abusing my otherwise generous hospitality. Please prepare me for the next visit.

GENTLE READER:

Do not have a next visit. A woman who calculates the expense of running her washer and dryer as being more significant than the convenience of her sister-in-law does not deserve to have family, let alone houseguests.

Toothpaste Proclivities

DEAR MISS MANNERS:

My partner and I have lived happily together for the past five years—until this past weekend, when her mother was with us.

When I first met my partner, I'll call her Boomer, she had the annoying habit of applying toothpaste to her toothbrush as if it were whipping cream on a sundae. I mean, we would go through a large tube a week. After watching her mother brush her teeth, I know where Boomer got the habit. I, being the sole support of the household, objected, and we agreed that I would put Boomer's toothpaste portion on her toothbrush every morning. This worked out fine until last weekend. Knowing that Boomer's family had a proclivity for using large amounts of toothpaste, I measured out individual portions on clean squares of wax paper and left them in the guest bathroom. (Boomer's family has an absurd idea that your teeth are not really clean unless you use large amounts while my dentist tells me toothpaste is not necessary at all.)

Anyway, nothing was said at breakfast, and Boomer's mother left quietly. Today I received in the mail a whole case of toothpaste, and a nasty note saying next time she would prefer to stay in a motel. Was I in the wrong, or is she acting rudely? Believe me, all I am trying to do is save money so that Boomer can go to graduate school.

GENTLE READER:

What a noble soul you are, out to educate the world. What have you planned to have Boomer study in graduate school? Obedience?

It had not occurred to Miss Manners before, but probably the definition of a rude host is one who notices how much of his ordinary supplies his guests use and broods about the cost. No, no. It is someone who lurks near the guest bathroom to observe how a middle-aged female houseguest brushes her teeth.

Houseguest Tug-of-War

DEAR MISS MANNERS:

Every time my sister visits me for a weekend, I get caught in a tangled social situation. She and her husband live about three hours away from me and my husband, and we are all close friends. They also have other friends in the area who rarely make it over to our house, but who invariably have a good reason for having us all over, like "Meet here to see So-and-So, who is also in town this weekend." And somehow, because they ask so nicely and so urgently, we all end up over there on Saturday night.

I feel that it would be better for all concerned if their other friends in the area, who are also friends of ours, would come here to party, so that the travelers could stay in one place. We end up making elaborate plans to eat, to rendezvous, to party. We live in a huge rural area surrounding a small city, so we end up driving at least twenty to forty minutes. For some of us, including my sister, and her husband, it gets to be nerve-racking. We don't talk about it, because when I do try to discuss how I feel, I come off sounding like the heavy, and it sounds like I'm not being flexible and I don't want to see the other friends, which is not true.

I am almost to the point where I feel like my sister and her husband are the rope in a twisted, neurotic tug-of-war between me and my husband and the other couple. (I tend to analyze everything, and I do not want to hurt anyone's feelings.) The tug-of-war is, of course, all very subtle and friendly and party-ish. So if I make plans for dinner or even think of planning, I am cautioned to "hang loose." On times when we have invited over other local friends (to meet my sis), my sis and her hub go over to the other friend's house anyway, and then return, and I get the feeling I'm somehow fouling things up because we had decided to stay home to entertain.

Even though it's only a few hours out of the whole weekend, I'm sick of it. I think the other friends are (unconsciously) putting us all in a power struggle—"Come over here" vs. "No, you come over here." I guess my feelings are kind of hurt because ultimately my sister and her husband don't just say to the couple, "We're staying this weekend at my sister's, and we'd love to see you, too, so come over if you can." I have tried including the couple, too, with no success.

Dear Miss Manners, can you please suggest some way I can simplify the situation without hurting anyone's feelings?

GENTLE READER:

Remarkably few people conduct their social lives for the purpose of insulting their friends. It is probably safe to presume that everyone in your circle means well, and to turn your attention to the practical, rather than the alleged psychological, aspects of the situation.

The fact is that most people assume that hosts who have houseguests are only too glad to get them out of the house once in a while, and to be relieved of serving some of their meals. Miss Manners sees no reason to assign your relatives and friends any motive but that of taking off your hands some of the chores of entertaining.

If you prefer to entertain at home, why don't you say so, in such a way that convinces them you mean it and are not insisting on sacrificing yourself to ideals of hospitality? Try saying, "I really find it a nuisance to drag all over to see everyone—I wish you could persuade them to come here." You will discover, Miss Manners is sure, that this is better, if less dramatic, than fretting.

The Family Circle

The Dull Uncle

DEAR MISS MANNERS:

How true it is that one can pick one's friends, but not one's relatives. Recently, we spent a holiday entertaining out-of-town relatives whose entourage included a terminally dull uncle. One-word answers are not our style, and the horror of one-way conversation soon grew to desperate proportions.

After exhausting our creative resources, we found ourselves unable to develop a two-way conversation with this docile man. Please offer some advice on how either to stimulate this lopsided exchange or to bring about its welcome end.

GENTLE READER:

You could redefine your terminally dull uncle as a good listener, and then unload on him all the stories you have wanted to tell without interruption, making him the object of all the rambling thoughts and reminiscences that livelier people have refused to sit still for. However, Miss Manners is perfectly aware that that will not solve your problem for long. That docile look of enduring whatever happens without reaction is pretty wearing.

As you say, you cannot choose your relatives. If you had a friend like this, you could either choose to have a friend like this no longer, or you could arrange to have that friend present only when inveterate babblers are also present. If you are related to such a babbler, by all means get into the habit of pairing them at family parties.

Miss Manners presumes you have tried questions about politics, the weather, and other such standard conversational stimulants. If you have not tried bombarding the man with questions about his own past, by all means do so. Few people can resist such curiosity, and boring as his tales may be socially, they should be of some interest to you as family history.

Failing that, you must fill the airspace yourself. To make the task easier, Miss Manners will relieve you of some of the strictures usually observed by society for the protection of guests—first because the burden here is an unusual one, and second because the man is a relative, and therefore must be presumed to have more toleration.

Tell him the plot of the movie you saw last week. Get the children to practice for their recitals with him as an audience. Recommend your favorite records, and then play them for him. Ask him if he can figure out why you are having trouble with your automatic garage door opener, and show him the problem. Complain that your grass isn't growing properly, and get him to watch it in hopes of detecting the problem.

One of three things is bound to happen if you keep this sort of thing up for a while:

1. You will hit upon something that interests him, and thus start him talking.

2. He will continue to sit there passively and silently, in which case you are no worse off than you were before, and even perhaps a little better off, as the children will have practiced, you will have been entertained by your own records or narrations, and you will have given needed attention to some household problem.

3. He will be unable to stand all this, and, in the interest of family harmony, will curtail his visits or come to them prepared to assume the function of entertainer himself, before you can spring something on him.

The Adult Temper Tantrum

DEAR MISS MANNERS:

What should I do with a close relative who throws temper tantrums?

She is my dear brother's wife, forty, and the mother of two really quite well-mannered teenagers. She is a dear in her own right when she wants to be, but her uncertain temper makes her a social liability—similar to, but not socially acceptable as, an epileptic who is subject to grand mal seizures just as I hand out the champagne in my best crystal.

The latest scene was just dreadful. Her whole family was visiting me with plans for supper out and an evening downtown—she, he, the two adolescents, and a friend of my nephew's. When my nephew and his companion lollygagged back to my house six hours after their arrival in town, my sister-in-law went into her fit, but not at the teenagers. Instead, she splattered invective at my brother and around my dining room for forty-five minutes. I left the room just as she got fired up, hoping she would regain her composure before I returned, but I finally had to come out of the basement and acknowledge the scene.

She spoiled the party. The evening resulted in my brother's returning to work as an escape, her sulking over a book at my house because she did not feel like going out, and my taking my niece, my nephew, and his friend to dinner downtown. The children were subdued, at best. I was trying to salvage something of the evening, with no success, mostly because we had planned the evening to be an ''easy family party,'' especially to benefit the children. You are ever so right about ''easy family outings''—they are much harder to achieve than full-scale formality.

I am still irked at her. It is unlikely that an apology will be forthcoming—she believes the Southern California claptrap that rudeness is enlightening. I know I cannot tell her that she was rude, boorish, ill-mannered, and a slatternly fishwife in my house, for heaven's sake. It was tacky of my brother to apologize for her behavior, I thought. It was also tacky of the two of them to expect me to enter the fracas.

Do you have any suggestions for how I can behave myself in the numerous family parties (my sister and her family and my parents live in the same metropolitan area) that are scheduled? May I disown relatives discriminately? Can I pretend that I had moved to Europe? Or that I'm out of town for the next six months? Can I pretend I died?

GENTLE READER:

Miss Manners has never cared for the widespread use of the medical model in describing disgusting behavior. In her opinion, your situation is in no way comparable to that of someone with a relative subject to epileptic seizures. All decent people accept manifestations of physical illness as a fact of life, in which embarrassment is inappropriate in both the ill person and the witnesses, as no social transgression has been committed.

Miss Manners will now pause for a chorus of protests by those who consider themselves decent, and Miss Manners indecent, because they believe your sister-in-law's behavior to be evidence of emotional illness, equally worthy of being treated with tolerance.

Very well. Those people will have to explain, then, your sister-in-law's philosophical justification for her rudeness, which indicates to Miss Manners that it is nothing more nor less than what you call it—an adult temper tantrum.

But this is a side issue, because the social solution here involves treating the behavior as an illness—hypocritically, in Miss Manners' case, but effectively. Say to your brother, ''I'm afraid dear Marietta is not at all well, and we simply cannot expose her to the criticism of those who don't understand that she can't help behaving the way she does. I know I'm helpless in knowing the best way to treat her. Perhaps we'd better not subject her to these gatherings until she is herself again, and able to handle them.''

Refusing Hospitable Relations

DEAR MISS MANNERS:

I am a liar and a sneak, completely lacking in any sense of loyalty or duty. It is my special goal to be mean to self-sacrificing old ladies who live alone and have few pleasures in life. If you don't believe me, you can ask either one of my aunts.

What seems to be the trouble here? you may well ask. You're such a nice chap, you would say if you knew me—mild, self-effacing, hardworking, honest to a fault, a comfort to your aged parents. A closet scoundrel? Preposterous! Aha, Miss Manners, that is only because you do not know my vile habits. Let me tell them to you, if two dear little old ladies have not already beaten me to the punch. (Curses!) You see, I live in New York City. That is not the crime, although in some quarters it is considered a contributing factor. Every once in a while, I have business in Washington, and—are you ready? here it comes!—I come to Washington for the day, do my business, and return home. *Without going to see my aunts.* No, it is worse: without even calling my aunts.

Even that isn't all. Sometimes (I told you I was a liar) I have more than I can do in one day, and I actually spend the night. In Washington. In a hotel. Get it? Can you think of any reason that a decent man would spend the night in a downtown luxury hotel that his firm is paying for when he has one aunt who has a perfectly good house in Arlington with a spare room that all you have to do is move the sewing machine out and all the stuff being worked on, and you can have it all to yourself; and another aunt who has an apartment just across the Maryland border with a perfectly good sofa bed in the living nook? Both of these establishments serve nourishing meals, too, and excuses about doctor's orders to diet are hospitably pooh-poohed.

Having only my health and welfare in mind, my aunts insist on feeding me not only well but early, if I visit either of them, because they don't want me to exhaust myself with a long work day. Dinner is on the table at sunset, and if I am delayed, it sits there and congeals, as does the temper of the hostess. If I try to go home to New York after dinner I am told that I will probably get a heart attack from rushing about too much, or give a dear lady one from the aggravation of watching me. One aunt will, if pressed, drive me to the airport after assuring me that no taxicabs are willing to make an excursion, and entertains me with predictions of her being robbed, beaten, *and* attacked (raped) on the way home.

Coward that I am, I have taken to sneaking through town. But crime will out, and I have been spotted by the Old Lady Spy League, and also my children have innocently given away my whereabouts (I am not so depraved as to instruct them to lie) when an aunt happened to call at the wrong time. Please, Miss Manners, help me. I honestly used to like these hospitable tyrants when I could visit them by choice and at leisure. I would like to maintain friendly family relations. Just, please, tell me what are the rules, and I will try to obey them.

GENTLE READER:

Your aunts' rules seem to be that the greater Washington area belongs to them, and that entering requires obeisance at telephone, table, and sofabed, depending on the length of the trip. To disobey them is to acquire trouble and shame, as you have discovered.

However, these rules are nowhere engraved on pasteboard, as we say in the etiquette business, and you may frankly admit that you cannot operate under them. If you wish, you may blame your employer, who expects you to be available by telephone at late hours, insists that you stay in a hotel where he can reach you, requires business dinners, and so on.

The important thing is to show that the rules you recognize do not exclude affectionate family relations. Call your aunts, every once in a while, from New York, just to say hello. Invite them to visit you at home. Send a postal card for no particular reason. The point is to show that your thoughts of them are in no way related to your geographical location. Once you have established your unwillingness to submit to their system, you will be able to appear gracious, rather than guilty, by an occasional Washington dinner, sometimes at your hotel, perhaps rarely at their homes. In the end, they will be more flattered because you will be seeing them voluntarily rather than under compulsion. Miss Manners wishes you luck in getting to that end.

Must One Sit with In-Laws?

DEAR MISS MANNERS:

My husband plays on a community men's softball team. Several times each season my in-laws show up at the games. I usually sit with other wives of the players; however, when my in-laws show up, I feel an obligation to go sit with them. In fact, they usually try to come sit by me if there is room.

I get along very well with my in-laws, but I don't care to sit with them at these games, and listen to stories about their health, gossip, family, etc. I would prefer to sit with my friends.

What exactly are my responsibilities in this case? Am I obligated to sit with them, or can I stay put? They come to several games a year and know other people in the stands. We also spend a lot of time with them other than at the ballpark, so it is not as if this is our only time to talk.

GENTLE READER:

Miss Manners has never done a seating plan for a community softball game before, but is quite willing to try. Perhaps if you are satisfied, you will recommend to the team that they allow her to do the batting order.

The object here is to have your in-laws feel that you are being gracious and attentive to them, without your having to sit with them. To a person of Miss Manners' prowess, this is child's play.

Greet them warmly, and say, "Let me find you a good place to sit." When you have established them, ask such polite questions as "Are you sure there's not too much sun here?" and "Can you see all right?"

During their appreciative nods, say, "Great—I'll be right over there in the wives' section," or "Good—I'm just going to run over and sit with Marianne there.'' The impression given is that you have put them in the best place and taken a humbler one for yourself, or that custom requires you to sit elsewhere. If you find them looking at you across the stands, give them a friendly wave. Miss Manners defies anyone to make a family fight out of that.

Financing Family Reunions

DEAR MISS MANNERS:

My cousin Susan has a lovely home just made for family reunions. Last year, she had the first reunion, which was attended by members of the family within a two-hundred-mile radius. It was a great success, and Susan would like to have a second reunion this summer, this time including a cousin and her husband who live across the country.

At Christmastime, an invitation was extended to her and she responded that her present financial situation prevented her and her husband from traveling so far.

My cousin Susan would like to know how to approach our cousin, offering to pay her transportation to the reunion this summer, without embarrassing her—how to make her feel she is doing us a great favor by accepting the gift of transportation.

GENTLE READER:

This is such a charming gesture that Miss Manners hates to have to bring up the possibility that the financial excuse is merely an excuse. Very likely, it is the literal truth, but a sensitive person would also allow for the possibility of its being a polite way of getting out of spending time and emotional energy as well.

The tactful thing for Cousin Susan to write would be something like ''There is a little extra family money for those who have trouble coming, and we would be delighted if you would take enough for your transportation. Don't bother paying it back—we hope to make a regular thing of this, and you can do the same for younger people some years from now if you want.''

If they then thank you but protest that they expect to have the flu that week, please consider the matter closed.

The Virtue of Respect

DEAR MISS MANNERS:

An older relative who was invited to dinner at my house went around the dining-room table after I had set it and brought to me—I was in the kitchen cooking—all the silverware she considered ''extra.'' She told me to put them away, as we did not ''need'' them and there was no point in dirtying them. I have a dishwasher, but I did as she wished. While we were eating, I realized that I don't like buttering my roll with the knife I use to cut prime rib and I don't like eating chocolate mousse with a teaspoon.

When this relative, who is a nice person, older, and deserves my respect, comes to my house as a dinner guest again, should I set the table her way? Or should I set it my way and insist on having all the silverware stay on the table if she tries to take it off?

Another older relative calls our house and when I say "Hello," answers "Hello." Then I say "Hello" again, and he says "Hello" again. This goes on until I recognize his voice and say, "Oh, hello, Uncle Bob."

He is a perfectly nice man and he isn't trying to be funny. He has never had any social life, other than with his family, and I think he expects anyone he calls to recognize his voice. I am getting better at this, but he doesn't call often enough for me to be really familiar with his voice (he is my husband's uncle). Next time, should I try to tell him in a polite way that he ought to give his name when he calls? I am fairly certain he would be insulted and think I was acting uppity, no matter how polite I tried to be.

GENTLE READER:

Allowing your elderly relatives to drive you crazy is a virtue known as "respect." Miss Manners greatly admires the patience with which you have practiced this so far, and your concern that a change of policy would be upsetting to them.

Nevertheless, she must protect these old people's true interests against their immediate satisfaction. Even if you are a saint, the day will come, if you continue to endure these practices, when you will go after Aunt Martha with the steak knife, or tell Uncle Bob—heavens knows what. It is just such petty irritations that, if repeated often enough, drive their victims to madness.

Of course, you will be kind. "I'm used to eating this way," you will say apologetically to Aunt Martha as you take the silverware from her hand and put it back on the table. "Who's calling, please?" you will ask Uncle Bob, adding, when he huffily states his name, "Oh, Uncle Bob! How nice to hear from you! Forgive me—I'm just so stupid at recognizing voices."

A Mother's Monetary Requests

DEAR MISS MANNERS:

I have a problem that concerns giving gifts to my mother-in-law. She is from another culture, and prefers receiving money as her gift from my husband and me, and has told us so to our faces.

I, on the other hand, hate to give money as a gift, and have always considered it to be in poor taste. After many lengthy discussions with my husband over whether a giver should give what he wants to give or what the recipient wants, I have reluctantly closed my eyes to the proceedings, and he gives her a check as requested.

Now she is adding fury to my embarrassment by announcing the check amount in front of the other family members gathered for the occasion. Please, Miss Manners, tell me what to do about this awful situation. Christmas is approaching, and I cannot go through another session of her opening her card and exclaiming, "Ah, forty dollars!"

Do we return to our former practice of giving her unwanted gifts, which she verbally rejects, or go on as we are, trying to ignore it all? Unfortunately, my husband will not consider giving her only our presence at Christmas, as I would wish to do.

GENTLE READER:

Miss Manners quite agrees with you that using Christmas as an opportunity to make cash demands is in poor taste, but, then, so is using Christmas as an opportunity to reform one's mother-in-law. Here are a few feeble suggestions for compromise:

1. Send the check before Christmas, so that she already knows the amount, which may discourage her from announcing it.

2. Tell her you have made a donation in her name to an organization or cause in which she has shown interest.

3. Give her a blank check, and tell her in front of everyone to fill it in for whatever she feels she needs. (Miss Manners is counting on the shame principle here, but you know better whether you can afford to take this risk.)

4. Shut your ears during the presentation, as you have already shut your eyes.

Miss Manners feels obligated to tell you that only suggestion 4 will work.

Presents for Relative Relations

DEAR MISS MANNERS:

I find myself faced with a dilemma regarding the etiquette of gift giving. My brother is living with, but not quite married to, a woman who is more than a roommate but less than a wife, which is to say she shares bills, board, and bed, without the benefit of legal sanction. Henceforth she will be referred to as his convivant, for lack of a better term.

My relationship to this convivant and hence my social obligations to her are not clear to me. What is an appropriate Christmas gift for a person who is neither in nor out of the family, related by neither blood nor marriage, but living among us in an intimate yet ill-defined manner nevertheless? Is any gift at all required, or even wise? I do so want to do the proper thing.

GENTLE READER:

You have no idea what satisfaction it gives Miss Manners to know that in these interesting and trying times people such as you are out there determined to do the proper thing. Merry Christmas to you, and may your New Year be filled with propriety.

Do not, repeat not, give this woman your great-grandmother's pearls. If she and your brother are not willing to commit themselves to a permanent bond, there is no reason why you should make a commitment you will regret if their relationship is dissolved.

Otherwise, Miss Manners sees no reason why you should not give a present to a member of your brother's household, and would consider it obligatory if she comes to the family Christmas celebration. If one withheld such privileges until any attachments, including the legal, were proven permanent, the stores would be empty right now.

A Creative Present

DEAR MISS MANNERS:

I live in a popular winter vacation city, half a continent away from where the rest of my family lives. For Christmas, I would like to give my grandmother an airplane ticket so that she could come and visit me in my new home, an opportunity which she might not otherwise have. Since the whole family, myself included, gets together on Christmas and opens presents together, and as we are all in the same income bracket, how might I best give her this gift, which will be uncharacteristic, without appearing, at best, overly generous, or, at worst, lickspittle? Should I give her a small present in public, and later slip her the ticket as a surprise after everybody leaves, or should I be creative (lie) and say that my friend the travel agent got me a terrific deal? I would really like to do something like this for her while she is living, rather than only something like a memorial or flowers when she is not.

GENTLE READER:

Surely we can be creative without lying. Give it to her, saying, "Grandmother, this is not really a present for you—I'm asking you to cooperate in a present I am giving myself. It would be a great treat to me to have you visit me in my new home."

Sharing Happiness

DEAR MISS MANNERS:

If this isn't the weirdest manners question you've ever had, at least it must be one of the strangest situations. Here is the problem: Everything is going really well with me.

In the last year or so, my life has fallen into place. I've had my share of trouble and then some, including losing my wife when my boys were small, periods of unemployment, etc., but my luck has changed. I was able to take advantage of early retirement to pursue my hobbies, one of which is to write down the histories my father and grandfather told me of my hometown, and the local newspaper is publishing them and even paying me. Another is gardening, and now I'm winning prizes at shows! Also, I helped organize a teen club at my church to do volunteer work, and the youngsters kind of took to me, and like to tell me their problems and things, and so my house is always full of young friends.

Best of all are my own boys. The older one went through a rough time, and there were years when he seemed headed straight for nowhere, but he's married a fine young woman who's straightened him out, and he has a good job and two of the brightest kids you ever saw. My younger boy is a senior in college on his way to becoming a teacher. (His old man barely made it through high school.)

One more thing, in case you're not feeling sorry for me already. I'm the most sought-after man in town. Loved, pursued, cooked for, brought presents, hounded almost. You might wonder why to look at me, but maybe if you looked at the number of widows and divorced ladies in this town, you would understand. All I'm saying is, no movie star ever had it so good.

Now I'll come to the point. Good things happen to me all the time, and I've got no one to share them with. Bad things are another story. Once I blacked out, and it turned out to be nothing, but for weeks afterward my house was crowded with friends, kids, my daughter-in-law, flowers, fruit baskets, etc. I appreciate knowing that if things had turned out bad, I would have had more help than I needed.

But if my grandson says something cute, his uncle is too busy with schoolwork to care, my young friends think such talk is boring, and my lady friends consider it an invitation to recite all the cute things their grandchildren ever did that I heard a dozen times before and acted interested about at the time. Same if my college boy gets all A's—his brother isn't interested because he didn't go to college, and neither is anyone else. If I get a compliment on a story from an editor and try to repeat it, the most I get is ''That's nice'' before they tell me some compliment they got, or should have but didn't.

I know it's wrong to brag, and boring to others, but I sincerely share the ups and downs of lots of people, and only want to know if it's too much to expect them to return the favor. I'd get married tomorrow if I found a lady who took the time to look genuinely happy for me for two full minutes before what I was telling her reminded her of something in her own life.

GENTLE READER:

Bragging is an attempt to make others think better of you by reciting your own accomplishments, or those of people associated with you. It is not an attractive form of behavior, and is therefore best done with the false modesty of disbelief or undeservedness.

But you are talking about something different. Swaggering, which is the sharing of happiness with others who have already professed the deepest interest in one's welfare, is a legitimate activity. You have properly confined it to people in whom you demonstrate a reciprocal concern.

Miss Manners has never understood why people who rush to any announcement of emotional depression as if responding to a fire alarm are not at least equally eager to share their loved one's elation. Perhaps you might serve notice of the proper reception you expect by prefacing your statement with ''I've had some good news, and I'm sure you'll be pleased for me.'' A lady who gets it might be a good candidate to share your fortunes in general.

The Full Cycle

DEAR MISS MANNERS:

I am sitting here seething at my eighty-five-year-old mother. She is, to the rest of the world, a darling. She is perky, appreciative, sociable, and beloved by everyone, from those who invite her to umpteen cocktail and dinner parties to the check-

out woman at the supermarket and the shampoo girl at the beauty parlor. *But* (where to start?) she is simply frightful to her children and grandchildren.

I am fifty. She comes for a visit at my house. All is (defensively) scrubbed and polished to a fare-thee-well, and she is wined and dined and shown a delightful time. When she leaves, she leaves a nice note saying what a fine time she had—plus a lengthy list of things that need doing or fixing around my house.

Friends think this is hilarious; I think it is dreadful. After my daughter spent a month with her, painting and doing many odd jobs, I received an angry letter detailing my daughter's sins and inadequacies. An expensive present we sent her was returned, with the request that we take it back as she really wouldn't use it. These are just a few tiny examples. Why would a gently bred woman who has never left a thank-you letter unwritten in her life treat her family this way? She would not dream of criticizing a friend or a friend's present. You may well give this answer: She feels responsible for the deplorable condition of her daughter's home and responsible for the behavior of her granddaughter.

So I guess my real question is, how does one make a parent realize one is a fully grown individual, for whom the parent is not—and has not been for decades—in any way responsible? Bluntly, how do you get a mother to mind her own business, and offer advice only when it is specifically sought?

GENTLE READER:

There is a way, but it is so cruel that Miss Manners begs you not to use it. Some of the things one can accomplish with careful politeness ought not to be accomplished. The business of a mother *is* child-rearing. Most mothers eventually notice that the people on whom they practice this are no longer children and allow the function to dwindle, but if you are fifty, Miss Manners cannot hold out much hope to you that this will come to your mother's attention. You could change the relationship by fussing over her and her household—"Mother, dear, let me just mop here a bit; you always kept such a lovely house that I can't bear to see it not quite right"—in such a way as to convince her that you are now the ruling adult. But do you want to undermine the confidence of a perky, appreciative, sociable, beloved eighty-five-year-old darling?

Your friends' approach is infinitely better. By humorously recounting stories of an impossible family character—Miss Manners would prefer you to keep these stories strictly within the family, but that is another matter—you turn that person from a villain into a comic eccentric. Not only does this remove the hurt, but it enables you to endure her transgressions peacefully, knowing what pleasure you will have in sharing them with your own daughter.

Extra Credit

Ethics

The Dutiful Child

Before the objective of child-rearing came to be producing a happy child, it was producing a dutiful one. Miss Manners does not notice any increase in the number of happy children, or in the happiness level of children, since this switch.

Perhaps it is because the satisfaction of having done one's duty is unknown to children whose parents are always nagging them to do whatever makes them happy, an annoying request if ever there was one. Miss Manners does not claim that doing one's duty is higher on the scale of satisfactions than, say, getting one's own telephone line, but it is fulfilling, nevertheless. The child who is taught that "not everything has to be fun" is more likely to know what fun is when he sees it.

Here, then, is a child's list of things that are not fun to do on a rainy day, and still less fun on a sunny day, but that must be done at certain times, because they are one's duty. Parents are welcome to try to convince children that they're all really jolly, but it won't be easy.

· Visiting, behaving well for, and even pretending to enjoy the company of cantankerous or otherwise unpleasant relatives. To find certain relatives difficult, boring or repulsive is not unnatural, but does not change the fact that they are relatives. Grown-ups are allowed to start family feuds, but children cannot, and therefore must be agreeable to all upon the request of their own parents.

- Attending, dressed as requested and behaving respectfully, whatever religious services the parents decree.
- Answering all invitations immediately, and writing prompt and imaginative letters of thanks for presents not given in person, and for hospitality exceeding the simple overnight-in-sleeping-bags—that is, weekend and holiday visits. "Imaginative," in this case, means that the body of the letter cannot start with the words "Thank you for the . . ."
- Treating the sick compassionately, which includes notes or visits to sick friends or relatives, and refraining from saying "Yuck" at their wounds or claiming to be made ill oneself by sickrooms.
- Suspending their own recreational activities when there is a death close in the family, and learning to consider the bereaved—by writing or visiting—rather than their own distaste for the event, when someone they have known well has died.
- Taking part in the chores of their households, not only upon direct command— it is as much of a chore to a parent to nag someone to do something as to do the work—but because they acknowledge it is necessary to contribute to the establishment, as well as to reap its benefits.
- Accepting, with some cheerfulness, the fact that there are duties to be performed in life, that no one is truly crazy about them, and that the less said about many the better. This means eschewing the classic whine "Aw, do I have to?" and its companion "But I don't feel like it," which carries the annoying suggestion that the child, unlike the adult, is discriminating enough to know the difference between pleasure and duty, and sensitive enough to be allowed the special privilege of enduring only the former.

Selfishness

As if it weren't shocking enough that people now routinely neglect the most routine social duties, they will also offer excuses for this that are simply inexcusable.

"I got so many presents that I don't have time," says the bride who didn't write a thank-you letter.

"I was depressed," says the friend who failed to show up when expected.

"I knew it would upset me," says the friend who failed to pay a hospital visit.

"I don't feel up to entertaining," says the widow who complains of social neglect but doesn't reciprocate invitations.

The translation of each of these statements is: "It was your feelings against mine, and I decided that mine were more important." However accurate and logical this may be, explaining it does nothing to mollify the feelings of the person whose claim was so dismissed. The polite response to one of these explanations, which is "Of course I wouldn't want you to trouble yourself," can also be easily translated—into a few short words, and they are not kind ones.

Miss Manners happens to believe that people who force themselves to do what they know is their duty, in spite of inconveniences or distaste, benefit enormously from the exercise. The only relief we have from the rampant selfishness of our time, which does not deliver the self-fulfillment it promises, is the habit of occasionally entering sympathetically into the feelings of others. A fortunate person increases his or her chance of prolonged happiness by cultivating the habit of gratitude, rather than considering that tributes and favors received are merely his or her due. An unfortunate person increases his or her chance of escaping from unhappiness by concentrating on pleasing others rather than on the unpleasantness.

At the very least, a clear lapse from duty should not be compounded with a self-serving and self-justifying excuse. (We are talking here about duty that is acknowledged by both sides to be valid. For refusing invalid claims that are presented as duty, no excuse is necessary, as in ''I'm flattered that you thought of volunteering me when I didn't even go to the meeting, but I'm just going to have to decline, because although it breaks my heart, I'm afraid I simply won't be able to do it.'')

Miss Manners hereby withdraws, as excuses for failing to live up to legitimate expectations; (1) busyness, and (2) malcontentedness.

You may take it as a general rule that everyone considers himself to be busy—overburdened is more like it—and that unless you are in the midst of a demonstrable emergency, such as giving birth, people will never acknowledge that your busyness is more pressing than their busyness. The same goes for feeling low, to which anyone not in an obvious state of crisis can make equal claim.

The unspoken replies to those people with the inexcusable excuses are:

''If I was not too busy to choose, buy, and send you a present, you cannot be too busy to spend two minutes acknowledging it.''

''If I was prepared to receive you graciously, regardless of what mood I might have been in, you should have been prepared to fulfill your commitment graciously, regardless of your mood.''

''If I am in the hospital, I assure you that my illness is more serious than the discomfort you may get from observing it.''

''If you feel up to being my guest but not my host, what you mean is that you don't feel like doing the work involved but you figure that I should.''

Whining

Lovely, tolerant, and sympathetic as we, as a society, pride ourselves on being, it was probably a mistake to dignify whining by calling it depression. Miss Manners would like to take a step toward correcting that by declaring a new rule: Whining does not take precedence over merrymaking. Merrymaking takes precedence over whining. This means that one does not enliven other people's holiday festivities with tales of one's own loneliness, or teach them to appreciate their good fortune by comparing it with one's own miserable fate. This peevish outburst on Miss Manners' part is essential, and has to do with the annual outcry from those who want the national whoopee lowered out of respect to their own fallen hopes. Already depressed, they are depressed even more, they say, by knowing that others are dancing around the Christmas tree or singing in the New Year—and still more by being asked to join in.

Well, pooh. If they can't be jolly, at least they can behave.

The very principle of the season—spreading true charity and cheer, true or false, to those even less fortunate than oneself—is the classic antidote to unhappiness. If everyone will promise to give it a try, Miss Manners will regain her customary good spirits and acknowledge that whining is a natural instinct and has its proper, if limited, place. She just wants it understood that the drawing room has never been the proper place for the satisfaction of natural instincts.

Strictly speaking, whining is the tuneless, illogical and repetitive recital of one's belief that fate persistently has it in for one. It should not be confused with grief, which has a specific cause in proportion to the misery it creates. Society makes allowances for true grief, recognizing that it requires human contact but is unable to meet ordinary standards of sociability. That is why those in mourning receive visits from their friends, in their own homes where they set the tone, and need not go out. When they do venture forth, they are expected to make an effort, but some lapses are forgiven. Miss Manners is not so coldhearted as to condemn the inappropriate sniffles of the bereaved or the feverish flirtations of the newly divorced.

Whining, however, is banned from social events. Doleful people are expected to simulate the tone of buoyant guests, not the other way around. Whining is properly directed only at one's intimates. The way you can tell whether particular relatives or friends are intimate enough to stand for it is to ask yourself whether, if you had a bad head cold, they would still be inclined to hug you, or at least sit at your bedside within range of your sneeze. If not, they won't want to listen to you whine and take the risk of catching your mood. Even then, it must be reciprocal. Miss Manners fails to understand why people who keep careful track of who has invited them to dinner so that they pay back the exact number of beefs Wellington forget to end their whinings with "And how are you?" Whining must also be strictly limited. Everyone has an occasional whining mood, but the person who is always sure of being ill-used by life eventually convinces his or her listener that life knows what it's doing.

When Form Precedes Feeling

DEAR MISS MANNERS:

The other day, my son wanted to visit a friend who had injured himself. The sole reason for the visit was that my son wanted to stare at his injury. As parents, we thought this was not a satisfactory reason and would not allow him to go. In the course of discussing why he could not go, we said that doing so would show no class. He asked us what "class" meant in this context. How would you answer this question in words a seven-year-old boy could understand?

Dear Michelle,

How perfectly ghastly for you to be sick now and miss all the holiday fun. Zuel bummer. Maybe they'll let you bow next year, instead of being a post-deb; after all, you'll be the only one of us with a new white dress by then.

Let me know when you're not catching, so I can come and visit you. Do you want me to keep an eye on Christopher for you while you're out of circulation?

Get well soon. We all miss you.

Love,
Heather

A LETTER TO A FRIEND IN THE HOSPITAL. *To encourage such compassion as this, Daffodil Right gave her step-daughter her very own paper. Well, almost. This is the personal paper the first Mrs. Right left behind. Only the middle initial is wrong. Heidi Right's middle name was Constance, until she changed it to Devi. Heather's middle name is Emily, and she once teased her father into buying her towels marked HERS, promising to sew in an apostrophe before the S, which she never actually got around to doing. Now she tells anyone who asks that her middle name is Charge-it.*

GENTLE READER:

"Class" is not a terribly clear word in this context, even to Miss Manners, who is unlikely to see seven again. She supposes you mean that "class" means visiting a sick person because you are concerned with that person's feelings, rather than your own.

Miss Manners disagrees with your decision not to allow your child to visit his friend because his motives were not noble. Send him off with strict instructions to pretend to be sympathetic with the illness, but apparently not unduly curious. (Some interest in the nature of the illness is usually agreeable to patients.) Perhaps his sympathies will truly be aroused. If not, he still will have done better by his friend than he would have by ignoring the friend. Form comes first in matters of class, and while one hopes that feeling will follow, going through the form well without it is more acceptable, more classy if you will, than eschewing the form because the feeling is not there.

Being in the Wrong

Being in the wrong is not a geographical position in which Miss Manners has much first hand experience to offer. She has heard the statement "Everyone makes mistakes," but has always assumed that, as in the case of "Everyone does it," not necessarily everyone is meant.

Nevertheless, the ability to be in the wrong so gracefully that you will be graciously assisted on the journey back to the righteousness in which we are all so much happier to dwell is a useful social skill.

Neither of the most popular methods of dealing with being in the wrong seems to Miss Manners to be any good at all. Both are attempts to deny being there, when one plainly is, and to counterattack that it is the other person who is in the wrong.

One of these is for the person who is in the wrong to redefine wrong as right, and to establish the recognition of wrongdoing by the other person as being the true transgression. In its crudest form, it begins with a version of "I have a right to if I want," and ends with "Why are you always picking on me?"

The second method is based on the idea that only motivated wrongdoings can be validly counted against one. Thus the original accusation is countered with a belligerent "Well, I forgot" or "Oh, for heaven's sake, I didn't mean to."

The trouble with these methods is that they positively enrage the person who has a legitimate cause of complaint. This may be of some use, in that it eventually transfers the conflict onto an emotional plane where the facts of the situation are irrelevant, thus putting the committer of the wrong on an equal level with his opponent. But it does not clear the air. And since Miss Manners considers peace to be the only acceptable state of affairs, between relatives and friends as well as among nations, this has to be counted as failure.

Let us say, for example, a friend has asked you to mail a letter, and you have cheerfully and thoughtlessly used the letter instead as a bookmark. Upon asking your commiseration on the fact that someone else got the job for which he had applied and been ignored, your friend spots his own return address peeking out the top of your reading matter. Typically, you try method one and say, "You shouldn't have asked me to mail the letter when you knew I was busy and could perfectly well have done it yourself," and then go on to method number two by saying, "How was I to know it was important?—I just forgot, that's all." End of friendship.

The alternative Miss Manners suggests is abject craveness of the nonstop babbling variety. Suppose, for example, in the case of the letter, you say, "Oh, no! How could I have done such a thing? I must be losing my mind. I'll never be able to look you in the eye again. I'll never be able to live with myself! I'll never forgive myself. I probably ruined your life. I wouldn't blame you for dropping me forever. What a terrible thing to do. I can't believe this happened . . ." and so on. What does your friend reply? Well, there is only so much of this incoherent self-flagellation that a body can stand. After a sufficient dose, your friend concedes, "Oh, I probably wouldn't have gotten that job anyway. Deep down I don't even think I wanted it. Never mind. Let's just forget it."

And you can.

Learning About Lying

Do not regard it as trespassing into the area of morals, as opposed to manners, if Miss Manners explains to you how to teach children to be honest. You know that Miss Manners does not mess around in that morass known as morality. If you do not want your children to be honest, you are welcome to skip this, once you give Miss Manners back her wallet.

There are ways to achieve honesty that fall under the general category of child-rearing, which is very much in Miss Manners' territory; civilizing the young is the first obligation of etiquette. She will not accept the need for kindness as an excuse for forgoing honesty, or vice versa.

In its natural state, the child tells the literal truth because it is too naive to think of anything else. Blurting out the complete truth is considered adorable in the young, right smack up to the moment that the child says, "Mommy, is this the fat lady you can't stand?" At this point, the parent rightly senses the need to explain kindness. Parents who have made a pretense of basing their precepts on inviolable logic are hopelessly stuck at this conflict, and some never recover the strength to resume authority. The wily parent, however, explains the importance of what others want to hear as a factor in selecting truths. Crisis No. 2 therefore occurs when the youngster, correctly assuming that the parent would like to hear that it did not get into the cooking chocolate, applies the new principle.

Nature sees to it that this experiment is performed at an age when the child is not yet alert to telltale evidence, i.e., has chocolate all over its face and the wrappers in its bedding. It unfortunately does not ensure that the parent has reached an age when he has wisdom enough to deal with the lie. The problem comes from a failure to distinguish between the literal statement of all known facts, and social conversation. Miss Manners does not like the term "white lie," because it suggests that it is sometimes right to lie. What it actually attempts to name, however, is the skill of interpreting and responding to a complex exchange of ideas and feel-ings in polite society, without which civilization cannot exist. Lying to protect oneself, which is the motivation of almost all true lying, is not civilized behavior. Responding to conventional phrases and situations in terms of what they really mean, rather than what they are on the surface, is. One must teach the two skills simultaneously, or they will cancel out each other, and you will have a child who is not only dishonest when it serves his purposes, but rude as well. Not a good combination.

Basic honesty is taught by catching the child at that early stage when his cover-up is clumsy, and pouring out an awesome stream of righteousness, augmented by endless examples of honesty-over-convenience in one's own life. (If this in itself is a lie, the situation is hopeless.) At the same time, one teaches the more inter-esting lesson of society's being composed of the exchange of kind reassurances that everyone finds everyone else reasonably agreeable. Thus, "How are you?" means "I trust you are fine," rather than "What's your health record?" "I had a marvelous time," is used to say "I appreciate your efforts," and "Did I make a fool of myself?" means "Are you going to hold what I did against me?" and requires the answer "Why no, of course not," which translates as "I'm still willing to be your friend."

It is an interesting, not to mention essential, language to learn. But as with all matters of etiquette, it cannot be used as an excuse for behaving badly.

A Response

DEAR MISS MANNERS:

If I understand you correctly, one is allowed to instruct servants or others to tell polite lies to unwelcome callers. Since children will frequently witness such lies, how shall I explain to them that there is something like a principle of saying the truth?

GENTLE READER:

You have heard, Miss Manners trusts, of "the truth, the whole truth, and noth-ing but the truth." Well, you must explain to the child what each of the three is, and when we use only one, as opposed to occasions, such as those following subpoenas, when we use all three.

The whole truth is the moral answer to such questions as "Did you take a cookie after I told you not to?" Such an answer might be "No, but I ate the cook-ing chocolate." One must always speak the whole truth when morality is at stake.

Nothing but the truth is more useful on social occasions. For example, the ques-tion "How do I look?" may be answered with "Beautiful as always," even though the whole truth would require adding "except that your dress makes you look like a truck."

The truth is the most complex of all. It means getting to the truth of the situa-tion, rather than the crude literal surface truth. To answer the question "Would you like to see some pictures of my grandchildren?" with the direct literal truth— "No! Anything but that!"—would be cruel. But is that the real question? The question, if one has any sensitivity to humanity, is "Would you be kind enough to let me share some of my sentiments, and reassure me that they are important and worthwhile." To which a decent person can only answer, "I'd love to."

To say that someone was not at home, in the days before the telephone demanded the right of entrance to anyone at any time, was the conventional way of saying something that everyone understood: It is not convenient for Madam to receive visitors right now. We are the poorer now for not being able to say that in a way that doesn't hurt the feelings of the caller.

Respecting Adults

"Respect your elders" was always the favorite etiquette rule of the adult population, which has unaccountably allowed it to fall into disuse. It is surely the rule most regretted by parents who neglected to teach it to their children.

Actually, Miss Manners never quite liked it in exactly that form. To claim, even to the smallest children, that all adults are worthy of respect seems to her unsupportable in view of the evidence. The rule that she prefers is "You must treat all adults with respect." You see the difference. Manners wisely do not attempt to regulate the thoughts and feelings of those they seek to govern. They restrict themselves to demanding proper behavior.

It is reasonable and wise to require children to address adults with the appropriate formality of family title ("Aunt Candy") or civilian rank and surname ("Mrs. Heppzapittle"); to expect them to rise when adults appear; to refrain from beating them to a seat on the bus and to surrender one when in possession; to answer their questions and remarks civilly, even if they are silly or repetitive; to restrain themselves from inappropriately pointing out their errors and from analyzing what powers could produce such errors; and so on.

It is neither wise nor reasonable to expect children to think that adults are, by definition, smart, right, or admirable. Such an attempt will quickly lead a child of even average powers of observation to the conclusion that at least one adult, the one who makes this claim, is either dim-witted or mendacious. It also takes all the fun out of observing the adult world. A child who is never allowed to betray the belief that any adult has done anything wrong is one who will quickly lose interest in the idea of being among such deluded fools.

On the contrary, Miss Manners recommends encouraging critical discussions of outside grown-up behavior in the privacy of the family. It is the reward for having restrained oneself while these people were present. It also teaches both manners and charity. A child who can delight in watching an adult misbehave, and receive confirmation later that the conduct, which was politely allowed to pass without comment at the time, was noted, will pride himself on the superior practice of good behavior.

At the same time, he should be taught that judgment is no easy matter. People who, although ignorant perhaps of etiquette refinements, have hearts of gold or other redeeming qualities should be duly credited. Most important, the child who learns to observe the adult world as complicated theater, which he gets to help criticize, will have the incentive to enter that world. If he is permitted to have polite arguments and discussions with the appropriate adults—parents, other fond relatives, teachers—based on critical observations of the sophisticated world, he will have an interest in the ways of that world, and a desire to participate in it.

The credentials for doing so are being able to know what is right or wrong, and at the same time to develop the skill of politely pretending that one sees only the right. A child who can do that may be trusted to get safely through his parents' parties, college interviews, and life.

Words of Respect

DEAR MISS MANNERS:

I am an old lady and would like to know if it is still correct to say "Yes, sir" and "Yes, ma'am." If not, how long has it been out of date? I seem to be behind in my thinking.

GENTLE READER:

Certainly it is still correct as an address of respect to one's elders, but Miss Manners is aware that one can grow old waiting to hear it. She will try her best, ma'am, to revive the custom, so that instead of feeling behind the times you may claim credit for being ahead.

Addressing Children

DEAR MISS MANNERS:

I have two grandsons, ages eleven and five, and one granddaughter, age four. At what age should I stop addressing their mail as "Master" and "Little Miss"?

GENTLE READER:

You do not state what age you are, but the time to cut out that "Little Miss" business is right this minute, before you find yourself with a granddaughter who tap-dances uncontrollably, mouths the words to old Shirley Temple records, and develops tinselly fantasies. Female children are addressed simply as "Miss." Male children are addressed as "Master" (by sweet, old-fashioned people such as yourself and Miss Manners) until they are old enough to object, which may be as old as ten if they are not socially alert.

Coping with Good Fortune

Elitism

Is it rude to be rich? Does this state require constant apology from any sensitive person so unfortunate as to be caught in it?

Is etiquette a luxury item, the opposite of which is kindness? Is its sole function to humiliate the poor?

Miss Manners does not really care for any thinking that equates manners with money or the lack of it. It seems to her that there is an unlimited supply of vulgarity in the world, and that anyone can partake of it freely, and most people do. What politeness she sees is apparently randomly distributed at different income levels. Nevertheless, she recognizes that many aspects of etiquette are directly or indirectly related to a wealth-based social structure, and that they are often used to judge the worth of individuals, monetary and otherwise.

These standards are applied by both rich and poor. The possession of a good heart does not count for much, in any society, in a person who licks his dinner plate. Presumptions are universally made about the social value of people who ignore conventional rituals of drinking wine because they prefer to take theirs outdoors from bottles wrapped in brown paper bags.

It is true that many of these forms were invented by the affluent (because they could afford to be genteel), and in some cases, the reason was indeed to reinforce class barriers rather than to "make everyone feel comfortable." Thus, in times and societies where social mobility is possible, there is always a proliferation of new rules and of guides to these rules, which explains what Miss Manners is doing among you.

Should a democratic people eschew such elitist forms? Only if you also spurn all of the other goodies and niceties of life, from cars and stereo equipment to education, because you refuse to enjoy something that everyone else does not have. Manners differ from luxury dry goods in that they can be learned for free. Why not have the best when you can afford it?

To the extent that they are used as passwords to prevent the merely rich from entering the upper classes (which consist of the children of the generation that the generation before that did not succeed in keeping out), they can also be used to get through the gates. Acting rich is a well-known first step toward getting rich. It is for no such crass purpose that Miss Manners recommends that everyone enjoy the very best manners and pass them on to the next generation, all at no cost to the consumer. It is simply that there is nothing you can buy that soothes and embellishes life so easily.

The most satisfactory of these, such as the rituals of greeting and introducing and thanking and apologizing, require no expensive equipment. Resistance to them is mere proletarian snobbishness.

When artifacts are required, one masters the skills as one encounters the objects. It is not difficult. If you can use a metal knife and fork, you can use silver ones, and even successive forks with specialized functions. One learns the rituals of the society one participates in, as one learns the jargon and behavior of the profession one chooses, and resisting either only hurts oneself.

It is also fraudulent as a populist stance. Miss Manners does not notice the same people who refuse to acquire genteel manners spurning the really costly dry goods—the fancy gold watches, the furs, the limousines, the designer clothes—when they can get them. Actually, doing so would be the thriftiest possible way of displaying the best manners. Refraining from all ostentation is, after all, behavior that the top and bottom of the social scale have in common. For different reasons, perhaps.

Privileged Households

There are two theories about the effect on children of growing up in a household that has servants. One is that the child will never learn to do anything for himself and will therefore live like a pig when out on his own without help, and the other is that he will get used to living in a well-cared-for environment, and will therefore even stoop to the level of using his own labor to achieve this when none other is available.

Miss Manners has two different observations to offer. One is that most children live like pigs if they are allowed to; and the second is that eventually many children who are used to neat households crave them, sometimes to the extent of helping create them if they can't persuade anyone else to do the work.

Her conclusion is that it is not necessary to fire the servants for the sake of the children, and have the family undertake all the housework or risk producing people who will pollute the world. You weren't planning to do that anyway, were you?

There are, however, special etiquette rules to be taught to children in staffed households. It needn't be a full staff in livery; the behavior is equally adaptable to the cleaning woman or baby-sitter. As a matter of fact, it is useful to anyone who hopes, sometime in life, to pay someone to do work he doesn't want to do himself. Have we left anybody out?

The basic concept is that one has a special obligation to be nice to those who are not in a financial position to declare immediate independence if they are treated badly. Children ought to understand this, being in the same position themselves. Talking back to any adult may be forbidden, but talking back to the help is worse, if such a concept is possible.

Nevertheless, the time will come when the child will do it. It wouldn't be any fun having rules if no one ever tested them. What a surprise it always is to the child that his dear and loyal parent, who adores him and defends him against all adversity, sides with the servant to the point of refusing to consider the child's grievance until the principle of his being polite is reestablished and an apology is made.

A favorite such taunt is "I'm going to get my parents to fire you." This should be as transparently ineffectual to the employee as it is nasty. A child does not properly share the position of employer with his parents, and should be so informed. The servant, in turn, should understand what the true employer's requirements are, and be empowered to perform them without regard to instructions from the young. As with any child supervision worth the name, this should include the ability to make decisions within the basic framework. In other words, don't tell me that your father lets you stay up all night, kid; I know better, and what's more, I say you go to bed this minute, and I don't want to hear any more about it.

In the well-appointed household, even if it has two shifts of upstairs maids and a nanny for the dog, the fiction is always maintained that they are overburdened. This is for the benefit of encouraging the children to be compassionate, as well as to serve as an excuse for making them do some work, anyway. Pitching in on weekends or other short-staffed periods, caring for pets, and learning that there are certain things one human being never asks another to do for him, such as picking up his dirty underwear from the floor, are useful ways to teach household work to privileged children. Defining extra tasks as beyond the servants' job descriptions, so that the child either has to do them himself or must plead with the help to do him a favor, is another useful exercise. In medieval times, the nobility would regularly send out their children as servants in the castles of their neighbors, which was a good way to find out how it felt; the modern equivalent for the rich is a skimpy allowance and encouragement to get a menial summer job.

Part of the reason to take all this trouble instead of letting the employees do all the work is, of course, to teach compassion. Part is to prepare the child for reverses of fortune. And part is to encourage him to be the kind of person with whom another person can stand to live.

The overriding reason, however, is to make sure that the rich kids are not cheated of one of the two skills that Miss Manners believes no child should be sent out into the world without knowing. The first is that everyone, male and female, must have a way, when grown-up, of earning a living for himself and for any dependents he may acquire. The second is that each fully grown child, male or female, must be able to take care of his personal needs, such as cooking and keeping a household.

The idea is that none of them, no matter what misfortunes may occur, will then have to marry just to get one of these tasks performed. If, however, any of them then want and are able to get someone else to do these things—well, more power to them. Miss Manners would not dream of opposing free enterprise.

Mere Gentility

DEAR MISS MANNERS:

I was the son of a minister with no money, and went to the best schools where almost everyone else came from well-off families. This can be an immense problem for a child, even into college, and it can be a problem, too, for the child who befriends a poorer child. What do you advise? Offering sympathy? Explaining that money is nearly as primal and private a matter as sex, as apt to cause embarrassment, as unique to the situation and personality, etc.? After thirty-odd years, I'm still hypersensitive on this matter.

GENTLE READER:

So was Miss Manners' dear friend, Anthony Trollope, writing about similar experiences forty-eight-odd years after they occurred. It is now, by Miss Manners' calculation, one hundred sixty years since the dear man left Winchester College, and although she hasn't spoken to him in far too long, she is quite sure he is still as hypersensitive on the matter as you.

His was admittedly a more extreme case. The Trollope family had gone off to America without him in vain pursuit of a fortune. (Mamma Trollope invented the shopping mall in Cincinnati, unfortunately many decades before anyone could see the sense of wandering around a huge building buying things they didn't need. She only did all right by coming home and publishing nasty things about the state of American manners, an occupation that Miss Manners, being a lady, doesn't want to discuss.)

"My college bills had not been paid," he reminisced bitterly, "and the school tradesmen who administered to the wants of the boys were told not to extend their credit to me. Boots, waistcoats, and pocket handkerchiefs, which, with some slight superveillance, were at the command of other scholars, were closed luxuries to me. My schoolfellows of course knew that it was so, and I became a Pariah. It is the nature of boys to be cruel. I have sometimes doubted whether among each other they do usually suffer much, one from the other's cruelty; but I suffered horribly! I could make no stand against it. I had no friend to whom I could pour out my sorrows. I was big, and awkward, and ugly, and I have no doubt, skulked about in a most unattractive manner. Of course I was ill-dressed and dirty. But, ah! how well I remember all the agonies of my young heart; how I considered whether I should always be alone; whether I could not find my way up to the top of that college tower, and from thence put a stop to everything?''

And so on. Miss Manners does not mean to top your own painful memory, nor to make light of the pain of children now in this predicament by implying that it is good training for a novelist.

She brought it up as evidence that it is, indeed, in the nature of children to judge one another callously by material standards. One job of child-rearing is to change this nature to something more civilized by instructing children of all financial backgrounds how unimportant fortune is in assessing people's worth, and how capricious it is—and therefore how precarious a matter for bragging. The wise rich have traditionally kept their young children on strict budgets. Miss Manners remembers from her school days that what the major heiresses had in common was a need to borrow quarters for the laundry machine from the overflowing pockets of the daughters of the middle class.

Few parents seem to do this, and Miss Manners hears far too much instead about money forked over for frivolities because ''everybody else in school'' has one fad item or another. Miss Manners doesn't doubt this, but is surprised that parents continue to give weight to such a silly argument. The true class division in America, it seems to her, is between those who ''make statements'' with dry goods, and those who don't bother.

The poor child who is in a school where consumer competition is common will have social difficulties that one hopes are compensated by educational advantages. A strong character, bolstered by his parents' values, may be able to ignore or even triumph over the disadvantage, but strong characters do not often develop at tender ages.

If possible, the child should be allowed to approximate the ordinary standard of clothes or equipment at the school—one sweater like his classmates' instead of several cheaper ones, for example. He must also be given instructions on the futility of trying to keep up and the necessity of employing quiet techniques for avoiding debt. He can't go along on expensive outings, because sooner or later the others will resent paying for him, but he can be as hospitable with lemonade or coffee; he can play ball rather than polo; and he can suggest walks or museum trips with friends, rather than shopping and restaurant expeditions.

There will also be times when he will simply have to say, without any apology, ''No, I can't afford that.'' Of course, in a sophisticated school, this means he will also have to put up with being suspected of being outrageously rich.

Serious Subjects

❦ HEALTH, HYGIENE, AND SEX

Not Being Embarrassed About You Know What

When the question of teaching sex education came up at the parent-teacher meeting, the school's headmistress looked around the room at the assortment of adults whose private lives she knew better than she cared to—from stories told by the children, from the successive instructions about where to send school bills and the not-always-businesslike explanations of why, and from the all too frequent use of her conference time for the outpouring of parental social problems.

"Well," she said, "we could teach sex education, I suppose. Of course we would want to teach the standards of this community. Suppose you tell me exactly what they are." That was the last of that. She heard no more about teaching sex education in that school.

Miss Manners does not recount the incident for the foolhardy purpose of debating whether sex education should be taught in schools. (Well, all right, she is feeling reckless, and will be just foolhardy enough to declare that she believes this is a parental function, and that schools that use their time to rear children won't have enough time left to educate them. This does not mean that she is not fully committed to the idea that some responsible adult must perform this important function, or that she is not sympathetic with the schools' attempts to make up for parental neglect in this and other areas, even including the teaching of manners. It is just that she knows that child-rearing is harder for teachers to do than for parents, impossible for teachers to do in a way that satisfies a varied community, and often done at the sacrifice of the school's proper function.) Back to sex. How easily one is distracted.

Sex education begins by teaching affection, and by teaching that there is a connection between that and touching. In other words, you are supposed to kiss and hug your children. Miss Manners trusts that will not be too much of a hardship. Nature being what it is, the only flaw is that after a few months during which you may do as you like because the child has no means of locomotion, you must catch him first when you want to kiss him.

That there are all kinds of laws, natural and otherwise, governing this form of expression is a concept that may be taught long before the more interesting details. In an ordinarily affectionate family, a child learns through experience that lip kissing usually occurs between romantically attached adults, kissing the air next to the cheek is generally reserved for people whose names his parents can't remember, and that the finger, nose, and toe kissing he had been receiving as an infant has turned into mostly cheek and forehead kissing as he grew older. These are only the general customs of our society, of course, and may vary elsewhere and within many different kinds of American subgroups.

A sense of appropriateness in regard to time and place is also easily explained to a child who doesn't want to be kissed in front of his friends. This should lead to discussions of discretion and of privacy, which will be useful when the child starts asking for homegrown examples. (Miss Manners hopes that the traditional embarrassment parents are supposed to feel about explaining sex will be somewhat relieved when she tells them that there is a blanket rule, as it were, that such discussions never draw on personal experience. We can either learn what sex is about, or we can learn what our parents' lives are really about, which is not necessarily what a parent ever cares to have his child learn, but we cannot learn both at the same time.)

Sex education begins when the child begins to be curious, and the flow of information stops just after his attention has been observed to have wandered off. Ideally, this means that the basic physical process is described when the child is young enough to top it with that common question that always throws parents: "Why would anyone want to do *that*?" The mind unfogged by eroticism can understand the utilitarian necessity of performing such an act, but not why any reasonably fastidious person would enjoy it.

Unfortunately for modern society, one must also at this time explain the concept of child-directed perversion, and the urgency of the child's recognizing any sign of it and seeking instant help. Otherwise, the variations on the basic theme are explained on demand. A child who only wants to know where babies come from should also be told about stopping them, but need not be bored senseless all at once by hearing the complete list of possibilities for use of the human body.

Miss Manners hopes that all parents will remember to teach their concept of sexual morality, whatever it is (no, no, Miss Manners doesn't want to hear it herself, please), at the same time that they teach the physical part. A parent who pretends that sex is a physical activity unrelated to thought is concealing vital information out of a prudishness that saddles the child with the false belief that there is something dirty about the natural human interest in forms of morality.

Besides, in a decent explanation of sexual behavior, it is the only chance parents will get to brag.

The Birds and the Bees

DEAR MISS MANNERS:

In telling children about sex, what terms do you use? Most of my friends feel strongly about using the "correct" terms, because the whole idea about sex education is for them to know the truth, but I have a deep prejudice against hearing small children talking about "penises" and "vaginas." Yet, I admit that the euphemisms are wrong, often cute in a sickly way, and misleading.

GENTLE READER:

If you are to teach the whole truth about sex, you cannot possibly stop with naming parts and describing what goes where, but must also fearlessly explain prevailing social attitudes. One of them is certainly that it is not always proper to blurt out things that are nevertheless proper to know. This is a secret from many modern children, whose parents, teachers, and therapists have actively worked to keep them from developing the essential social and intellectual mechanism to judge a thought or observation—for appropriateness, perhaps just for sense —before expressing it to others.

The fact is that not everything is acceptable everywhere. There you are, teaching that sex is beautiful, no doubt, but neglecting to indicate that the police do not consider it so when practiced in a public park. An essential task of child-rearing is developing in the child a sense of what vocabulary, behavior, and dress are right for what occasions.

Yes, you do teach the child the correct names. But you also teach him the current euphemisms. Giving him one without the other is unfair. (A consequence of being too euphemistic was dramatized for Miss Manners by the most mesmerizing social incident she ever experienced, unfortunately as one of the principal characters. The child of her hosts at a dinner party showed her a tender book designed to instruct children about lovemaking, but giving the idea that hugging, handholding, and something called "being close" were about it. Later in the evening, Miss Manners was sunk in an armchair, on the arm of which the host was perched. As he got to the point of an amusing story, he leaned forward and draped an arm companionably on Miss Manners' shoulder. "Mommy!" shouted the newly educated child, observing this. "Daddy is having sex with Miss Manners!" Miss Manners has never so completely captured the attention of a roomful of people before or since.)

Actually, by the time you are explaining sex, you should already have taught the child the difference between descriptive language and euphemisms. The person who grows up saying "I'm going to have a bowel movement now" is not going to have much of a social life.

The Polite Child's One Exception

DEAR MISS MANNERS:

I am badly shaken, and appeal to you, although I know this is not a question of etiquette. My daughter has always told me she hates my brother-in-law, and I have scolded her for not being nice to him anyway, but this evening, when I was doing the dishes, I went into the television room and saw him jump away from her in a way that makes me understand why she was keeping away from him. I ran to my husband, who dealt with his brother in a way that has made him understand that we will turn him over to the police if he ever comes near her again. We did not handle this one politely. But what bothers me is why Carrie never told me about this before. All she would say is that she didn't want to be near him, but never why, or we would have stopped this at the beginning. We have tried to encourage her to communicate her fears, and she tells me about nightmares, school problems, etc. How can we urge her to be more open with us about what is really bothering her?

GENTLE READER:

Actually, it is exactly an etiquette problem that you have here. You have taught your child to respect adults and consider their behavior as a standard, and so it did not occur to your child that the situation was caused entirely by evil adult behavior.

It is the unfortunate duty of a parent to mention, before the child encounters such a situation, this important exception to the general principle of allowing adults to set the rules. This is a lecture known as Don't Take Candy from Strangers, but you had better spell it out in more detail than that, to include a description of acceptable and unacceptable affection in relatives and friends, exhibitionism, obscene telephone calls, and other such refinements of modern life. The polite child, in particular, needs to know what criminal behavior is, and that ordinary rules of politeness are suspended in dealing with it.

Borderline Cases

DEAR MISS MANNERS:

I am writing this letter on behalf of my daughter, who is eighteen. We have a very touchy situation, and we don't want to hurt anyone.

All of our parents and grandparents passed away within the past six years. The only family close to us are an aunt and uncle in their mid-sixties. They have been like parents to us, and we love them dearly.

However, my daughter has been reluctant to visit them lately. Asked why, she said, "Uncle is too affectionate." She is a very pretty and well-developed young lady. She is also a warm, loving, caring person, but she says that "the hugs and kisses are just too much," and she feels molested. She has tried "Ouch! Sunburn!" and complaining of scratchy whiskers, dodging and leaning over to pet the

dog. None of these maneuvers works. How do we handle this without hurting anyone's feelings?
Gentle Reader:
	Touchy is right.
	Miss Manners trusts that your daughter is old enough to know the difference
between a manners problem, in this regard, and a morals one. Younger children do
not and will sometimes suffer outrageous abuses for fear of being disrespectful to
an elder—a principle Miss Manners endorses in general, but to which she takes
hearty exception in these matters.
	Yours is a manners problem because it involves overenthusiasm of acceptable
gestures, rather than the practice of unacceptable ones. (Miss Manners trusts she
is not being too delicate for you to understand what she means.) In this case, you
do want to be careful to avoid hurting feelings.
	Take Uncle aside yourself, and say, "You know, Lucinda is at the age when
she's funny about being touched. I think she'd be more comfortable with you if
you treated her as you would a young lady, instead of a child." This is a perfectly
polite statement, even seeming to put the blame on your daughter, but if you sense
that there is an implied threat in it, you are correct.

✿ AGING AND DEATH

Senility

	No tragedy of life strikes Miss Manners as so hopeless as to be without redeem-
ing value as an occasion for teaching etiquette. The need to deal politely with a
person whose memory and perhaps emotional stability have eroded with age is,
in that light, a rigorous course in the exercise of patience and compassion.
	Without suggesting that it is a priceless opportunity no one should miss, Miss
Manners will go so far as to say that it would be a mistake for a parent who has
such a problem, perhaps with his or her own parent, to keep it hidden from the
next generation down. You might someday be personally terribly grateful to have
taught your child to be kind to the senile.
	Comparisons with childhood, as when dotage is referred to as a second child-
hood, are, in Miss Manners' opinion, harmful. That idea suggests more than the
similarity of caretaking services which may be necessary; and treating a grown-up,
however incapacitated, with parental authority is undignified. It is difficult to
remember to observe the forms of independence to someone who has actually become a dependent, but tact demands it. One says "Oh, do have some more, please"
rather than "Eat up, and stop wasting my time" and "Ooops, let me clean that
up" rather than "Now look what you've done."
	The place where a grown-up lives is always treated as if it is under his com-
mand. One knocks to enter, even if it is not practical to stand upon the reply;
and one asks permission to help out, even if that encompasses taking charge of
things.

The childhood simile is also harmful in creating expectations that things will improve. Impatience is sometimes justified toward the young, because one expects them to make progress and wants to prompt them along to accelerate the pace. When the movement is, instead, in the other direction, an attitude geared toward learning can only be frustrating for everyone. The cover-up remark ("Those appliances are tricky") is of more use here than the instructive one ("Pay attention while I show you so next time you'll know").

One of the worst consequences of memory loss is the accompanying humiliation. The civilized reaction, when anyone is having any kind of embarrassing difficulty, is to fail to notice the problem, and, at the same time, to offer help while apparently unaware that that is what one is doing. In this case, you seem to supply missing names or other words as a conversational gambit. It is amazing how many people think it more fun to play guessing games, along the lines of "Now, do you remember who this is?" Such people, like those who push their way through parties saying "I bet you don't remember me," deserve what they usually get.

As recent memory sometimes goes before what was stored earlier, the most successful conversation is about the past. It generally is, anyway. From the smallest child who fails to understand why he gets a laugh by opening a story with "When I was little," we are all fond of reminiscing. Under circumstances when one's past is more rewarding to dwell upon than one's present, it is particularly enjoyable. Repetitiousness is not exclusively a fault of age, either (Miss Manners has the awful feeling she's already said that), and the knack of listening politely to something one has heard before, even a few minutes ago, is a social skill.

The visitor to the impaired elderly might find himself burdened with an increasing amount of the sociability. This could be the one polite opportunity of a lifetime to hog the conversation, with only an occasional rhetorical question. To someone unable to carry on a conversation, it may nevertheless be pleasant to feel that one is part of an apparent exchange. Miss Manners does not mean to suggest that it all need be sacrifice. It is no small thing, nowadays, to have someone willing to listen to you, perhaps even sympathetically.

That is not, however, always the case. Teaching one's children to be tactful, patient, and unilaterally sociable with the elderly is simple; explaining why an older person who once cherished them is now indifferent or hostile is close to impossible.

"Grandma is not really herself" is the usual explanation, and as good as any. Why, then, one has to treat her as if she were can only be answered by a lecture on respect. And you certainly do want to teach your children to respect their older relatives, regardless of merit.

The Other End of Life

DEAR MISS MANNERS:

At what age should children be taken to funerals? Should they, in any way, be involved in mourning—being present when people call, even taking off from school?

My mother-in-law, who was very close to our six-year-old, is dying. We have told him that she is in the hospital, but he keeps asking when she is coming home, and we're beginning to think it's time we prepared him by telling him that she isn't coming back. But he's too young to be troubled with what is really happening. How can we say as little as possible, without leaving him at the mercy of people who might, intending to be sympathetic, scare him? We don't want to give him nightmares. We were told that the best thing is not to interrupt the routine of his life, but he won't be able to help noticing that ours is different, and that his father, who has already been quite upset by all this, is bound to be emotional when it happens.

GENTLE READER:

It is nightmarish enough for all of us to face the fact that people we care about will no longer be a part of our corporal lives, without suggesting that a cherished person could vanish without anyone's knowing or inquiring what happened. Would you prefer that your child be surrounded by people, including his own father, who behave as if nothing had happened when his grandmother disappears?

In some rudimentary way, you must explain what death is. Perhaps you can soften it by talking about the life cycle, including birth. Offer what comfort you can from your religion, or at least from the belief that the person survives in memory and the heritage of her descendants, including your son. It is not an easy task, and never will be.

Children do not do heavy mourning duty. But to exclude or excuse them entirely from participating gives them the dreadful feeling that they are helping push the deceased into oblivion. A child under ten need not attend the actual funeral; if he does, he should be close to his parents but also in the special care of someone who is emotionally able to direct attention to the child's needs—holding his hand, answering his questions, helping him reply to remarks addressed to him.

He should certainly not be kept to his normal routine. Sending him off to school or a play group would not only burden him with worry about his family and subject him to the remarks of other children, but would establish the idea that he is not an important part of the intimate family circle. These are the reasons that formal bereavement existed for everyone: so that the erratic fluctuations of grief should not be exposed to comment, so that people who understand one another's feelings can be together, and so that no matter what one's actual feelings about the death are, one could have the satisfaction of having behaved respectfully.

When you speak of "natural behavior," as people do all too glibly these days, it is well to remember that it is natural to want to shrink in horror from any unpleasantness, even if it means betraying a loved one. The child who is allowed or encouraged to do this is going to be unhappy about it later.

Nothing Can Be Done

DEAR MISS MANNERS:

Please let me know the correct procedure for the following: My daughter-in-law's father died, and she received dozens of condolence cards, Mass cards, flowers, etc., and she doesn't feel duty-bound to reciprocate with a thank-you card to those folks. She feels that they wanted to send everything, and there was no need to thank them. What is the correct procedure in the above matter?

GENTLE READER:

For whom? For your daughter-in-law, as you well know, it is to write a letter in her own hand, even if it consists only of the words "Thank you for your kindness." However, she is not going to do it, is she?

The correct procedure for you is to do nothing whatsoever. You cannot correct her, because she is a grown-up, but you needn't feel responsible, as you did not rear her. For her father, who presumably did, the correct procedure now is to roll in his grave.

Notification of Death

DEAR MISS MANNERS:

What is the proper way to notify friends and relatives of the death of a member of the family?

In the past five years, I have gotten greeting cards on the back of which was written that some member of their family has died. It is most upsetting when it comes at birthday or Christmas time.

GENTLE READER:

You are quite right that "Happy birthday! Did you know that Jesse died of a heart attack?" is not strictly correct. A more subdued version, such as a suitably melancholy letter saying, "I was thinking of you on your birthday," may include something like "You may not have heard our sad news . . ."

Relatives and close friends of the deceased should have been called when the death occurred. Making these calls is an excellent way to employ all those people who say, "What can I do to help?"

Indifferent Siblings

DEAR MISS MANNERS:

My brothers and sisters all left home years ago, and have not maintained more than a Christmas relationship with our parents for more than ten years. When my father was hospitalized with a terminal illness last year, I called and urged them to come home and make their peace while there was still time. They refused. It's been ten months now. My first instinct is to not call them when our father dies, and to not permit them to come to the funeral. I know Miss Manners would never permit this, so I'm asking your advice. I've also lied to my parents by making excuses for the other kids. I tell them they call me to check in, but can't get away because of sick kids, money, jobs, etc. Is this wrong?

GENTLE READER:

Miss Manners cannot disapprove of an effort designed to comfort one's dying parent; but neither can she approve one that will dramatically open the feud you know they dread, the minute your father is dead. You cannot withhold the information of your father's death, or the details of the funeral arrangements and their part in it as his children. Allow him to rest knowing that at least one of his children knows how to behave. (Miss Manners will, however, permit you a dry, ironic tone when you say, ''Father died last night—I thought you ought to know,'' and to respond with silence when you are then told how grieved they are.)

Wearing Mother's Rings

DEAR MISS MANNERS:

We are adult sisters whose mother passed away last fall. Our father survives. Our parents had been married more than fifty years.

One of the sisters was awarded Mother's modest diamond solitaire and gold wedding band (and let's not go into that!). Sister shed a few pretty tears and sped off to a jeweler. She had both rings resized for herself and wears them on her right hand, her own wedding set being on her left hand. Mother had a very small hand—Sister's hand is quite large, which necessitated cutting the wedding ring and adding a larger piece.

We other sisters were outraged and grieved at the destruction of Mother's sacred wedding band, as that is how we see it. We felt the wedding ring should be kept as a keepsake only. We have no quarrel about the diamond. Sister is not destitute, and could have afforded a different ring for her right hand. She said the jeweler told her it is usual and customary to wear one's mother's rings on one's right hand. But we felt he just saw a good chance to sell some expensive gold. To add to the hard feelings, Sister flashed the remodeled rings under our father's nose before Mother had been gone two months. She was insensitive and callous to do this, we think.

Would you please comment on the propriety of wearing one diamond engagement ring and one wedding ring on each hand? I have never heard of such a thing before, and if I'm so abysmally ignorant that I don't know what's proper, I'd like to know.

GENTLE READER:

When Miss Manners first saw your ''let's not go into that'' notice, precluding a discussion of why that particular sister was given the rings, she was relieved, thinking that at least she did not have to get into that nest of worms. An innocent person who steps into a family dispute like that can end up more battered than any of the participants.

But upon reflection, she has to point out that it is the crux of the matter, the inspiration of the belligerent tone of the argument, and, indeed, the motivation for your questions.

Miss Manners cannot say why this sister was chosen, but either your mother or your father must have intended her to have the rings. (If not, she stole them, and you can take this mess to a policeman, rather than to Miss Manners.) It is considered more flattering to make use of a sentimental legacy than to put it aside.

Thus, her decision to wear the rings (which you call flashing them) is only proper, and her decision to have them resized for her hand (which you call destroying them) is only sensible.

Posthumous Generosity

DEAR MISS MANNERS:

A dear old aunt of mine died in Germany a couple of months ago. She was a part of my childhood and my early adult years.

Now my eldest daughter, seventeen, who went to see friends and my family in Germany, brought back a big antique silver candlestick this aunt had left me in her will. My daughter repeated that my family continues to discuss this inheritance, finding it unfair, claiming the old lady was not responsible, having mistakenly put my name in her will, because I hadn't seen her for five years. Nobody else got anything except my aunt's inner family. She owned a castle they are selling now.

I have felt like the black sheep of the family for years for many reasons, and now I am hurt by this activity and rather want to return the candlestick to my aunt's children. But my husband thinks that would not improve my position in my family because "the damage is already done," and they are just jealous.

GENTLE READER:

Why would you think that your family duty consisted of gratifying the mean wishes of the living, rather than the clearly and legally stated generosity of your late aunt, who, incidentally, is also being insulted by these people?

By all means, keep the candlestick, and try to associate it with the kindness your aunt felt for you, rather than the unpleasantness of your cousins. Miss Manners' only regret is that your aunt did not leave you the castle and them the candlestick. Then we would have had some fun, wouldn't we?

Mealtime

Family Breakfast

It has come to Miss Manners' attention that there are people who have not mastered the etiquette of breakfast, but who nevertheless think themselves entitled to go right ahead and eat lunches and dinners. First things first, if you please.

Miss Manners is not even talking of such complicated and interesting activities as the hunt breakfast, the wedding breakfast, or the all-day Bloody-Mary-and-quiche Sunday breakfast. Plain old everyday family breakfast at home, the least structured and most permissive of the day's meals, is being abused daily in breakfast nooks everywhere. Just because the rules for breakfast are different from those for other meals, that does not mean that anything goes. What a dreadful precedent that would be for getting through the day.

Family breakfast is the only meal for which people can show up as their schedules or inclinations allow, instead of everyone's being expected at the same time. But only the first person down is excused from saying ''Good morning'' before entering the kitchen or breakfast room. Each new person initiates an exchange of greetings with those already there.

Minimal dress for breakfast is a robe. Miss Manners does not want to hear any coy remarks about the pleasures of appearing in less. Anyone who finds black lace or bare chests appetizing at the breakfast table either has no standards of sensuality or has not concluded the previous evening, in which case taking a break for food, however much daylight there is, cannot be considered legitimate breakfast.

Brushed teeth and brushed hair are also required. Slippers probably should be, also, but Miss Manners is lax about checking under the table.

Breakfast is the only meal at which menus may be different for people at the same table. The eccentricities of taste that would be considered finicky at other meals are tolerated at breakfast, where they are believed to be closely related to the emotional stability of the eater. There is nothing wrong with a breakfast table at which one person is having grapefruit, toast, and tea, another orange juice, cereal, and milk, a third cantaloupe, eggs, and coffee, and so on.

Provided, of course, it is all properly served. Cereal boxes, milk cartons, and other such commercial packaging do not belong on the breakfast table. That rule is absolute. There will be no excuses tolerated about being rushed in the morning. If you must set the alarm earlier in order to have time to pour the cream into a pitcher before placing it on the table, then do so.

At lunch and dinner, the entertainment must consist of conversation. Reading is forbidden when there is more than one person at the table. But at breakfast, one can have conversation, reading, or a combination, depending on the taste of the participants. Miss Manners' preference is to read the paper and periodically announce the news to the other people at the table, but she is aware that there are households in which her life expectancy would not be long.

People may leave the table at different times, but never in silence. Instead of "Excuse me," the customary remark at breakfast is "Oh, gosh, look at the time, I'd better go now or I'll be late." The correct response to this is " 'Bye," rather than "Well, then, hurry up—you remember what happened yesterday."

That is the civilized way to start a day.

The Compartmental Theory of Selective Hunger

The stomach of a child is a very delicate organ, as has been well proven to parental, if not medical, authorities. The number of children whose stomachs ache on school mornings in this country (French children's stomachs do not ache, but they have crises of the liver at the same time) is frightening.

The exact anatomy was discovered by a gentleman of Miss Manners' acquaintance when, as a scientifically alert child, he noticed the lack of provable truth in the parental dictum "If you don't have room for the eggplant, you're also too full for dessert." It was, he was able to demonstrate, entirely possible to be too full to eat another bite of eggplant, but to have quite enough room for even seconds in dessert.

How is that possible? asks the aging inquiring mind. "The biological theory, never disproved to my satisfaction," wrote the gentleman, "is that one's stomach is divided into compartments. In my case, the good Lord gave me no mushroom compartment at all, and I could therefore not eat them (although I later developed such a compartment). Fortunately, my mother had a sizable one, and took care always to seat me to her right when mushrooms were part of dinner, she not being inhibited about jabbing a fork into a neighbor's plate, provided it was her son's.

"To return: My eggplant compartment was very small, so that one or two bites of eggplant filled it to bursting. My roast pork compartment, however, was the size of an attaché case, my strawberries compartment the size of a Boeing 727, and my ice cream compartment was a veritable Carlsbad Caverns."

This explanation, he reports, worked for about a week. It is a well-known curiosity of parental anatomy that a parent who is laughing is incapable of barking commands. It is this kind of cleverness in the young that leads Miss Manners back to that school of child-rearing of which the motto is "Very funny. Now do as I say." (Other adages for the defeated parent's recovery include "That's enough talk; now eat" and "Don't talk with your mouth full—but please finish your dinner immediately; you're keeping us all sitting here.") She will not therefore abandon the time-honored dicta for training the palates of children:

- "How do you know, if you don't taste it? That's not enough. You can't tell from one bite."
- "Don't play with your food."
- "Your likes and dislikes are not conversation. Just eat your dinner and let's talk about something else." (Rule suspended for the statement "Mommy, this is delicious.")
- "I never said you have to like it. I just said you had to eat it."
- "It's good for you."
- "This is an acquired taste, and once you get used to it, you'll love it. But how are you going to enjoy it if you don't get used to it, and how are you going to get used to it if you don't give it a fair try?"
- Finally, the great classic: "If you don't want that, you're not hungry, and if you're not hungry you certainly don't want dessert."

Never mind the clever answers. Adults have strong stomachs or they wouldn't be able to function as parents, but they have a remarkable number of headaches brought on by being outwitted by their children.

Family Conversation

Rules for conversation, like those for eating meat from a bone, are different at the family table from what they are in public or with guests. "Keep your fingers out of your plate—how many times do I have to tell you?" and "That is really disgusting—stop it this minute, or you'll make me sick" are, for example, remarks Miss Manners considers inappropriate among even the closest of friends. But they are obligatory, from parent to child, at the family dinner table.

This is far from saying that anything goes at family dinner. It has its own etiquette, and a running commentary of instruction after the traditional openings ("Turn that thing off and come here before everything gets cold" and "You call that washed?") is part of that. But if this were unrelieved, it would be even more revolting than the children's natural eating methods.

Therefore, we have conversation.

In polite society, conversation means topics of general interest, not individual recitals of experience with no wider point. But just as you are allowed to pick up the bone at the family dinner table, you are allowed to lose the conversational thread.

Telling what one did, bragging about the successes and fishing for sympathy on the difficulties, is acceptable, even valuable, family conversation. Not only is it one of the great joys of family life to have a daily cheering section and supporting cast, but it teaches the others at the table to listen, or pretend that they are. It also teaches parents to refrain from seizing on a child's newly acquired knowledge and topping it by delivering a lecture showing off the parent's wisdom and knowledge on that subject. That is a very difficult lesson for parents to learn.

In company, it is rude to challenge another person's views or knowledge. One must say things like "Oh, really? That's funny, because I read that . . ." in order to undercut another person's position politely.

But at the family dinner table, conversation standards should be rigorous. Miss Manners will even make a major exception to the rule about not leaving the table for anything other than an emergency, in order to allow a disputed fact to be quickly checked. (Ones that take longer must be deferred, but the volunteer researcher can usually escape helping with the dishes if he reads aloud from the reference book in the kitchen while the others are working.)

Opinions, in Miss Manners' opinion, are also subject to challenge at the family dinner table. She believes that the child who is allowed to get away with baseless opinions, or who is congratulated for mouthing a family opinion without having thought it through, is destined to grow into a fuzzy thinker and a bore.

It annoys her no end to hear of children's being credited for "discussing" nuclear warfare, for example, when they have merely been told of the disastrous possibilities, so that they can then produce the "opinion" of being against it. She would hope that the most active anti-nuclear-weapons parent would insist that the child understand that the issue is not whether one is for or against destruction of the universe—how smugly children accept congratulations for coming out against it—but how countries can live in peace and how protect themselves from aggression. We all want our child to share our opinions because they are so wise. But if we want the child to be wise, as well, we will not accept his arriving at these opinions without knowing what he is saying.

All this can make for a rather stimulating dinner table. And whatever excitement is generated, it's bound to be more tolerable than "We're all going to sit here until you finish your spinach, so you might as well get to it."

Self-Expression for Grown-ups

DEAR MISS MANNERS:

We agree with everything you say about family dinnertime being a time to share experiences and exchange thoughts. But how much should this interfere with adult needs? My wife and I both work, and with taking work home, seeing to it that the children get their homework and chores done, and getting them bathed and into bed, we're pretty tired and just want to watch the news and go to sleep. When, except at the dinner table, are we going to discuss office matters, and even things having to do with the children? Also, we sometimes use some language that we don't let them use. That we know we shouldn't do, but it's the way most adults talk now, and it just comes out when we are talking about the office.

GENTLE READER:

Miss Manners realizes that many things have happened to the old cocktail hour, such as Perrier, and both parents getting home from the office just in time for dinner. Nevertheless, a quick private chat, details to come, is essential. If you use the dinner table for private adult conversation, the children's eyes will glaze over, and they will get into the habit of not listening to anything you say, except the swear words. (Miss Manners is sorry to have to tell you that the vocabulary you use is the one you are going to hear back from the children. That's how you taught them to talk in the first place, remember?)

You may, however, discuss matters concerning the children that you don't want them to hear, provided you and your wife speak a foreign language that the children do not. Many capable linguists today owe their abilities to the desire to find out what their parents were saying that they didn't want them to hear.

Miss Manners hopes you will also cultivate the habit of listening to the children's conversation, not just their transgressions. You are allowed to break in occasionally with "Don't tell us the whole plot, just tell us briefly what it was about" and "That's very interesting, but finish your dinner now and let's hear what your brother did today," but not to the point of discouraging them. Many a generational "communications problem" was caused by the parents' failing to listen to the children until the children had something so interesting to report that they decided it was better to continue the habit of keeping things to themselves.

Dinner Is Served

DEAR MISS MANNERS:

I work hard to make good hot meals for my family, which is not easy because I also have a part-time job and don't get home until the afternoon. I could take the easy way and serve them convenience foods, but I don't. It seems to me that the least they can do is come when I call them, but every night I end up yelling at them until they finally get themselves to the table, and then I have to send my youngest back to wash her hands, or my oldest to put something on over her underwear, which is what she wears to do her homework in. Don't you think they owe me the courtesy of coming to dinner on time?

GENTLE READER:

Certainly. However, Miss Manners would prefer it if you would separate your perhaps justified self-congratulations from the etiquette problem.

Unless you serve dinner at the exact same hour every night, you owe them the courtesy of a warning, so that they may come to a natural stop in homework or other tasks, and fulfill requirements of dress and hygiene. The usual sequence of announcing dinner is:

1. Dinner's almost ready!
2. I'm about to dish up.
3. Dinner's ready; please come to the table now.
4. All right now, I mean it. Everything's getting cold.

If you issue the first three statements, the fourth should not be necessary.

Culinary Conversation

DEAR MISS MANNERS:

If a salad or other part of the meal is served on a bed of lettuce, is it not proper to eat that lettuce as part of the meal, or is it more appropriate to leave it untouched on the plate after having consumed whatever was on it? What about the parsley garnish that often accompanies a dish, particularly in restaurants?

What is proper behavior if one absolutely abhors something, let us say, for example, ripe olives, but finds it mixed in whatever dish is served at table? Should one be obligated to consume such an item out of politeness? Is it permissible following the example above, to fish the ripe olives out of the rest of the dish and leave them in a neat little pile by the side of the plate? What if the item in question causes an allergic reaction or raises havoc with one's digestion, liver, or whatever? Must one still simply eat it and suffer quietly, or would it be permissible then to fish the item out, perhaps with an apology to the host or hostess?

GENTLE READER:

Miss Manners blames herself for the absurdity of the current preoccupation with what should or should not be eaten.

Time was when it was considered polite to leave some food on the plate—"for Miss Manners," as children used to be instructed. Well—ugh. Miss Manners got tired of eating the leftovers of revolting children, and the style became "joining the Clean Plate Club."

Each of these positions assumes an intense interest in how much people do or do not eat, when everyone knows that it is the society and conversation that is important at dinner parties and other such events, and not the food.

In fact, Miss Manners is rapidly getting to the point of reviving another old rule, which was that one never discussed the food at table, even to praise it. (This rule dates from the time when even moderately well-off people employed cooks, and therefore could take no direct credit for their accomplishments. Miss Manners can just hear the screams of protest from the kitchen-mad hosts and hostesses of today who, having labored all day over a hot pasta machine, want nothing else discussed at their dinner tables. It is just such people who are driving Miss Manners to outlaw food conversation. You know who you are, so please take warning.)

Of course you can eat lettuce and parsley if you want, and of course you don't eat something that makes you turn blue and drop dead on the tablecloth. It is not necessary to fish offending objects out—just leave them where they are. And please raise your attention from your plate to the people around you.

Dinnertime Noise

DEAR MISS MANNERS:

There are very few traits that I can complain about in the father of my four children, but I would like your opinion as to whether one of his habits is crude, offensive, and insulting. When we sit down to dinner, all six of us together, my husband insists on wearing his hearing protectors—you know, the sound mufflers that people wear to operate power tools or to signal pilots where to park their aircraft. He is mild-mannered about it, asserting that he is not annoyed or spiteful, but that just brings the noise level down to where he can tolerate it and enjoy the conversation. He does seem to understand everything, but we feel he is screening us out. Is wearing sound mufflers at dinner sound etiquette? If you think so, I will stop objecting, but I can't promise not to feel offended.

GENTLE READER:

What's that you say? Just a minute, till Baby stops banging his spoon so Miss Manners can hear what you're saying. Stephan's trying to get your attention; can you ask him to wait a minute until we finish our conversation? Who left the TV on in the other room? All right, answer the phone, but tell whoever it is that we'll have to call back after dinner. Now—what were you saying? Oh, about that rude man over there, tuning out. Well, Miss Manners has some sympathy with him. *Can you hear that, sir?* Some sympathy. Not an unlimited amount.

No, he certainly may not wear sound mufflers to dinner, a patent offense to all. On the other hand, let us all help in removing the offense from his ears. First, ban all mechanical noises at dinnertime. Then attempt to teach rules about one person talking at a time, taking orderly turns, and so on. That is what child-rearing is all about, and your husband must participate, not tune out. Eventually, peace will settle on a table of cheerful but intelligible babble. Miss Manners only hopes your husband has not gone deaf by now.

The Grace to Bow One's Head

DEAR MISS MANNERS:

I often spend the weekends at my aunt's house. Whenever they sit down at the dinner table, they pray before they eat.

I do not pray before meals, and constantly find myself uncomfortable before them. I always feel out of place, as if I was doing something wrong by not bowing my head. How should I approach this situation when it arises again?

GENTLE READER:

With head bowed. As is sometimes the case, you felt wrong because you were wrong. Bowing the head does not constitute praying, nor even endorsement of the prayers of others. It is simply a sign of respect for the religious activity being practiced in your presence. It is equivalent to standing at attention in silence while the national anthem of a country not your own is being played. Etiquette does not regulate whether you use the time for sacred or profane thoughts—only that you keep respectfully still and refrain from getting a head start on the food.

Chicken at the Family Table

DEAR MISS MANNERS:

Tonight at the dinner table, my father said it was all right to eat baked chicken with your fingers. But my stepmother said it wasn't all right. So we (the four kids) want to know who is right. My brother agrees with my father, but we three agree with my stepmother. If we lose (stepmother and three kids) we have to wash the cars. But if they (Daddy and brother) lose they will take us out for pizza and ice cream.

GENTLE READER:

First wash the cars, and then go out for pizza and ice cream. There is something wrong with each of your arguments. (Miss Manners could have put it that each of you has a point that is correct, but in that case, the cars would stay dirty and you would have liver and onions for dinner.)

It is not how the chicken is cooked that is important here; although there are some messy chicken dishes that can never be eaten with the fingers, baked chicken is up for grabs, so to speak. The deciding factor is where the chicken is being eaten. At the family dinner table, other highly informal meals, or picnics, chicken may be eaten with the fingers. In restaurants other than the least formal, fast-food type, or at meals with company at your house or when you go out, chicken is eaten with the fork and knife, even if it is cooked in such a way—deep-fried, for example—that this is a struggle for all concerned, including the chicken.

Miss Manners intends this as an argument for: (1) cooking chicken with some nice sloppy sauce when company is expected; (2) ordering the Coq au Vin at restaurants; and (3) preserving the family.

Reviewing Table Manners

DEAR MISS MANNERS:

My parents did their best to impress good table manners upon me, but being the cheeky devil that I was, I refused to heed their advice. Consequently, while I have pleased my parents in every other respect, my table manners are atrocious—slightly below the level of barbarian. I have just graduated from law school and I am terrified of going out to eat with associates and clients.

A list of my table etiquette faults could cover several pages, but I have questions about two situations that have occurred more than once.

1. Eating fish or chicken, small bones are found. Do I:

    a. chew them until they are ground fine, then swallow them?
    b. hold a napkin to my mouth and spit them out?
    c. pick the bones out with my fingers?
    d. order steak and avoid the problem altogether?
  2. Cutting something, it will skitter off my plate and onto the floor. Do I:
    a. pick the food off the floor and place it back on my plate?
    b. pick the food off the floor and place it somewhere other than my plate, like an ashtray?
    c. kick the food under the table leg so that nobody will notice it?
    d. ignore it?

GENTLE READER:

How often does your food leap off of your plate? Never mind. Miss Manners will endeavor to (d) ignore it.

Miss Manners is happy to answer your questions, provided that you understand that we are using a system based entirely on precedent and that argument is therefore useless.

1. It depends on the identity of the victim. Solution (a) applies to very small game birds and pickled herring; (b) applies to nothing; (c) applies to fish; and (d) depends on who's paying.

2. This depends on the scene of the crime and the likelihood of your being caught. Solution (a) is for dining in a private home, where you can contrive to make others believe that the only thing you dropped was your napkin; (b) depends on the size of the evidence (a grape could be placed in the ashtray, but a corncob could not); (c) applies only to open-air hunt breakfasts; and (d) is passable in restaurants, although it would be kinder to call the waiter's attention to the fact that there is a fish on the floor before he discovers this with the sole of his foot.

Tucking Napkins

DEAR MISS MANNERS:

I wear fine clothing, and although I have good table manners and am careful, sometimes accidents do happen and I get food stains on my shirt or necktie that are impossible to remove.

My mother maintains that it is acceptable to wear a napkin tucked into one's collar in all but the finest restaurants or at formal occasions. I assert that this isn't done by adults, except in the privacy of their own homes, perhaps at a picnic, or when eating lobster. When dining out, I purposely avoid ordering foods that are particularly potentially dangerous.

I wouldn't tuck a napkin under my chin at a fast food restaurant, much less anywhere else. My mother wonders why I am so concerned about what other people think. What do you say?

GENTLE READER:

Not being concerned about what people think is a poor blanket lesson for mothers to be teaching is what Miss Manners thinks.

The correct version is: In moral matters, you need not concern yourself with the opinions of others as long as what you are doing is both honest and kind. (Miss Manners brings you this one directly from her own dear mother.) In matters of etiquette, however, you do what is accepted unless, as in the case of civil disobedience, you wish to make a protest and accept the consequences.

Of course, adults do not wear bibs, or make their napkins into them; nobody does who has passed the toddler stage. Life is not free of risk, but there are limits to how much one can protect oneself. Why doesn't she just serve you when you are in the bathtub?

Napkin Rings

DEAR MISS MANNERS:

A difference of opinion has arisen among my friends concerning the nature of napkin rings.

One faction holds that napkin rings serve a purely decorative function by enhancing the beauty of the table setting. The other faction (the minority) contends that napkin rings are a holdover from earlier days when families (among others) dined together several times a day. In this bygone era, neither paper napkins nor even automatic washing machines had been invented. It being impractical to wash napkins for every meal, it became necessary (for sanitary reasons, if no other) to distinguish the diners' napkins. Hence, each regular diner's napkin ring was emblazoned with his or her symbol or initials. The slightly used napkins were safely stored corraled in their appropriate napkin rings. A nonuser, unique supply of napkin rings would be necessary when guests dined, for obvious reasons.

We await your answer in anticipation of resolving this longstanding question. It is worrisome to consider what we will discuss after we lose this topic.

GENTLE READER:

If you think that is worrisome, how would you like to have a normal routine of your household described as the custom of a bygone era?

Of course the purpose of napkin rings is to distinguish among the family napkins. Their use, like so many things in life, represents a compromise. In an ideal world, everyone would be issued a fresh napkin at every meal. In this unfortunate world, some people have to make do with that distasteful invention the paper napkin. Thus the genteel compromise is to reuse family napkins for several meals. (Extra rings are needed only for intimate houseguests who partake of family-style meals.)

Your other friends are also correct that some people do use napkin rings vestigially, as it were. As this only reminds people who know the function of the compromises necessary in this imperfect world, it would seem to Miss Manners to add a depressing, rather than a festive, touch to the table setting.

Spoons 101

DEAR MISS MANNERS:

What are the etiquette rules regarding the use of a regular teaspoon? My husband persists in using his spoon to eat vegetables such as corn and peas. He also sometimes uses his spoon for mashed potatoes and stew (not soup). I feel this is improper, but he maintains the spoon is on the table to be used.

If the use of the spoon is improper, I would like to know before our sons start copying Dad!

GENTLE READER:

Unbeknownst to you, and probably also to himself, your husband is gently making a satirical point about the way you set the table. Why, indeed, is a teaspoon put on the dinner table, if not to be used?

The answer is that it simply does not belong there. It is a very common error to place the teaspoon next to the knife, presumably to use in eating the dessert. Place settings are even advertised in that arrangement. But it is wrong. Dessert is correctly eaten with a larger oval spoon and/or a small fork. You will recognize this spoon, because you use it for soup. At least, Miss Manners hopes you use it for soup. That statement about your husband worries her. The teaspoon is used for—surprise!—tea. Unless you have the most formal service, the dessert spoon is placed above the plate, parallel to the edge of the table, with its handle toward the knife and its bowl toward the fork; a dessert fork is placed between the plate and that spoon, facing in the opposite direction. Try this, and please let Miss Manners know if your husband persists in using that spoon for his mashed potatoes. She will have a stern talk with him.

A Misdirected Fork

DEAR MISS MANNERS:

Today at lunch someone reached across the table and stole my french fries. I proceeded to stab him with the fork I was holding. For future reference, I would like to know the correct response to this breach of etiquette.

GENTLE READER:

"Ouch." Oh—you mean *his* breach of etiquette.

Your response to that was all right as far as it went, but it omitted the final touch that makes a vicious, although provoked, gesture impeccably correct. After stabbing the interloper with your fork, you should have looked in horror at the row of tiny holes you had made in his hand and exclaimed, "Oh, I'm so terribly sorry! I thought that was my soft-shelled crab!"

Never on the Table

DEAR MISS MANNERS:

Is there anything wrong with leaving a hairbrush face-up on a table, even if it isn't going to be eaten on for three more hours?

GENTLE READER:

Yes.

Correcting

DEAR MISS MANNERS:

Is there a polite way to handle the problem of well-mannered parents who do not insist that their children use proper manners also? I refer specifically to table manners as an example, because it ruins my dinner. Children (over three) who grip the utensils in a "fist" (rather than balance them in three fingers), and lean down to the plate to "shovel" in the food like starved truck drivers. Also the talking and/or chewing with a full and open mouth; the placing of gigantic portions on the fork, then biting off hunks instead of cutting food into smaller amounts; the refusal to use napkins on messy fingers and faces; picking up non-finger foods in their fingers—the list goes on and on.

When these people are guests at your table, at home or in a restaurant, is there anything you can say to them about it? What if these are relatives?

GENTLE READER:

The only thing you can do while you are actually at the table is to make a mental note for the future to invite your friends only after their children's bedtime. You cannot correct your guests, even if they are disgusting children, and that also means that you cannot correct your friends on their child-rearing techniques.

Far be it from Miss Manners to sympathize with people who shovel, chew, and bite in the manner you describe, but three is rather a low cutoff at which to expect finished table manners. Between three and six may, in fact, be considered prime training time for table manners, when the parents of such people should be spending a great portion of their family dinner hours doing the training. They may elect not to conduct this training when others, such as yourself, are present. They could figure, correctly, that doing so would add embarrassment to the other difficulties of the process, and also that a steady stream of instruction to the children might not provide you an amusing evening.

Of course, it is possible that no such training is taking place, in which case you may want to avoid these children all their lives. But if they are relatives, or the children of very close friends, you may supply the lack yourself if you do it tactfully. This means inviting the children without their parents, in some way that will make them feel privileged and grown up, and then explaining to them, in a kindly way, that the custom at your house is to chew with the mouth closed, take only one mouthful of food on the fork at a time, and so on. (You must be careful not to criticize their parents, and to say, "Well, dear, they do things differently, but this is the way I prefer it to be done at my house.") If the occasion is pleasant enough, they will try to live up to your standards, and you will have done humanity a great service.

Restaurant Rights

It will astonish restaurant employees and patrons alike to hear this, but even the best restaurants are commercial establishments where people pay to be served meals, and not temples of social behavior where they submit themselves to be judged.

It astonishes Miss Manners to hear that many people who are confident of their behavior among family and friends become terrified of embarrassing themselves before the imposing figures of maître d's, as they call themselves, or other high officers in the restaurant service. One would think that if the people sitting at one's restaurant table are satisfied with one's manners, one would hardly care about the opinion of those standing behind it.

This odd state of affairs, a reversal of the usual customer-serviceperson relationship—paralleled only among patients and the doctors they hire—seems to have come about by design of restaurant managers. Many of them believe that their patrons are sycophants who only respect those who look down upon them, and their success has proven them often correct.

The fact is that few restaurants, no matter how outrageously expensive, can provide formal service as it is known in social circumstances. It is rare, indeed, to dine in a restaurant where the service people do not interrupt the diners, where filled plates are never put before one, and where trays, rather than hands, are used to bring needed equipment. To those who believe that a fancy restaurant represents dining of a class higher than that to which they are accustomed, Miss Manners must explain that there is no need to feel inadequate. Good restaurant service may be pleasant and smooth, but it does not represent the equivalent of butlers and footmen.

As you are paying for your meal in a restaurant, it is perfectly proper to:
- Request a table in an area you prefer, say, near a window or away from musicians. For a customer to accept employees' or owners' ideas of "good" tables and "bad" tables and compete to be favored with their choices is childish.
- Sit next to whomever you want among those in your group. Unless one is giving a party in a restaurant, the social rules about seating do not apply. If couples want to sit next to, rather than across from, each other, or with the gentleman, rather than the lady, against the wall, Miss Manners cannot see why they should not be permitted to do so.
- Know what is being offered, in the way of food and drink, and its price. If a list of "specials of the day" is recited, it is sensible to ask how much a dish will cost.
- Expect to be supplied with correct flatware, and resupplied, discreetly and tactfully, with replacements for dropped or misused implements.
- Talk only with those with whom you are dining. If strolling musicians, itinerant fashion models, or sociable waiters or other servicepeople present themselves, they may be dismissed with a pleasant but abstracted nod.
- Remain ignorant of the personnel hierarchy of the restaurant. If a restaurant employs an army of captains, waiters, headwaiters, priests of wine, busboys, and hostesses, that is its privilege. But the customer should not be expected to recognize and treat according to rank the entire service. He may address any request to whoever presents himself with the expectation that that person, if not designated to perform the task, will find the person who is. Unless some

special favor is given, the client should only leave one tip, to be divided by those involved according to their own standards.

· Enjoy your dinner, free of worries about the help's criticizing your manners. Only Miss Manners is allowed to do that.

The Middle Menu Rule

DEAR MISS MANNERS:

Last week, my fiancée's parents took us out for dinner two nights in a row, and it was understood that they were treating us. The first night, two of us had steak at $18, and three had lobster at $36. The next night, at another restaurant, three people had entrées of $13 to $18, and I had lobster for $36. I had previously raved about this dish at this restaurant, and though I don't go there often, it's the dish I usually order there. As a matter of fact, when I am paying, I customarily have an expensive meal, lobster or steak or both.

The next day, I was told that I was rude to order such an expensive meal, since the other people ate more modestly.

On the third evening, it was understood that I was paying. Since there were seven of us, I took them to a less expensive restaurant. The same party who made the comment that I was rude ordered the most expensive item on the menu, as did I. Wouldn't this also be rude? Please be aware that it is not a question of affordability.

When you go out to dinner, is it rude to order one of the most expensive items, even if it is what you customarily order?

GENTLE READER:

If Miss Manners settles this for you now, will you promise not to involve her in the money disputes that will arise out of your wedding arrangements? They are bound to be doozies.

When being taken out to dinner, it is customary to order "from the middle of the menu," which is to say neither the most nor the least expensive item available. However, if the host himself orders the top item, it is a sign that everyone else is free to do so. Therefore, the lobster choice having been sanctioned on the first night, you were within your rights to order it the second night, and your guest was entitled to order as expensively as you on the third night.

What is highly improper is the fact that everyone kept such detailed notes of how much each of you consumed financially at each setting.

Tasteful Treatment of Ice Cream

Ice cream, like a fourteen-year-old high fashion model, can look very innocent or very sophisticated, depending on how it is presented, although actually it is neither. But it always looks good.

Ice cream is a tease, because to enjoy it in the way one would secretly like best would be highly improper. And although there are many different ways of attacking it, none of these will be fully successful. (N.B.: Metaphor used in first two sentences does not apply to this paragraph.)

The truth is that ice cream tastes best when it is smushed. That means working it onto the side of the bowl with the back of a spoon and pounding anything else— syrup, whipped cream, nuts, fruit—into the slime. Naturally, no well-mannered person would dream of doing this.

Among the tools supplied for conveying ice cream into the willing mouth are cones, straws, dessert spoons and forks, special ice cream spoons that look like shovels, special ice cream forks that look like spoons in drag, parfait spoons, iced-tea spoons moonlighting in sodas, and flat wooden pallets that look like spoons that have been run over by ice cream trucks.

None of these does the job. They fall into two categories—those that leave ice cream on your plate, and those that leave ice cream on your shirt.

However, as no one is willing to give up the attempt and eat something coopera-tive, such as whipped prunes, instead, here is a guide to eating ice cream, from the most informal to the most formal methods. The aim is to achieve a mixture of manners, safety, and enjoyment as satisfying as, for example, soda water, syrup, and ice cream.

Cones

Lick in swirling motion, dealing first with the overhang at the rim of the cone. When no one is looking, dart out tongue, snake-fashion, and push middle of scoop into cone. The ice cream cone is designed to teach children about symmetry and fairness, as anything but strict impartiality in the licking and the cone-nibbling is disastrous. Biting off the bottom of the cone and sucking the ice cream through it is illegal.

Bowls

Patience is the best method for getting the ice cream served in a bowl to the proper consistency, but this may be speeded along discreetly by idly separating spoonfuls from the central scoop. If more vigorous mixing is required, for a sundae, for example, the best method is to fix the attention of witnesses by a penetrating stare and animated talk, while apparently absentmindedly dragging the spoon around the dish.

Parfaits

Same as above, only moving vertically.

Sodas

Eat enough whipped cream with spoon to make it safe to lower the spoon into the glass without invoking Archimedes' principle all over the saucer. Alternate

sipping, stirring, and spooning (the last not to be confused with the social behavior of the same name, although it is hard to say which is more exciting) until
all that remains is beyond the reach of these techniques. Because of the exceptional
nature of this treat, Miss Manners then allows three free slurps. A fourth would
be vulgar.

High-Level Offerings

This category includes Baked Alaska, ice cream rolls, Peaches Melba, bombes,
Cherries Jubilee, and other such desserts. The fork, in the left hand, conveys everything into the spoon, held in the right hand. If the ice cream should be pounded
insensible on the trip, so much the better. Otherwise, this is the time to enthrall
the company with brilliant stories, while your dessert gradually weakens.

Other

No instructions are given for eating ice cream out of the carton with a spoon
while standing in front of the freezer, because Miss Manners does not believe that
anyone would do such a thing.

The Great Cookie Debate

DEAR MISS MANNERS:
Our home is racked by great debate over how one properly consumes a sandwich
cookie. Our son and my wife both agree that you must separate the two halves
first. But my son feels that you should lick off the icing first, whereas my wife feels
that the uniced side should be the primary target.
I don't eat sandwich cookies myself, but would like to settle this matter.
GENTLE READER:
Miss Manners is sorry to disillusion you about your entire family at once, but
it is never proper to separate a cookie horizontally, and therefore the question of
which part to attack first is moot.
Mind you, Miss Manners is not disputing that sandwich cookies taste better
when pulled apart at the icing. We are discussing propriety here.

Foods Only a Child Can Eat

DEAR MISS MANNERS:
I desperately need to know how to eat tacos, chili dogs, Big Macs, and the like,
so I will not make a fool out of myself. Also, is there a correct way to eat with
plastic knives and forks?

Gentle Reader:

The answer to part two of your letter is no. Those things were invented for the express purpose of making fools out of well-meaning, earnest, mannerly people. There is nothing that tickles the manufacturers of plastic flatware more than the sight of a hungry person trying to pick broken plastic fork tines out of his food.

As for the foods you mention, they at least give the eater a fighting chance, although many people who attack them end up covered with something other than glory, especially on the shirt fronts and laps.

Just about every society in the world has at least one popular finger food in which the part that, although edible, can be safely held in the hand is substantially smaller than the part that cannot. A classic example is the ice cream cone; an outstanding example is the double-scoop ice cream cone.

The basic strategy for attacking these unwieldy items, which are unfortunately often delicious, is to go for the overhang first. In the case of the taco, that means nibbling off everything sticking out beyond the base of the taco itself, taking a bite from one corner, eating whatever sticks out after that bite, and then working one's way across the open end, alternately biting the taco and then eating off the new overhang. Anything in a hamburger bun is nibbled from the top, and then the bun is pinned down at the bottom to approximate the closed end of a taco. For chili dogs, anything really oozy should be left on the plate and eaten with—aren't there any real forks in this joint?

Art and Sport

Cultivating Children's Taste

Many people nowadays won't even agree to meet anyone until every taste and characteristic has been checked out, and there is a guarantee that the candidate will be slender, nonsmoking, fond of good restaurants and walks in the country, financially and emotionally secure, and fun-loving. (Sloppy, smoky, insecure fun-haters who support mediocre restaurants get married all the time, so there must be a great demand for them, too, but presumably they are able to meet their mates effortlessly, in dancing class.)

What surprises Miss Manners is that this finickiness is totally abandoned when it comes to the smaller people with whom adults agree to share their households and lives. One can argue, on behalf of parents who claim to be helpless to prevent the alien culture of their children from taking over their domiciles, that they are victims of a bait-and-switch ploy. Few newborns smoke in the hospital nursery, after all, and it is always presumed that their other nasty habits will soon disappear. But it seems that they no sooner learn to sleep through the night and bring up a burp than they are making it impossible for the parents to sleep through the night—and are bringing up heaven knows what.

Miss Manners tries hard to sympathize with parental wailings that their standards of language, noise, dress, and decorum are being violated under their noses by their immediate descendants. But she keeps wondering why they didn't bully and brainwash the children to acquire their own tastes when the children were too innocent and helpless to know any better. Many parents are too nice and understanding to do this. They accept the principle that the children will have different tastes from theirs, and they pretend—right up to the moment that they get blasted out of their own houses—that the children's tastes are just as valid as theirs. (Miss Manners' own cultural preferences are seeping out here, but, then, adults who share their children's tastes don't need her consideration, because they haven't any such problem.)

There is no innate reason why children should prefer certain types of culture that we shall collectively call junk. What is natural and inevitable in them is only the taste to spurn what the parents have pushed as being good for them, and to indulge in whatever produces that interesting reaction of driving the parents up the wall. The wily parent will therefore make every effort to conceal his or her desire to share. Far kinder, in the long run, are callous positions: What's good enough for you isn't good enough for me, so keep it to yourself; the luxuries I enjoy would be wasted on you.

You don't, for example, try to encourage the children to watch "good television," cut viewing hours, or be selective about programs. You simply say, "I don't see how you can stand that boring stuff—I can't even bear to have it in the background." Therefore, there is a rule that the set is never on when the parent is home, which generally means nights and weekends. The child is free to watch at other times—say, after school and homework but before dinner—and will, at first, be overjoyed when the parent is going out for an evening. But the habit of not expecting any television otherwise will be established early. It might be helpful to note here that whatever the parent wants to watch is, by definition, important, and therefore an exception.

What the parent goes out to enjoy is also defined as good—but much too good to waste on the children. "Take you with me? Don't be silly. In the first place, I'm going out to a good restaurant, for good food, and you'd be much happier with a hamburger; then, you would look out of place in the clothes you always insist on, which are all right among your friends but not for anyplace important. Afterward, I'm going to the theater, which would probably bore you, and anyway, I'll be out of the house, so you can watch television instead. Toodle-oo. Have fun."

What self-respecting child can resist a challenge like that? The next thing you know, they'll all be whining that you aren't fair, and demanding to horn in on the treat. Anything to annoy a parent—and the parent's only problem then will be to continue to look annoyed while sharing his enjoyments with a nicely dressed, well-behaved, open-minded child who is straining to prove he is sophisticated.

Unassigned Reading

DEAR MISS MANNERS:

My wife and I are concerned about the fact that our children never read for pleasure. They all do reasonably well in school, but would never think of taking up a book just for the fun of it. Our own childhoods were very different. We were both shy kids, and always in libraries or curled up somewhere, escaping into more interesting worlds. A teacher told us that children learn by example, that if there are books in the house, children will get into them, but we are practically crowded out of our living space by bookshelves, and always reading ourselves—it's a big joke, even, that Mom or Dad can't even go to the bathroom without a mad search for glasses and reading matter to take along—and yet the only things they ever read are joke books or collections of comic strips in book form.

It is not, as our friends complain, that the kids can't unglue themselves from the television set. They watch, but not as much as other children apparently do. Partly this is because we always limited the amount of time and programs they could watch, but also its because by now (they are nine, eleven, and twelve) they find most television predictable and boring.

Also, we do read aloud to them, and have since they were very small, reading the classics we each enjoyed as children (*Oz*, *Alice*, and even our old Nancy Drew and Hardy Boys books, and now *Robinson Crusoe*, *Gulliver's Travels*, and things like that). They enjoy this, and even plead with us to read to them more often, but just don't make the step of doing it themselves. It's not, you see, that they're not interested, because they are really bright kids.

As I said, lots of our friends tell us about the same thing, but they always have a theory of why, and none of these apply to our home, which is book-lined, and filled with good stories. Perhaps it does have something to do with the times, but what?

GENTLE READER:

Miss Manners has heard all those theories and more. One way or another, they all have to do with the influence of television—if not because the children are watching instead of reading themselves, then because they have no friends who can share an interest in books with them. It is, Miss Manners keeps being told, a picture world now, not a word one. As the printed word replaced the spoken word in human communication, film has replaced books.

Nonsense. Human knowledge is still stored in writing. If you succeed in teaching your children the love of books, they will never reach that boredom they got to in only a decade of television watching.

Of course, you did ask Miss Manners how, didn't you? And you have already followed the known methods, of example and the enticement of reading aloud.

All right, let's get rougher. Start reading some book they will all love, and, just when you get to the juiciest part, cut the session off abruptly, claiming that you have other things to do and will get to it again some vague time when you are free. Miss Manners apologizes for stealing this method from film, it having done years of service in getting people to return to movie theaters to see successive installments of serials, but we take our learning wherever we find it.

Then you must forbid them to read in bed after the official bedtime—and provide them with flashlights.

Background Music

Dear Miss Manners:

I have a friend who says it is rude to have soft music playing in your car when she is in the car. She even reaches over and switches it off.

Soft music soothes my nerves when I drive, and I keep it low enough to have a normal conversation. She also says it is rude to have soft background music in your home when you have guests. I always enjoy it when I go into homes where it is playing, and the television isn't blaring. I think it makes for more light, pleasant, happy conversation. What do you say? Am I rude?

Gentle Reader:

"Rude" is a harsh word for what you claim is soft music. Nevertheless, Miss Manners shares your friend's feelings, although she would not dream of employing her rude method of expressing them. "Do you mind if we turn that off so I can pay attention to what you're saying?" is more polite than switching off someone else's radio.

If you really cannot drive safely without the radio on, then your driving license should state that, as others' say they cannot drive without wearing glasses. However, if you cannot have pleasant conversation without a mechanical background, that is a dreadful affliction, and perhaps your guests should be warned of it. Many people, Miss Manners foremost among them, find such conflicting noises distracting, and an insult to both the conversation and the music.

Indeed, having television on when guests are present is worse, but the principle is the same: You may invite guests for the specific purpose of watching something on television, or of listening to records or the radio. But you should not allow them to believe that their conversation is to be the sole entertainment, and then, apparently thinking it not sufficiently amusing, supplement it with other forms of entertainment.

Competition

Having children is not, Miss Manners would have thought, a competitive sport. And yet there are so many parents who go in for it as such that she hopes they will at least gain the experience to teach their children the mannerly way to handle competitions.

Your truly competitive parent loses no opportunity to enter his child into competition, beginning with its birth weight. One measures the child's performance against charts and live competitors—including those available in the hospital nursery, the other products of one's childbirth class, the memories of former champions, and total strangers who are minding their own business, taking the air in their carriages and strollers at parks and zoos. What the child eats, when he performs certain actions or pronounces new words, when he learns not to perform certain actions—every detail can be used to check the child's rating against the competition. It does not sound to Miss Manners like an entertaining or useful sport, but then tennis sounds foolish, too, when its rules are explained to a non-participant.

The time comes, however, when the child is inevitably pitted against others, for academic or athletic tests, for spots in classes, teams, plays, and other prizes and honors of the society. He must therefore be taught to be a brave loser and a graceful winner. The basic attitude to be taught is that there are enough goodies in the world for everyone to be blessed (although the distribution system may be somewhat slow and haphazard), so that one must be pleased at the success of others even if that seems to delay one's own triumph. The illogic of this position, flying in the face of the simple fact that you got what I wanted, is apparent to the tiniest child. Nevertheless, it is one of the tenets of civilization, and subscribing to it produces first nobility and then happiness.

Let us say, for example, that your child tries out for the part of the prince in the school play, as does his best friend, who gets it. Your child doesn't get a lesser part, either, but is told that being an usher is just as important as being a star. Having wished his rivals to be run over on their way to the audition, the child is now furious at (1) his friend, (2) the teacher who distributed parts, and (3) fate, in that order. He is behaving naturally, but not civilly. By citing the litany, one must persuade him to:

- Wish the others success beforehand and with some degree of plausibility, which does not include saying sullenly, "I just know you'll get it, I just know you will."
- Compliment others on their attempts, regardless of whether one considers them to have messed up or to have been threateningly good.
- Make his best try, measuring himself against his own ability, not against the probable achievements of others.
- Congratulate the winner with some heartiness ("That's great, you really deserve it"), no sarcasm ("Well, of course you were picked—you always are"), and no bitterness ("I didn't want it anyway").

Should your child be the winner, he must still encourage and compliment the others, but with more subtle delivery (acting ability is why he got the part, isn't it?) that excludes a triumphant tone. The correct comment to make when others acknowledge the victory is "Yes, I was really lucky this time."

Any child can learn this valuable technique. Whether a competitive parent can, when informed that a younger child than his is doing calculus while his child is still trying to figure out how to get his thumb in his mouth, is another question.

The Proper Stage Mother and Little League Father

If a young person shows persistent interest in a field of endeavor that is considered both rigorous and glorious—dancing, skating, drama, classical music, soccer—society tends to blame the parents.

That is because everyone agrees that the natural pursuits of teenagers are (1) boredom and (2) junk culture. If a child has been diverted from these, it can only have been through the machinations of warped parents, who, disregarding his birthright of noisy ennui, push him into a pretense of appreciation for skills that show such perverted adult values as discipline and development.

We thus recognize such stock villains as the Stage Mother and the Little League Father, parents who are perceived as engaging in only one activity: that of pushing. It is, however, Miss Manners' observation that many such adults are being pulled, rather than pushed, and that she had better set some standards for their protection.

It must be the parents' official position, no matter how much they share the child's goal and admire his achievements, that they are allowing the child to follow his interest warily, and that the privilege could at any moment be withdrawn. If this sounds mean and at variance with the enthusiastic support a parent should also give—encouraging the child, attending his recitals, games, and performances, cheering successes and sympathizing with setbacks—it is. But it works.

You don't nag a child to practice, you simply offer to stop his lessons.

You don't complain that schoolwork has been neglected, you simply use scholastic troubles to make the point: "Well, of course, you can't manage both, so I'm afraid you'll have to give up the team and concentrate on your work unless there's an improvement."

You don't tolerate tantrums, you say, "Look, the emotional strain is too much for you, and if you can't handle it, let's get you back into a more normal life."

Miss Manners is not above suggesting that you even grumble occasionally about the parental hardships of driving children to these activities, buying equipment, and adjusting schedules around theirs. It does wonders to create feelings of determination and, incidentally, responsibility. Look at all the other lessons you can slip in:

Dealing with a person of authority (a coach, balletmaster, employer) whose job description does not include sympathizing with the problems and erratic standards of children gets the children out of the habit of developing creative excuses and into the habit of doing what they are supposed to. (This is one reason that it is essential that the parent never step into the middle of such a relationship; part of the deal is that the child do his own negotiating and apologizing.)

Competing can be made to teach that others who share your ambitions are more useful to you as friends and exchangers of information than as rivals.

The inevitable ups and downs teach the value of maintaining a sensible emotional level, and not throwing oneself out of whack with discouragement or triumph.

The ability to receive and to give compliments is a skill of value in any life, but most easily learned when one is exposed to more than the usual "My, you have pretty hair" or "Did you really make this potholder yourself?"

In short, the experience of striving in a difficult field is an opportunity to learn perseverance, graciousness, generosity, responsibility, and keeping life in perspective. Only a status-mad parent would allow his child to be exposed to such influences when he could be spending his time in the healthful pastime of lying around complaining that there is nothing on earth worth doing.

The School Play

There are certain cultural events at which the etiquette is so exacting and the consequences of a mistake so shattering that Miss Manners does not wonder that those who must attend are filled with fear and dread. She is referring, of course, to the school play. Having an extensive wardrobe of clothes appropriate for first nights at the opera and knowing from birth the proper nod to give from the royal box at the ballet are of no help there. One must learn a different set of rules to manage gracefully—or at least in an inconspicuous manner that will not confer terminal embarrassment on one's family—as a member of the audience at a school Christmas pageant, recital, or annual play. Yet these are performances to which the audiences are commanded, as anyone knows who has asked to be excused on the flimsy plea of having to earn the money to maintain the performer at the school. If one can't attend, it is charming to send flowers, a telegram, or at least a surprise note in the lunch box.

It is difficult for children to learn that while only the deepest affections could induce a grown-up to attend such an offering, the reverse—that absence indicates a lack of affection—is not true. While generally acknowledging the right of theatrical producers to lure in audiences by any means, Miss Manners would like to enlist the aid of those producers who are also teachers in teaching this lesson.

Dress, at school events, is noneccentric in terms of prevailing community standards as explained by the student. One does not do one's usual self over just to go to a school, but one may do oneself slightly under. No social credit goes to the child with the most chic parents in his home room. Behavior, with one notable exception, should be restrained, bordering on the timid. The parent who arrives quietly, accepts without complaint whatever seat is conveniently available or shrinks against a wall if none is, and saves any socializing until after the performance is a credit to his home environment. The exception is in showing appreciation for the show. At professional cultural events, gentlemen clap by hitting their flat palms together and ladies clap by holding the left hand out and hitting its palm with the fingers of the right hand. At school plays, both must cup their hands, which amplifies the sound.

Raucous laughter is appropriate to intended jokes, but a look of serene oblivion is required for forgotten lines and other stage accidents. Afterward, compliments should be extravagant and generously distributed. Miss Manners does not believe that child performers are immune from criticism if they willingly perform frequently, but that all performers are, for the duration of the day on which they perform.

Appropriate statements include "You were fantastic!" and "Why, this show was wonderful!" This is not time for such values as truth, moderation, or aesthetic standards. Any professional can tell you that even such slightly reserved remarks as "Mostly it was terrific" or "Well, you looked just great" spell doom. What is more, these extravagances should be directed at everyone—your children's playmates, unknown children, producers, costumers, set builders, directors—not just at your own child. You probably needn't request the usher's autograph, but you could. In the tradition of the theater, such remarks are interpreted and valued as the disinterested admiration of strangers.

What is the reward for all this exertion? A happy child, possibly, or at least one who has not suffered public humiliation. Most of all it is the right to impose one's own standards of dress and behavior on the child for that Christmas-vacation visit to the office.

Unpleasant Congratulations

"I suppose you're tired of hearing this," people say with surprising frequency when offering their congratulations upon the successfully realized dreams of friends or acquaintances.

Miss Manners is puzzled by their assumption of what is boring. She admits that boredom is a factor that defies logic—why, for example, does she slide sleepily into her soup plate when her dinner partner volunteers information about his own sexual proclivities, but wake up suddenly if he offers similar information about someone sitting across the table?

But how could anyone be bored at receiving complimentary congratulations? Miss Manners would prefer not to speculate on what, then, would bring that little glow of warm pleasure to the cheeks of such people.

She supposes, however, that this strange but widespread idea that pleasant remarks are anathema to those who receive them accounts for the current fashion of offering unpleasant congratulations.

The best congratulatory remarks are the simplest and most conventional: "Congratulations," "I'm so happy for you," "You deserve the best," and so on. (You may take it for a general principle that the things one is happiest in life to hear —"I love you," "You just won the lottery," "The lab test came back, and you're fine"—are worded in time-honored, and not new and cute, ways.)

Here, however, is partial collection of currently fashionable congratulations:

"You might as well enjoy it—it doesn't last."

"I hate you." (This is cheerfully offered, with an explanation available of how the congratulator would have preferred that it had happened to him instead of you.)

"You'll be happy to hear . . ." followed by a recital of someone else's having attempted the same success but failed.

"How does your family take it?" (Sometimes this is directed toward family members, in a sympathetic tone.)

"We're all terribly jealous of you."

Why, thank you. You're so kind to say so.

That is the reply Miss Manners recommends for any form of compliment, but she can imagine that the recipients of the ones mentioned would have a hard time producing the proper facial expression of shining delight to go with it.

Perhaps it is true that the world is so bad that good things are only felt in the grudges of others. Perhaps there are people so mean-spirited that they truly resent the successes of their friends, that family members are presumed to be discomforted by the triumphs of their relatives, and that the benefactors of good fortune themselves only enjoy it by savoring the contrast with the less fortunate. Miss Manners does not believe this. It strikes her that any addition to the sum of happiness in the world is of benefit to us all, and that even the most selfish analyst would rejoice in such a sign of abundance. Even if it is true, she would wish that those who feel so would put a decent garment of courtesy and pretended kindness on their feelings. It is not easy to thank someone for having assured you that your happiness is making everyone around you miserable and that you are no doubt deriving immense satisfaction from that.

Advice for the Stagestruck

DEAR MISS MANNERS:

My problem is somewhat unique. I'm a very pretty fourteen-year-old, and my problem has me very depressed. Ever since I was ten years old, I have been longing to be a professional singer. Recently I went to a concert starring one of my favorite entertainers. About a week before the concert, I bought his new album. Every day, when my parents were at work and my little brother had gone out to play, I'd line some pillows on the sofa and pretend they were an audience, turn on the stereo, and pretend that I was with his group. Although I've done this every day almost since I was ten, I still feel a little silly. Finally, Friday night came, and I thought I'd forget all my problems and enjoy the concert. I didn't. As soon as the group came on stage, I got chill-bumps and I almost cried because I couldn't be up there.

Almost every night, I think of how I'd look and feel onstage. I often try to picture myself leading a normal, boring life—finishing high school, going to college, and being a teacher or something along that line. But for the life of me, I can't see myself being something I'm not made for. What I really want to do is to make people laugh and cry with music. I've heard so many people say that it's not an easy business, and that you have to be able to handle rejection. That's okay, too. I've handled rejection all my life. All I need is a chance. If I can't have that, I might as well be dead! Please help.

GENTLE READER:

If there is one thing that the wish to become a star is not, it is unique. Neither is being pretty at the age of fourteen, nor even feeling discouraged at that age because one is not a star. You may rest your mind about all that.

Probably you are aware that Miss Manners is not in the business of giving ''chances'' to potential stars of any description; she, for her part, is aware that yours is not exactly an etiquette problem. Nevertheless, there you are, like a pillow on a sofa, so she will give you what plumping she can. The people who told you that performing is not an easy business, and that one has to be able to handle rejection when aspiring to it, are correct. Miss Manners only wonders that they neglected to mention that in order to succeed in the entertainment business, one should be entertaining. It is not reasonable to expect people to pay money to watch someone whose chief characteristic is the desire to be watched. Depressed and self-absorbed teenagers can be readily observed for free.

The best thing in your letter is the desire you express ''to make people laugh and cry with music.'' Why don't you work on that? All you have to learn is music, what makes people laugh and cry, and how to produce these effects. It will not help to sit and cry for yourself while the very people you most admire are performing, instead of using the opportunity to study what it is that they do that makes you and others admire them. It will not help to dismiss normal life as boring, since it is the very people who lead those lives whom you will need to learn to please.

It will not help to eschew education. One reason is that the more you know, the more you have to offer others. Another is that teaching, which does not appeal to you, is nevertheless a profession that involves skillful performing, and the best chance you have now of daily observing what commands attention and what loses it. The chief one, which your advisers also neglected to mention, is that all performers who expect to eat (Miss Manners knows some dancers who don't) must have other marketable skills to exercise while they are handling rejection and wishing they were dead.

The Loudmouthed Fan

DEAR MISS MANNERS:

My son is on two basketball teams, one at his elementary school, the other at the YMCA. Invariably, there is some father attending the game who yells out instructions and very rude comments to all the players, coaches, and referees. This type of person disrupts the game, embarrasses the children, and, by his actions, shows poor sportsmanship. Please tell us quiet parents how to deal with this loudmouthed fool without being rude ourselves.

GENTLE READER:

One person's loudmouthed fool is another person's sports enthusiast. The etiquette of sports audiences is somewhat different from that of concert-goers (although not too far from that of diehard opera lovers). Miss Manners is not saying that there are no rules, nor that this gentleman has not violated some, but let us sort them out first. ''Git 'em,'' addressed to a player, is an instruction, for example, and ''Kill the umpire'' is certainly a rude comment. But both are within the etiquette of the situation.

Where children are involved, you may, and should, set higher standards than are normally practiced. Children should not have to listen to obscenities, embarrassing criticisms, confusing instructions, or recommendations of poor sportsmanship while enjoying a bit of healthy recreation. If there is one person to whom a loudmouthed sports fool (oh, dear, there goes Miss Manners' pretense to neutrality) will listen, it is the coach. You parents should pass on your complaints to him. If he steps menacingly in front of the offender and says, ''I'm in charge here, and I won't have you throwing my players off their game'' (or whatever it is they say—Miss Manners has difficulty sounding like a menacing coach), your problem will be solved.

Conclusions

A Final Word

If you have less than perfect children, what went wrong?

Miss Manners believes this should not happen if you follow her instructions. However, she does feel for those who had the misfortune to produce their children before she produced this book, or who listened to other supposed experts with child-rearing theories differing from hers and perhaps not even including the holy subject of etiquette, which is so essential to the rearing of children. (Some of them are so misguided that they even speak of the "raising" of children. You raise vegetables but rear children.)

It may be that you have a mistaken notion of what a perfect child should be. A perfect child need not have the ambitions, opinions, taste in friends and other attachments, or housekeeping habits of its parents. The idea is not to reproduce yourself, or rather your better self as you might have been, but to assist in the development of a separate human being.

Besides, no child can be considered a finished product while the parent is still alive, no matter how old the child. Therefore, the imperfections you cite may simply be just another stage—middle age, for example—the child is going through on the way to perfection. Stages are what we call the unbearable things children think of to do while waiting for child-rearing to take effect.

If, however, your child is in jail for grand larceny or has provided himself with a fake lineage and pretends he can't remember your name, the chances are that something did go wrong. Your choice then is to feel guilty or rationalize about it before you get back to your proper task, which is to continue to do for him what you can. As Miss Manners has always had a fastidious distaste for guilt, which she associates with boring people who have unattractively hangdog expressions on their faces and no idea of the proper time to make telephone calls, she advises rationalizing.

Miss Manners, along with a few friends like Plato, believes that the rearing of children is the most important of all human tasks. However, she does not believe that our society really believes that, whatever people say. Her dear father, who was an economist, taught her to analyze history in terms of finance, so she cannot help thinking that a nation that really cared about children would find the money for day-care centers, education, health care, and benefits to both otherwise employed and unemployed parents.

Nevertheless, she never fell for the argument, popular some years back for paralyzing parents with guilt, that a child is a clean slate and every bad mark that shows up later must have been put there by the parents. Children are human beings, not toys, and contribute almost from the beginning to their own development. "You were fine as long as I was bringing you up," Miss Manners' grandmother used to say to Miss Manners' dear mother, apparently before that lady reached perfection, "but then you started bringing yourself up." Children are also, as are we all, vulnerable to countless influences from nature and society that are beyond the parents' control.

Is that a sufficient rationalization? All right, then, here, for the parent whose child is less than perfect, is the last rule of child-rearing:

Never give up.

Proceeding Normally

DEAR MISS MANNERS:

I have two parents who nag me all the time. They nag me about things like eating Brussels sprouts, lima beans, and asparagus. And things like practicing the piano, doing homework, and cleaning up my room. I can't stand to do anything of that nature. *I need help fast!*

P. S. from Parents of the Above:

From our perspective, we have struggled eleven years to raise our son to appreciate the virtues of education, music, and homegrown produce (not to mention spelling), and it appears that we have failed. He has learned only that "work" is a four-letter word, and has decided that the world owes him a living. Assuming we got the right baby at the hospital, what have we done wrong, and how can we correct it?

GENTLE READER:

It sounds to Miss Manners exactly as if you are doing everything right, and that the child's development is proceeding normally. If you grow produce at home, you should know that it takes a long time before things come up, and, until then, the juiciest vegetable just looks like a piece of dirt.

Pursuit of Perfection

DEAR MISS MANNERS:

I'm always trying to be neat and quiet, but I'm always making mistakes. What should I do?

GENTLE READER:

Keep on as you are doing. The nobility of striving for perfection and the charm of not quite succeeding are a perfect combination. Miss Manners always is neat and quiet, and her family and friends assure her that they find this behavior frightfully provoking.

Review

A review of pertinent subjects from *Miss Manners' Guide to Excruciatingly Correct Behavior*.

Names

The practice of parents' teaching their children to call them by their first names comes into vogue from time to time, as people think it sounds sporty. Miss Manners has no violent objection to this on the grounds of etiquette, but can't imagine why a grown person would want to seek the semblance of equality with an infant or an adolescent, or an unruly middle-aged child, for that matter.

As to names for the children, parents should realize that the names will not remain as they are given, no matter what the parents say. Miss Manners believes that there is nothing wrong with children's playing with their names, provided that they clean up the mess when they are finished. She recommends that parents give their children the proper equipment—middle names, good combinations of initials, nicknames, names that have alternate spellings—to use when the children inevitably decide that they can no longer tolerate their childhood identities.

Like all children's games, this one must have rules, and Miss Manners is happy to provide them:

Up to the age of seventeen, children are allowed free play with their names, even to the point of changing names that end in y to i and vice versa, which of course they all do anyway.

Upon leaving high school, they must each pick a permanent first name. On beginning college or employment, they must tell everyone the new name, pretending they have always had it, but they are not allowed to chastise relations and childhood friends for using the old one.

When they either marry for the first time or settle on a first serious career, they must pick a permanent last name. It is wise not to associate these names with philosophies or spouses likely to prove fleeting, because this is the surname they must keep. Miss Manners suggests sticking to the original family surname—but in the female line. The system of the matriarchal line worked fairly well in ancient societies, before women made the mistake of telling men that they had anything to do with the production of children.

If you must name your child after yourself (otherwise known as "carrying on the family tradition"), Miss Manners begs you to do it properly. In America, where people go down in history by virtue of their deeds, rather than by being XVIth in a long line of men named Louis, the terms "Junior," "III," and "IV" (or "3d" and "4th," a form Miss Manners prefers) are simply place markers, to differentiate one holder of the name from another. The oldest William Wellborn is therefore numberless (and no, he's not "Senior," either; that's for his widow, as in "Mrs. Wellborn, Sr."), his son is "Junior," his grandson, "3d," and so on. When he dies, everyone moves up a notch. Miss Manners gets rather suspicious when she hears of a "VI" running around, as he's either implying that his great-great-great-grandfather is still alive or claiming connections to royalty.

The only rule that supersedes this is that people should be addressed as they choose. If a gentleman is very fond of his "III" (and one can grow fond of a numeral, if one has had it most of one's life), he may call himself "III" even if he is the oldest holder of his name, and not even Miss Manners would contradict him. That is why she urges you to get it right at the start, before your descendants start producing Williams the 12th.

Birth Rites

The Christening. The baby at a christening is both the undisputed center of attention and completely free from social responsibility. (The only other occasion at which the guest of honor has these distinctions comes at the extreme other end of life.) It may cry, turn purple in the face, or drop off to sleep in the middle of the festivities—actions we have all been tempted to perform at other social events, but mustn't—without being disgraced. The burden of behaving well thus falls on the parents, the godparents, and the guests. In addition to producing the baby, the parents must:

· Arrange with a clergyman a time and place for the ceremony, either at church or at home. A home christening requires a formal table with a bowl, usually silver, for the font.

· Send out informal invitations (time, place, the baby's name, and a sentence of urging, such as "We hope you will be able to join us"), handwritten on the parents' paper or cards, to relatives and close friends. A christening is an intimate ceremony, and not the occasion for pseudo-formality or casual acquaintances.

- Give a small party afterward, such as a luncheon or tea party. White cake iced with the baby's initials, and Caudle, a hot eggnog punch, are traditional, but most people prefer champagne.
- Decorate the house in flowers and the baby in white. A baby wearing the traditional elongated christening dress gives the whole thing the charming look of a postscript to the wedding.
- Choose the godparents, two of the baby's sex and one of the opposite, from among their closest friends.

The godparents' duties are to:

- Hold the baby at the christening.
- Give it some lasting present, traditionally something silver, engravable, and of unknown utility.
- Act as second-string parents to the child, providing moral and religious instruction, birthday and Christmas presents, and asylum when the child has a teenaged quarrel with its parents.

The duties of guests are to:

- Put on dressy street clothes (no black for women) and attend the ceremony and party.
- Declare convincingly that the baby, though alternately dozing noisily and yelling itself purple, is perfectly beautiful. That is not a lie. All babies and brides are beautiful by definition. That is a fact of nature.

Bris and Circumcision. The berith milah, or bris, like all the great ceremonies of life, is designed to be enjoyed by everyone except the guest of honor. It is traditionally performed on the eighth day after birth, and may be done either in a return visit to the hospital, with a reception there, or at home.

Needless to say, this cannot be done for a girl. A daughter is formally named at services on the Sabbath after her birth, with a reception at the temple or at home afterward.

A firstborn son may also have a pidyon haben ceremony, in which he is dedicated to the service of God and then redeemed by his parents. The receptions to follow all these ceremonies are customarily small, with only relatives and close friends invited, and refreshments of just wine and cake. This is to give the parents' extended circle and the caterer time to prepare for the child's bar or bat mitzvah. (Please see pp. 380–381.)

Baby-Sitters

Baby-sitters are members of the workforce like the rest of us, and equally deserving of decent working conditions, especially with what they're paid. They should not be expected to do housework, other than cleaning up for themselves, unless there is extra compensation involved. Employers are generally expected to provide transportation, some food, and some mild form of amusement, such as television, for the employee to enjoy after the children are in bed. Wages should be agreed on beforehand, and standard information such as feeding and disciplining instructions, emergency numbers, the parents' whereabouts, and their expected time of return should be provided as well. A phrase such as ''I don't feel that this is a job that allows you to entertain others during working hours'' is an appropriate way to head off the possibility of a clandestine rendezvous with the employee's boyfriend, or the entire tenth-grade class, for that matter.

Table Manners

In the Great Fork Debate, the rule is this: Use the one farthest to the left. That's all there is to know. The knives follow along in kind, from the outside in, one knife and fork per course. If you do use the wrong fork (an event that happens far less often than Miss Manners' mail would suggest), lick it clean and slip it back onto the tablecloth when no one is looking.

In terms of the actual handling of knife and fork, in America, one cuts food with the fork held in the left hand and the knife in the right, and then lays down the knife and switches the fork to the right hand to eat the bite thus produced. Miss Manners prefers this to the European method, in which the knife remains in the right hand. It is an elaborate, time-consuming, and therefore impressive procedure, actually more advanced than the European method, because it is more complicated and less practical, always a sign of refinement.

In American eating, also, one does not use bread, rolls, knives, fingers, little silver hoes, or, indeed, anything to push the food onto the fork. The fork acts alone, and if a few peas must remain on the plate as a result, so be it. This is a marvelous opportunity to improve the motor skills of small children, and will stand them in good stead later in life.

Small children are, of course, not expected to master these refinements immediately. They should be expected to learn to wait until their mother begins eating; to sit up straight with their elbows off the table and their hands in their laps when not in use; to use their forks, knives, and napkins as God meant them to be used; to refrain from mentioning their dislikes on the menu; to pretend to listen attentively when others are speaking; to ignore the toy potential of various food items; and not to leave the table without permission. Older children should be expected to have table manners as good as or better than their parents'.

Expectations are not always fulfilled, of course. What Miss Manners really means is that children should be repeatedly reminded to do these things in such a way as not to interfere with the opportunity for pleasant family conversation, but as to make basic table manners such a constant requirement that they become automatic before the children reach maturity. (Please see also *Mealtime*, Chapter 8.)

Rites de Passage

Bar and Bat Mitzvah.   Something strange happens to children when they turn thirteen years of age, and Miss Manners is not sure she would call it adulthood. Nevertheless, this is the time of the bar mitzvah, for Jewish boys, and the less traditional (but only fair) bat mitzvah, for girls, which mark the religious coming of age. It is also an excellent time and opportunity for inculcating the social duties of adulthood. No thirteen-year-old should be permitted to begin whining, "But I'm not a child anymore," let alone to call itself by the dignified title of adult, without having mastered the ability to:

- Accept the idea that no social event is so important as to justify subordinating all else to the pleasure of one person. Parties are always a compromise, and learning this early will spare the child much grief on wedding days, retirement parties, and whatever other milestones are stepped upon.
- Realize that there is a relationship between the financial resources of the family and the amount of money it can spend, and that things the child needs, such as

THE FAMILY DINNER, *with Appropriate Place Settings for Different Ages and Numbers of Teeth.   The family dining table is where one learns that there is, indeed, a style of eating somewhere between putting one's hands into cartons in front of an open refrigerator and being served by powdered footmen. Proper family dining requires appearing promptly in a clean*

tuition, can be as important as things it wants, such as live bands.
· Produce a proper guest list, taking into account that there are things more important than whether the child likes a person, such as blood relationship, or whether his parents like the person.
· Sit still for invitations in the proper form, which for the ceremony is:

Mr. and Mrs. Alexander Wise
request the honour of your presence
when their son
Guy Noah
will be called to the Torah as a Bar Mitzvah
on Saturday, the first of April
at half after ten o'clock
Brookdale Hebrew Congregation
Brookdale, Connecticut
Luncheon following the services

state, using the basic tools of eating correctly, and pretending to take a sympathetic interest in the adventures of each person at the table. However, napkin rings, picking up drumsticks, and bragging are permitted.

and for the evening party is:

Dinner dance
at half after seven o'clock
125 Primrose Path
Brookdale, Connecticut
The favour of a reply is requested

and to reply promptly and correctly to all friends' invitations to luncheons, dinners, or receptions for their bar and bat mitzvahs.

· Accept a compliment, no matter how silly. The answer to "What does it feel like to be a (heh, heh) man, sonny?" is a smile.

· Stand in a receiving line looking pleased to see everyone, no matter how detestable; and circulate, in both talking and dancing, without distinguishing between those one likes and those one was forced to invite.

· Perform proper introductions. No person who cannot correctly introduce the chief troublemaker of the eighth grade to his grandmother, concealing all terror of what each might carelessly say to the other, can be considered an adult.

· Behave as if age were not the most important distinction among people, and act as if it were perfectly natural to have a room full of members of different generations who are not even all related to one another.

· Write prompt thank-you letters, each with an opening other than "Thank you for the . . ."

Please note that this is a minimum list. Any child who can master these skills, and add on top some grace and sense, Miss Manners will consider a full-fledged human being.

Communion and Confirmation. First Communion, among Roman Catholics, is usually celebrated when the child is about seven, with confirmation four to five years later. Among Protestants, the two are generally at the same time, at around age thirteen. Both are marked with religious services, followed by a small reception, at church, at home, or sometimes in a restaurant. Relatives, godparents, and close friends who attend should give the child a present. The rule that all such presents should be strictly religious in nature has been relaxed somewhat, but Miss Manners urges that they be appropriate to the occasion, and not, for example, a doll in a silver jumpsuit who looks as if she could get into church only as a bad example.

The Debut. In modern times, it has become fashionable for a young woman, upon reaching the age of eighteen, to signify her membership in adult society by announcing that she refuses to make a debut. This innovation has many advantages over the old debutante system, including being a lot cheaper.

The reason for this surprising acceptance on the part of Miss Manners, whose usual custom is to fight fiercely for the preservation of outmoded rituals, is that the surviving debutante tradition often makes a mockery of its original purpose, which was to introduce one's daughter to one's friends. If they happened to have sons with good prospects, so much the better.

In some private dances given by close relatives of debutantes, and in some church or civic groups, where cotillions are organized by members who know one another well, this idea still prevails. Far more often, the cotillion is run by a competitive committee, more or less in business for the purpose, which allows debutantes to bow to an artificial society composed of people their parents don't know and will probably never see again. It is not uncommon to have an ambitious debutante presented to strangers in a strange city by parents who have to add their hotel bill to the already substantial costs.

In such a determinedly organized setting, debutantes are usually required to dredge up two or three "escorts" each. Remember that these are supposed to be innocent young girls making their first appearance in the world among eligible men, and then ask yourself how they are supposed to have acquired several. Standards are necessarily lowered for this dragnet, and the young men begin to understand that they are at a premium. So, for the expense and trouble of the debut, fond parents are able to attach a permanent date to their daughter's youth, have her scrutinized by strangers, and arrange for her to meet a lot of young men who have come to believe that the world owes them free champagne. That is why Miss Manners will not be offended if you decide to skip this particular tradition.

Those still contemplating making a formal debut should remember that manners are of paramount importance for debutantes, because debutantes have most of the responsibilities and problems of brides without the job security. They are also subject to the same delusions of grandeur and fits of self-indulgence, feeling that no expense should be spared in their honor, and that everyone else should be subservient to them for the period of their glory.

The principle that tends to be forgotten is that the debut is a presentation by the parents of their daughter to their society. It should therefore be in their style of entertaining, according to their tastes and standards, with the adult guest list considered to be as important as the young people's.

The responsibilities of those young people include presenting only known people as candidates for invitations, forms of which include the following for a tea:

Mr. and Mrs. Geoffrey Lockwood Perfect
Miss Daffodil Louise Perfect
At Home
Saturday, the first of April
at five o'clock
123 Primrose Path

And the following for a ball:

> Mrs. Plue Perfect
> requests the pleasure of the company of
> [space for guest's name to be handwritten]
> at a small dance
> in honour of
> Miss Daffodil Louise Perfect
> at half after ten o'clock
> Society of Early Dames
>   Kindly send response to
>   127 Primrose Path

Their responsibilities also include acknowledging all other invitations, flowers, presents; dressing properly (which means, for the debutante, a white dress appropriate to the occasion and her age) ; engaging in as many duty dances as ones for pleasure; being hospitable to all guests, regardless of age; discouraging disruptive behavior in themselves and others; and especially for the debutante, remembering that her tea or small dance is but a party, that her parents are the social heads of the family, and that the occasion marks her assumption of the privileges and responsibilities of adult society. The young lady who can do all that should find adulthood to be child's play.

A Glossary of Parental Expressions, Traditional and Useful

BECAUSE. Answer to "Why?" Variants: "Just because," "Because I say so," "Because I'm the parent and you're the child."

BECAUSE IT'S GOOD FOR YOU. Reason given to make child eat food it does not want.

BE NICE TO HIM (HER) ANYWAY: HE (SHE) MIGHT HAVE A NICE SISTER (BROTHER). Essential last-minute social instruction to child going out on blind date, especially if with child of a friend of the parent's.

BUT HE'S SUCH A *NICE* BOY. Admonition to daughter meaning "We like his parents."

DO THAT ONCE MORE AND I'LL KILL YOU. Mild reprimand.

DON'T MAKE ME SAY IT AGAIN. Last warning before parent violates his own standards of behavior.

DON'T MIND ME. Notification that the only weapon the parent has left is that of sulky disapproval, and that he plans to use it.

DON'T TALK WITH YOUR MOUTH OPEN. Although this appears to be a corruption of the simple mealtime instruction "Don't chew with your mouth open," it actually means what it says, which is "Now eat; it's someone else's chance to talk."

GO ASK YOUR FATHER (MOTHER). Reply to request, meaning, "No, you can't, but I don't have the time to argue with you right now." Can be used only by parents who have maintained a united front in child-rearing.

GO PUT ON A SWEATER.   Order to child whose parent is cold.

HOW CAN YOU STAND TO LIVE LIKE THAT?   Clean this place up.

HOW DO YOU KNOW IF YOU HAVEN'T TRIED IT?   Prelude to ordering child to eat something he claims not to like. From that taste on, the statement is "One more bite won't hurt you."

HOW WOULD YOU FEEL IF SOMEONE DID THAT TO YOU?   Superfluous philosophical prelude to enforcing rules.

I DON'T WANT TO HEAR ANY MORE ABOUT IT.   Assertion of parental authority after parent has lost argument with child.

I TOLD YOU TO DO THAT BEFORE WE LEFT THE HOUSE.   Self-explanatory.

LOOK IT UP.   Answer to any scholarly inquiry, ostensibly used to promote good study habits.

IF ALL YOUR FRIENDS JUMPED OFF A CLIFF, WOULD YOU DO IT, TOO?   Reply to "Everyone else is doing it."

IF YOU WANT TO SEE HOW A MAN WILL TREAT HIS WIFE, LOOK AT HOW HE TREATS HIS SISTER.   Attempt to warn daughter about beau who is undesirable for any reason, even if he doesn't have a sister. Also may be used to warn misbehaving brother, who replies that he doesn't want to get married anyway.

IF YOU WANT TO SEE WHAT A GIRL WILL TURN OUT TO BE, LOOK AT HER MOTHER.   Gender reverse of above; Miss Manners is sorry about the sexist differences in the statements, but we are dealing here in folklore.

I'M NOT GOING TO ASK YOU AGAIN.   Do it now, or you'll never hear the end of it.

I'M NOT YOUR SERVANT.   Reply to request that the parent do something the child ought to do. (See below for variant if there are servants in the house.)

IT'S YOUR LIFE.   Warning that the parent plans to crow about it if course of which he disapproves is followed anyway.

OKAY, THEN BE YOUR *OWN* BOSS.   Threatened revocation of parental authority when the child won't do what parent wants anyway.

OPEN WIDE.   Announcement to baby that parent is about to open his mouth wide and push loaded spoon toward baby.

OR ELSE.   All-purpose, nonspecific threat.

SOME DAY YOU'LL THANK ME.   Statement made by parent who has successfully asserted authority, in order to soften the victory.

STOP PLAYING WITH YOUR FOOD.   Dinnertime refrain, thrown in whenever there is a lull in the conversation.

THAT'S ALL RIGHT, DEAR—SOMEDAY YOU'LL FIND A BOY WHO APPRECIATES YOU.   Unhelpful advice given to unpopular teenage daughter by mother who fails to appreciate the appreciator when he finally appears.

THE SERVANTS HAVE ENOUGH TO DO.   Notice that the child will be expected to behave as well as an underprivileged child.

THINK OF ALL THE STARVING CHILDREN IN (CURRENTLY PATHETIC NATION).   Line that succeeded "Leave some on your plate for Miss Manners" when wasting food ceased to be fashionable.

TOO BAD, YOU GOT THE ONLY ROTTEN PARENTS ON THE BLOCK. Answer to ''Everybody else's parents let them.'' Alternative, with snobby overtones: ''Well, we're not everybody else.''

WE'RE NOT MADE OF MONEY. Explanation of refusal to purchase something; may be used at any income level.

WHEN I WAS YOUR AGE . . . Signal to children to cease listening.

WHEN YOU'RE A MOMMY (DADDY), THEN YOU CAN————————, TOO. All-purpose excuse by which parent explains breaking any of her or his own rules.

WHERE WERE YOU BROUGHT UP—IN A BARN? Humorous criticism of manners directed at children, ironically, by the parent who did the upbringing. Neither funny nor correct when directed at the children of others. Related pastoral expressions, used in rearing children who have never seen a farm, include ''You must feel right at home in this pigsty,'' ''Do you like having your room smell like a stable?'' and ''Why bother with the fork at all—why not put your face directly in the trough?''

WHY DON'T YOU DO THAT RIGHT NOW. Announcement that parent is approaching brink.

YOU HAVE TO BE NICE TO HIM (HER), HE'S (SHE'S) YOUR BROTHER (SISTER) or . . . HE'S (SHE'S) YOUNGER THAN YOU. Reason given to enforce humane treatment of younger siblings; confirms older children's opinions of the newcomers as spoiled usurpers of parental affection, enjoying favored status.

YOU'LL FREEZE THAT WAY. Request that child stop making faces.

YOU'LL GET PNEUMONIA. Announcement, on the first day of autumn or winter, that clothing requirements have changed, or (in early spring) that they have not. Does not bear medical scrutiny, as most cases of pneumonia originate in hospitals and are therefore unconnected with the wearing of mittens.

YOU'LL UNDERSTAND WHEN YOU HAVE CHILDREN. All-purpose retort, the truth of which is proven in that no child understands it, but all parents use it.

YOUR RIGHTS STOP WHERE MY NOSE BEGINS. All-purpose reply to the preposterous idea of children's rights on any issue.

Final Examination

An hour examination, prepared by Miss Manners' teaching assistant, Jennifer Georgia. Use No. 2 pencils only. Please choose the most nearly correct answer to each of the following questions:

1. Miss Manners agrees with dear Mr. Plato that:
   a. Oedipus' problem was primarily one of etiquette, rather than psychology.
   b. A body immersed in water will not clean behind its own ears unassisted.
   c. Child-rearing is the most important task of civilization.
2. When a child comes home from school proudly bearing a report card containing four A's and one B, the parent should say:
   a. "Now, dear, you know it's not nice to brag."
   b. "Why that's marvelous, dear! We're very proud of you."
   c. "What's the B for?"
3. When introduced to redheaded twins, one should say:
   a. (To the mother)   "Can you tell them apart?"
   b. (To one child)   "Hello. Do you like sports?" (To the other)   "Hi, where do you go to school?"
   c. (To the mother)   "Wow! you must have been taking some amazing drugs when you were pregnant."

4. When informed by a friend that she is pregnant, one says:
   a. "How wonderful! Congratulations. I'm thrilled for you."
   b. "Oh. Was it planned?"
   c. "Don't you care at all about overpopulation?"
5. When a bride's parents are divorced and both have married again, the proper seating arrangements at the wedding are:
   a. The original parents together in the first pew on the left, with their spouses seated directly behind, all having promised to drop any feuds for the duration of the day.
   b. The custodial parent with spouse in the first pew, with the other parent and spouse in the second pew, all having promised not to fight loudly enough to upstage the principal event.
   c. Each couple seated comfortably in their own house, to be informed by telephone of an elopement.
6. The bridegroom's parents are required to contribute:
   a. Half the wedding costs, of which they are notified by a bill at the conclusion of the festivities, not having been consulted beforehand, as the planning is the bride's family's responsibility.
   b. A rehearsal dinner for the bridal party, their spouses, lovers, and friends-of-the-week (a total of sixty-five people), equal in elaborateness to the wedding itself, plus a silver tea service.
   c. A bridegroom, and their warmest compliments (at least in public) to the bride and her parents, upon whom they called when informed of the engagement.
7. The proper response to a sulking child is:
   a. Ignore it.
   b. "What's the matter now?"
   c. There is none.
8. The proper response when a guest's child is destroying one's home is:
   a. (To the parent) "Could you please rein in your darling child? He's about to break my Boehm porcelain Elvis statuette."
   b. (To the parent) "You're such a nice person—how could you produce such a hoodlum?"
   c. (To the child) "Aaron, dear, why don't you go out and play in the traffic?"
   d. Extreme concern for the child, as in: (to the parent) "Please make him stop—I'm afraid he'll hurt himself," or (to the child, through clenched teeth hidden by a fake smile) "You'd better stop that—you might get hurt." (Especially effective when holding the child's wrist so tightly that his hand turns blue.)

ANSWERS:

1. (c). (a) and (b) are true, but Plato cannot take credit for them.
2. (b). Those who chose (a) had the right idea but the wrong locale—home is the only legitimate outlet for the bragging instinct.

3. (b). Not brilliant, admittedly, but at least better than (a) or (c).
4. (a). Would she be telling you if she weren't happy about the situation? But that question is rhetorical. Even if she is unburdening her soul, the correct answer is (a). If there ever is a time for a conventional answer, this is it.
5. Either (a), (b), or (c), depending on the demeanor of the participants. Miss Manners is fond of answer (a).
6. (c), with as much of (b), or a toned-down version of it, as the bridegroom's family cares to offer, which may quite properly be none.
7. (c). (a) or (b) will only make the sulking worse. Sulking is the only weapon the perfect child has, so the parents must simply take this punishment as long as the child sees fit. Luckily, children have short attention spans.
8. (d). Any Gentle Reader who doesn't know this by now has not been paying attention.

ESSAY QUESTION

Compare and contrast Miss Manners' method of rearing perfect children with the common method of allowing them full expression of their natural creative impulses. Which is more conducive to the preservation of civilization? Give reasons and examples. You will have a lifetime in which to answer this question.

Index

Miss Manners is a perfect lady whose column is internationally syndicated by the United Feature Syndicate.

Judith Martin, however, also indulges in novel-writing and child-rearing. A graduate of Wellesley College, where she majored in Gracious Living, she is the author of Miss Manners' Guide to Excruciatingly Correct Behavior, Gilbert: A Comedy of Manners, The Name on the White House Floor, *and a forthcoming novel,* Style and Substance. *She lives with her husband and their two perfect children in Washington, D.C.*